The Guardian Year
2000

The Guardian Year
2000

Introduction by **Harold Evans**
Edited by **Michael McNay**

First published in 2000 by
The Guardian
119 Farringdon Road
London
EC1R 3ER

Copyright © 2000 by Guardian Newspapers Limited

The right of Michael McNay to be identified as the editor of this work has been asserted by him in accordance with the Copyright, Designs and Patents Act 1988.

A catalogue record of this book is available from the British Library.

ISBN: 1 84115 424 5

Cartoons by Steve Bell
Country Diary illustrations by Clifford Harper

Typesetting and layout by Blackjacks
Printed in Great Britain

Contents

Michael McNay *Preface*   xi
Harold Evans *Introduction*   xiii

Aubade

Combined front page and leader *Dawn of a new millennium*   2

People

Michael White *Chancellor meets convergence criteria*   8
Duncan Campbell *As Kim Bassinger wasn't telling me the other day*   10
Sabine Durrant *Enduring love*   11
Michael Foot *We just love that woman*   14
Jonathan Romney *The little fellow*   16
Martin Kettle *A kinder, gentler, better America*   18
Euan McCaskill *The left's Lawrence of Arabia*   21

War and peace

Maggie O'Kane *A blacked-out vehicle, a piece of Irish history*   26
John Mullin *This couple fled their farm in fear of the IRA 27 years ago.
   Today they are urging their fellow unionists to vote for peace*   28
Hugo Young *Words were not enough*   30
Vikram Dodd *Last voyage into legend*   36
Maggie O'Kane *The army pledged to fight to the end*   38
Chris McGreal *Mozambique's misery goes on*   41
Maggie O'Kane *Carla's court*   42

Nemesis

Alan Rusbridger *Farewell to Have-a-go Hamilton*   48
Jonathan Freedland *Windows close for capitalism*   51
Simon Hoggart *The latest Archer: Queen Trixie and her fertile pigs*   54
Simon Hoggart *Widow Twankey ends the peers' last show*   55

Country matters

Alex Bellos *Out on a limb*   58
Virginia Spiers *Apple days: A Country Diary*   61
Paul Evans *Beholding the fort: A Country Diary*   62
Maev Kennedy *Time runs out for station steeped in myth*   63

Contents

John Valins *Mendip lead: A Country Diary*   65
A Harry Griffin *The SOS box: A Country Diary*   66

Online and offline

Anna Vaux *Get your hands off my husband*   68
Alexander Chancellor *Internet fever*   69
Corrections and clarifications *Sorry, we'll say that again*   71
Ian Mayes *A short history of style*   71
Polly Toynbee *Guarding the Guardian*   73
Ian Katz *Final edition*   75
Ian Mayes *Name dropping*   80
John Ezard *Oxford English Dictionary to go online*   81
Matthew Engel *Consultation is not for real people*   83
Julie Burchill *Julie goes online*   85
Letters   87

Art beat

Fiachra Gibbons *Effing is off, rules theatre computer*   92
Letter *You're effing wrong*   93
Michael Billington *Crowning glory*   93
Birthdays *Don McCullin*   95
Gordon Burn *Walking the plank*   95
Andrew Clements *Hector's nous*   101
Matthew Engel *It's titwillow, titwillow, for hours on end*   103
Jonathan Freedland *Oscar gets serious*   105
James Fenton   107
Maev Kennedy *Tate and style*   108
Martin Kettle *The oldest singer in town*   110
Bel Littlejohn *Bloomin' Bloomsbury*   112
Adrian Searle *Brush hour*   113
AC Grayling *The last word on Art*   116

Take me to your leader writer

Là ci darem la mano   118
Labour's monument   118
A pother of pedants   120
The policy isn't working   121
Cold comfort   123

Contents

The sex war

Julie Burchill *'Suicide is a side-effect of affluence.*
    You didn't get many suicides in Jarrow in the 30s'   126
Leanda de Lisle *Boys will always be joys to me*   128
Bel Littlejohn *Men, you're miserable*   129
Peter Preston *My daughter is just fine*   131

Honi soit qui mal y pense

Catherine Bennett *The appeal of Camilla*   136
Leanda de Lisle *The king and I*   139
Simon Hattenstone *So what exactly do you do for a living, ma'am?*   140
Saira Shah *Plain tales from the hills*   144

Here and there

Nick Davies *The great divide*   148
Catherine Bennett *Best at self loathing*   157
Owen Boycott @ *Murmansk*   160
Duncan Campbell *Jackrabbit's last raid*   161
Stephen Cook *Fool's paradise*   165
Michael Ellison *I don't feel defeated: I still seek justice*   167
Jonathan Freedland *Wackos in white coats*   169
Gary Younge *Stand in line*   171
Hugo Young *The folly built by our leaders that makes fools of us all*   173
Roy Hattersley *Britain can't make it*   175
Jon Henley *Tide of oil pushes Brittany to the edge of despair*   179
Christopher Hitchens *Beautiful behemoth*   181
John Hooper @ *Berlin*   185
Bernard Kops *A letter from America*   186
Jon Henley *A century of eating has left Michelin overstuffed*   189
Martin Woollacott *Our past is diminished but the future remains unclear*   191
Gary Younge *Strangers at the gate*   193
Sam Wollaston *Harley Street*   196

Telly ho!

Nancy Banks-Smith *Let there be light entertainment*   202
Peter Preston *History hopping*   203
Nancy Banks-Smith *Police, fire brigade, or veterinary?*   206
Gary Younge *Is it 'cos I is black?*   207

Contents

Letters *'Nuff respect* 210
Nancy Banks-Smith *Tacky, but the girl just can't help it* 211

Wonderful world

David McKie *On the road to nowhere* 214
AC Grayling *The last word on Age* 215
Madeleine Bunting *Let's wear our frills with pride* 217
Leanda de Lisle *My brief encounter* 219
Francis Wheen *The paranoia pantomime* 220
Dea Birkett *No shelter from the swarm* 223
Tim Radford *Not for the squeamish* 225
David McKie *Far, far from Bohemia* 227
Smallweed 229
Peter Tatchell *Homo heaven* 231
Polly Toynbee *Time to turn cameras on the media mob* 233
Francis Wheen *Champagne socialists unite* 235
Michael White *The name game* 238

Sporting strife

Matthew Engel *Early risers marvel at new dawn* 242
Ian Aitken *Cricket for comrades* 243
David Davies *Seve puts the lid on his own trophy* 245
Jacqueline de Gier *The beautiful, deadly game* 246
Matthew Engel *Why I'm quitting Wisden* 252
David Hopps *Leicestershire left armer bowls Wisden a googly* 254
Ian Malin *Technicolor game* 255
Jamie Reid *Jumping to the summit* 257
David Lacey *Even the last resort is better than a return to Heysel* 259
Donald McRae *A hard day's night for Billy Schwer* 261
Michael Walker *One-time safecracker captures the Cup* 263
Frank Keating *The sportsman of the century* 265

Passing through

John Mortimer *Dear John* 270
John Ezard *A hero passes into folklore* 272
Francis Beckett *One woman's journey from revolutionary idealism
    to Stalin's slave labour camps* 274
Robin Denselow *Essex philosopher* 276
Simon Hattenstone *Flirting with happiness* 278

Contents

Leading article *Alastair Hetherington*   281

Letters   282

WL Webb *Leader writer who split the Guardian*   283

Harold Jackson *A masterful eye for gentle ridicule*   285

Melvyn Bragg *A lifelong devotee of the Lake District,*
    he mapped its geography, history and culture   287

Duncan Campbell *So long Charlie Kray*   289

Norman Shrapnel *A comic writer in the English tradition*   291

Envoi

Michael Frayn *Late night final*   298

Michael McNay
Preface

As I was making a final selection for this volume, I noticed an advertisement in the London Review of Books from a body styling itself the Farringdon Therapy Group asking, Are you a loyal but disgruntled Guardian reader? and requesting like minded disgruntleds to respond to an email address. The notion that Guardian readers might be both loyal and disgruntled would not come as news either to the readers' editor (who is a daily ombudsman mediating between newspaper and readers) or the letters editor. Or even the editor. What caught my attention and prompted me to apply to the email address was the depth of concern that would cause a body of readers to react in this fashion. I was, I told them, a loyal reader all right, but on the whole a gruntled one.

I had a reply very quickly, laying out the current orthodoxy: that The Guardian is, like all broadsheet newspapers, dumbing down; that foreign coverage is inconsistent, criticism has been replaced by hype, and that The Guardian was "promoting airheads like Julie Burchill" (Ms Burchill's outrageous irreverence, I'm proud to say, figures in Guardian Year 2000). To all this I can only say from my experience of assembling this book that this is simply not so, even though, as has been said, journalism is the first rough draft of history, not the closed volume; but I understand the concern. For five years I was part of the team putting the front page together. One day at a news conference someone suggested that news of the death of Kurt Cobain should figure on page 1. "And who, pray, is Kurt Cobain?" I asked in, admittedly, a slightly less measured phrase than that (for disgruntled readers, it should be explained that Mr Cobain was an American rock music eminence who had killed himself). I felt by the frosty silence that greeted my sally that my long nights on the front page were numbered; and, indeed, shortly thereafter I found myself helping to produce a new sports tabloid.

But until I retired in March 2000, I had worked for The Guardian since 1963 and had been a reader since 1949. The first editions of The Guardian Year (then The Bedside Guardian) were published in the 50s; ominously for those of my generation, teenage girls were wetting their knickers at this time as Bill Haley rocked around the clock; I was in the army, hero worshiping Alastair Hetherington for moving The Manchester Guardian into outright opposition to the disastrous Suez invasion and, be it remembered, Labour's craven acquiescence in the tawdry adventure. When I joined the paper in Manchester, Alastair was still the editor, but about to up sticks for London. The core values he espoused have not changed from that day to this, and probably haven't since CP Scott was at the helm.

The difference is that The Guardian, like all newspapers since the advent of journalist-input technology, has expanded hugely. So has financial clout and the ability to employ round-the-clock legal backing to sustain perilous investigative reporting of the sort that brought down Jonathan Aitken and Neil Hamilton. The Guardian's coverage of everything from the mechanism of European Union affairs to the Balkan and Chechnya wars has never been surpassed in analysis or eye-witness veracity by anything in the paper's history. Criticism, far from having degenerated into hype, is more incisive all round than in my years as arts page editor (1970-5).

The other difference might be put as a gloss to CP Scott's often cited epigram: Opinion is free but facts are on the internet. The net is the growing challenge for today's staff journalists. Good luck to them. Meanwhile, because the Guardian electronic archive is accessible to all, The Guardian Year 2000 can revert to being, not a portrait of the last year of the 20th century and the first of the 21st (we can safely ignore here the view of the estimable columnist Smallweed, who believes that the new millennium begins on 1 January 2001: he cannot count), but a collection of the finest writing in the Guardian on any subject in that period. Or rather, which is different, what I consider the finest writing, because my heart bled as I discarded pieces which other readers, not to mention their authors, would have included. Kurt Cobain might not have made it to these pages, but another dead star, Ian Dury, has. How's that for progress?

Harold Evans
Introduction

When Neville Cardus was 18 he performed a ritual known only to himself. He would go and stand, fairly late on Monday nights, on the pavement at the dark and deserted corner of Cross Street and Market Street in Manchester. In our own fretful times, when loiterers after dusk are apt to be in the retail sex or dope business, one hastens to say that Cardus's mind was on higher things. He spent his time looking up at the lighted windows of the Guardian building which stood at that crossroads. "I would imagine that behind any one of them Montague was at work on a dramatic notice; that Agate was adding a finishing touch; that Samuel Langford, greatest of all writers on music, was meditating on Brahms over his desk".

I know the feeling. A few decades later, when I was growing up in Manchester, I regarded that city junction as the crossroads of civilisation. The divinities of my youth were Sir John Barbirolli at the Hallé orchestra just a little way down the road, Stanley Matthews, and The Manchester Guardian. Cardus was by then writing as the "Cricketer" about the mischief done to England by Don Bradman down at Old Trafford; and there was HD "Donny" Davies on the magic of Manchester United, and Harry Boardman up aloft in the parliamentary gallery at Westminster, watching Winston Churchill, the lion in winter. What a treat every morning! Such style, such wit, such an eye for the memorable detail. It was only journalism, but journalism rubbing shoulders with literature and with history.

I mention these icons of the Guardian tradition because fifty years from today somebody will be saying much the same thing about the writers collected here and many that the editor has had to leave out. It is a very varied collection. Lord Cecil once said the Guardian made righteousness readable and it's true here: the full fire-and-brimstone works from Alan Rusbridger and Hugo Young are enhanced by zest. But what is most attractive about having a selection of these Guardian writers available for instant replay is the cultural kaleidoscope they afford us as serious minded viewers or bedtime voyeurs. So this is our world. A mass murderer looks on his accusers. An 'effing computer at the Royal Court brazenly erases the word Alastair Hetherington and the Guardian first made history printing in the 60s Lady Chatterley case. Every week two women are killed and hundreds of thousands every year injured by the men they live with. An Indian theatrical troupe enraptures villagers with its version of the loves and life of the Princess of Wales. Britons lap up a television rural soap opera with mayhem round every maypole. Carlo Bergonzi at 75 finds Verdi's Otello an aria too far. A father brilliantly and sensitively ponders a moral code that asks him to disavow a daughter who lives the life of a lesbian. Kim Basinger tells all – or does she?

Introduction

Most journalism is perishable. The writing here has no read-by date. If you missed the articles at the time – and the likelihood is that you missed a fair proportion – you can read them with as much pleasure and enlightenment as if the ink were still fresh on them. I recommend peering through the fog of the Troubles with Maggie O'Kane and John Mullin. But if that's not your mood try Frank Keating on the sporting greats or Ian Aitken's revelation of why cricket failed to catch on in Red Square, or Michael White on seeing the Chancellor of the Exchequer attempt a kiss.

It is notable how much good writing is written against pressures of time and space; conciseness and clarity are an imperative. The style is very much the Guardian style of Cardus's day, simple, lucid and direct, vivid with personal observation, and wearing its learning lightly. It is the opposite of the mandarin style characterised by Cyril Connolly as assuming that neither the writer nor the reader is in a hurry and both are in possession of a classical education and a private income. The Guardian's prose is everyman's, demotic but luminous, and it is well represented in the familiar bylines of the contributors to this book.

We can't any longer imagine them at their desks behind the lighted windows in Cross Street, but dipping into the The Guardian Year 2000 is a happy alternative.

Harold Evans is a former editor of *The Sunday Times* and *The Times*, and was president and publisher of Random House. He is the author of *The American Century.*

Aubade

....

1 January 2000

Dawn of a new millennium

T here have been billions of dawns since earth was first formed. But, according to the calendar most of us share, with today's dawn the human race enters the third millennium.

We may feel awe and humility, and even surprise. For more than two generations we have survived our power to destroy all life while slowly engineering the planet's asphyxiation. Somehow we have made it.

The sceptics will say that today's date is only a number; the pedants insist it is not even the right one. But for everyone else, just as the dawn marks the start of a new day, and January 1 announces the start of a new year, so today's dawn opens a new chapter in the human story.

We do not wake this morning to a blank slate: there is something deathly in that idea. We wake instead aware of the long past we leave behind. But the turn of the millennium requires us to pause a moment, turn around, and ready ourselves for the future . What will it be? Can we possibly imagine it?

The perspective of the lens in space is denied us. The century just gone is too close to disentangle its miracles from its horrors. Even the still beauty of the image is a lie because its gleaming perfection masks the potential for catastrophe.

But a millennium offers renewal. "To make an end is to make a beginning," wrote Eliot. "The end is where we start from."

Attempting to predict the coming century is more than usually foolish. Even 10 years ago we could not have imagined the internet, the speed of computing (currently doubling every eight or nine months), genetic mapping or cloning. While the mystery of consciousness may elude us for many decades, there are other large areas of our make-up which are about to be revealed. Last month scientists announced the decoding of the first of 23 human chromosomes. It is, as yet, only a rough sketch, but they will be reading the entire genome soon enough, decoding every human characteristic, working out the genes or combinations of genes which are responsible for musicality, schizophrenia, left- handedness, height, athletic prowess and aggression.

It feels uncannily as though human beings are finally getting to the roots of the tree of knowledge. No wonder today's scientists feel they are living at the most exciting time in history. While Charles Darwin discovered the probability that we evolved by natural selection, we did not understand the mechanics of that change. Soon we will. We are learning from this string of genetic information what life was for our predecessors, how it works for us – and even catch a glimpse of what we might become. In short, we will read the story life is telling us.

This new knowledge will bring untold medical benefits and pose awesome ethical dilemmas. It may be that within two decades traditional surgery will largely be replaced by gene therapy – the injection of chemical messages into diseased or malfunctioning parts of the body. The predisposition to life-threatening diseases in certain patients will also enable doctors to anticipate illness in their patients. The same technology may enable the rich to give their children enormous advantages – enhanced athleticism, height, mathematical ability, the absence of asthma. A scrap of DNA will tell any authority anything they want to know about any person. Who is to determine how this knowledge is used?

It is easy to dwell on our fears. The geniuses of genetics have opened Pandora's box. But people forget the end of the story of Pandora. At the bottom of the box was hope, waiting to break out. Our new ability to eat from the tree of life need not trigger a fall from grace. Take, for example, the fears that the science of genetics would revive the science of eugenics and give intellectual underpinning to crude racism. In fact, advanced genetics teaches us not about the biological origins of our difference s, but how strikingly similar we all are to each other. Two groups of chimps found 20 miles apart differ more from each other than one human being does from any other, even those who resemble each other least: our brains are remarkably similar. As we open the book of life during the coming millennium, we should see how much we all share – and how bogus are any notions of racial superiority left over from the last century.

Nor should we blindly fear the prospect of doctors toying with our genes. We need to keep a vigilant eye on what they do, of course, but we can also afford to look forward to a world where diseases such as muscular dystrophy or Huntington's chorea can be tweezed out before they have ruined a life. Would the world really be worse off if those plagues were banished? And if genetics enables human beings to stay alive for longer, and life becomes less of a risk – with less need for the insurance policy of multiple children relied on in the developing world – then perhaps world population might start to fall, easing some of the strain on the planet.

The implications are so vast that we can barely sketch their outline. Where does God, already in retreat after 600 years of modern science, sit in a world where we feel we may one day know the innermost secrets of human existence? Will ours become an entirely godless world? The scientists do not seem to think so. Indeed, some of the most imaginative thinkers speculate that we could eventually discover the concept of right and wrong alongside our genetic instruction manual, that we will realise that the notion of good and evil exists in the universe, as real as the concept of a number: both are real, independent of our perception of them.

Cutting-edge studies of physics – of light, energy and matter – can also feed, rather than choke, our mystical impulses. Now that we can describe the entire physical history of the cosmos for all but the first thousandth of a second, scientists have c oncluded that, in the words of one, "it looked as if the universe knew we were coming". Somehow it seemed ready to welcome life. The result is that religion may be different in the new millennium, it may have to speak in a different language, but it will not be dead.

The possibilities are thrilling. Space exploration will continue, reaching beyond our solar system to discover... who knows what? Once we have cracked the code for life, will we be able to construct a machine that mirrors it perfectly? Will we crack the riddle of consciousness, so that computers start resembling brains – or will we discover what exactly it is that makes us so different from them? These are just some of the dilemmas that await us.

Still, there is a question that has to be solved first, one that underpins all the others. If, uniquely among all the creatures on earth, our evolution is in our own hands – thanks to our understanding of our genes and our mastery of our physical environment – what will we do with it? How will we ensure it is just? And this, tough as it may seem, is not a question we can leave to the experts. This is one for all of us. For there is a risk here that, as science accelerates ever faster, our human institutions fail to catch up. We have the brainpower to see how our lives could be improved beyond our dreams, to be rid of much pain and hardship, yet we struggle to spread these new riches fairly. So scientists develop a treatment for Aids which gives those in America or western Europe once written off as the living dead a new chance of life, and yet Aids still kills millions in Africa. This is not because our scientific creativity hits some conundrum it cannot solve in Africa: it is because one part of the planet is so much poorer than the rest. We could be about to repeat the mistake with genetic medicine. The rich countries of the north may discover how sto abolish a raft of hereditary diseases forever, but in the south (or among the poor anywhere) those genes could continue to kill. If the new millennium sees us eating from the tree of knowledge, we need to work out how we can share out the fruit.

Our starting point is not easy. We live in a world where economic wealth has grown in ways few ever imagined possible – but where it has become concentrated in fewer and fewer hands. Rich countries such as the US are getting fantastically richer, but the poor ones are not just shut out of the new wealth party: they are getting poorer. Life expectancy, so long assumed to be ever-increasing as man and medicine become more sophisticated, is actually falling in the planet's poorest countries. Genetic research may be discovering the secret of making clever babies in London and New York, but in Mali and Malawi children are going blind for lack of basic eye cream. If science has put humankind's destiny in our own hands, we are getting it horribly wrong.

In the past 50 years we have been so concerned with individual rights, with self-expression and personal liberation that we have quite forgotten what we are doing to the planet in this binge of self-gratification. Capitalism becomes more global; so does the threat to the environment. What were once local problems of pollution have now merged into a huge general threat to the planet's delicately balanced ecosystem. The oceans rise along with the steady increase in global temperatures; the atmosphere is more polluted than at any stage in human history; and hundreds of plant and animal species are becoming extinct. Our need for fuel, food and living space increases every day and yet we do not have the slightest inkling of how we are going to cope as the world's population leaps from 6bn today to 10-12bn through the next century

From the industrial revolution until a projected date of 2050, we will have obliterated half the species on earth. Whether it is tiny plants, fungi or insects, we are destroying about 27,000 separate creations a year. It is a programme of devastation unlike anything the globe has witnessed before. Climate change is making the problem worse, with arid areas getting more arid and wet ones getting wetter. Land currently used for farming will become unviable, either too dry or with vital top soil washed away. Some geographers predict a kind of runaway meltdown, as global warming becomes a self-fuelling process, galloping ahead beyond our control. The melting of the glaciers will not solve our other looming problem: a world shortage of water, which could see whole swaths of the Middle East and Asia running dry within 40 years, perhaps warring over H_2O the way they once battled for oil.

What can we do about this glaring paradox, which has led us to understand ourselves so profoundly and yet still organise our world so badly? Science can offer some help. It may be that a nudge in the direction of genetic modification will eventually be required to avert a food crisis, compensating for the once fertile areas ruined by global warming. Nanotechnology, the use of tiny robots to perform miniature tasks like microsurgery, could also help: the world will consume fewer resources the more adept we become at manipulating matter. The real answer, however, may be globalisation, since even the most highly developed nations seem incapable of addressing the destruction that is going on. Not the globalisation of the world economy, which currently serves to widen the gap between rich and poor, but a new, as yet unformed idea of globalised politics.

HG Wells saw the point a century ago: he realised that modern problems are world-wide, requiring worldwide solutions. Only a kind of politics which weighs up the needs of the entire human race could begin to address the water question, for example, insisting that the water-rich countries use no more than they need, while the water-poor get no less than they need. At the moment we do nothing because the problem seems too large or the cause too obstinate. This is because the growth of the most developed economies depends on the pillaging of natural resources. It is a global problem which will eventually have to be sorted out by powerful global institutions, rather than national governments. This will be the only way to prevent the Brazilians from burning their rainforest, the Americans from polluting the atmosphere with their factories and the British from dumping nuclear waste in the oceans. Each nation bears a responsibility for the terrible state of the world's environment at the end of the 20th century, but it is way beyond the powers and will of individual nations to right the damage.

The anxiety we may feel about such things might just be alleviated if the west, which has never been richer or economically more self-confident, began to construct a proper programme of third world aid, as well as taking real action on the vehicle and factory emissions, and the pollution of the seas. If we can decode DNA and invent the internet, we should be able to do pretty much anything. The experience of the past decade in producing global answers to global problems has not been encouraging. Last month's fiasco in Seattle suggested a fatal dislocation between the ambitions of the developed world and the needs of the developing world. Europe has been at peace for more than half a century, but the struggle to establish successful pan-national governmental structures shows the difficulty of reconciling international aspirations with local cultures. The UN security council has so far been unequal to the task of dealing with the problems thrown up after the collapse of the old communist bloc and the consequent erosions of the 19th and 20th century concepts of state sovereignty. The wars in Kosovo, Bosnia, Rwanda and Chechnya all illustrated the international community's inability to intervene quickly and decisively.

But pessimism should be tempered. The emergence of global consumer power, thanks to the internet, could bring a company like Monsanto to its knees. The web is creating new political communities, scattered across the globe, but working together. To hint that all this might one day lead to a global government, democratically elected, sounds laughable now. If anyone had suggested votes for the masses at the beginning of the 19th century they would have been ridiculed, too. But it happened.

We need to pull off a shift as profound as that modern move to democracy, this time at the global level. And yet we must still remain mindful of the local. A challenge for the new century is to keep alive the belief that individuals can shape the world around them, whether it is the planet or their village. The new technology can be a friend or foe in this process – daunting us with information overload or enabling us to reach out and connect with others. We need to make sure the internet and its allied innovations work for us, not against us.

Where might our own, small island fit into all this? The answer could be quite well. Our mother tongue puts us at the forefront of the web, whose first language is English. We are also neatly situated between the old and new worlds, perfectly placed to be the pivot between Europe and America. In the effort to give birth to a new global aware-ness, we could be in just the right position. We will need to resolve our dilemma over our relationship with the continent once and for all, and we should do that sooner rather than later. That, in turn, may require a new understanding of Britain itself. In the imperial age it was clear what the union of England, Scotland, Wales and later northern Ireland was for. At the start of the new century, we are much less certain. But we need to work out the purpose of the union if we are not to watch it unravel in the coming decades. Until we do, it is hard to see how we can enter into any other arrange-ment, with Europe or others, with any self-confidence.

So vast changes are ahead of us, perhaps an unending cascade of them. A new rela-tionship between women and men began to emerge in the past century, at least in the developed world. That process of struggle and debate will continue into the new era. But we should embrace it all. For as the scientists will keep telling us, change is in our nature. We are evolutionary creatures, granted a unique ability to ask questions about ourselves. Indeed, it is this very pursuit of understanding which distinguishes us from the animal. We should cherish this fact about ourselves, just as we cherish the intricate beauty of our existence. To quote Eliot once more: "Last year's words belong to last year's language/And next year's words await another voice." We are blessed to live now: let us make this a blessed century and a blessed new millennium. •

People

4 August 2000

Michael White

Chancellor meets convergence criteria

It may have been his wedding day, but for once it was hard not to feel sorry for Britain's Iron Chancellor. Gordon Brown and his bride, Sarah Macaulay, had been within 18 hours of pulling off the private family occasion they had so carefully planned when they were hit by the matrimonial equivalent of a Budget leak.

And this was the result. Instead of 20 or so close family, friends and assorted children gathering for a quiet nuptial at Mr Brown's redbrick home, high above the Forth bridges in North Queensferry, there was a media scrum at the gate.

Their prey cornered, nearly 100 photographers and reporters waited for the nod from Inspector Benny Byers, then streamed up the gravel drive and walked all over the back lawn (as we'd promised not to) for the agreed photo-call.

Prompt at 11.30am, it became another Brown promise delivered, but it was proof that a man may have nerves of steel when macro-managing a £1 trillion economy and still be painfully shy about his private affairs. The chancellor's face looked happy but his hands were all awkwardness.

"A kiss, sir," cried the snappers after the newly weds came diffidently through the back door following the Church of Scotland service (no hymns, no vows of obedience). "Is this the happiest day of your life?" shouted the Sun, eager to strike up a conversation. No answer. You could have attacked the comprehensive spending review in detail yesterday and still not got a word out of him.

The new Mrs Brown, whose long term investment strategy has proved every bit as clever as her husband's, wore an elegant cream silk suit by Louise Kennedy, Mr Brown looked as neat as he is ever likely to in his usual dark blue suit and white shirt. He was wearing a pink I-bought-it-for-the-wedding tie, smart enough but knotted so that it hung halfway to his knees. It is something else for Mrs B to take in hand.

"Another kiss please," they cried after Gordon, 49, and Sarah, 36, had whispered briefly (an "informal bilateral" in Whitehall-speak) before engaging in a tentative peck. They tried three times without getting it quite right. A month on Cape Cod will do wonders.

Those of us who cover all the big social weddings remembered that, back in 1981, Prince Charles had responded more convincingly to the challenge – and look where that got everyone. So perhaps the Browns' reticence was a good omen.

Twenty-fours hours earlier nothing of this was supposed to be happening. As the Daily Record, the Mirror's Scottish sister paper, gleefully reported yesterday, "ill-informed speculation" in London had even suggested that the workaholic politician and the PR exec's six-year affair had broken up – like all the others.

Now we learned from Ian Austin, the chancellor's normally tight-lipped Brummie spokesman, that he had proposed in January. Hang on there. Surely the brooding Heathcliff of the Heather was busy in January? All his energy was focused on the Budget, the CSR, the Transport Plan and the NHS Plan. But no. He was also nursing a Romantic Plan. What a polymath!

It was the Record which was to blame for yesterday's bunfight in the back garden. Locals in the chancellor's Dunfermline East constituency, 13 miles north of Edinburgh, had spotted the banns notice for "James Gordon Brown" and "Sarah Jane Macaulay" a fortnight ago. Amazingly, only yesterday did someone tip off the Labour tabloid. No one was taking credit for handily diverting the press pack, first to St John's church in nearby Inverkeithing at first light, then to its neighbour, the more imposing St Peter's outside which the constabulary (this was deemed significant) had placed two traffic cones.

The media pack tramped between the two churches like City investors dashing between equities and gilts on Budget day before the penny dropped. Under Scottish law the Rev Sheila Munro did not have to use any of her three churches to do the deed. She could do it in a private home.

So that was why the bridesmaids and pages, the aged parents, the friends and Treasury aides had all turned up at the chancellor's famously minimalist home. The pack headed south and arrived in time to hear the wedding was over.

At last the day belonged to Sarah, not to Prudence, her rival for the chancellor's heart during many a Budget cycle. She had waited longer than the average spending minister for Mr Brown to decide to ditch Prudence in favour of commitment and investment for a purpose. The time was finally ripe. "A wonderful day," said the bride and groom, but only in a statement.

Apart from Ed Balls, the chancellor's righthand man, and his wife, Yvette Cooper, the junior health minister, no political heavyweights were invited. From London the Blairs sent congratulations. Even Michael Portillo, the chancellor's Tory shadow, refrained from calling it a "stealth" wedding.

Touring the television studios the chancellor's former spin doctor, Charlie Whelan, called it posthumous vindication of his own oft spun, much disbelieved claim that it had been love all along. New Labour had delivered 100% more Downing Street babies than the Tories, even allowing for inflation. Now Downing Street was delivering 100% more Treasury weddings than John Major had managed, real weddings, not ones promised for 2003-04 as long as the economy holds up.

As the media was treated to a glass of Sainsbury's champagne (at £11.99 it reflected Prudence's lingering influence), the chancellor's friends expressed quiet glee that he had finally taken the plunge. "About time too," they murmured. •

29 May2000

Duncan Campbell

As Kim Basinger wasn't telling me the other day

In his satirical classic The Devil's Dictionary, the late American journalist Ambrose Bierce defined an interview as "a confession where vulgar impudence bends an ear to the follies of vanity and ambition". Now a ground-breaking new definition of the form is being offered in Hollywood.

The German magazine Süddeutsche Zeitung has published an apology to its readers for what it describes as "a betrayal of monumental proportions". It has had to admit that one of its Los Angeles freelance writers, Tom Kummer, has been, perhaps, too creative in some of his "interviews" with the stars.

It all came to light when other German journalists were asked by their editors why they were unable to come up with such spectacular exclusives. "We had our editors ringing up and saying 'why can't you go fishing with Bruce Willis, riding with Robert Redford and playing golf with Kevin Costner?'," said one journalist in Los Angeles last night. "He was coming up with all these great exclusives – being invited to Kim Basinger's cottage and things like that."

Holger Hötzel of Focus magazine decided to do some checking after an interview with Courtney Love, famously protective of her privacy, who was "outraged" to discover that she had supposedly been sharing her thoughts with Kummer. Many of the interviews turned out to be bogus. "They were conversations with himself. A lot of quotes came from a book he had written."

When Hötzel confronted Kummer, the latter attempted to justify his technique. "He is not apologising. He said that what stars say is an insult to any person's intelligence."

When the Focus article appeared two weeks ago, Kummer's own magazine pressed him for tapes of a supposed interview with Christina Ricci, star of The Opposite of Sex. He was apparently unable to provide them.

In an interview in Der Spiegel, Kummer explained his style as "montage reporting", part of the school of "borderline journalism". He explained: "Readers of my generation want to be entertained."

Last night he was said to be in Heidelberg giving a lecture on "Modern Myth". But in the spirit of borderline journalism, we joined him and Marlon Brando for champagne on the roof of the Beverly Hilton just before his departure from LA, where he told us: "Hey, that's showbiz." •

7 February 2000

Sabine Durrant
Enduring love

"**H**er house," says Michael Foot, standing alone in a sitting room in Hampstead. "Her garden." He is leaning against the door jamb, the weight of his body seemingly held in one gripped hand. He says this in a curt, matter-of-fact way. He nods his head towards the bay window, but he doesn't look through it. "Her garden. Nothing to do with me. All hers. I'm afraid." And then he makes a strange noise, a sort of audible full stop, "ny'hem", which sounds like a laugh but could be a groan.

He is very rickety. He bangs his body with his hands as if reminding himself where it is, thumps his knee as if urging his other limbs to be still. When he loses a word he puts a finger in his ear as if trying to retune. And when he walks, it's a negotiation between the world and his one good eye, one arm out to judge the distance. You have to keep remembering that he is 86 and that he has always been frail; that even as Labour leader during the 1983 election, he had the appearance of an old man. He does it to clothes too. There was the famous donkey jacket back then and today there is a voluminous knitted cardigan, coffee-stained and ink-splattered, that looks as if it's 50 years old. He got it for Christmas. But, for all this, everyone always said that in the company of his wife he lost years, that he twinkled, that they teased and flirted, that he always had one arm on her. Now that arm flails in the empty air.

He took a time getting to the front door (and opening it, but that, to use one of his phrases, "is another matter altogether"). He had been looking at Byron's Letters, which he had read with her in Venice. "It was 1978 when I was supposed to be in the bloody government and have no other interests but that. But we had a wonderful holiday. I suppose that's how we could afford it. We had some great holidays together. We've been to Venice many, many times. And then more recently to Dubrovnik, but that's another matter. Come to that later. But it was in Venice, in 1978, I first got on to Byron. Very late in life. I'm sorry to say. She was critical of him on some matters but gradually I put the case. So that was done with Jill. As everything." He slows down and takes a deep breath between each word. "Pretty. Well. Was."

It is less than two months since the death of Jill Craigie, film-maker, feminist, socialist, political and literary sparring partner. She was 85. She and Foot had been married for 50 years. She made her last film, Two Hours from London – a documentary about the Yugoslav conflict, paid for out of their life savings – only four years before. This time last year, she was giving sprightly interviews about her rape by Arthur Koestler in 1951. (She had always kept quiet about it, but the matter surfaced in a spat between David Cesarani, Koestler's biographer, and Frederic Raphael, who believed Craigie and Koestler's other victims should have been "honoured".) "A good witness," said Foot fondly of his wife at the time.

Then, last summer, she slipped in the bathroom and fractured her hip. There were complications with her heart, and for her last six months she was either in the Royal Free or in a bed in this sitting room, a room like all the rooms in the house, full of pictures and faded colour and books. Foot read to her every day.

"I still thought, you know, that we would have three or four more years when she'd come back," says her husband. He is talking with the same declamatory cadences one might use to give a political speech. "Especially in the garden which was looking wonderful all the year so . . ." He waves towards the window but still doesn't look up. "BUT," the word comes as an explosion, out of the side of his mouth, "when it actually happened finally there was a complication with her kidneys and the rest of it. Didn't work. SO it happened much more suddenly."

They had talked a bit in the past about who would go first. "We thought the chances were just about even." They had no children together, though she had a daughter from a previous marriage. Would she be worrying about you? "Huh." He looks down at his hands, which are doing invisible crocheting. "I don't know. She'd be laughing." I ask rather hopelessly if he still sees her in the house around him. "No," he says. "Both of us had the same views on these matters. We didn't believe in any afterlife or that kind of stuff. So . . . aaaaa, aye . . . aa . . . no, she's, you know. I'm not saying we didn't have a number of quarrels at varying times, I'm not going to go into that. But over the last 10 years I suppose we were getting closer on many things. So. It knocks the charm out of life."

They married in 1949 – "up there at Hampstead town hall" – but had been lovers since they had met four years earlier in Plymouth, where Craigie was making a film and Foot was an MP. There were holidays even then, first in Nice. "It was just after the end of the war and we were in this huge great palace hotel and hardly anyone else in the bloody place. But we were so nervous about bloody scandal we had to book two different rooms and I crawled around this big hotel late at night . . ." When they got back to Hampstead there were reporters on the doorstep. "And I said if they print anything derogatory about us, we'll print something derogatory about their proprietors in Tribune the week after. I knew about Beaverbrook, obviously, and even more so about the antics of Lord Rothermere. And they dispersed."

Jill, "My Jill" as he says at one point, charmed everyone he knew. Beaverbrook, who employed him on the Express. His father, who adored her. Tom Driberg, "who would come back from one these escapades in Moscow and used to walk up and down this room and pour things out to Jill he wouldn't mention to me". Henry Moore and Stanley Spencer, about whom she made a film. Everyone fell in love with her, then? "You bet. Yes. You bet. The whole lot." And did he find that difficult? He gives a grim laugh. "That's a different question altogether."

When he talks about their life together, it is people, but mainly books, that come to mind. The things they read, the things they talked about, disagreed about, came together over: Byron and Oscar Wilde and William Morris, and Rebecca West, whose rehabilitation he is adamant is due to the friendship and encouragement of Craigie. He refers to the last book Craigie read to herself, Francis Wheen's biography of Karl Marx ("and she was very much in favour of it"); the last book he read to her, Rebecca West's Letters in typescript.

Politics, on the other hand, seem to impinge very little on his memory. Political discussions, yes. Craigie's arguments with Barbara Castle: "Many here in this room". Watching Nye Bevan speak in Devonport, and Craigie saying "here's the chap to lead us". Friendship with Donald Dewar, who used to live in the flat upstairs: "not exactly a raging leftwinger, but a very fine chap". But on the nitty gritty, the victories and the massive defeats of his political involvement, he is supremely detached. Of his own involvement he says "supposed" a lot, and is free with his expletives. "When I was leader of the House of Commons and responsible, I suppose, for the legislation that was going through the bloody House of Commons . . ." he says at one point. When, just after he had been elected leader of the Labour party, he went into hospital with a broken leg, "I didn't want to take those damned Blue Books, so I took Don Juan." People often said, he goes on, that Jill had "put me up to standing as leader, but that's not true at all". However, she would, he says, "have run Chequers very well, believe me".

Was she happy with Blair's government? "N'yaaaaaaa," he says. "I don't see it. No, she was anxious about a lot of things, you know." Her main disagreement, he says, "was about the bomb and all that, because Jill is still, both of us, strong CND supporters. The government could certainly do much much more along those lines, and we still think they might. I miss her terribly on that front. Everything that happens . . . since . . . I'd like to have known what her views are."

In her last few weeks she was very interested in the Hamilton trial. "I used to go in there every day for the last week and say, 'What do you want first? The Hamiltons or not?' Not that she was a sadist – she was quite the opposite – but she was also interested in gossip and she thought the business of politicians taking these bloody bribes was a disgrace and she was very glad to see it exposed. She would have been very satisfied, in my opinion, with the result but I fear that it happened just two or three days after her . . . death."

Foot has been holding a cup of coffee during the interview, which at times has looked as if it might spill on to the sofa cushions below his waving hand. Only now does he take a long gulp. He wipes his mouth. He says he has things he can get on with. The memorial service is behind him now, but there is to be a celebration of Craigie in Dubrovnik, where she is "the uncrowned queen". There is talk of a biography. He has a "junket" to Bermuda. Something else in Paris.

Was she as proud of you, I ask, as you obviously were of her? He stutters for a while. He taps his leg. "I don't know. She was wonderful to me without any doubt. Most of the fun I've had out of life is due to her and the things we did together. Was she proud of me? I don't know. She was not . . . ah . . ." He opens his mouth but nothing comes out. Finally, he starts again: "On political questions she was in agreement with what I wanted to do."

There is a long silence while he fiddles with his ear. Then he says, "She said, 'Lots of people will come and look after you, you know.' And I said, 'You're the only one I want.'" And we both look out at the garden then. •

15 April 2000

Michael Foot

We just love that woman

Selected Letters of Rebecca West
edited by Bonnie Kime Scott
Yale University Press, £25, 479pp

"I just love that woman," Jill Craigie would say of Rebecca West, and Rebecca would eagerly repay the compliment. Their friendship blossomed only in the last dozen years of Rebecca's long life, but since it was chiefly on Jill's prompting that Rebecca returned to the journalism of her flaming youth, the two of them together took the century in their feminist strides. Like Jill, Rebecca was an artist in everything she touched and saw. Each had a specially sharpened visual sense, which Jill could translate into films and pictures, and Rebecca into words.

Again and again throughout our own quite lengthy lives, Jill and I found ourselves bumping afresh into some revelation of the HG Wells-Rebecca West saga. I first met him at a weekend party at Max Beaverbrook's country estate in the late 1930s. He was the hero of my early twenties, having completed my conversion to socialism with Tono-Bungay and several other of his titles. At his side on that occasion was not Rebecca but his last and maybe truest love, Moura Budberg. She became for me a heroine, too, keeping alive my connection with HG until he died eight years later.

The HG Wells of the second world war fought with all his might for the rights of man; Beaverbrook's Evening Standard played a notable part in that victory, proudly printing every one of his red-hot revolutionary words. Both Jill and I fell victims to Max Beaverbrook's charm. Outside observers could not understand the relationship, but he was a firm friend to both of us until the day of his death. No topic of conversation seemed to be banned between us – especially his interest in the worlds of HG Wells, Arnold Bennett and so forth – but in all our conversations, one name never cropped up: that of Rebecca West.

Not until years later, when HG and Max and Rebecca were all dead, did Rebecca's posthumously published novel Sunflower tell the story of how the slightly ageing HG was displaced in her affections by the magnificent young Max. It was a delicate, matchless love story, intelligently told. But no one could know about this at the time; Rebecca was presumably resolved to give offence to neither of her lovers.

What happened between Rebecca and Max in their original affair is not finally clarified either in the novel or in these letters, but every later development is honourable to them both. He helped her directly in her journalistic career, and would do his best to assist when her more outrageous friends, such as the anarchist leader Emma Goldman, were being pilloried in the newspapers.

If you have not yet read Sunflower, order your copy now. Don't be deterred by some of the jealous reviewers who dismissed the work as inferior when it did finally appear; Rebecca knew better.

Her suppression of the novel must have been all the more galling when she saw that her literary opponents showed no such reticence. Enemy number one was her own son by HG, Anthony West, who wrote a damning autobiographical novel, Heritage, while Rebecca was still alive, and pursued his vendetta even after her death with an unrelenting fury that can still turn the stomach.

In these pages she can defend herself against all his accusations. "Posterity will never forgive a bad mother," she would sometimes say to Jill. Here she is vindicated; Anthony gets his due. He had, for example, a terrible quarrel with his father in HG's last days which he wretchedly tried to blame on Rebecca; in fact, it was much more the result of his own imperfect sympathies with his father.

Along with many writers of the century, headed by HG himself, Rebecca understood the importance of Anglo-American associations – she made her name in the US in the 1920s, and ever after kept a foot on both sides of the Atlantic – so the editing of this volume by the American Bonnie Kime Scott is all the more appropriate.

Some of the best liberal spirits of the age became her closest friends. A few of them at moments of stress might have questioned her allegiance, but, if need be, she could counter-attack with all her polemical might. Her insights take command at the most appropriate moments: "The Statue of Liberty," she said at her first glance, "is a washout – she gets her stays at the same place as Queen Mary's."

A most prolific letter writer herself – she claimed sometimes to write several before breakfast – she had a special appreciation of how full volumes of letters could inform a proper judgment of the greatest writers. She had not always been as aware of Oscar Wilde's genius as might have been expected, for instance, but after his letters were published she sent his son Vyvyan Holland a glowing response, full of fresh understanding: "I don't think anyone could read the volume without liking your father more than before." These words were intended to bring comfort to Merlin, Oscar's grandson, as well as to his father. The Rebecca who wrote this letter and several more of the same quality truly knew what love was.

But what of her relationship with HG, the most significant of her life? They had their rows, but nothing to compare with the savagery of those with Anthony. For several years after their first meeting, HG drew on his own new knowledge of Rebecca to portray the new woman – from Fanny in The Dream to Helen in The World of William Clissold – and what a wonderful breed she was. The literary connection between the two was brilliantly unravelled by JR Hammond in his HG Wells and Rebecca West, published in 1991. He showed how each was indispensable to the other, and where each could claim to be innovators.

The last book I read to Jill was this collection of letters from the woman she so greatly honoured. No hardship, I can assure you: the wit pours forth on every page along with the lamentations. Jill sometimes suspected me of treating her Rebecca less kindly than I should – especially when HG was misbehaving in a big way. And yet, having read and re-read every word, the main conclusion is unchallengeable. The love between them triumphed over everything else: the reconciliations were always much more significant than the ruptures.

The last of these came in the 1940s, when they shared a vision that the England they both loved could rejoice in a victory over the forces of evil. Anthony failed to join that period of exhilaration: he even helped to spread the insinuation that his father's mind was failing. The reality was nothing of the kind: with Moura on one side and Rebecca on the other, he was celebrating the freedom which he had done as much as any of his countrymen to secure. ■

5 January 2000

Jonathan Romney
The little fellow

The end of the 20th century was a good time for what used to be known as the Little Fellow. Comedian Norman Wisdom – a favourite of the Queen, and a living legend in Albania, where he's known as "Pitkini" – was listed for a knighthood. And Mickey Mouse made a comeback in what many consider his finest hour, the Sorcerer's Apprentice sequence from Disney's Fantasia (1940), now incorporated into the bigger, louder Imax extravaganza, Fantasia 2000.

Although critics over 18 didn't rate the film much, prepubescent viewers vox-popped by this paper enthusiastically agreed that the original Mickey sequence was the best in the film. That ought to prove the undying appeal of Mousehood, but I have my doubts. The Sorcerer's Apprentice and its star may well be timeless, but only in the particular sense in which a cultural phenomenon is entirely of its time, absolutely represents its age, and is therefore dated, albeit in a transcendental way.

Standing specifically for the last century, Mickey has no chance of making it as an icon into the 21st. He's a curiously repellent figure in ways that only the professionally lovable can be. His history is one of rapid institutionalisation and embourgeoisement, from the surreal elastic imp of the 20s to the tolerant suburban patriarch and corporate spokesman he had become by the 50s. The lanky, rubbery hero of 1928's Steamboat Willie is a bizarre, elemental creature, but it didn't take the corporation long to make him stocky and leaden, formalise his costume and turn him into a smiling yes man, glad-handing theme-park punters. Mickey became not just the company's figurehead, but its very being, its chairman by proxy. It's no accident that Variety still routinely refers to Disney as the Mouse House or, tellingly, just the Mouse.

Fantasia 2000 shows today's Mickey still playing the obliging corporate mascot, dashing on between musical sequences to make cheeky, squeaky backchat with the conductor. This only underlines the conservative lesson of the Sorcerer's Apprentice sketch. Mickey is warned by the beetle-browed magician not to make trouble, but quite reasonably wants to harness the boss's magic for his own ends, so borrows his hat. He brings a broom to life and makes it carry buckets of water for him, but the brooms multiply uncontrollably, and an army of them floods the cell with water. At last, the angry sorcerer restores order, retrieves his hat, and sends Mickey – who shoots the boss the very definition of the shit-eating grin – scuttling ignominiously back to his corner. And we're still supposed to be charmed by this "timeless" parable of the workers knowing their place.

Mickey's original persona was rooted in the mythology of modern industrial society, no less than the other Little Fellow archetype, Charlie Chaplin. His early battles were against technological chaos: Mickey would be the one malleable yet stable figure at the centre of a storm of clattering stovepipe machinery. Objects would malfunction and mutate around him, but Mickey would genially bend to the chaos, at once master and servant of technology's rhythms. Through him, the art of animation – the unnatural cinema technology par excellence – dramatised its own mechanical nature and in a roundabout way advertised its approachability.

While Mickey was promoted to the board, the Disney hero who still seems contemporary remains an outsider – Donald Duck, no one's idea of the resiliently accepting Little Fellow, but a crazed romantic rager against the inconveniences of the world, whether natural or technological, who might at any moment erupt into a libidinous cataclysm in his own right. Donald is the precursor of Jack Nicholson, Travis Bickle and Seinfeld's sidekick George Costanza, yet – shame – even he has been co-opted by Fantasia 2000, pressed into service as an obliging steward on Noah's Ark.

Similarly, the silent comedies that don't seem timeless, as Chaplin's do, but of the present, are Buster Keaton's, whose battles can't be reduced to those of the early-21st-century industrial struggler. Paradoxically, what makes Keaton modern is that he is a parodic hangover of an archetype from an earlier age, a comic avatar of the 19th-century Byronic hero – the loner in the wilderness, racked by the elements, impassioned, unbowed and above all, never submissive to the audience's approval. Where Chaplin was forever tipping a winsome wink to the crowd, Keaton acted as though the audience simply wasn't there – he seemed as unconcerned by the mechanisms of entertainment as by the industrial mechanisms that defined the plucky toiler hero, whether Chaplin, Mickey or Norman Wisdom.

Mickey's last stand, and Wisdom's knighthood, surely represent an adieu to the archetype of the eager little loner – cloth-capped, bowler-hatted or big-eared – on the shop floor. Is it too early to hazard a guess on the comic archetype of the coming age? For that, we do have a model: Jacques Tati, like a distracted stork legging and pecking his way through the attractions of the post-modern consumer metropolis in his underrated 1967 masterpiece, Playtime. Tati couldn't be a more timely icon, a model for the punters sceptically and bemusedly inspecting the variously mystifying and ludicrous attractions of the Millennium Dome. •

22 February 2000

Martin Kettle
A kinder, gentler, better America

Garrison Keillor is sitting in his dressing room reading sonnets. Three thousand at the latest count, he says, and rising every time the postman calls. All because he suggested on the radio that listeners might try their hand at a Valentine's day poem.

"There are depths of love out there that we barely knew about," Keillor says. "It's not the simplest thing to sit down and write 14 lines. All these people, overcome by the need to write a sonnet. Just imagine that." Imagining it is easy. A Prairie Home Companion – the programme that Keillor hosts each week – inspires levels of devotion that few radio shows can rival.

There are people who plan their holidays around A Prairie Home Companion so as never to mis s a show, and people who plan their holidays so they can attend live recordings at the Fitzgerald Theatre in St Paul, the show's Minnesota home. So if Keillor asks these people for sonnets, he should expect sonnets.

A Prairie Home Companion goes out every Saturday across the US's National Public Radio network, just as it has done since it first started in 1974. This is therefore the silver jubilee season, and, to celebrate, Keillor and his team are bringing the show to Scotland and Ireland over the next couple of weeks, beaming it back live to the US and recording two episodes to be broadcast on Radio 4 and Ireland's RTE.

The show is a mix of all kinds of music and comedy sketches, culminating in a set piece "News From Lake Wobegon" monologue delivered by Keillor to about 3m rapt listeners. The show begins with and returns to Keillor. At 5pm Central Time he starts it, singing "Oh, hear that old piano/ From down the avenue..." Two hours later, as he announces, "And that's the news from Lake Wobegon, where all the women are strong, all the men are good-looking and all the children are above average," the audience know it's home time.

A Prairie Home Companion is an expression of Keillor's personality, his imagination and his values. Though the show is very funny, and the music is great, in some ineradicable way it is Keillor's loving and funny evocation of a kinder, simpler, better US that is at the heart of its appeal. "It's based on a kind of show that existed in my youth," says Keillor, who grew up in 50s rural Minnesota. "It's a live variety-show broadcast, but with some important differences." Like the range of its music, which can run from a cappella chorus through jazz, bluegrass, Cajun and Celtic, and occupies at least half of each show. And like the fact that Keillor devised and writes much of the show himself, sometimes finishing his script only just before the show airs.

Watching Keillor in rehearsal and then as he hosts his show, it's hard not to wonder why he subjects himself to it. What would make this bespectacled middle-class Minnesotan gentleman of 57 stand on a stage and perform Great Balls of Fire for the millions? What would make a man with a new marriage and young daughter rise every morning at 5am to write? Whatever else Keillor keeps hidden about himself, and there's a sense of a dark side to him, you know that this is a driven man.

He says that doing the show is "good work". He says it's "a little harder than you'd like to be doing ideally in your late 50s", but that it would be "a terrible waste to just drop it". He says he finds it easier to do these days. "One of the great secrets that they don't tell you is that your declining years are really a lot more fun than when you were riding high and you were nervous about losing your touch."

"In my view," says producer Christine Tschida, who has worked with Keillor for the past 10 years, "Garrison just has a need to stand up in front of an audience every Saturday."

People in Britain know Keillor mostly as a writer – which is also how he likes to see himself. Lake Wobegon Days, published in 1985, was the first – and in many people's eyes the best – of a succession of novels and comic writings that have appeared at regular intervals ever since. His latest – Me by Jimmy (Big Boy) Valente as Told to Garrison Keillor – is a satire on the other iconic Minnesotan of the present era, the state's improbable governor Jesse Ventura, the man they call the Body Politic.

Lake Wobegon is Keillor's Minnesotan never-never land. It permeates his books, and it has the honoured place in A Prairie Home Companion. "It's both real and imaginary," he explains. "But it does exist, it very much exists. Even here in Minneapolis and St Paul."

"All these rural people have come to live in the city, but they like to live on the outskirts, and they like to have an acre of land, two acres, three acres. These are Lake Wobegon people and they are a part of midwestern culture that's describable, and I think that I describe it.

"I write about it with love," he continues, "but I also write about it satirically, because the people themselves have a satiric mind. They're very ironic people. But I think their reticence is funny – their dishonesty, their inability to tell the truth to each other, the great length they go to. And they are stoics. Stoics I think are comical. They never give up. They keep at hopeless tasks. And these people don't believe that they are entitled to happiness."

Like the man himself, the writings may leave Minnesota from time to time, but it is to Minnesota that they always return. And the same is true of A Prairie Home Companion. Every year it goes on the road, occasionally, as now, overseas. But most of the shows are broadcast live from the Fitzgerald, the century-old theatre in downtown St Paul that Keillor helped to save a few years back, renaming it after the greatest of St Paul's literary sons. Keillor is an enthusiast of the author of The Great Gatsby – his cat is named F Cat Fitzgerald.

The on-stage understanding between Keillor and his house band (led by keyboard player Rich Dworsky), actors Sue Scott and Tim Russell, and sound-effects man Tom Keith, speaks of years of respect. But there's no disputing that the only real place to see the show is at the Fitz, in winter, on Keillor's home ground, with snow in the streets and a theatre full of cheering devotees, which is where I saw it earlier this month.

The weather looms large in Minnesota, and thus in the Lake Wobegon fantasy, and thus in A Prairie Home Companion too. "It's a neutral place for a conversation to start," Keillor says. "The show is about ordinary things. You don't need to have seen movies, or watched TV, or read books to understand the show."

Winter is a big deal in Minnesota – bigger than anyone in the Britain can really know. "Growing up in a place that has winter," Keillor has written, "you learn to avoid self-pity. Winter is not a personal experience – everybody else is as cold as you – so you shouldn't complain about it too much."

That passage is reprinted on a coffee mug that I bought in what must surely be the only store in the world devoted wholly to a radio show. Lake Wobegon USA is in the largest shopping mall on the planet – the Mall of America, outside Minneapolis airport. Dave Edin, who runs the shop, will talk Garrison Keillor with customers for as long as they are willing to listen. Which, in most cases, is a long time.

"I think about America every day," Keillor once wrote, "and imagine a town, an avenue of old frame houses, a boulevard of tall trees, a June night, lawn sprinklers swishing across the grass and popping the flower bushes by the porch. A dog on the porch. Lights behind the curtains. Rock'n'roll in an upstairs bedroom. Charcoal smoke in the air, a whiff of burgers. A gang of kids skidding around on gravel, giggling. A screen door slaps and a dad marches out to the garage. Yard after yard, block after block, every sight and sound and smell utterly familiar. This is the American neighbourhood of childhood comfort and fantasy, of teenage ambition, and of the tenderness and misery and splendour and comedy of marriage. Movies and novels of brutality and greed may sell a zillion copies, but they're irrelevant to the life of this avenue, which is based on faith, hope, love and humour."

In a sense, that's the key to the appeal of A Prairie Home Companion. "I hope you enjoy the show," Keillor tells the Minnesota audience just as they go on air. "And I hope I do too." It is great entertainment with a high purpose – and if you can come up with a better working definition of art, then you're welcome to it. •

16 March 2000

Euan McCaskill
The left's Lawrence of Arabia

The Labour MP, George Galloway, smoking a large Cuban cigar, rolled up at the Jordanian border this week. In a Range Rover flying the British and Iraqi flags, he looked out across no man's land to Iraq. "There is the holy land," he said, with genuine affection.

For many, such a remark would be regarded as inflammatory – the "holy land" is the land of Saddam Hussein? And such enthusiasm for the country could be viewed as treacherous at a time when British warplanes, along with some from the US, still fly sorties over Iraq. The war is not over.

Galloway has no doubts where his loyalty lies on this issue. The Iraqi people are suffering on a devastating scale from the UN sanctions imposed after Iraq invaded Kuwait. He says: "One million Iraqis, many of them children, have died, more than Pol Pot murdered in Cambodia."

On arrival at the Iraqi border post, a 50-strong welcome committee was waiting for him, holding up portraits of Saddam and chanting "Galloway welcome." He waved a victory sign from the car window. Another chant followed: "Saddam, the Americans shake at the mention of your name." They broke into song: "With blood and soul, we will sacrifice for Saddam."

The 45-year-old MP for Glasgow Kelvin, who for eight years has been campaigning for the lifting of sanctions, originally wanted to fly medical supplies from London to Baghdad but the flight, which would have been the first between the two capitals since the war, had to be cancelled after a row between the anti-sanctions campaigners on the one side and the British government and the UN sanctions committee on the other. In defiance, he and a handful of others went anyway, flying to Amman in Jordan and leading a small convoy 600 miles across the desert to Baghdad on Tuesday. He told those gathered at the border: "We are determined to break the stranglehold the Americans have on the country. One day we will win, because God is great."

He arouses strong emotions and has made lots of enemies. A British foreign office source, dismissive of the trip, described him as a "buffoon". But there is a lot of warmth for Galloway in the Arab world, much more than might be believed back home in a sceptical Britain. While the meeting at the border was stage-managed, elsewhere in Iraq, where he is almost universally recognised, and in other parts of the Middle East, the welcome is spontaneous and genuine.

In Jordan, sitting in traffic, a man in the next car rolled down his window to reach out and shake his hand. At a petrol station, another man walked up and offered him a sweet. It does not sound much but the man did not look as if he had much. Close to the Jordanian Iraqi border, a Bedouin, Sheik Abu-Hatam, who runs herds of sheep, insisted that he stop for lunch. Galloway told him he could not stop but eventually relented, agreeing to go in for a minute. Time passed, and a full-scale lunch appeared, the sheik saying: "Because you did not want any formalities, I have killed only one sheep."

Galloway, who joined the Labour party aged 13 and is on the left, has a wide range of interests, from Cuba to Pakistan through to Scottish devolution, but it is the Arab cause that he first embraced with a passion and for which he is best known. Born in Dundee, he left school at 16 to work in a Michelin tyre factory. By his mid-twenties he had transformed himself into the most prominent and passionate British champion of the Arabs – socialism's answer to Lawrence of Arabia.

His life was changed by a chance encounter when he was 21. He was sitting in the Labour party's office in Dundee when a Palestinian came in, saying he represented Palestinian students at Dundee university and wanted to put his case to someone in the party. When the Palestinian left two-and-a-half hours later, he had made an important convert.

Galloway spent three months living in the Lebanon with Palestinian refugees, and had a Palestinian girlfriend. He now lives with a Palestinian, though not the same one as in the Lebanon. His partner now is Amineh Abu-Zayadd, a 33-year-old scientist from Jerusalem: they share a flat in London.

Back in Britain after his stint in Lebanon, he organised the twinning of Nablus and Dundee, where the Palestinian flag flew over the Labour-controlled council headquarters.

Earlier this week, on the Jordanian shoreline, looking across at the sun setting on the blue hills of what was once Israel but is now Palestine, he said wistfully: "I used to dream I would be part of the force that would wade ashore, Kalashnikov in hand, and return it to its rightful owners ." Such rhetoric stems in part from romantic socialism, echoing heroes such as Lenin, Mao and Che Guevara, but in the main from a belief that the Palestinians are the victims of a huge injustice.

Eight years ago, he visited Iraq for the first time and was appalled by the condition he found people in. He had a new cause. Coming so soon after the formal end to the Gulf war, his involvement brought accusations of being a quisling, a traitor and Saddam's stooge. He was dubbed the MP for Baghdad Central.

At a public meeting on the Crusader hilltop town of Karak in Jordan on Monday night, packed with people fiercely sympathetic to Iraq and its president, he said bravely: "Saddam is not my hero." A shout came from the audience: "He's mine."

Galloway draws a distinction between Saddam, whom he does not support, and his campaigning on behalf of the Iraqi people. But he is valued by the Iraqi government. When he arrived at the border, the deputy prime minister, Tariq Aziz, unexpectedly sent two Mercedes to whisk him to Baghdad.

As part of his anti-sanctions campaign, Galloway took a young Iraqi girl suffering from cancer, Maria Hamza, to Britain for treatment, highlighting the crucial shortages in Iraqi hospitals. Back in Baghdad now, the six-year old is still alive with the cancer under control, but is blind. Last year, he embarked on another stage of his campaign, driving a London double-decker to Baghdad.

He sees a connection between his espousal of the Palestinian cause and the Iraqi campaign. He says both were part of "the Project" aimed at keeping Arabs divided – a cause pursued by Britain for the first half of the 20th century and by the US in the second. He describes himself as being in sympathy with Egypt's ex-president Gamel Abdul Nasser and with Iraq's ruling Ba'ath party, both committed to the idea of a united Arab nation and describes Israel as having been "implanted" to maintain the divide. "Israel is there to stay but I believe it should not be there," he says.

He insists he is not anti-Jewish, though he expresses disappointment that the Jewish people, who he perceives as being in the vanguard of the progressive movement in Europe for much of the last century, have been turned by Zionism "from being this bright shining light to being guilty of some atrocious crimes".

As one of the best speakers in the Commons and with a talent for publicity, Galloway had the potential to rise far within the Labour party. But he has proved too controversial, too outspoken, too hot to handle, with a row involving War on Want, where he worked, through to a libel action against the Mirror, which made an enemy of the prime minister's press secretary Alastair Campbell. He has not given up hope, and would like a crack at becoming Glasgow's first mayor.

At nights when he is late at the Commons he phones Amineh at home and asks her to prepare a hookah by lighting the coals. Most nights he has a smoke while watching Newsnight. As one Jordanian said this week after the Karak meeting, he is "more Arab than the Arabs." •

War and
peace

27 June 2000

Maggie O'Kane

A blacked-out vehicle, a piece of Irish history

When Cyril Ramaphosa arrives at his office in Johannesburg at 11.30am today, he will have completed a seven-day journey that has taken him across the world and into Ireland's history books. He is a witness to what may finally be the end of 30 years of violence, human loss and private agonies in Northern Ireland.

It is a place reserved for him and the former Finnish president, Martti Ahtisaari, as the only two outsiders present on a warm summer's day in Ireland when the IRA opened three arms dumps to them.

The journey of the two international inspectors began on Monday last week when Mr Ramaphosa flew north out of Johannesburg airport and met his colleague, the former Finnish president, in London.

Their movements over the next three days in the Republic of Ireland may have taken them to the south, to the slopes of the Magillycuddy Reeks and the Slieve Bloom Mountains where the IRA has historically stored arms, or perhaps they tramped the Co Cavan border.

What they saw was the first ever voluntary display of IRA weapons to outsiders. Yesterday morning they confirmed that they believed that the IRA weapons had finally been stored and could not be used without their knowledge.

It is a huge step – the closest the IRA will ever come to decommissioning its arms.

The details of exactly what the inspectors saw when those dumps were opened are reserved for the next chapter of the history books.

Did they see what remained of the three tons of semtex brought in from Libya to the Wicklow Coast between 1984 and 1987? Perhaps it was just a couple of the kalashnikovs the IRA have been buying in eastern Europe since the Bosnia war ended. Perhaps the dump, like the one discovered by the Irish police under a farmhouse in Co Laois, had its own electricity supply, air vent and heating system to keep the weapons at optimum temperature.

The IRA drove the inspectors to the dump. The vehicle's windows were blacked out. There were no blindfolds. Mr Ahtisaari, who ran the negotiations between Nato and Russia during the Kosovo war, and Mr Ramaphosa, one of the most influential black leaders in South Africa, are not men who travel blindfolded.

"These are international statesmen and there is trust there," a source who spoke directly with the IRA after the operation told the Guardian. "The whole basis of this operation is trust and secrecy."

Even the inner cogs of the Irish government were unaware of what had taken place late on Friday afternoon. "This is unprecedented, uncharted water. In 24 years in the job. I haven't seen anything like it," said one of the men at the heart of the Dublin government.

After the inspections the dumps were sealed using one of three techniques – a wax seal, stamped by the inspectors (most unlikely), an electric current run across the entrance to register an interference (also unlikely), or concrete.

They will be back in three months to check that the arms have indeed been "put beyond use"

"You can be sure of one thing. This is as good as it is going to get. You will never see IRA arms being put through the metal grinder. They will rust in the ground but never be handed over," the source told The Guardian yesterday.

What the IRA still has to rust under the ground is somewhere in the region of 600 detonators, six flame throwers, a Sam surface to air missile, 50 rocket launchers, 20 heavy machine guns, 12 machine guns and three sniper rifles. Most of these came courtesy of Colonel Gadafy some time between 1984 and 1987; the Armalites and 600 AK47s also hidden are a spin-off from the Balkans.

In a small cottage along a coast road in Co Donegal is a shabby single storey cottage with its kitchen and dining room windows blocked out with white paint. It is the summer home of a 58-year-old man who, last Monday, finally issued the invitation for his foreign visitors to come and visit the dumps: Brian Keenan, once described as "most intelligent, energetic and resourceful military operator the modern IRA has yet produced".

He's not been seen much around the cottage, where the garden is full of wild Donegal cotton. He has been busy, spending two years persuading the IRA to put their "arms beyond use".

There are two important things to note about Brian Keenan. He has always said the IRA will never decommission. But they also say that if you get Brian Keenan's pulse, you get the pulse of the IRA. Yesterday in the early morning Donegal sunshine, his home looked like that of a man who had finally reached a quiet place. •

27 November 1999

John Mullin

This couple fled their farm in fear of the IRA 27 years ago. Today they are urging their fellow unionists to vote for peace

John McClure still thinks of Johnny Fletcher. He expects something of his friend to flit into his mind today as he prepares to make a decision he thinks will determine Northern Ireland's future path. It might be their days together at Knocknashangan primary, or the cards schools where they would play poker for hours, just for pennies. He might recall the laughter when they helped each other on their farms, and then nipped across the border for a pint in Kiltyclougher.

They were brought up in a different era in the Fermanagh farmlands. No one, he says, cared what religion anyone was back then.

Mr McClure, 66, hopes these days can return, for the sake of his five children, 10 grandchilren, and the memory of his old friend. That is what wil l motivate him most when he votes with his wife, Ivy, at the Ulster Unionist Council meeting in Belfast.

The IRA came calling for Johnny Fletcher on March 1, 1972. He was 43 and married to Edith. They had no children. He had a 20-acre farm and had taken another job, as a forestry worker.

Leaving home, he stopped his car to open the gate across the lane. He was seized and dragged back to his house by four men who wanted his guns. After finding a pistol and a shotgun, they assured his wife they were taking him hostage merely to ensure they made it to the border.

Mr McClure says: "They shot him 33 or 34 times. They dumped him on the river bank, and strolled across the border into Leitrim."

Two days after carrying his friend's coffin, Mr McClure fled the small border community of Garrison with Ivy, and their five children, aged 12 to three, and went to live in Churchill. It was a run-down house, without a lavatory. The three other Protestant families then living in Garrison decided to go too. There were no problems with their Catholic neighbours, but threats were coming thick and fast from the IRA just south of the border.

Mr McClure was a member of the recently founded Ulster Defence Regiment. He netted at most £20 a month, and had joined out of duty. So, too, had Johnny Fletcher. Mr McClure knew it could just as easily have been him executed and dumped on the River Kilcoo.

When he and Ivy left the home where their children were born, they thought they would be back soon, that the Troubles would be over. Instead, they moved several times, scrimping to improve the houses. Mr McClure took work as a lorry driver. They live now in Springhill, 18 miles from Garrison, and would love to return to the 100-acre farm.

The three-bedroom bungalow is a ruin these days. A horse bridle lies in the middle of the floor; an old radio and tilly lamp to the side. Still hanging from one door is Ivy McClure's coat, mildewed. They had left in a hurry.

Mrs McClure was lost in her thoughts yesterday in the yard where her children used to play. She fretted over the driveway, once a tidy gravel path, now a mud bath.

The McClures were regular attenders at the Church of Ireland in Garrison, where there is now a plaque to Johnny Fletcher. They met at the Sunday school, and married there.

Mr McClure, who was to see several friends killed in the UDR, says: "Life was simple then. Religion didn't matter at all. You helped everyone out no matter what. I know my Catholic neighbours would really like to see us back home.

"If you were Protestant, you were Unionist. There was only the one party then. The man would come around ever y now and again and collect a few shillings. You paid him and he'd be on his way.

"We've both been in the party all our lives. Now we are delegates to the council."

The party's 858-strong ruling body will decide at the Waterfront Hall today whether to back leader David Trimble's call to support proposals by the former US senator George Mitchell meant to lead on Thursday to Northern Ireland's first ever inclusive government. They believe IRA decommissioning of weapons will follow early next year.

Mr McClure, who voted for John Taylor for leader four years ago, said: "We have had a fairly turbulent life. We want better times for our family. None of our children has ever wanted to leave Northern Ireland, and we want our grandchildren to feel the same.

"Do we trust Gerry Adams and Martin McGuinness? If we go along with Mr Trimble, we won't have long to wait to find out.

"If the IRA fails to deliver, then Mr Trimble can pull out [of joint government]. There will be nothing lost. We will only be back to where we are.

"Those who are opposed to the compromise have taken no part in the talks. I have no time for them. We are both agreed. We trust David Trimble, and so we will both be backing him. We hope the council does the same." •

15 April 2000

Hugo Young
Words were not enough

A hazard of the writer's trade is that writing is sometimes not enough. Great writers know there is nothing else to do, and most lesser writers would probably be incapable of any other way of life, however sketchy their literary satisfactions and paltry their rewards Whether novelists, historians or general-purpose hacks, we know our limitations, and usually find that these do not extend beyond the filling, one way or another, of the unwritten page. But there are exceptions. An engulfing aura of pointlessness is capable of sinking the author whose two-year labours produce sales of a couple of thousand copies. Might it not be better, for heaven's sake, to do something, to act, rather than spend more years in futile toil at the word-processor screen?

The writer who wants to change the world could be particularly vulnerable to this temptation. But succumbing to it seems a kind of betrayal. One writes one's piece, perhaps one's several pieces, filled with sincere outrage and all the literary power one can muster – and then passes on to the next subject. The writer has to write. The reporter has merely to report. In journalism especially, the line between writing and acting should be guarded with professional severity. Crossing over, in the short term or the long, is an offence against the canons of the trade. The battlefield reporter doesn't stop to pick up corpses.

Anyone Here Been Raped And Speak English? – the title of Edward Behr's memoir sums up the code of the disaster correspondent hurtling to meet his deadline. Dominique Lapierre spent plenty of time as such a writer. A senior reporter on Paris Match for 20 years, he covered the Algerian war and many other catastrophe zones on the front line. He has also been a staggeringly successful author. From the 60s, his mega-works of popular history, several written with his American confrère, Larry Collins, piled the shop-shelves high for months and years. The two men developed a uniquely accessible line in documentary reporting, with a strong human interest. They were early practitioners of total research. Is Paris Burning?, their first effort, reconstructed the liberation of the city from the Germans, based on interviews with no fewer than 1,200 witnesses. They wrote the life of a Spanish matador, El Cordobes, and, among other things, a celebratory history of the military operations behind the foundation of the Jewish state – O Jerusalem.

The subjects, it is apparent, were picked for their commercial possibilities, as well as thematic grandeur. The Paris book, without the apparatus of scholarship, was revelatory as well as humanly gripping, and eventually had s ales of five million, which at the time was just about unprecedented for a work of non-fiction. It was a classic of reconstructive history, personal and graphic, before television developed the genre and seized it, however fitfully, for itself. What counted most, though, were the numbers. These were in a league that almost any other author would consider justification enough of his life. Lapierre is a writer with no reason to feel frustrated that his passions and concerns are not exposed to a substantial part of the reading universe. When he branched out on his own, he became an even bigger name for publishers to boast of. City Of Joy, a book built around the poor children of Calcutta, which later became a Roland Joffe film, has sold eight million copies worldwide.

Lapierre's books are the work of a reporter, but they always had an intensely emotional undertow. He plunges into his subject with a degree of sympathy that is sometimes disorienting if one approaches the books expecting dispassionate narrative. Though public events are his subject matter, the human stories come out more strongly than the political and diplomatic complexities. Perhaps he always was a candidate for going over to the other side. His style of hot-blooded engagement was halfway to expressing the need he later felt: to be quite extravagantly much more than that distanced, all-seeing but nothing-doing creature, the professional writer.

His start was orthodox enough. There was no conflict between the quest for evidence and any distracting compulsion to react to it as a human being. He was no different from any other reporter, and was very good at it. "In Algeria," he told me recently, "I did some very tough reporting on people dying. They were wounded and I did not pick them up. My first loyalty was to my paper, and my first problem if I had a camera was to do the photos and make sure they got back to my office." Did he feel nothing beyond that? "My compassion for the victims may have been total," he now reflects, "but I just had no time. I couldn't stop to pick up a child who was bleeding and bring it to hospital. I discovered on the battlefield that one cannot at the same time be Hemingway and Mother Teresa."

Forty years ago, I guess the Mother Teresa aspect of things featured hardly at all. As for the laconic Hemingway, any comparison with Lapierre's voluble excitement seems somewhat inapt. But it's clear enough what the macho newsman's priorities were. The facts, lady, just give me the facts. Those were wars in which reporters, with rare exceptions such as James Cameron, felt no more need to carry a stretcher than they did to propagandise – even between the lines, let alone as openly as happened in Bosnia in the mid-90s – about the rights and wrongs of the conflict. By the time he was 50, however, Lapierre began to think he had had enough of that life. This wasn't a case of the kind of physical fatigue that might overtake a reporter who had been 30 years in the field, so much as a certain kind of inconvenient moral enlightenment that had come from writing certain kinds of book. "I experienced, suddenly, remorses," Lapierre said, in an arresting departure from his fluent English. "I had seen so many things, and done nothing about them. It was a great moment to make retribution for all the things I had left undone."

The retribution he made – if that's the right word for someone whose books, while perhaps over-effusive, hardly deserved punishment – was more spectacular than any writer has ever, to my knowledge, performed. Dominique Lapierre's leap from writer into actor has so far involved him in the sacrifice from his own earnings of around five million dollars. The catalyst was direct and personal: a benign reversal, one might call it, of the biblical law that approves an eye for an eye. Lapierre decided to repay, hugely, the very sources of his own prosperity – the subjects who made his latest books pruriently fascinating, the victims out of whom he might have made another fortune. He couldn't escape the emotional logic that said writing did not suffice. He may not have saved a single child from dying in Algeria, but, in the 70s, the producer of best-sellers, which had by now acquired an almost routine inevitability, found the new gold-mine from which, as he thought of it, to make amends: India.

The place caught him at the time when he already suspected he had to change, and was looking for a way to shift the focus. "India lends itself particularly well to that kind of psychological process," Lapierre told me. "It is a very touching, very warm country. Maybe if the same thing had happened in Germany, I would not have been as touched by the sufferings of the Germans as I was by the hard lot of some of those Indians I met during my research." Freedom At Midnight, an account of the run-up to Indian independence, led fast to City Of Joy, his Calcutta epic that has nothing but common humanity as its theme and finally excludes all trace of the reporter's conventionally sceptical mind-set. It scrutinises deeply – in a way, almost celebrates – the human consequences of Indian poverty. The writer's life was not the only one this book changed for ever. Giving the money, however, turned out to be only the start. Lapierre's journalistic instinct, rather than being discarded, was put to service in a different way. He began as a disgorger of his gains, but soon became a ferocious polemicist. Examining what he has done with his five million dollars, one finds roughly equal portions of pity and fury.

Let the fury come later. Not long ago, I was in Calcutta and went to see some of the fruits of his pity. He has been giving half his royalties to projects around the Ganges delta for 20 years, and has collected through the publicity he can generate – virtually unheard in this country, but loud in France, Italy, Spain and the US – another $200,000 a year over the past five years. Topped up by his own giving, the projects take around half-a-million dollars a year. In the bottomless ocean of human need in West Bengal – one of the poorest, most densely populated, disease-ridden, flood-prone, weather-beaten places in the world – it seems a tiny contribution. But it certainly rates against, say, a leader in The Guardian about third world debt.

He began with lepers. India has a quarter of the world's sufferers, and their children, mostly living in slums and filthy, secluded compounds, have little chance. Contrary to most people's impression, once leprosy is diagnosed, it is quite easily treated and cured. But finding the victims and hoisting them out of the filth is another matter. Lapierre kept seeing them while researching the Calcutta life of Mahatma Gandhi, the key character, of course, in Freedom At Midnight. Mother Teresa herself told him that if he had money to spare, they should be his target. It was the beginning of an odyssey that has taken him into alliance with characters that would fit as well into a Joseph Conrad fiction as the most florid reporter's notebook.

On the edge of the city, an hour's honking, heaving perilous bus-ride from the centre, sits the Resurrection Home – Udayan – for children of the victims of leprosy. Its founder, major domo, podgy and eagle-eyed superior is a former British businessman by the name of James Stevens. Between them, these two benevolent western autocrats – one who now says he never calls England home, the other who makes sorties to India three times a year from his house in St Tropez, to watch over his social investments – have made quite an impact on leprosy.

Stevens got to Calcutta in 1968, intending to stay for a couple of years. But he couldn't get the leprous children out of his head. When he met Lapierre, who was fresh from Mother Teresa, he told him Udayan was about to shut down because he'd run out of cash. The Frenchman and his wife were electrified. They were ready for the trans-formation. "My wife took out of her bag the bundle of dollars we had brought with us," Lapierre recounts in his recent autobiography, A Thousand Suns. "'This initial donation will enable you to pay off your debts.' I said, and before really thinking, I added: 'We will fight to see that you never have to close the Resurrection home.'"

It is now a paradise of calm, which has seen 6,000 boys pass through it, cleansed of leprosy and fitted up with a basic education. Married to an Indian, Stevens has left Bristol far behind, though he did become an Anglican priest somewhere along the way. Collecting me from the city centre, he sits up front in the bus, the patriarch of a six-acre spread, chanting hymns to himself, gesturing almost regally to the throngs who see him approaching.

Udayan began with 11 boys, and now houses 300 at a time, along with a handful of girls. The atmosphere and buildings come straight from a modest English public school. There can't be a more orderly, obedient, pacific collection of children east or west of the playing-fields of Eton, all of them seemingly grateful for their temporary rescue from the compounds and roofless hovels of those who are literally untouchable.

Indian officialdom isn't sure it likes this kind of independent enterprise. It seems, after all, very European, even while being wholly Indian. There's been talk of infil-trating some party overseers, and Stevens spends a fair bit of the day hooked to his mobile telephone, grappling with Bengali bureaucrats. But the facts are there, that nobody else made. Some of these boys, going back a few years, have become teachers and civil engineers. At Udayan now, they live in clean, well-lit pavilions, eat regular meals, have regular lessons – and sleep on 300 beds and mattresses that suddenly turned up one day at the dockside, a gift from the Australian cricket captain, Steve Waugh. The name of Dominique Lapierre is splashed lavishly around the property, which would collapse without his money. It seems, in the circumstances, a modest replace-ment for the ego-trip of writing.

So are the Dominique Lapierre dispensary boats that ply the remoter tributaries of the Ganges delta. A day on one of these takes you back to the simplicities of medicine. The door marked Pathology, below decks, covers a room no more than six feet by six, in which the equipment consists of a single microscope. The room marked X-ray, on this particular boat, still awaits its apparatus. Here is a health service, carried from the little mainland port of Raidighi to places that may take three days to reach and do not even appear on the maps, yet contain thousands of people who otherwise would see no doctor and get no medicine.

After the former British businessman, enter the former Naxalite terrorist, who has become another Lapierre protégé. Wohab is the leader of SHIS, the Southern Health Improvement Samity, who shows that writers aren't the only ones in need of some form of displacement activity. At one time, Wohab ran among killers, but in 1980, under the influence of a Swiss priest, he changed sides. "He persuaded me to change from taking life to giving life," Wohab told me as we eased down a mercifully quiescent Ganges towards the village of Lakshmi Janardhanpur.

"I was from the extremist group of the Marxist-Leninist party," he said quite solemnly. His extraordinary health work he sees as a kind of socialism in action, Marxism with a human face. Wohab is still intensely political, fired up by the myriad injustices you can never get away from in West Bengal and least of all here in the Sunderbans, which have changed little from the description given by one of the early Victorian mapmakers who first came across them: "a sort of drowned land, broken up by swamps, intersected by a thousand river channels and maritime backwaters".

An embryonic system of floating dispensaries was under way before Lapierre came along. But he has made it grow hugely, on the back of Wohab's zeal. This time the enemy is not leprosy, but tuberculosis. Arriving at the village, we climb the mud bank into a throng of scores of women and children, for whom this day has been long awaited. The doctor sounds and probes, the nurse – Sabitri, whose pioneering work with these people was the beginning of SHIS, of which she is now president – dispenses, Wohab himself supplies his own confident inexpert diagnoses to women who may have walked five hours barefoot to get here. More than 150 people were queuing up. "I lost so many friends from TB," Wohab told me. "I declared a holy war against it."

Not without some victories. These SHIS dispensaries and clinics now serve some 400 riverine villages, and 1,600 on the mainland – the largest non-governmental TB control project in India. In 1998-99, more than 40,000 people were treated for it, all the poorest of the poor. What Lapierre's money bought, as well as a couple more boats, was technology and power-supplies, especially for X-rays.

"I went myself to negotiate the purchase of radiology equipment from the Siemens representative in Calcutta," writes Lapierre. Its arrival in the remote countryside "provoked the sort of stupor a UFO falling out of the sky might have occasioned". But in 10 years, he reckons, TB disappeared from more than 1,000 villages, and 100,000 sick people were cured.

All this is good work. Far better than you or I could do, or probably would do, even with five million to spare. It's not, however, the work of an idealist who is starry-eyed, or unfailingly nice. Alongside the pity, we have the fury, which includes a certain vanity, directed at what the author-amateur sees as the excesses of professional aid organisations by comparison with his own. He, indeed, has no organisation. That is his point. As well as giving, he has the donor's interest in ensuring that the money doesn't go astray. "I find it an absolute scandal that so many welfare organisations spend so much money on running their activities," he said. "My readers, our supporters, know that when they send us a hundred dollars, it is a hundred dollars which will go to Calcutta."

I have no way of verifying that. A Canadian donor, with experience inspecting such projects all over the world, told me as we chugged back up the Ganges that this was nothing special. Indeed, the 600 workers employed – inefficiently, as he thought – by SHIS made it sound like an aid-recipient itself, perhaps a Lapierre-financed exercise in outdoor relief in a social context where one job is commonly reckoned to keep a dozen family members alive. Nothing wrong with that, said my Canadian friend, but why didn't they spend more money fitting out the boat with better equipment for, say, minor surgery?

What nobody could dispute, though, is that this kind of individual effort stays close to the people. There are no layers of offices, stretching back from Calcutta through Delhi to Geneva. Nobody flies first-class, checking into the local Oberoi. "When I read that Ted Turner gives a billion dollars to the United Nations for the poor of the world, I think it's fantastic," Lapierre said. "But I could tell you down to the last dollar what's going to happen to this billion dollars. These big organisations are not equipped to determine the real needs of the people. They don't know what a Bengal farmer really needs. How could they? Unless you have lived as a Bengal farmer, slept in his house, gone through the monsoon with him?"

Here, by contrast, the donor-in-chief is the scourge of all suppliers. "There's no other way than to be extraordinarily attentive," he said. "That begins with the banks in Paris, reducing the commission when you transfer $100,000. Then getting the banks in India to get a decent rate of exchange. Then making sure the contractor who is building your school is really doing what he says in his estimate. One brick in India can be four rupees if it's a good brick, three-and-a-half rupees if one corner is cut, three rupees if two corners are cut, and only two rupees if it is broken in two. Which brick is he going to put in your school and charge you for?"

Equally, he has few illusions about his own people. "You give an ambulance to a centre, you create a problem. Who is going to be the driver? Is he going to steal half the diesel fuel? Is he going to put air in the tyres? When you come next year, is the ambulance going to be running?" As the ambitions expand, so do the problems. "You still have to monitor these extraordinary people very closely. This Wohab is a fabulous person. But he is now asking me for a scanner. A scanner! Many French cities don't have a scanner, and we're in the middle of Bengal!"

To this kind of end, nonetheless, Lapierre is now planning to sell his house outside St Tropez, and provide still further for people who will be depending on him when the literary stream dries up. The action man is approaching 70, and A Thousand Suns sets down a life from which all cynicism has departed. The "pornography of poverty", a phrase sometimes used to classify works, usually TV films, that exploit the poor for little more than voyeuristic ends, cannot conceivably apply to a man with five million dollars in the virtual Bank of Recompense. He doesn't dismiss the ongoing value of the profession he used to follow. "Reporters must tell the world about Rwanda, Kosovo,

Chechnya, Venezuela," he said. "It's their duty to make the world aware of those tragedies, to move opinions, to force political leaders to take action. For a battlefield reporter suddenly to drop his camera and become a nurse would be a beautiful individual gesture. But I think, ultimately, his photos would be more important than holding an IV bottle."

He himself just moved on. He discovered that, by becoming an actor, he could change things. To him, it is just another way of dealing with reality. "I still faced reality, like a reporter. But this time with the idea of changing that reality." Anchored defiantly in the world he left, one can't escape the trace of feeling humbled. •

Dominique Lapierre's core charitable fund is:
Action Aid for Lepers' Children of Calcutta, 26 Avenue Kleber, 75116 Paris, France.

3 June 2000

Vikram Dodd
Last voyage into legend

Sixty years on from their finest hour, a flotilla of small boats yesterday made their passage across the English Channel in a pilgrimage to Dunkirk, honouring those who evacuated 338,000 British troops.

The vessels came to commemorate what Winston Churchill called "a miracle of deliverance", when the cream of the British army, trapped on the beaches, were saved from capture by the Nazis.

Just after 9.15am the first of 61 small boats eased out of Dover harbour. As they emerged they were set against a horizon dominated by the undulating white cliffs of Dover. As it was 60 years ago, the weather was near perfect for sailing and the wind moderate. The crests of the low, greenish-brown waves were turned silver by a warm late-spring sun.

Among the hundreds watching the departure was Dunkirk veteran Bill Hinchliff, 81, who was rescued from the French sands after three days trapped by incessant enemy fire.

Bearing witness yesterday brought back the horror that left only 60 of his battalion of 908 young men alive. "It was the most scared I've ever been in my life. We were under enemy fire all the time, being shelled with Stukas coming down. I was petrified by the noise of them.

"We just buried ourselves in the sand. We couldn't go in the basements of the houses because there were the dead bodies of troops in there."

After this anniversary, the Dunkirk Veterans' Association, defeated by ageing, will wind itself up. That fact added poignancy to yesterday's graceful commemoration by the Dunkirk little ships of the role that they played in rescuing so many.

Eight hundred craft, some barely 30ft long, were involved in Operation Dynamo, which it was hoped would save at best 45,000 troops. Some carried soldiers all the way back, avoiding heavy enemy fire and minefields, but most ferried troops off the beaches to larger ships anchored further off shore. Their role was invaluable.

The former TV presenter Raymond Baxter, 78, is honorary admiral of the Association of Dunkirk Little Ships, which masterminded the commemoration. Yesterday was his seventh voyage of pilgrimage to Dunkirk, which is held every five years. The first was in 1965.

Sixty years ago his motor yacht, L'Orage, ferried bloody troops, 34 at a time, off the beaches and to safety. He said: "It's a celebration of one of the two turning points of modern world history, the other one being D-Day. If Operation Dynamo had been a disaster it's highly probable that Britain would have sued for peace."

Sailing towards Dunkirk yesterday, as 60 years ago, were yachts, motor cruisers, barges and a cockle boat. All flew the defaced flag of St George, which vessels involved in the rescue earned, on which the Dunkirk coat of arms sits in the middle of the Red Cross of St George.

One vessel was more than 100 years old, another sat barely 2ft out of the water. It was this flotilla of wood, glue and nails that played a role so much greater than the sum of its parts in preserving this island in an hour rich only with darkness.

Some boats nearly failed to make the pilgrimage. Shrapnel was discovered in the hull of Firefly when it was being repaired. Four years ago the Southern Queen was a day away from being put on a bonfire, such was its disrepair, when Phil Hammond rescued it to stop "another part of our history being destroyed".

Since then he has restored the craft estimated to have saved 1,000 troops, spending more than £10,000 to join yesterday's convoy. It went back into the water only 10 days ago.

During the voyage Mr Hammond, 57, said: "Coming across has been so emotional. I am very elated we could be part of the celebrations, but there is also a lump in my throat about what happened 60 years ago. We've been on board living history today."

From a few hundred yards away these dots of history in the channel were guarded by HMS Somerset. It was needed, as to reach Dunkirk from Dover the flotilla had to cross shipping lanes in one of the busiest maritime areas in the world.

They sailed at between four and six knots. Most tankers, which dwarf them, dropped anchor and stayed out of the convoy's way as a mark of respect. The flotilla at times stretched 1.9 miles long, becoming more compact when the danger from other vessels was at its greatest.

HMS Somerset, a type 23 frigate, also ferried over Admiral Robert Timbrell, 80. As a 20-year-old acting sub-lieutenant he captained the yacht Llanthony, which with five Scottish trawlers saved 900 troops. The day before setting out he had been in naval school.

Mr Timbrell had hoped to be reunited with the yacht, owned in 1940 by Lord Astor, but bad weather prevented it from reaching Dover in time.

But watching the armada sailing across the channel yesterday brought back to him memories from the last century, of dead troops floating off Dunkirk, of the three trips he made in darkness at the wheel of his vessel. In the chaos, he, like other captains, had to decide how best to effect the rescue.

Mr Timbrell, a Canadian from Nova Scotia, said that his role in the rescue was his finest hour. "The Dunkirk evacuation for a 20-year-old acting sub-lieutenant, who dare I say successfully lifted 900 troops, was a major event in my life."

Halfway across the channel the RAF paid its own tribute to the heroism of the little ships.

The blue sky was pierced by a lone Spitfire coming out of the sun, which flew over the convoy as low as mast height. Sixty years ago that was how close German fighter planes were getting.

After six hours, the first of the 61 vessels reached Dunkirk to waiting crowds.

The cruiseboat Papillon limped in on one engine after its starboard engine failed two miles from Dunkirk. Its owner, Ian Gilbert, 49, an avionics engineer, spent £20,000 to join this ride. It was a small price to pay, he said, to honour those who ensured liberty. "The boat is a unique part of our heritage. It's a living symbol of the Dunkirk spirit."

He added: "It is not just about commemorating troops being evacuated from Dunkirk, but that people were prepared to sacrifice huge amounts, including their lives, for the freedom of Britain.

"It's commemorating that selflessness and the ability of my 12-year-old son to grow up in a peaceful world. That's why it's important for the memory to be kept alive."

Soon the baton of remembering the little ships' heroism at Dunkirk will pass to a new generation, to hold or not as the brightness of memory allows. •

....

14 December 1999

Maggie O'Kane
The army pledged to fight to the end

We are summoned at short notice by a group of guards who take us to a large villa in a secret location in southern Chechnya where the president now lives surrounded by a core of trusted staff who sleep on makeshift mattresses in the dining room.

He is dressed with surprising elegance for someone in the middle of a war zone, in full military uniform. Behind him, tacked to a wall carpet, hangs the green, white and red of the Chechen flag.

We have come to talk to the man who the Russians say is the head of a terrorist band of insurgents. But that is not how President Aslan Maskhadov, head of the self-declared independent Chechen nation, sees it.

During our hour-long meeting he portrays himself as the leader of a Chechen people so united in the face of Russian aggression that they will win the war within the next six months. Yes, his fighters are outnumbered by overwhelming Russian force, but they have the benefit of belief.

"They have a bigger army, but that doesn't matter. We have spirit and we are fighting for our country. Chechnya has God on her side and the Russians have got vodka and cigarettes."

President Maskhadov claims that only 158 of his fighters have been killed by Russia's relentless bombardment. Certainly, his contention that his troops are determined to win has been born out by four days spent inside Chechnya among them.

They would have to be determined to put up with the privations. The mountain air and the sun in the early morning makes the cold almost bearable. But then, in the twilight time between night and day when the stove has gone out, there is ice on the windows. They have just come back from a night on the mountain, trying to kill Russian pilots.

Their food comes as stacks of cans, which are packed under the rock shelves. Tins of wobbly pink beef imported from Holland usually mixed with watery ham. Refugees as they pass donate food for their army – the latest offering two geese caught beside the river.

The mountain soldiers kill at night, sleep in the day and pray again before they go to kill. A strange sight. A dozen soldiers in military fatigues pray on the floor asking God to give them victory. They have all the zeal of recent converts.

"I had a car business in the last war. Didn't give a damn about any politics and then something just got to me about it all," said Ali Iskhanov, 24. The fervour with which men like him have embraced Islam is clear in this army – it is part of their identity. Part of what it means to be a Chechen for a generation whose parents were born in Stalin's icy exile camps after being packed into railway carriages one bad weekend in 1946 and decamped to Kazakhstan.

Time to leave the mountain camp with its warm wooden stove and dirt floor. The journey south out of the mountain camps into the Chechen plains usually takes five hours. Tonight it will take 11 hours. Beslan has done it three times in three days. "Alluh akbar – God is great," he says, lighting a Marlboro, before he kicks the badly camouflaged Soviet minibus into gear.

The Chechen soldiers mostly buy their own weapons. One thousand dollars for a good sniper, a couple of hundred for an old Kalashnikov.

Tonight, Beslan and Idrise will share the way. They always travel two to a truck, in case of breakdowns. All along the road the news of what's ahead is relayed on walkie-talkies. If they're scared they don't show it. Despite the fatigue, despite a night in which the skies are full of planes trying to strafe them with rockets, and Russian tanks are targeting the road, they laugh.

The trucks that bring arms and medical supplies to the capital creep along the mountain walls and valleys out of sight.

Chechnya now is two worlds. On the ground the scrabbling small people in their vans and trucks; above the planes and helicopters. In the daytime, they seem almost benign. A helicopter hanging like a fat lazy dragonfly in the sky – it is at night when they can't be seen, that the sound is different.

The reason the Chechens believe they will win this war can be understood on a night-drive with Beslan and Idrise. Everything moves at night.

"If you die a martyr you can have 49 wives," says the camp cook, Ali, who used to fight in Azerbaijan and says his war is a Holy jihad. Even at night the bombing on the road is clear – bridges are missing, great hunks of soil have been gouged out by missiles.

The country is without electricity and the only things that move in the black village is the beam of the passing trucks and lorries. Then suddenly it begins. A horrible gut-turning boom – the giant upstairs has got out bed – and then another, as the booms get closer.

Beslan and Idrise are in the ditch, heavy and wet with winter mud. Other drivers from the convoy join them and in the beginning they chat in the darkness. But as the flashes and booms move closer, they fall silent.

The road has disappeared. Now they are driving in darkness through a riverbed. Any second, a great tank round could punch through the side of the truck. Beslan drives at 80km an hour, crashing through the riverbed.

The minibus is old, the water is splashing into the engine. The sound of the starter motor screeching helplessly and a dead engine seem to echo through the night. On Beslan's brow, the sweat pours. His hands are shaking as he tries to dry the engine – finally it starts.

Afterwards, inside a safehouse, soldiers snooze on their break on the way down south. The food on offer from a local farmer is gherkins and cold potatoes.

"In this war, the whole country is united behind our soldiers," President Maskhadov said back in the villa.

"The people are feeding them, giving them their beds. Remember, our soldiers are volunteers fighting for their country and the Russians have to pay convicts from the prisons in Moscow to go to the front – that is why we will win." •

30 March 2000

Chris McGreal
Mozambique's misery goes on

The lakes of floodwater that consumed whole towns are trickling back into Mozambique's rivers, but the television cameras have gone, and with them the international attention that set off the scramble to rescue a drowning people. In the next few weeks Mozambicans will have good reason to wish that the cameras were back.

It is now, at just the moment when the world's focus has moved on, that foreign governments must decide how far their commitment goes. Do they walk away, having completed the job of saving lives? Or do they stop and face a far greater task – to help Mozambique rebuild and save its once-shining economy?

In Ilha Josina Machel, a town still marooned in a sea of water, people are surviving at the end of a clattering lifeline of British, American and South African helicopters delivering food. Once the water drains away, the future of the town will be determined by how quickly the roads are rebuilt.

The floods wrecked or damaged the homes of about 250,000 Mozambicans. Their livestock drowned, their crops rotted and their tools washed away. It will take years for many to recover.

But the destruction is not, at the moment at least, a catastrophe for Mozambique's much-vaunted economic revival, fuelled by generous dollops of aid, rising foreign investment and a government surrender of financial control to the World Bank and International Monetary Fund.

Most factories and other export earners were largely untouched by the floods. But there was considerable damage to the roads and railways that underpinned the boom.

The government estimates that it will need another $280m to rebuild more than 1,000km of roads and long stretches of railway tracks that were swept away. Then there are the electricity and telephone lines, and more than 600 schools in need of repair.

An appeal for money to reconstruct the infrastructure will be made at an international donors' conference in Rome in four weeks' time. Mozambique's foreign minister, Leonardo Simao, is betting on his country's status as a favourite son of Western governments and global financial institutions.

He says Mozambique is seen as too much of a success story to be allowed to fail. "Our success was a source of inspiration for many countries in Africa. If this example is left to die, we are killing their hope. This economic growth is a major condition for peace and stability in the region."

But Mozambique has failed to persuade foreign creditors to write off its debt, although a number of governments have unilaterally scrapped outstanding bilateral loans. And there are concerns that donors will use money earmarked for development to pay for reconstruction.

"What we require is additional aid, not at the expense of development money," Mr Simao stressed.

The outcome of the meeting will be decisive for towns such as Ilha Josina Machel. Two months ago rains flooded the Incomati river and laid waste to part of the southern end of the town. A month later a surge of water swept down the Limpopo river to the north and cut the town from the rest of Mozambique.

It is now an island, accessible only by helicopter or boat, and wholly reliant on the outside world for food. Even when the waters recede, the town will count on aid from the World Food Programme for at least three months. But its mayor, Samo Timoteo Samo, is stoic.

"More than 1,000 homes were destroyed in the town and surrounding villages. For those people this is a disaster," he said. "For the rest of us it is merely difficult".

But difficulty could turn to disaster for the region. In recent years the town prospered, selling sugar cane to a factory a few kilometres away. Now the crop is almost completely destroyed. The factory is helping with an advance on future sales, so people can buy tools to replant the crop. But the roads were destroyed, and the town can only get its crop to the factory with great difficulty.

Mr Simao argues that the floods caused more devastation than the 16 years of civil war between 1978 and 1994. "It's much worse than the war if you look at the losses in terms of human beings in a short space of time, the losses of houses, schools, telecommunications systems, power lines," he said. "If you look at the losses of cows – more than 1m dead. We never had 650,000 people dependent on food aid in such a short time."

"There's also the psychological impact, because those who suffered are the survivors of war. They had seven years of hope and now they are back to square one. It is very easy to get discouraged." •

···

1 May 2000

Maggie O'Kane
Carla's court

Three judges sit up on the bench looking straight at the witness who is screened from the public by a large cream venetian blind. Everything is blue except the polished teak veneer benches. The stenographer is dressed in jeans and a white shirt. The three judges – male, female, black, white – talk soothingly to the witness. Would you like a break? Another glass of water, perhaps? How is the hotel? The International Criminal Tribunal for the former Yugoslavia is a haven of political correctness and human civility.

Then you sit for a while in one of those blue seats and listen. Or catch snippets of the short circuit television broadcast that wafts along the corridors where people chat about where to go for lunch.

A lawyer on the TV screens asks the witness: "When the bodies were laid out, dead, on the football pitch, did there seem many more of them than when you had seen them alive and crowded into the gym?"

A 23-year-old man, the only survivor of the massacre of 7,000 men and boys in a field near Srebrenica, is asked by the judge if he wants to say anything. "If I could speak in the name of the innocent victims, I would forgive the actual perpetrators of the executions because they were misled," he says. Inside the blue courtroom, the weight of justice is palpable.

"Do you recognise the man who raped you?"

"Yes, I can recognise him."

"Can you look around the courtroom and let us know where he is?"

"He is there, with the security guard on his right."

"For identification purposes, can you describe him? Please take your time."

"He had a light blue tie and a dark blue suit."

"What is the name of the man who raped you."

"His name is Zoran Vukovic."

The guard tries to hold his gaze straight ahead, but the temptation to sneak a look at Vukovic is too much. Vukovic sits still, only the fingers of his right hand fumbling with the papers in front of him.

Unnoticed by the world, dramas like these are being played out five days a week in the Hague. It has been a good spring for the tribunal. Last month, for the first time in the history of war, a United Nations court focused exclusively on rape as a war crime. The trial was running simultaneously with that of one of generals accused of the massacre of 7,000 Muslim men in Srebrenica. Two weeks later, the champagne bottles were cracked open following the arrest of a top political aide to Radovan Karadzic, the psychiatrist with the big hair who led the Bosnian Serbs in the bad, bad years.

Thirty-seven suspected war criminals are already here. The last one was delivered only a week ago to chief prosecutor Carla Del Ponte's remand centre by the sea. At a cost to the United Nations of £116.14 per day, each prisoner gets art classes twice a week, video, a coffee machine, satellite TV and conjugal visits. Such is the backlog, these men will wait for at least two and a half years before they step into one of the Hague's three courts.

But the prisoners do not include any of the three big names: Karadzic; his creator, Slobodan Milosevic, president of Serbia; and their loyal, brutal general, Ratko Mladic.

When Graham Blewitt, an Australian lawyer who specialised in the prosecution of Nazis, arrived as deputy prosecutor in February 1994, he found an empty office with a desk and chairs: "I started making calls around the world, to Scotland, England, the United States, trying to recruit the right people. We had stacks of applications, but they were from lawyers who had no skills in this area. In the end, it was the old Nazi network that took on the core of the work here."

Six years later, Blewitt has built an institution with a budget of almost $100m, with 832 staff working as judges, lawyers, intelligence analysts, field investigators, forensic experts and translators. Others have come and gone, but on a Saturday afternoon you can still find Blewitt in his office, trawling through papers and listening to classical music.

"You get bitten by the war crimes work. It gets into your blood. It has been so exciting, just getting this thing started and off the ground. When we got here, there was nothing."

Next door to Blewitt's third floor office is his new boss, Del Ponte, a Swiss-born judge who has already taken on the mafia and corrupt Russian politicians. Today she's in a good mood. George Robertson, Britain's former defence secretary and now secretary general of Nato, has just visited her office. Robertson has power and is one of the strongest supporters the Hague has ever had.

Normally, Del Ponte hates the press, but today she's happy to pose in front of her wanted poster with a "watch this space" look in her eye. She won't talk about when she expects Karadzic, Milosevic and Mladic to arrive at her jail, but gives the impression that Karadzic, at least, could be here quite soon. "Come back and talk to me in a couple of weeks," she says.

Unlike her predecessors, Del Ponte is now also getting cooperation from the French, who were once so indifferent to picking up war criminals that their soldiers rented houses from them. "President Chirac was here in February and she handed him a new arrest order," says a Hague employee. "Ten days later we had the guy here."

The man Del Ponte wants most is Milosevic. If he is arrested he will be the first democratically elected leader to face the justice of an international court, theoretically laying the legal framework of a system that could try Russia's president elect for Chechnya; could have tried Nixon for Chile or Cambodia. That would not make everyone happy; the US is the most fervent opponent of a permanent international court.

In these old insurance company offices in the centre of the dull, well-organised city of the Hague, generous salaries mean that some of the staff can earn double what they get in most of their 68 home countries. Jeffrey Nice, 52, a wealthy English barrister, abandoned his practice in London for a year to prosecute war criminals. Part of his work involved the prosecution of a man who called himself the Serbian Adolf and whose favourite method of execution was to ask his victims to kneel on the ground and place their heads on a grate so it would make less of a mess.

Nice, who lives in Canterbury, says the two things that shock him about his work are the "ease with which a common criminal turned into a killer once you put a mobile phone in one hand and a gun in another", and the bewildering submissiveness of the victim. "It seemed like they queued up and waited to be executed. One minute they are well nourished people living in comfortable homes and the next they've got their head on the grate, waiting to be executed.

"You'll never, in England, have cases of such sheer scale. Here your overall project is to deliver international justice."

Terry Cameron, a field investigator in Bosnia who also served during the war, used to wake up sweating from nightmares. "The worst thing was dealing with the sniper victims who came in. Some were as young as eight.To see the guys responsible being brought in is a tremendous feeling ."

Glenn Morgan came from the West Midlands police and has worked as an intelligence officer for six years. His job is to work out the command structures of military operations. His training was in British Army intelligence in Northern Ireland. "It's like working on a jigsaw puzzle. You've got 40 pieces and you need to get a good idea where the other 60 pieces fit in."

Every fact they uncover is processed into the Hague's computer system, which is sealed to the outside world. On most desks there are two computers, one that accesses the internal computer files, a second for everyday use with email connection and internet facilities. The computer unit has almost 100 staff and 2m documents on file, new ones coming in at the rate of 16,000 a month.

But getting Karadzic will be the real signal to the outside world that the Hague is serious. Milosevic and Mladic are more likely to die in the bloody civil war that is brewing in Serbia than surrender to international justice.

"I will have room for a hundred more of them," says Del Ponte. She points to a poster offering $5m (£3.2m) for the capture of Bosnia's big three: "There, they are my three."

After the Blair government came to power in 1997, the SAS carried out the first arrest. Until then, western governments had been worried more about body bags than justice for the battered Balkans and the crack squads of the SAS, the US Delta Force and commandos from France, Holland and Germany sat around on their well-trained hands and watched the war criminals drink beer in Bosnian bars.

Another reason Del Ponte's cells are filling up fast is that nobody in Bosnia seems to care very much that their former leaders are being kidnapped and brought to trial. Initially Britain, France, Germany and the US were all worried about a backlash against their soldiers on the ground. "So far we've had car tyres slashed, but that's been about it," says Terry Cameron.

Del Ponte doesn't want to talk about why it is taking so long to get the big names. "What I care about is when they are going to bring them in. Come to me the day after Karadzic arrives and I will explain everything. I am doing things a prosecutor should not be doing."

Such things include visiting George Robertson in Nato headquarters to discuss plans for a special international snatch squad to speed up the pick-ups.

When, if, Karadzic arrives in the Hague, the hood and earplugs he has been forced to wear during the two-hour flight so he will not recognise the nationality of his captors will be removed. He will be met by a Dutch immigration official who will sign him into Holland. Tim McFadden, a tall Irishman and his chief jailer in the prison, will be on hand to take charge of him.

"The biggest success with Karadzic will be getting him here alive," says Morgan. "The worr y is that there are a couple of Milosevic stooges waiting to put a bullet in his head before he gets here."

Karadzic will then be dispatched to a cell on one of three floors, where he will be watched on a security camera in case he attempts suicide. At 7.30 the next morning, over breakfast of muesli and fruit juice, he will be reunited with some old friends and enemies, for there is no segregation.

"The funny thing about these guys is that they are pussycats to handle," says McFadden. "They are not idealists. They don't seem to believe in what they were fighting for."

From the press gallery, we couldn't see the 19-year-old giving evidence. But Zoran Vukovic could, and for two days he listened to her tell the tribunal how he had been part of a group of soldiers who had gang-raped her over a period of five weeks. How, at the end, he had taken her alone to a deserted apartment, to a room on the left hand side of the hallway and raped her again.

"Then, when he had finished, he sat down on the armchair and lit a cigarette," she said. "He said to me, I could do much more to you, but since you're the same age as my daughter, I'll leave it at that."

Vukovic again scratches desperately at the paper in front of him with his blue Biro.

The older women are tougher, merciless in telling it as it was. Vukovic was the kind of a guy who forced them to give him oral sex because he couldn't get an erection. Then he got a gun and became a big guy. The women and girls leave the bench devastated and high, so high.

Tejshree Thapa, a young Nepalese woman lawyer, spent more than two years preparing the rape cases. "After they've given their testimony and left the stand I have broken down and cried," she says. "The older women are better able to cope – they have some sort of social structure. It's the young girls that get to me. They are just completely bewildered by what has happened to them.

"Their best friends are the girls who were raped with them. They are all traumatised, but they end up in refuges in different countries where they don't speak the language.

"They have been terrified of coming into court," says Thapa. "But as soon as they get into the witness box, their anger replaces the fear. All of them have been glad they have done it." ●

Nemesis

22 December 1999

Alan Rusbridger
Farewell to Have-a-go Hamilton

Forget Neil Hamilton for the moment and remember, if you can, Tim Smith. Mr Smith was MP for Beaconsfield in the last parliament and until 1994 a minister and respected pillar of the Conservative party establishment. On the quiet Mr Smith took bungs. A leading businessman was in the habit of paying the member for Beaconsfield £2,000 a throw to ask questions on his behalf in parliament. Cash in brown envelopes: easy money, easily deniable.

One day an enemy of the leading businessman got to hear of the bungs and wrote a menacing letter to Mr Smith threatening to unmask him. Mr Smith took fright and confessed all to his chief whip. The chief whip received his confession in private and sent him on his way. He took no note of the conversation. He told no law officers. He did not inform the privileges committee or the prime minister. He did nothing. Shortly thereafter Mr Smith was appointed a vice-chairman of the Conservative party as well as party treasurer.

That was the way the political class liked things at the time. Actually, it is the way the political classes like things generally. It is, for perfectly understandable reasons, altogether more comfortable to do these things away from the public glare.

Lip service will always be paid to the principle of the "public's right to know". It is the practice that politicians often find difficult. Jack Straw's first attempt to frame a freedom of information bill – crammed with exemptions which would have even kept hidden reports to do with accidents and health and safety – is eloquent proof of that.

Tim Smith was no Oscar Wilde. He had no intention of risking ruin in the libel courts and quietly left public life after admitting the allegations which the Guardian first published in October 1994. But for more than six years now, Mr Hamilton has remorselessly persisted in his denials, smearing whoever refused to believe them.

The Guardian's reporters were corrupt. They forged their evidence. Alison Bozek, a single mother who had trained to become a solicitor in her spare time, was a liar in the pay of Mohamed Al Fayed. The parliamentary commissioner, Sir Gordon Downey, became Sir Gormless Dopey – too stupid to see that he was being gulled by Mr Fayed. The MPs on the standards and privileges committee were biased and useless. None of this now matters very much. Three separate tribunals – the parliamentary commissioner, parliament and the courts – have all decided that Neil Hamilton was corrupt. Indeed, the more Mr Hamilton twisted and turned, the more unpleasant the truths we learned about him.

It began as a greedy binge at the Ritz while doing the business for Mr Fayed. Then we learned he was taking cash, too. As time passed we learned he was also taking undeclared fees from other companies, including covert fees for promoting carcinogenic chewing gum. He charged his own constituents to represent them while picking up "introductory fees" from lobbyists. If he could dodge tax on his fees by converting them into paintings or a holiday, he dodged tax.

And then there was cash for amendments. The £10,000 he took from Mobil to move a six-word amendment to the finance act in 1989 revolted even the Mobil executives he was working for. Hamilton knew this would be terminal for him if it ever became known.

He was fully aware of the 1695 resolution of the House of Commons, which specifies: "The offer of money or any other advantage to any member of parliament for the promoting of any matter whatsoever depending or to be transacted in parliament, is a high crime and misdemeanour and tends to the subversion of the English constitution."

So, once again, he either misled or openly lied about it to anyone who inquired. Asked why he concealed it from Sir Gordon, he confessed that he considered that: "I was released from whatever obligation of candour I might have had towards him."

The more light that has been cast on the political climate of the late 80s and early 90s, the more unappetising it looks. That is why it is always useful to remember Mr Smith and his quiet word with the chief whip. Or rather remember Jonathan Aitken's quiet pledge to Sir Robin Butler. Or Jeffrey Archer's quiet assurances to Michael Ancram.

Left to itself parliament would never have purged itself or taken any of this remotely seriously: that was left to newspapers. Sir Gordon Downey and the Nolan commission into standards in public life only made an appearance as a result of the Guardian's original stories as well as the Sunday Times's parallel investigation into MPs on the take.

Which brings us to the libel laws. After Aitken's downfall – and now after Hamilton – people ask in bewilderment: "Why did they do it?" The answer is obvious: they wouldn't dream of doing it if they didn't know that this country's libel laws are stacked in favour of a plaintiff – particularly a plaintiff who is happy to conceal evidence or lie on oath. It is well worth a last roll of the dice.

The burden of proof is on the defendant. There was – until last month – no protection for writing about public figures. Plaintiffs have been known to dispose of juries if they find them an inconvenience. The costs involved in fighting an action to trial are prohibitive. Plaintiffs find numerous ways of avoiding discovery (Aitken's credit cards, Hamilton's Mobil evidence). Witnesses (see Aitken and Archer) can be persuaded to come to court and lie themselves blue in the face.

One decent jury verdict in the face of overwhelming evidence does not change any of that. One can certainly hope that the triple examples of Archer, Aitken and Hamilton may well suggest a pattern to future politicians who are contemplating seeking vindication by perjury. But one shouldn't bet on that either.

Imagine for a moment what Mr Hamilton and his small but resolute band of admirers would have made if the jury had found against Mr Fayed. We would have heard a lot about trial by newspapers and how the media had hounded a decent (if greedy) man out of public life. There would have been demands for apologies, maybe even demands for more damages. Red-faced columnists on the fringes of the right would have spilled much green ink thundering about cutting the overwheening fourth estate down to size. They had the same pieces ready-to-go halfway through the Aitken trial.

Those pieces will once again be quietly spiked. But here are some tricky questions for those who drafted them: was the Guardian right to take the decision to publish the claims about Tim Smith, or should we have shelved that story when he lied about it to our reporters? If we were wrong, what evidence is there that anyone would have done anything about Mr Smith's misdeeds or that they would ever have come to light? If they had never come to light would British public life be better as a result? If we were right to publish the story about Smith, were we wrong to publish the same claims about Neil Hamilton (about whom the evidence was rather stronger)? If so, why?

If we were right to publish the stories about either Smith or Hamilton, should we have had any protection from the courts in defending the claims? Should we have been able to argue – as American papers can – that this was a serious matter in the public interest which deserved the shield of qualified privilege? Or should newspaper editors and broadcasters only publish material which they are absolutely confident will stand up to weeks, months – even years – of minute forensic legal scrutiny?

To pose these questions is really to answer them. A newspaper editor cannot possibly predict what will emerge during the discovery process or how witnesses – of whom s/he might have no knowledge – will perform in the witness box. The hotel receipt that destroyed Jonathan Aitken only emerged from the shoebox of the Hotel Bristol in the Swiss Alps, well into the 11th hour of that action. We could not possibly have predicted that: nor that Mr Aitken would submit a dishonest witness statement from his wife and daughter. The Star could not have predicted that Lord Archer would have persuaded one or more friends to cook up false alibis on his behalf. The Times could not have known what every document in the DEA files would reveal – or not reveal – about Michael Ashcroft. The Telegraph may well be feeling the same misgivings as it sets about to investigate Romano Prodi in the face of threats of legal action.

If editors felt inhibited by having to operate to the standards of proof required by unsympathetic courtrooms, we would have to settle for the cosy world of quiet conversations and assurances behind closed doors. The penalties for doing otherwise are too forbidding for most editors to behave otherwise.

The chilling effect that results from the punishment aspect of libel (often the huge costs rather than the damages), is one of the reasons that the US supreme court held that the common law of libel was incompatible with the first amendment guarantee of freedom of speech and of the press.

A leading American commentator on defamation law summarised the position of the press thus: "Because of the risks and uncertainties in the process of ascertaining and demonstrating factual truth, a rule that penalises factual falsity has the effect of inducing some self-censorship as to materials that are in fact true."

Happily, the law may finally be moving in a more reassuring direction as a result of the law lords' decision in the Reynolds case. The leading judgment by Lord Nicholls contained this crucial passage which – for the first time – made some allowances for the conditions in which journalists often work. "Journalists act without the benefit of the clear light of hindsight," he said. "Matters which are obvious in retrospect may have been far from clear in the heat of the moment.

"The press discharges vital functions as a bloodhound as well as a watchdog. The court should be slow to conclude that a publication was not in the public interest and, therefore, the public had no right to know, especially when the information is in the field of political discussion. Any lingering doubts should be resolved in favour of publication."

Less happily, the Nicholls judgment also erected a 10-bar gate over which stories may in future have to leap before they can qualify for protection from the courts. They include consideration about the source (even though the source may not be revealed), the "status" of the information, the urgency of the matter, the circumstances and timing of publication and the "tone of the article".

All this is territory to be fought over during the coming years. But Aitken, Archer and Hamilton do have a lesson for us, and it is a lesson about openness and the absolute necessity of giving the public the right to see what the people they elect and pay for do in their name.

If Mr Straw can see a lesson here for his pallid freedom of information bill as it wends its way through parliament, then these three chancers may not have sued – and been ruined – in vain. ∎

5 April 2000

Jonathan Freedland
Windows close for capitalism

Karl Marx always said capitalism contained the seeds of its own destruction – but perhaps it contains the seeds of its own salvation, too. Is that too optimistic a reading of Monday night's US court ruling against the computer behemoth Microsoft? Maybe. But it is a tempting one.

For in the most capitalist nation in the world, a judge nominated by the most conservative president in living memory has plunged an arrow into the corporate beast. Judge Thomas Penfield Jackson, a free-marketeer appointed to the United States District Court by Ronald Reagan in the go-go 1980s, has achieved in an instant what leftwing activists have dreamed of for years. He has branded one of global capital's biggest players a corporate lawbreaker, a bully which abused its monopoly power to stifle creativity and innovation in an industry which relies on those qualities for its survival. He lambasted Microsoft for keeping "an oppressive thumb" on the computer software market, forcefeeding consumers Microsoft's operating system, Windows, and then its internet browser, Explorer. These were not the words of some crunchy, eco-warrior shaking his fist at the big boys of Seattle: this was the measured judgment of an American judge, administering American law.

It could not be more important – or more heartening. For what Judge Jackson has done is place a limit on corporate power. He has drawn a line and told mega-capitalism, "This far and no further." That counts as a blow not just against boardroom greed – but against the twin diseases of our globalised era, fatalism and passivity. By his ruling, the judge has reaffirmed the power of consumers and citizens. He has reminded us that, even in a world dominated by economics and market forces, politics – and the law – still matter.

It could not have come at a better time. Defeatism in the face of the market is rife just now, especially in Britain. We watch the 50,000 workers of the west Midlands facing redundancy thanks to BMW's sell-off of Rover, and we feel powerless. People want the government to do something, but few know what. Most of the current demands amount to requests to soften the blow.

We see Barclays close up to 4,000 bank branches, thereby stranding rural communities across Britain, and we feel just as impotent. Chris Mullin, a junior minister, gamely suggests a boycott. It's a good idea – but few of us are convinced it will make much difference. Whether it's Barclays or BMW, we feel the market has an iron logic and it would be quixotic, Scargillite madness to buck it.

Not now. Judge Jackson, with the help of the US statute book, has proved capitalism need not run wild: it can be tamed. He has not had to craft some new, interventionist ideal from the bench. Instead he has simply enforced America's anti-trust (or anti-monopoly) laws. These are the same rules which in 1911 took one look at John D Rockefeller's Standard Oil – which by then had gobbled up 90% of the American petroleum industry – and demanded the company break up. In 1984 it was AT&T's domination of the telephone market which fell on the wrong side of the anti-trust rules. "You're getting too big," said the law. "It's time to break up." If Judge Jackson's ruling is not overturned on appeal, he may well end up prescribing the same medicine to Bill Gates.

Is it just America that boasts this protection against excessive capitalism? Does it work like a vaccine, so that a nation where capitalism courses through the collective bloodstream is somehow uniquely protected against its ill effects? Not necessarily. The European Union cannot claim the scalps won by America's anti-trust laws, but Articles 85 and 86 of the Treaty of Rome are darts that can be fired at corporate bullies who try to choke competition. In 1997 Brussels struck out at Boeing whose $14bn merger with McDonnell Douglas would have handed them a virtual monopoly in the world market for aircraft. The merger went ahead, but only after Europe had attached some useful strings. The continent's arsenal may not be as mighty as America's antitrust law, but it does exist.

Britain's own defence against the big boys is a work in progress. For years Britain seemed like a place where mega-business could do what it liked: witness the green light repeatedly shown to Rupert Murdoch as he gobbled up more and more of our national media. Now there is an effort to tighten the rules. Starting last month, the Office of Fair Trading has been given tougher powers to root out the Microsofts of British industry. It can now demand documents, launch dawn raids on recalcitrant firms and even slap instant fines on companies deemed to be playing with loaded dice.

We are still some way from Judge Jackson, but Labour might be heading in that direction. Last year Yvette Cooper, the impeccably modernising junior minister, published an essay on competition, wondering whether the government would "pass the Microsoft test". Would it be willing, she mused, to take on a flagship national company if such a firm were getting too big for its boots? Gordon Brown's chums say he's already passed that test: threatening last month to eat in to BT's monopoly on local calls. Monday's ruling might help him stand firm.

The logic of all this is not anti-capitalism. On the contrary, America invented this vaccine to protect enterprise, not to kill it. The authors of the antitrust laws understood that a truly free market requires competition; without it monopolies expand, before growing slow and flabby. The true capitalist is on the side of the new, cheeky Davids buzzing around the ankles of the corporate Goliaths. That, as Judge Jackson understood, is why the friend of business has occasionally to take an axe to this or that company. To promote the US software industry, Microsoft may have to tear itself apart. Eventually BT might have to shrink – not to satisfy old Labour spite, but to keep Britain a dynamic, competitive place for capitalism.

This is not exactly socialism, but for those anxious to tame the corporations who increasingly shape our world it may be the next best thing. It certainly beats giving up. The global campaign against Monsanto and its genetically-modified food had already showed that consumer action can work: in December the company bowed to pressure, spun off the GM wing of its business and quietly folded itself into another drugs firm. Now Judge Jackson has proved that the law can make a difference, too. And lest we give up on electoral politics we ought to note this: Republican George W Bush has hinted that, if he becomes president in November, he will do his best to halt the war on Microsoft. Al Gore takes the opposite view. The vice president may not want the endorsement – but you can guess who old man Marx would vote for. •

24 March 2000

Simon Hoggart

The latest Archer:
Queen Trixie and her fertile pigs

How do politicians cope with the concept of shame? Some don't have it; their brains aren't wired that way, just as colourblind people don't know when the traffic lights have changed. Ken Livingstone is one; that's why his apology to the Commons this week was so perfunctory, so like a teenager's " sor-ee!"

Tony Baldry, the Tory MP for Banbury, who pushed a City lawyer for an honour without revealing that the fellow had just lent him £5,000, comes out of the other box. Yesterday in the Commons he pleaded and scraped and grovelled. "This was an error of judgment on my part, for which I have already apologised unreservedly in person to the committee," he said. "I fully accept that I deserve to be criticised. I wish to say 'sorry', sincerely, to the House without reservation or hesitation of any kind."

Nothing would stop the tidal wave of contrition. "I should wish to apologise to each and every member of the House." Was he going to go round on his knees and beg forgiveness from every single MP? Or grab Ken's legs and let him drag him into the lobby while blubbing out yet more remorse?

Thank goodness, no. So I cut across to the Lords to catch the most shameless legislator of the lot.

Labour spin doctors could strap Frank Dobson to a table and surgically remove his beard and whiskers without exposing more bare-faced cheek than Jeffrey Archer generates in five minutes.

When he turned up at the House of Lords a fortnight ago, for the first time after the latest scandal, he sat on the steps to the throne. This was brassy enough, but yesterday he went one further – he not only sat on the Tory benches, in spite of the fact that he has been expelled from the party, but he even had his man phone us beforehand to tell us he was going to do so. This is chutzpah on rye bread with a side order of pickles and sour cream.

He placed himself gingerly between two grand dames, baronesses Seccombe and Miller, both of whom were Tory fund-raisers during the Archer glory years.

He stared ahead as if fascinated by the questions. Perhaps he was gathering material for a novel about a successful writer who is forced out of public life by tiny-minded Pecksniffs, but who braves their jeers and so boldly reclaims his rightful place at the top.

"He was impeccably dressed in a silk tie from Giorgio of Goodge Street's closing down sale, and a worsted suit from the Scope charity shop..."

Questions began with rail safety and signals passed at danger – "spads". Hmm, yes, that's it, our hero had lunched at the Euston Spad U Like, where the maitre'd, Paolo, had welcomed him as an old and valued customer.

Next Lord Mackie of the Benshie spoke about pig fertility: it seems they multiply too quickly. He blamed the strong pound for the crisis. Something there, perhaps.

Baroness Gardner of Parks, an Australian dentist whose real name is Trixie McGirr, started talking about female circumcision. Yes, the plot was almost in place. The heroine, who has her own suite at the Ritz, has discovered a plot by Australian republicans to replace Elizabeth II with a native monarch, Queen Trixie. They have sent a squad of evil north African female circumcisors to terrify her into silence.

But she has been away, skiing in Gstaad. In the meantime her pet pigs have multiplied. Ravenous with hunger they set upon the gang, whose gored remains are found...

The plot perhaps complete, Lord Archer scurried out. None of his former colleagues acknowledged him on his way. •

....

12 November 1999

Simon Hoggart
Widow Twankey ends
the peers' last show

The end of the peers show happened yesterday afternoon at around half past five. Lords vied with each other to say the most historic, the ultimate, the most resonant final words.

But the resonant final mumble was left to the Commons. Summoned by Black Rod to the red and gold magnificence of the upper house, the MPs stood at the Bar as the Lord Chancellor – superb in scarlet and ermine and a massive tricorn hat, so he looked like a character in a cheap panto, obliged to dress as both Baron Hardup and Widow Twankey – read out the bills to which the Queen had agreed.

"House of Lords bill," he said. "La reine le veult!" said a clerk in the traditional Norman French, and with those four words, 800 years of lawmaking by hereditary peers was abolished.

The Commons rumbled with noisy, lip smacking pleasure, and the remaining lords and ladies – life peers, elected hereditaries, departing hereditaries – glowered at them angrily and impotently. It had been a curious final session. Lord Grenfell asked a question about cleaning up the Danube.

Lady Scotland, the incredibly elegant black foreign office minister, who was wearing an ankle-length grey crushed velvet riding coat, paid tribute to his lordship. "He will be greatly missed for his sage counsel," she said.

"Sage counsel" is a very House of Lords phrase. You don't hear it anywhere else. "He said take the 36 and get off at Asda. It was really sage counsel," is something people never say, except in the context of "what herb goes well with roast pork?"

The House was noisier than usual, though not what you or I would call rowdy – more like the hubbub you get in a library reading room when someone turns the pages of What Hi-Fi? too loudly.

Matters weren't helped by the chaos which attended the final debate on the House of Lords bill itself. No one seemed to have the faintest idea which clause was which. Peers would stand up and speak on amendment 4, until someone courteously rose to point out they were still on amendment 2, whereupon another peer would inquire whether they were not actually debating amendment 13.

In the end it didn't matter, since they had decided to give way to the Commons on everything and hope for better luck next year, though they did not yield without some protest. Lord Erroll declared: "We got steamrollered. The government is trying to rail-road us. They want to ramrod things through," so made them sound like baddies in an old-fashioned western.

With slightly more elegance, Lord Strathclyde scoffed at the government's promise not to use patronage to stuff the new House. "'Trust Tony' may be an article of faith in the Labour party, but it cannot be elevated into a constitutional doctrine," he said, in a voice as dry as manzanilla sherry.

Even those who will remain looked dejected. Baroness Strange was wearing a poppy big enough to pick up the England–Scotland game. She won re-election to the Chamber last week on a platform of bringing flowers, but still looked as miserable as if her favourite retriever had fallen off Megginch castle.

Lord Archer seemed glum. Lady Thatcher, whispered one of my colleagues, "looks as if she's been worked on by Damien Hirst."

Baroness Jay, the Marat of this revolution, paid moderately graceful tribute to the departing hereditaries. The clerk read the message of prorogation from the Queen, including the bills she had "accepted as good and perfect acts of parliament".

"Oh, get real, your majesty," the peers must have thought as they trooped off for their final consoling drinks party. •

Country
matters

17 December 1999

Alex Bellos
Out on a limb

We turned off the highway on to a dirt track, on the trail of the rarest bird in the world. The earth was stony and reddish; the landscape typical of this remote, drought-infested corner of north-east Brazil – low, wiry trees and fierce-looking cacti.

We got out of our car and crept quietly to the bank of a small river, where a few tall caraibeira trees emerged from the bank. A camouflaged hutch about a metre high and a metre wide had been cobbled together from branches and leaves. The guide, the photographer and I squashed in and started our vigil.

Shortly after dawn, right on time, we heard a distinctive caw. The guide, a biology student, caught my eye excitedly. Then an elegant blue parrot alighted on the caraibeira opposite. For about 20 minutes it watched us watching it, before it slipped into its nest in the tree's hollow trunk.

In the animal kingdom there can be few sights as poignant. The bird, a Spix's macaw, is one of a kind, the sole member of its species left in the wild. Thanks to the predatory habits of humans – who reduced its habitat through colonisation and then captured the birds for private aviaries – the remaining male Spix's macaw that lives near Curaça, 1,300 miles north of Rio de Janeiro, is the last step before extinction. To paraphrase Monty Python, the species is almost no more. It is almost an ex-species.

Its unique, exaggerated situation, however, has made the parrot an international cause célèbre. It has become a symbol for nature conservation and the battle against animal trafficking. The lonesome Spix's is possibly one of the most closely observed living things. Four people are employed full-time to observe the bird during all daylight hours. They make a log of its movements every two minutes. Local people, most living in extreme poverty and many barely literate, keep notes of whenever they see the bird flying nearby.

"People always ask why we have all of this just to save one bird. But it's a call to arms," says Yara Barros, in-field coordinator of the Spix's Macaw Project, who has spent most days of the past three years huddled in the wooden cabin looking out for her blue-feathered friend. "It's an alert to the world about how close to extinction you can get. The Spix's is a figurehead."

Macaws are the long-tailed poster-birds of the parrot family. Living in a region stretching from Mexico to Argentina, they are an emblem of the American tropics. But their beauty has been their downfall. Thousands have been captured for the international trade in wild animals, now considered the third largest illegal market after drugs and guns. Of the 16 species left, nine are considered at risk of extinction.

The Spix's is the smallest of the three blue macaw types – in Brazil it is known as the ararinha azul (little blue macaw). It has never been seen in large numbers, and it is perhaps fitting that the man who in 1819 gave the macaw its name, Austrian naturalist Johann Baptist von Spix, only did so after he had shot one down. Even before traffickers began stalking them, the population is assumed to have been about 60. For almost a century after the Austrian visited Brazil, none were seen, and by the 1980s, naturalists assumed that the only Spix's alive were the handful kept in private zoos.

Then, in 1990, a Brazilian farmer from near Curaça turned up with photographs of a bird – its long tail dark blue and its head bluey-white.

The excitement in ornithological circles was so great that the Permanent Committee to Save the Spix's Macaw – set up the previous year to link owners of the 15 birds in captivity – set up a base camp in the Brazilian outback.

Since then, the project has dedicated itself to researching the bird. The hope is that the Curaça Spix's can be used in a programme to reintroduce other Spix's to the wild. "This male is the only one who has knowledge of how to survive," says Barros. "He has memory of where there is food, of which cactus to sleep on. "

The project has concentrated on finding the male a family. The soap opera of his marriage guidance and family planning has enthralled bird-lovers, zoologists and environmentalists. The starting point was to find him a wife, and then hope that the couple would produce offspring. Macaws pair for life, but there was a problem – there was an "other woman". When the Spix's was discovered in 1990 he already had a girlfriend: a bright green Illiger's macaw. With none of his kin around, he had no choice but to date the nearest species.

The odd couple had a typical domestic life. The Spix's would sleep on the central pole of a facheiro cactus – the macaw equivalent of a gated condominium – then fly to meet the Illiger's, who lived in a hole in a tree trunk. The couple would fly together during the day, than at sundown the Spix's would escort his lady back to her tree and then scoot off home to the cactus.

Researchers decided nevertheless to find a same-species candidate. They located a female Spix's in Recife, 400 miles away, who had spent seven years in captivity. She was taken to Curaça, where the head biologist gave her a crash course in non-sedentary life, feeding her food from the wild and building up her wing muscles.

In March 1995 she was released. The researchers were in two minds about whether to capture the Illiger's, to give the female Spix's a clear run. "We decided against this because we thought it might disorientate the Spix's," says Barros. The result was, at first, very positive. The female Spix's quickly started courting the male, and the two Spix's and the Illiger's went around as a threesome.

The honeymoon lasted a month. One day, the female Spix's disappeared. A search party of 30 people failed to find any trace. Only recently has the truth come out – a local cow herder spotted the dead bird but was afraid to say for fear that the project would stop.

Researchers devised another tactic. They decided to have faith in the cross-species couple. In 1996, for the first time, the Illiger's laid some eggs. When researchers noticed that one of the eggs was cracking they took it out and analysed it. It contained a hybrid embryo, but it was dead.

During the reproductive season of 1997-8, the project took to playing God more directly. The Illiger's produced some eggs, but they were infertile and were replaced with fertilised Illiger's eggs from another couple. Unfortunately, the eggs were eaten by predators.

A year ago Barros tried a variation on the theme. She swapped the again-infertile Illiger's-Spix's eggs for wooden eggs for the period of incubation. The Illiger's sat on the eggs and on the day that real eggs would have been due to break, Barros took a pair of newborn Illiger's chicks and sneaked them into the nest when the Illiger's was taking her daily stroll.

"When we had a peek in the nest the next day, it was full of food. In other words, she had accepted it. This couple has parenting skills."

The pair brought up the chicks and flew with them until they were old enough to leave. Although genetically completely Illiger's, the young birds developed voices identical to that of their foster father, the Spix's.

Last year's experiment has led Barros to hope that the same would work with Spix's chicks. The problem is that all the reproducing Spix's couples are in the northern hemisphere and so their reproductive season is six months out of sync. Next year, however, six Spix's are to be moved to an aviary near Curaça to try to induce them to produce young at the correct time.

The Spix's-Illiger's couple are still a couple. They still mate, they still fly together and the male still picks her up and drops her off at her home. But he is now about 15 years old. In captivity the species can live to 35, but in the wild the lifespan is thought to be less – and if he dies, the project dies. But recently, another strategy for preservation of the species has emerged. The idea is to train captive birds by keeping them in larger and larger aviaries, feeding them food from the wild, and then eventually releasing them. Two years ago an experiment was started, again using Illiger's as the test. Nine were given a year to adapt to the wild in a Curaça aviary and were then electronically tagged and released. A year later, seven are still alive.

The Spix's Macaw Project has not just helped birds. It has transformed the poor, sleepy town of Curaça by providing it with a primary school, renovating the town theatre and giving it a sense of pride. Children parade dressed as Spix's macaws.

"Without the support of the local population, the project would never work. We rely on people to keep monitoring the bird when she is flying a long way from the nest," says Alexander Gomes, the field assistant.

One 51-year-old cattle rancher has started to carve models of the bird and writes poetry in its honour. Another, Jorge de Sousa Rosa, 42, has swapped his life as a herder to be one of the full-time team of birdwatchers. "I like sitting here all day," he says. "I want to keep up with everything he does. When I was a teenager I remember about 10 of them flying around here. I also remember the traffickers who came. We didn't realise how valuable the birds were."

Barros adds: "It's great that we have taught people that it is important to keep a species alive. The first time I saw him the first sensation I had was fear. You see how fragile the situation is. But, at the same time, he was first spotted nine years ago and he's still here. There is hope."

Sick as a parrot? A little lonely perhaps, and possibly tired of being snooped on constantly, but for once it can take heart that the human race is on its side. •

15 October 1999

Virginia Spiers
Apple days: A Country Diary

TAMAR VALLEY

Queenie, Devonshire Queen and Queen's are different varieties of crimson, aromatic apples with pink-streaked flesh which can be eaten, relished or frozen as delicious juice. Ben's Red raised by Benjamin Roberts at Trannack, Cornwall, around 1830, still hangs on to its characteristic, knotty branches with aerial roots, burr-knots or bee-bunches. Grandfather Martin referred to these apples, growing on their own roots, without the need for grafting, as seedy limbs.

Also known as seedy warts or pitchers, they can be propagated in a damp climate by cuttings taken below the burrs. This year, Miel d'Or, another upright, bushy pitcher, was also loaded with fruit – juicy and very sweet. James and Mary have already picked some 50 varieties from their collection of local and old-fashioned apples. In the cool, dark apple-house, fruit has been stored in old boxes from Davidstow's cheese factory, chalked up with tantalising names. Each year they refine observations and notes concerning appearance, flavour, season and nomenclature. Up the hill, in the dense grove of mother trees, planted 17 years ago, late sun slants briefly through dripping, overarching branches, lighting up rotting, multi-coloured apples, a feast for pheasants, foxes, jays and red admirals.

Clusters of unpicked apples shelter ladybirds, shield bugs, small yellow or orange snails and even the occasional earthworm. Out on the lighter perimeter, trees have dropped distinctive, fully ripened fruits – Breadfruit, big and creamy-pink with a strawberry flavour; golden Early Bower and red-striped Tom Putt, once used for colouring cider. In the main orchard of widely-spaced trees, most apples have been picked and we look forward to munching unsprayed favourites like Ellison's Orange, American Mother and the handsome Blenheim which keeps until Christmas. Still ungathered is Longkeeper, spread out and laden for the first time with smooth, orange-flushed fruit. Mr North's "Pine" from Landue, a beautiful russeted red apple will be picked in time for Cotehele's apple day. •

29 March 2000

Paul Evans

Beholding the fort: A Country Diary

NORDY BANK, SHROPSHIRE

High above the village of Clee St Margaret, where the Clee brook runs down the main street, the skylarks rise through warm hazy sunlight. The track from Stokegorse across The Yeld follows old ways sunk under bracken and centuries of history. Breeze from the west swings over this shoulder of the Brown Clee hill, over the wild expanse of grass and bracken commons called Clee Liberty and Abdon Liberty which are the steep hillsides of the twin peaks of Brown Clee and Abdon Burf. On the lower slopes the boundary hedges are of ancient and solid holly, once used for winter cattle food.

The commons are packed now with sheep, so many that the sward is battered to bowling green height and nothing, except bracken, grows more than an inch high. Great swathes of dry bracken have been mowed and together with the relentless grinding teeth of sheep the strange topography of the land is exposed. There are remains of sunken lanes with banks on either side, quarry-holes with slabs of a old red sandstone poking out, odd formations of ditches, mounds and plateaux.

This land has been shaped by centuries of human labour; time and vegetation have a levelling effect and you can't tell immediately whether these ground forms are decades or centuries in age. But when you see the hill fort of Nordy Bank you know you are in a landscape which has been occupied since the Iron Age. The fort is on a flat promontory jutting westwards from the hill. Its earthwork ring and ditch are impressive even after two and a half thousand years. Once faced with sandstone from surrounding pits, which still shows through the soil of the wall, it would have been topped with a formidable palisade. The scattered farms and smallholdings are probably what remain of ancient settlements which looked to this place as sanctuary in times of trouble and the locus of their culture in this landscape.

As the skylarks rise from the noises of a working countryside, above Nordy Bank, the sky is shattered by the war-like blattering of a huge military helicopter. It swoops low, hawking, as if searching for insurgence in the wild Liberties. The ghosts of Nordy Bank reach for their spears. •

....

8 November 1999

Maev Kennedy

Time runs out for station steeped in myth

The station clock, an icon of British cinema, has stopped and time is running out for the trust struggling to restore Carnforth station, where the classic British romance, Brief Encounter, was filmed in 1945.

The film brings tourists from all over the world to visit the station in Lancashire: more will flock in when the movie is re-released for Valentine's Day next year. But they only find desolation. Like the wretched commuters, huddled on the platforms of a station recently voted the worst in England, the tourists can only dream of steaming tea urns.

The Carnforth Station and Railway Trust has magnificent plans for the station, but if it cannot raise the £1.5m needed before the Railtrack regeneration programme reaches north Lancashire early next year the buildings will be flattened. The trust is still about £1m shy of the target.

The buildings which sheltered the stiff upper lip tragic lovers still stand – just.

Every time a 110mph express screeches through without stopping little flakes of British cinema history drift down from the rotting platform roof. The refreshment room is locked and shuttered, its interior a mouldering ruin.

The last 30 years have been a chapter of disasters for the junction, which created a market town and once provided hundreds of jobs. Half the platforms were torn out in the 1970s in the electrification of the west coast line. The station lost its ticket office, then all staff. The station clock was also electrified (its 1870s clockworks were sold off for scrap), ran erratically for a few years and then stopped.

The only facilities now are two and a half benches – the vandals had the other half – and a square room, headquarters of the trust, which is manned daily by volunteers. It offers petition forms, tourist leaflets, and a brief respite from the savage wind from Morecambe Bay.

"This was the station master's office, and it always had a proper fire – fed with coal from the tenders," trust chairman Peter Yates said. "They had to film in the small hours of the morning, when the station wasn't in use, so it must have been bitterly cold. When she arrived at the set Celia Johnson used to stand in front of this fire warming herself"

Director David Lean scoured the country for a setting to film Noel Coward's script – originally a one-act stage play – about a middle-aged couple who meet in a station buffet, fall in love, steal a few afternoons at the Kardomah cafe and the Roxy cinema, and then part forever for the sake of their children and lthe sacred institution of marriage.

Carnforth was chosen partly because it was so remote the war office felt the film set's lights blazing in the blackout were unlikely to attract the Luftwaffe. David Lean's shrewd eye also spotted that the station had ramps to the underpass – Celia Johnson, who spends an unfeasible amount of the film running from her platform to her lover's and back, would have looked ludicrous scrambling up and down steps.

It was filmed in the last months of the war, and released in November 1945. It recently came second on the British Film Institute list of 100 great British films.

All the crucial scenes between Johnson and Trevor Howard take place either on the station platforms or in the refreshment room, ruled by Joyce Carey's magnificent Ivy, goddess of the tea urn.The trust has an agreement with Railtrack to restore all the buildings, bring back a stationary steam train as the star attraction of a visitor centre, and reopen the refreshment room complete with bentwood chairs, cast iron stove and mahogany counter.

However, the scheme was shot down last year by the heritage lottery fund because the unlisted buildings did not meet their priorities. The trustees believe their project meets all the government's objectives of conservation, urban regeneration, and promoting increased railway use.

The trust recently located the innards of the clock, which warned the lovers their time was up, in west London. The owner knew nothing of the film connection, and is happy to sell it back. It had been through dozens of hands since it was first sold, yet we managed to trace it, chairman Peter Yates said. If we can do that we can do anything. •

14 December 1999

John Valins

Mendip lead: A Country Diary

SOMERSET

A few miles before we reached Wells, on the road from Bath, we crossed a high Mendip plateau that, from its appearance, might have been somewhere near Chapel-en-le-Frith in the Peak District. Sheep were scattered across wide stretches of pastureland divided by dry stone walls. The weather was bright and cold. Where the bleak expanse began to give way to wooded slopes, we suddenly found ourselves on a level with the uppermost pinnacles of a finely decorated church tower that seemed to rear up out of a hidden valley.

Then the road pitched down past buildings at odd angles into the centre of the village, Chewton Mendip, past the Old Rectory and the Waldegrave Arms. From this level, a backward glance shows the church reappearing, now apparently high on a hill.

When you climb up and see the base as well as the top of the tower, you can better appreciate what Leland called "a goodly new high turrid steeple" set so dramatically among bewildering contours.

Not far away is Priddy, where potholers with lamps in their helmets were on the way to the caves in a high, rocky terrain with ancient stone circles.

A fair has been held on the green since the middle ages and still thrives. We stopped by a sheet of water where the landscape was harsh and bare of trees. There was no live-stock, the grass was tussocky and coarse and the surface pocked and scarred.

There were mounds that looked more man-made than natural. A notice explained that this was an area of special, scientific interest, one of four Mendip lead "minors" where lead extraction continued until as recently as 1910. The trade was one source of the wealth that built a church and tower of such scale and grandeur in a place that nowadays bears no obvious marks of prosperity.

The notice explained that no stock grazed here because of the high lead content in the vegetation. It described the unfamiliar marks in the landscape as pores, mounds, spoil heaps and "buddle pits". Another steep drop through woodland brought us towards Wells and the softer south of the county. •

....

8 November 1999

A Harry Griffin
The SOS box: A Country Diary

THE LAKE DISTRICT

Some time before Christmas a helicopter hovering above Dow Crag, the splendid precipice in the fells above Coniston, will gently lower a massive blue stretcher box to the foot of the cliff, where volunteers will carefully bolt it into place – ready for use in any emergency.

The new stretcher box is a memorial to my son Robin who, sadly, died suddenly 15 months ago, not long after a most successful first visit to the Himalayas. It also commemorates other climbers, remembered on the original stretcher box, who had died on the crag in earlier years.

The sturdy new box, containing the stretcher and other vital first aid equipment, was provided through generous donations from friends at Robin's funeral. He had often climbed on Dow Crag and had known the original stretcher box since it was installed many years ago. His widow, Mary, and I were kindly invited to the recent opening of the splendid, enlarged headquarters of the Coniston mountain rescue team, where the new box was on display. How well I remember the tragedy in the snowbound fells just before Christmas 1946 that led to the formation of the Coniston team, in which I was indirectly involved. This was the first mountain rescue team in the Lake District – set up some months before Keswick's.

Robin first went up Coniston Old Man and along the ridge to Dow Crag, with me, when he was four. At the age of five and a half – and I have a photograph of him at the cairn to prove it – he took his grandfather, my father, up the Old Man. At that time my father had never been up there, nor any other mountain so far as I'm aware, so Robin, knowing the hill, was the leader.

Strangely, the Old Man and Dow Crag were also Robin's last hills. Two days before his sudden and inexplicable passing, he took Mary around the familiar traverse high above Goats Water and, on the way up the crag, pointed out to her the little blue blob of the stretcher box at the foot of C Buttress. So the new box will be an appropriate memorial to a gentle man who loved all mountains – but especially the Coniston fells he had known all his life. •

Online and offline

23 November 1999

Anna Vaux

Get your hands off my husband

Rachel Garley's web page comes in, if you look it up on Hotbot, at number 6. Rachel Garley, it says in upper and lower case, six times. Rachel Garley Rachel Garley Rachel Garley... She is here, against a pink background, against a white background, breasts pushed together, white underwear, no underwear, black underwear, killer stilettos, a red rose, 80s hair (very 80s hair), wet-look mouth. There is something Vaseline-y about the photography, but you can zoom in closer when you click, and things seem less misty after that, at least to me.

I am staring and zooming because Rachel has been writing to my husband, a philosopher, on a philosophical matter – for she wonders, as did Descartes, if she exists. She places the origins of her existential crisis with the television presenter Kirsty Young, who has the habit of saying to the viewers of Channel 5 News, "Join me, Kirsty, after the break for more real news, real stories about real people" (enough to give anybody angst).

To tell the truth, Rachel didn't come quite clean in her letter, charming as it was. She didn't, for one thing, suggest anything like the career I imagine when I click on her page and am told "See Rachel stripped in nude cafe full length version in naked cafe what lovely long legs" – though she did, in her letter, describe herself as drinking down the Groucho Club, in her little sugar babe dress, and looking good.

Naturally, I have been pondering the image of Rachel in a sugar babe dress, and tried to imagine exactly what it is that a sugar babe dress might be – nothing like anything in my wardrobe, where there are rows of serge, suggestive – I had mistakenly imagined – of something thoughtful in my demeanour. I can't shake off the knowledge that where I come from, if a girl writes to a boy about something sexy, then sex is what it is.

My husband, who has written books on David Hume, Free Will and Mental Reality, appears to take a philosophical view of this – though he is visibly piqued by the thought of sugar babe dresses, I can tell – and wasn't/isn't sure if Rachel really does exist and is not a hoax. She might be someone else entirely. Anyone in the Groucho club for a start, where her letters suggest she spends a lot of her time. Certainly there is no denying that that would be a wheeze.

One other philosopher has succumbed already. He sent her a poem by Emily Dickinson, the one which starts: "I'm nobody! Who are you?/Are you nobody, too?" She included it in her letter to my husband, though she didn't think it a particularly helpful response. I, on the other hand, thought it a good reply and hoped for something similarly clever and detached from my husband, if he were to reply at all, which many parts of me hoped he would not.

But he did, and Rachel seems grateful for his response, for this time she enclosed not a poem but a photocopied clipping from Loaded magazine, from which I learned that

Rachel is an exhibitionist. She likes being watched during sex. She likes going out with no clothes on – especially when there are builders around; she is in love with S&M, and wants a slave. A much better picture this time too.

Much better hair. Very 90s. Still blurry, but good faux demure, face down, hands through hair, and great legs in black stay-ups (it looks like). The interviewer makes a point of calling for medical assistance in block capitals (MEDIC . . . STRETCHER . . . AMBULANCE . . .).

So, as I thought, sex and not philosophy. Or in any case not exclusively philosophy. And if it is not a hoax it is certainly a game (though she denies that) – a delightful one, perhaps, that contributes fully if not quite properly to the gaiety of nations.

Nevertheless, I can't help but wish that Rachel would pursue another branch of philosophy. Game theory perhaps. Or risk theory. Or even ethics. There's lots of good stuff around on that, I'm told. And I'm sure she'd be good at it. A course on English literature can be very enlightening. I did one myself.

But Rachel is down on traditional forms of art and expression. She says so in her letter. She was hanging out with Tracey Emin and asked her if she, Tracey, thought that traditional art was dead, and Tracey said yes. Rachel says she'd write a book, except that writing is dead too. She will do a book of installations instead.

Except, Rachel, you are wrong, as your letters show. They are very appealing. Nothing could be sexier than a letter. You should stick it out (though it is true, you have to stay in sometimes to write a book). Still, and for what it's worth, the installation-thing seems like a good idea. I'd buy it. Obviously. Especially if my husband were in it. His charming and considered response to the issue of whether or not Rachel Garley exists should be read by more than just Rachel Garley. As I'm sure it has been. •

11 December 1999
Alexander Chancellor
Internet fever

My constant companion nowadays is the invaluable *Guardian Guide To The Internet*, by Jim McClellan (Fourth Estate, £5.99). Together with an ear infection and other winter ailments, I have suffered an attack of internet fever. I have a desperate urge to grasp and control the internet in all its infinite richness and complexity. I don't want to be left out. I want to be a fully paid-up member of the global internet community, conversing urbanely with all the peoples of the world and discovering all the secrets of the universe. You can do that, you know, on the internet. You can find out everything there is to know. It is a wonderland at which even Alice would marvel.

But unfortunately, you will never be able to grasp or control it for, as Gertrude Stein once said of Oakland, there is no there there. As every internet beginners' guide points out, it isn't a thing. It's just a means of communication, used, at the moment, by about 150 million people with computers. You can no more control the internet than you can control all the telephone conversations going on in the world. Jim McClellan sagely advises us not to be too ambitious. "Getting online is not like signing up for some monolithic crusade," he writes. "You don't have to buy into the whole programme. You can pick and choose."

That's all very well, but how do you pick and choose on the internet without constantly stumbling into stupid, unpleasant and cocksure people who poison your view of the world? There is much nastiness out there, and not only of the unspeakable kind that landed Gary Glitter in jail. There is smugness and rudeness and ghastly technological jargon, which are the legacy of the early internet users who tried to hijack the new medium for an exclusive new culture that would frighten off normal people. They wrote ungrammatically and without punctuation. They invented words that only the initiated would understand. They responded to conventional language or technological naivety with sneers and abuse.

Recently, I received an incredibly abusive e-mail message from a reader of a column I write for an American online magazine. I replied with studied politeness and was rewarded with a grovelling apology. He hadn't meant any of it, the reader said. Being rude on the internet was just a habit that was very hard to shake. He was truly sorry. Here was evidence that the techno-elitists are on the run. Their bid for control of the internet has failed. They have been swamped by ordinary people, such as my mother-in-law who, at the age of 84, has started using a computer to send e-mail messages, which she writes with care and elegance and describes heretically as "letters".

In fact, the internet is seldom decried nowadays for promoting cultural barbarity. Instead, it has become fashionable to credit it with a revival of old-fashioned literary values. In its current issue, the New Yorker magazine claims that "the internet is the first new medium to move decisively backward, for it is, essentially, written". "When someone tells you that he has been online, what he has probably been doing is reading words that other people have written, and then writing some words of his own," it says.

The New Yorker points out that it has caused millions of people who, until recently, were communicating almost exclusively by telephone to start writing letters again. "Those who stubbornly insist that the internet is forward-looking point out that it's good only for a certain kind of writing – the 300-word burst, the quick hit," it goes on. "But this confirms how sublimely reactionary it is. It doesn't just look back – it looks way back, to around 1730. Swift and Pope and Lord Chesterfield, with a Web page apiece, would have been merrily scribbling short essays, anonymous accusations, and billets-doux. "Two of the most popular Web forms – the rant and the quote page, a miscellany of epigram – are pure 18th-century revivals."

There remains, however, a large gap between the language ordinary people use on the internet and that of the technical experts who make it work. These people are brilliant, of course, and without them the miracle could never have taken place. But they need to be much more self-effacing. You can use the radio or the telephone without any understanding of the technology behind them. That must become true of the internet as well if it is to embrace the Swifts and Popes of the modern world. I am now able to listen to music on the internet, but only after being instructed to download a tool known as a "Stuffit Expander". A Stuffit Expander?

I ask you. This is the internet's great challenge – to get itself to work without telling you how. •

Sorry, we'll say that again
Corrections and clarifications

2 June 2000
Apologies for the rude anatomical note introduced into yesterday's Country Diary, page 22, where we noted the common sandpiper's "whirring flight over the bum". It should, of course, have been "burn".

7 October 1999
On page 8 of Monday's sport section we captioned a picture: "Mark Rivers swoops in on Tranmere Rovers' Alan Mahon during Crewe Alexandra's 2-0 win." The Crewe player was Shaun Smith, not Mark Rivers. The Tranmere player was Dave Challinor, not Alan Mahon. Crewe did not win 2-0. They lost 2-0.

7 December 1999
The film starring Errol Flynn in which Gillian Lynne appeared, page 16, G2, December 7, was The Master of Ballantrae, not The Mask of Gallantry. •

11 September 1999
Ian Mayes
A short history of style

All newspapers fight a losing battle to achieve accuracy and clarity. But do we try hard enough? We published a note from a reader this week suggesting that the editor of the letters page favoured short letters because of the ever-increasing volume of corrections and clarifications accommodated at the foot of the page. That's amusing, but neither of its implied points is really true. The daily corrections take up anything from, exceptionally, a few lines to about 110, and that has been the case since they moved to their present prominence on the leader/letters page; but they are, let us agree, too many.

Fortuitously, a sheaf of papers arrived on my desk this week showing some of the efforts made by the Guardian in the mid-1960s to keep the number of errors and grammatical lapses under control. No point was too small to qualify for inclusion in the style notes which were then circulated to all senior staff who were expected to initial each sheet when they had read it before passing it on.

One that I have before me included the following contribution compiled from points submitted by Alistair Cooke: "We committed the old gaffe only a few days ago of using 'Texan' as an adjective. This is an ancient British error and worthy only of papers that are just catching on to American usage, like The Times and Daily Telegraph."

Cooke's little lesson continued, "A Texan and a Californian are always nouns. They describe the citizens of those states. Thus: A Texan States His Case. A Californian for President? Otherwise: A Texas Fiesta for Erhard ... A California Landslide ..."

His contribution concluded, "Please note that a native of Florida is a Floridian not a Floridan." (The lavish use of initial capitals may bring a tear of nostalgia to a few eyes: we shall come to the present policy of capitalisation in a future column).

One of these notes, which I shall make sure is preserved in the Guardian archive, is dated November 25, 1966, and signed A.H. [Alastair Hetherington, editor of the Guardian 1956-1975]: "nigger in the woodpile – cliché, and to be avoided".

Some progress has been made. But have we allowed the attention to detail clearly evident in these style pages circulated among Guardian journalists more than 30 years ago to be lost in the vast growth of the paper since then?

We make relatively few errors that cause serious damage or distress to innocent people. We make huge numbers of mistakes in our use of English and in minor facts that could easily have been checked. Among the latter are the misspelling of people's names, which is nearly always inexcusable: is it Catherine, Catharine, Katharine, Kathryn... someone should have asked. We should be warned by the precedent set on August 18, 1914, when a piece describing German artillery at practice appeared under the byline HD Lawrence, although reading it, it is difficult to see how the true identity of the author could have been obscured, which it apparently was for a period.

Readers who point out spelling mistakes commonly ask whether our journalists have yet to find the spell-check key on their keyboards. In a way I hope they haven't. No computerised checking system would pick up the use of real but incorrect words, or prevent the homophones that annoy and entertain us. The spell check that comes between the journalist and the dictionary is a bad thing. The dictionary at a glance provides a check on spelling and, more importantly, meaning.

Is there a cultural problem, something in the air-conditioning in Farringdon Road that encourages slack attention to these things? One of the paper's more senior subeditors thinks there may be. He is scathing about the condition of some of the copy submitted for editing, which suggests that its author has not read it over. I have had furious rows with writers who have sent unread copy to me: if you can't be bothered to read it why should anyone else bother?

It is a complicated business in which any or all of the following may be factors: the legacy of a time when expression was favoured above spelling and grammar in the teaching of English; changes in training, with fewer journalists coming through the regional press and more direct entries to the Guardian from university or other parts of the press, magazines etc; deficiencies in the Guardian's own training activities; the absence of proof readers at the Guardian and reliance on journalists correcting their own work; the emphasis on the Guardian as a writers' paper – do we give the writer too much autonomy, do we give editors the feeling that their activities are secondary or peripheral? And so on.

We are trying to work out the answer. ∎

....

10 September 1999

Polly Toynbee
Guarding the Guardian

The Guardian is not like any other national newspaper. It has no proprietor and is owned by the Scott Trust whose sole purpose, as handed down generously by the Scott family, is to devote itself to ensuring the paper's long survival "as heretofore". We have no proprietor, no Murdoch, Black, Hollick, Rothermere or O'Reilly capable of pulling our strings. And, of course, we make much of this. Indeed our enemies sometimes accuse us of being sanctimonious. Frequently we attack other newspapers for slavishly following their owner's self-interested line or distorting their apparently straight news columns to further their owners' business interests.

We have often been in the forefront of exposing and condemning political sleaze and dishonesty, whether over Neil Hamilton and cash for questions or Jonathan Aitken's public lying. We sit very comfortably on our high horse over any suspicion of the Honours list being used cynically by political parties to hand out rewards for large donations: cash for gongs is what finally sunk Harold Wilson's reputation in the history books.

We have also mocked the distribution of honours to journalists, editors and newspaper proprietors: Sir David English of the Daily Mail, Sir Larry Lamb of the Sun, Lord Deedes of the Telegraph, Lord Rees-Mogg of the Times, Lord Cudlipp of the Mirror, Lord Black (if he manages it) of the Telegraph or Rupert Murdoch's extraordinary papal knighthood. Gongs for craven parti pris journalism is as nasty an allegation as gongs for cash and for this reason reputable journalists do well to eschew them. They are always handed out by the parties that these journalists and editors broadly support, never by the other side and that must make them suspect, however much the recipients protest their independence. In fact the closer a journalist comes to agreeing with one political party or the other, the more jealously they should guard any suspicion that they have been or could be suborned. It was through a fierce sense of the Guardian's political independence that our editor-before-last, Alastair Hetherington, turned down a knighthood rather than risk tarring us with the same brush, even after his departure. CP Scott refused a peerage.

That is a long preamble to the difficult question of the Guardian's present dilemma. Bob Gavron, the chairman of the Guardian Media Group, parent firm of the company which publishes the paper, has recently made a substantial donation to the Labour party of £500,000. This follows a previous £500,000 given in 1996 before he became our chairman, an earlier gift of £100,000 to Neil Kinnock and life-long generosity to the Labour party he has always belonged to (contrary to unpleasant smears in the Spectator). In June this year, the same month he made his second donation, his elevation to the peerage was announced (he was told about it in March). There has been an entirely predictable and understandable outcry, amid some chortling from the rightwing press. What, they ask, would the Guardian have had to say if some Tory newspaper chairman had done likewise? Of course we would have clambered on to the old high horse and galloped into battle against gongs for cash.

Once the size of his recent donation was leaked in the Sunday Telegraph, gleeful accusations abounded, as they were bound to. The implication that Gavron only got his peerage because of his donation may be grossly unfair: he is a long time Labour supporter and a highly successful businessman who has built up a large publishing empire. He is also a big-league philanthropist who has given away more than £15m to charities for sick children, prisoners and the arts. He has just the kind of business expertis e Labour rightly seeks to harness and there is nothing secretive about his political affiliation. But as I write these words in all sincerity, I can hear how they sound – exactly like the apologies for many far more dubious titles given out over the years. This is mud that sticks, however unfairly, especially to a newspaper that prides itself on being better than the rest.

As bad is the allegation that the Guardian has been used as a stepping stone by a businessman keen to earn himself as title. The Times snidely wrote in June that Gavron, "who gave more than £500,000 to Labour's election campaign, is one of the party's most important benefactors. But it is not the influence he wields in boardrooms that makes Mr Gavron such a serious player in Labour circles but because he is chairman of the Guardian Media Group. He oils the wheels of the economic engine of the newspaper which is often not on the same side as the government despite its leftward leaning." The suggestion that he might be used to make the Guardian more "on message" with the government is absurd. But it is distressing to Guardian journalists if it undermines what we write. To have a chairman who is soon to take the Labour whip, pager-obedient to every twist and turn of Labour policy, makes many on the staff of this paper deeply uneasy. Those who do often support the government feel their reputation most threatened.

Of course anyone who knows how the Guardian's constitution works, knows that is impossible. The Scott Trust, chaired by Hugo Young, hires and fires editors but has absolutely no other say in the editorial content of the paper. Neither does the board of the Guardian Media Group, which manages the Guardian financially alongside many other local newspapers and magazines. So strict is this edict that one hapless businessman, put on the board in the 1930s, was removed for raising editorial matters. Gavron is a non-executive and unpaid chairman, under whose leadership the group has done phenomenally well financially. But the board may never discuss the paper's content with the editor, who answers to the trust alone.

In other words the Guardian's chairman is in no sense its owner: he cannot lean on the editor. Naturally all newspaper editors always claim their absolute independence – but how are readers to know if and when they are lying through their teeth? Public trust in journalism could hardly fall any lower. It is a commodity so rare that if the Guardian has managed to earn a little more than others, we need to nurture it with extraordinary scrupulousness. Perhaps one emblem of editorial independence is that it would be unthinkable for any other newspaper to print criticism of its own chairman or owner.

The very idea that the Guardian has been bought will no doubt draw ribald comments from Alastair Campbell, since we are not exactly this government's favourite reading: they tend to spit the paper's name. But we will be embarrassed by hypocritical attacks from others and possibly our readers' trust may be undermined. I do not believe Lord Gavron has done anything underhand but for the paper's sake it would have been better if he had refused a peerage. •

....

13 December 1999

Ian Katz
Final edition

A little over three years ago I wrote a story about Martin Dunn, then outgoing editor of the New York Daily News. Dunn was heading back to Britain to run Associated's fledgling new media arm and I suggested, knowingly I thought, that there had to be more to it than that, since his new job was plainly not a proper one. It was a line he gleefully tossed back at me when I followed him back to London a few months later to fill exactly the same role at the Guardian.

Back then the handful of us ink-stained hacks who had crossed the great divide spent much of our time explaining to incredulous colleagues why we had abandoned perfectly good jobs for the relative obscurity of a medium that seemed best suited to servicing unmentionable perversions and indulging teenage conspiracy theorists.

In the past few months all that's changed. Suddenly the new media departments of the major British papers are brimming with the kind of heavy hitters whose talents had previously been reserved for the print editions. Over in Kensington Paul Dacre's favourite lieutenant, Ted Verity, is beavering away on a digital interpretation of the Daily Mail; across town in Wapping, Andy Bull, formerly of the Mail on Sunday, and Andy Coulson, one of the brighter stars in the tabloid firmament, are toiling over online versions of the Times and Sun respectively. Closer to home, David Rowan takes over today as editor of this paper's Unlimited network of sites.

One of the things that has propelled the net onto the radar screens of executive bunkers across the Fleet Street diaspora is the realisation that the numbers of people using the online editions are beginning to look more like the circulations of national newspapers than specialist newsletters on tax harmonisation. Here at the Guardian, for instance, somewhere between 50,000 and 80,000 people tap into our sites every day, a number that no longer looks insignificant next to the paper's circulation of 400,000. And unlike the circulation charts that promise all of us the prospect of a gentle but inexorable decline, the graphs plotting site usage march reassuringly towards the top right of the page.

Everywhere there is talk of ramping up, shifting emphasis, integration. The Financial Times has assigned "web producers" to each of its desks and is busily recruiting online reporters; the Independent has unveiled a shiny (if creaky) new site; the Telegraph has hived off its new media business to allow it (among other things) greater flexibility in raising cash.

From the Times, meanwhile, comes news of a still more dramatic development. As part of the paper's Lara Croft promotion, the makers of Tomb Raider have created a level of the game featuring none other than the editor, Peter Stothard, himself. Users of the Times website will be able to download the groundbreaking sequence, explains an excited Bull: "It's the first time a broadsheet editor has appeared as a character in a video game."

Behind this flurry of activity lies a broad agreement that the future of newspapers is somehow entwined with the internet. There is general agreement, too, that this has something to do with the fact that classified advertising will migrate largely or entirely to the web where it works better and can be produced more cheaply.

But beyond that no one seems very sure of anything. A host of big questions hang, unanswered, in the ether. What should newspapers really be doing on the net? Will they have to change what they do in print to survive in a digital world? Will they exist in print at all, five, 10, 20 years from now?

The arrival of the first WAP (Wireless Application Protocol) phones offering direct access to the net in stores last week was a reminder of the scariest question of all: will the skills of newspaper journalists even be relevant in an online world where brevity and speed seem far more important than elegance or intelligence. (It was sobering that the first WAP phones from Orange offered access to headlines from ITN rather than any newspaper.)

To the extent that anyone is willing to venture answers to these questions, opinion is divided broadly into two camps which could be labelled, only slightly crudely: Don't Panic and Sinking Ship. Those in the first group invariably start by pointing out that no medium has ever snuffed out another, despite confident predictions first that radio would cripple newspapers and then that TV would sweep both of them aside. Next they list the many powerful advantages of dead trees. "No phones, no wires, no batteries, no dodgy screens, no slow systems..." said the Mirror's Piers Morgan in a piece in Media Guardian last week.

That kind of newsprint jingoism might not be surprising from Morgan, but what about this from Robert Kaiser, the former Washington Post managing editor who masterminded the paper's ambitious net effort: "Every month since I got involved in this stuff I kept finding new examples of what a miracle the invention of the newspaper was. Here's a product that is portable, clipable and easy to save for reading later. Every time Windows crashes on me I'm reminded how reliable my Washington Post is."

Sooner or later, proponents of the Don't Panic view come to what you might call the argument from serendipity. "It's kind of fun to stumble on adverts or stories you didn't know you were looking for," says Howard Kurtz, the Washington Post's media correspondent. "This may be a dinosaur's illusion but I still believe the 500-year-old medium of papers has its advantages."

The Sinking Shippers point instead to the clear advantages of the new medium: its immediacy, its searchability, its interactivity, its ability to deliver sound and video as well as text, its relatively low production costs. Why, they wonder, would anyone chose to wait 12, or even 36 hours after a football match to read a printed report when they could access the same report, along with video clips of the goals, on the net within minutes of the final whistle?

Central to the Sinking Ship view is the assumption that papers have essentially lost their primary role as deliverers of news. Where once they got all their news from their daily paper, readers now have access to a dizzying range of news sources from rumour mills like the Drudge report, via the wire services that were once available to journalists only, to the huge news factories like CNN, the BBC and MSNBC.

It cannot escape the notice of newspaper readers for long that many of the stories they are served each day are essentially tarted up versions of wire stories they have seen online the previous day – quite possibly on the same newspaper's own website.

Jon Katz, the American media critic, has been warning for years that newspapers would pay dearly for failing to understand that news moved quicker in a wired world. "When you put a story on the front page that's been on the net 24 hours before, you might as well take out a full page ad and say 'We're useless'.

"In an age where the Starr report is distributed to 55m people within hours you still have hundreds of people sitting around waiting for press briefings."

But what about the other things newspapers still offer: analysis and commentary, for instance? "The trouble is that I'm not sure the digital world is a good place to do those things," says Roger Green, managing director of Emap New Media and one of Britain's web publishing pioneers. "These are things which take time to read and if you look at how much time people are spending on the net it's like nanoseconds."

At the same time, Green warns, we are coming under attack from a host of specialist publishers – many of which didn't exist six months ago – picking off the consumer niches newspapers so successfully aggregated. Just look at the plethora of specialist sports sites which have largely crowded out the once formidable sports offerings of newspapers. And all this is before considering the likely impact of a generation of young people who have grown up more comfortable with screens than printed pages. Does Green expect us to be printing 20 or 30 years from now? "Well, there will always be annuals, won't there... The World in 2030, that sort of thing."

The fate of newspapers, and the ways in which they will have to change, depend to a large extent on how digital technology develops over the next few years. The arrival of WAP phones is seen by many as a milestone as significant as the development of the PC.

Bill Gates acknowledged as much last week by forming an alliance with Ericsson, the world's largest manufacturer of mobile electronic devices, and industry experts predict that by 2003 more people will be accessing the net through phones than PCs. "We haven't even launched our website yet and already we're out there doing deals with phone companies who want our headlines," says Claudia Jay, the 28-year-old managing director of thestreet.co.uk, the British offshoot of the hugely successful American finance site.

When I first started working on the web, friends would remind me constantly that the whole concept of net newspapers was doomed until we could read them on the bus. Well now we can – but only off a screen the size of a matchbox. Is learning to exploit this new hyper-abbreviated medium the key to our future, or does it really lie with the scientists searching for the Holy Grail of publishing technology: an ultra-slim screen that mimics the characteristics of good old paper? One thing is for certain, says Kaiser: "No model that you can imagine today is the model of 2020. Things are going to happen that are going to throw out everyone's thinking."

The key question facing newspapers is whether they should – or can – abandon the 24-hour production cycle around which they are organised. British newspapers have only dabbled with asking their print journalists to file for the web. Even the Washington Post, regarded as a trailblazer in this area, asks its print journalist to produce just a dozen or so stories each day for net deadlines.

On one hand it's easy to argue that a lurch towards rolling news would compromise what we're good at – putting news in context and breaking real stories – while throwing us into an unwinnable contest with the news giants like the BBC. On the other, it's hard to see how we can avoid the kind of increasing marginalisation Katz (no relation, incidentally) talks about if we simply opt out of the news race.

Each question spawns new ones. How important is sound and video going to be, and what do newspapers know about them anyway? How are we going to hang on to our talent in a giddy period where every journalist with an ounce of net savvy is being wooed by some start-up with the promise of virtual millions? And, the really difficult one, how are we going to balance the books when no newspaper in the world, with the exception of the Wall Street Journal, has yet turned a profit on the web?

My own guess is that hard economics, rather than any journalistic consideration, will make the really big decision for us quicker than most of us imagine. A drop off in print classifieds of the scale most people in the industry now expect will not only blow a multi-million-pound hole in newspaper budgets but will surely hit circulations too – even if readers still, miraculously, want us for news, they won't be buying us to find a job.

Falling circulation will mean falling display ad revenue leaving us no option but to hike up cover prices. And loyal as readers like those of the Guardian have been, that will force circulation down further. And so the cycle will continue until we either settle for a precarious future as high-price niche publications – or switch off the presses and jump headlong into cyberspace.

But while the sentimentalist in all of us will miss the old-fashioned pleasures of ink on paper, we should not be gloomy. The really important question is not whether the presses continue to roll, but whether we can still practise something like journalism as we know it in an online world.

And the answer to that one is yes, provided that we are sufficiently resourceful and adaptable. To date, our experience in the new medium has been so tentative and disorienting that we accept as gospel the dispiriting conclusions of the web pioneers – that no one wants long or thoughtful articles online, that good writing counts for little, that users don't even care much about our view of the world, happily gathering their news from "non-brand" suppliers like the wire services instead.

What we forget is that if we measured the value of content only in terms of circulation, we could draw a similar set of conclusions about print. We know that running lots more stories about two-timing soap stars and replacing our comment pages with extra sports coverage would sell more papers, but as broadsheets we choose – by and large – not to do that.

In time we will define a new role for ourselves online that will combine enough of what we consider important as print journalists with the things – like producing one sentence stories for mobile phones perhaps – that we need to do to survive.

Robert Kaiser, for one, is confident that quality journalism will still be relevant online. "The more information that's available, the more people need our help to sort it out. We still have this huge thing to offer, which is our sensibility and our judgment."

And here's another thought that should cheer us dead tree types. Of all the people I spoke to for this piece, it was the netheads who were most sanguine about the prospects for newspapers. Jay of thestreet.co.uk's was typical: "The funny thing is that I'm sitting here thinking, how am I going to convince all these conservative people who read newspapers to use my website?" •

....

26 February 2000

Ian Mayes

Name dropping

There is a dilemma in writing about unattributed pejorative quotes. Do you repeat them for the purpose of discussing them, thereby adding to their circulation? I repeated one that was at the centre of a complaint dealt with in this column last week and decided that its use in the context complained of was justified, a conclusion with which several readers strongly disagreed. We have to differ. That particular remark will, however, slip quietly into oblivion. It does not resonate in the journalistic mind.

The same cannot be said, unfortunately, about a grossly offensive remark made by someone from whom, in May last year, we sought a comment upon the appointment of Andrew Motion as poet laureate. That the remark was intended to apply, as our story said, to the decision and not to Andrew Motion personally, was a distinction too fine perhaps for any of us to grasp.

It was immediately regretted by almost everyone concerned, including the poet who made the remark. If you are going to write about it, he said, you might point out that the source of the quote, appalled at how the remark was being both misapplied and misattributed, fairly swiftly identified himself and apologised to Andrew Motion, that it was made by a vociferous advocate of Carol Ann Duffy's candidature who heard the news at 11.30pm as he emerged from the pub somewhat the worse for drink, and was staggered to hear that the government had failed yet again to appoint a woman to the post, and that he regrets having come up with such an unfortunately resonant phrase.

Let me add the reminder that it was the Guardian that started the controversy in the first place. Andrew Motion says, yes, he did have a very long and apologetic letter from the person who made the remark, but by then the damage was done. It is easy to see what he means. In the nine months since it was printed in the Guardian the remark has been run in at least seven other newspapers and, more to the point, it has been repeated at least six times in the Guardian.

Andrew Motion said he could understand the need to use phrases such as "Downing Street sources" in the context of political reporting but the use of anonymous pejorative quotes apparently aimed at an individual was a cowardly practice and "just deeply irresponsible". Perhaps our regret that we ever used the remark would carry greater force if we desisted from any further repetition of the remark.

We have to ask ourselves whether there is an anomaly in our demanding greater openness and accountability from others, on the one hand, and the prevalence throughout the paper of unattributed material on the other. It seems to me that there is. It is not a question of whether the device is useful or not. It is sometimes an essential tool, most obviously, perhaps, in political reporting. The question is, are we, through allowing its proliferation, creating a culture of anonymity?

That is overstating the situation. However, the deputy editor (news) made the general point, "It is quite objectionable that we are allowing so many people to voice their opinions under the cloak of anonymity." We had been speaking earlier about our front page lead on Tuesday (February 22) headed "Secret plan to ditch Dobson", which claimed that Tony Blair had drawn up a contingency plan to back Mo Mowlam, rather than Frank Dobson, as Labour's London mayoral candidate if Ken Livingstone stood as an independent. There was no specific attribution anywhere in the story, even though remarks which Mr Blair was said to have made at a meeting with Mr Livingstone were placed within quotation marks.

The deputy editor (news) said that in these circumstances he always asked reporters and specialists three questions: Did they know the person or persons giving them the story? Had they dealt with the source before? And was the source in a position to know what he or she was telling us?

Our political editor said, "I have what I call the jury test. If you were forced to divulge your source would a jury think you were justified in what you had written?"

The editor of the paper acknowledges that the use of unattributed quotes can sometimes be a device for getting at the truth. In the case of a pejorative remark he suggested the journalist had to ask whether it provided so valuable an insight that it justified the shield of anonymity.

He said that if a story was being built around unattributable sources it should always be discussed with a senior editor, and the printed story should be as specific about the sources as possible, both the nature and number of them.

One final thought. If you do not already know what remark was made when Andrew Motion was made laureate, is that knowledge that you can manage to live without? Or do you have a feeling that I have let you down? .

11 March 2000

John Ezard
Oxford English Dictionary to go online

You hear some unlikely stories if you walk into the neo-classical headquarters of the Oxford English Dictionary these days. The first is that the book's scholarly, white-bearded Victorian founder, Sir James Murray, is to be played in a Hollywood film by Mel Gibson.

That is true; and it is part of a world full of change for the OED, regarded as the supreme authority on the English language. On Tuesday the dictionary – on which work started 143 years ago – goes online, all 60m words of it.

It will instantly become the internet's biggest, most prestige-laden reference book, dwarfing the 44m-word Encyclopaedia Britannica which launched its own website last year. Yesterday Britannica said that its free site, financed by advertising, had 17m users last month.

To emphasise continuity, the button launching the OED site will be pressed by Sir James Murray's great-great-great grandson Thomas, aged five. But the boy's action means that one of the glories of the world's publishing history may die as a printed book.

Online, it will evolve into a creature different from Murray's – less venerable, monstrously larger, far quicker at reflecting shifts in the language. If its editors' vision comes true, it will be on tap electronically at every school and college as part of Tony Blair's national grid for learning rather than mouldering away on bookshelves at £1,800 for a 20-volume set.

But the web edition will depend chiefly on institutional or public authority subscriptions of £400-£1,000 a year. Its prime overseas markets are the US and Japan. And that has led to another unlikely story: the new US editor of these mostly chaste Victorian tomes is more famous as the author of a best-selling scholarly paperback entitled The F-Word.

This is true too. Moreover the editor, Jesse Sheidlower, a former Random House executive, is taking a hard look at the OED's definitions of the f-word and other obscenities on which he is an authority.

Embarrassingly for his new colleagues, some of these entries – like most of the 300,000 other main words – have lain in the dictionary unrevised since it first came out in 1928, or long before that.

They will have to go, he said. The word "bloody", in an entry thought to have been written by Murray in the 1880s, is defined as "now constantly in the minds of the lowest classes but by respectable people considered a horrid word". It appeals only to the imagination of "the rough classes".

You cannot say this kind of thing any more, especially not in the classless US, in Mr Sheidlower's view.

A combined entry for the f-word and th e c-word, written after the Lady Chatterley trial made it legal to print them in the 1960s, said both were "for centuries, and still by the great majority, regarded as a taboo-word; until recent times not often recorded in print but frequent in coarse speech".

Sadly perhaps, Mr Sheidlower said, you now might well have to acknowledge that the majority no longer sees the f-word, at least, as a taboo word and that it often appears in print.

Sales of the OED's second print edition in 1989 have so far grossed £36m. Of the revolutionary £35m move online, Mr Sheidlower said: "Sales of print encyclopaedias in the US have been going way down in the last couple of years. We had enough requests for an electronic OED to convince us that it is a commercial proposition."

John Simpson, chief dictionary editor, said of the f-word problem: "It's not how you would define the word now. It's a typical example of how the OED needs updating."

The website edition will play new tricks. Its search engine will tell you that historically the Guardian is the dictionary's fifth most quoted source for word usages, after scientific journals and the Times.

Most of all, in the biggest overhaul since 1928, it will enable 1,000 new word revisions and words to be added online every three months. Without it, readers would have had to wait until at least the year 2010 for a new print edition to update "bloody", the f-word or "hairbrush", defined confusingly by Victorian lexicographers as "a toilet brush".

On Tuesday the first 1,000 electronic revisions will be unveiled, between the letters Ma and Mah. New words and phrases are likely to include Mel Gibson's early film character Mad Max, who has entered the language as a byword for anarchic violence.

The director Luc Besson has cast Gibson – who won some respect for his film Hamlet – as Murray in The Doctor and the Madman, a screen version of Simon Winchester's best-selling book The Surgeon of Crowthorne.

The book is about how the dictionary patriarch travelled to Berkshire to meet one of his most brilliant contributors, William Minor, who turned out to be a psychotic, convicted murderer in Broadmoor. Robin Williams is to play the madman.

Minor's framed letters, in cramped obsessive handwriting, hang on the walls of the Oxford University Press archive in Oxford, which houses the millions of other public contributions the book has had since 1858; among them letters from JRR Tolkien, Thomas Hardy, WG Grace and the Peanuts cartoonist Charles Schulz (about the meaning of "comfort blanket").

And staff are beginning to foresee another unlikely story if their online OED proves a success in the century stretching ahead. Their mild and learned boss John Simpson will – they tease him – end up being played by Leonardo DiCaprio's grandson. •

....

18 April 2000

Matthew Engel
Consultation is
not for real people

On Easter Saturday – a date presumably chosen for minimum impact the way the government issues its most mendacious press releases on Christmas Eve – all London's phone numbers are to change. Four other cities plus Northern Ireland are also affected: more than 11m numbers in all.

This comes five years after Oftel (sponsored by Prontaprint) changed everyone's numbers, creating something like 45bn numerical options accompanied by a promise that they would never bother us again. Next year they will muck about with mobiles. Thanks a bunch.

The Sunday Times reported this week that 73% of the people affected by this week's nonsense did not understand what was happening. This is not surprising, since both codes and numbers are affected. I don't want to sound anoraky about this, but I think I've got this right: most Londoners believe they will be getting a new code of 0207 or 0208. In fact the code will be 020, and each number will have a 7 or 8 plonked in front of it. You will find out the difference the hard way the moment you try to ring your next door neighbour.

A drive round London would soon reveal shop fronts with six different types of codes: the correct new ones; the wrong new ones; the dying 0171 and 0181 sort; the old 071 and 081; the plain 01 that preceded them; and – I'm sure there are some left, examples welcome – signs still showing the evocative exchange-names that were killed off in the late 60s.

Such happy days! The exchanges in the Wembley area were named after poets: ARNold, BYRon, DRYden and WORdsworth. Other places were improbably nautical: Earls Court had FRObisher and Walworth was RODney. Where have they gone? ELGar and HOGarth; EMPress and ENTerprise; LABurnum and CHErrywood; SILverthorn and SPEedwell; VANdyke and VIKing. True, the lines were terrible and it took six months to get a new phone: I once had to pose as a doctor to beat the system. But a call to directory enquiries (DIR) provided history and mystery. British Telecom used to have a museum devoted to such delights; it was chopped two years ago.

The places that were elevated to seven-figure numbers in 1995 like Leeds and Sheffield are still uneasy with their new big-city status, and people there get very muddled about the spacing. This confusion represents a phenomenon that goes far beyond telephones. It is a manifestation of a country ill-at-ease with itself.

We can't even cope with our currency. In pre-decimal days, people talked easily about money even when they didn't have two ha'pence to rub together or were dealing with tuppeny-ha'penny organisations like Oftel. Now cashiers will ask you if you have "a one-pence piece". Coins no longer have comfy nicknames, like the tanner and the bob; they are replaced too quickly.

The government first tried to force us to use centigrade temperatures 40 years ago, long before we went into Europe. Still, the nation doesn't understand them – and with good reason. Fahrenheit is both more accurate in detail and more expressive in rough outline: if told the temperature is in the 50s or 80s, you know at once how warmly to dress.

Metrication has been a bad-tempered fiasco. We have been lumbered with the litre: too large for drinking; too small for motoring. Its main purpose has been to hide years of petrol price increases. The kilo, imposed with mad determination, is an equally useless measure. Don't tell me it's progress or necessary harmonisation: the Americans have stuck with what they know.

Successive half-baked administrative re-organisations mean that many people no longer even know – still less care – what county they live in. This partially explains both why local government is so hopeless, and why cricket has gone down the plughole. And, with the weather dreadful, we are about to have three bank holidays in 10 days. There will be none at all in the three months of high summer, between late May and late August, when most of us could actually enjoy them, and there would be a sporting chance of sunshine.

There is a simple explanation for just about all the above, and it has very little to do with Brussels. Any change that affects our lives which is not quite big enough to cause a blip on V the political radar comes after "consultation". This consultation involves relevant interest groups but not the rest of us. Do you even know anyone who has ever been "consulted"?

The vending machine makers are allowed their one-pence worth about currency changes. The tourist trade is allowed a say on bank holidays – and it suits them to have the dates spread thinly away from the warm weather, so they can chug along happily for longer. Oftel can get it spectacularly wrong, and there's no redress. It needs a WORdsworth or a BYRon to do it all justice. •

17 November 1999

Julie Burchill
Julie goes online

Julie Burchill: I'm sure I can get round to all of you, except the very rude and stupid ones and the ones who mention my WEIGHT!

PenmanX: I was very interested to read your column about suppressed homosexuality. I'm a gay man and I play football regularly but find the kissing after goal-scoring uncomfortable as I feel it's a front for all of us.

JB: I think that 60% of alleged straight men are gay, and that this is at the bottom of a lot of male violence, especially at football matches, because when they're drunk they just have the overwhelming urge to GRAB another man.

KennyGee: I think that 90% of women in this country are lesbians. But sadly that opinion makes me a thicko bloke instead of an astronomically well-paid columnist.

JB: I think you WANT 90% of women to be lesbians, as most men do when they're drunk.

KennyGee: I have to disabuse you of your fatuous prejudices. We want all women to be heterosexual when we're drunk. Otherwise we wouldn't be able to have sex with them.

PenmanX: A lot of people I've spoken to have the idea of human "fundamental bisexuality". Have you seen Fight Club? I sat there thinking: this is the MOST homoerotic movie!

nipper33: I've seen many a male get overly excited at the prospect of a goal and leap a fraction too early into the eager arms of their friend.

Shettany: Julie, why are all men b*stards?

JB: I like them a LOT! I know it's corny, but you'll meet a good one one day. Just practise BEING LOTS OF FUN and don't EVER cook for them.

Shettany: Sorry... was my bitterness showing??

Pantherxi: Why is it that despite your socialistic incantations, much of what you write conveys a rightwing perspective often tinged with racism or trashy cheap shots?

JB: I don't have a racist bone in my body, but it is true that I am not a mealy-mouthed middle-class liberal either. If I want to point out that African states seem to feel a burning need to chop off peoples clitori, I'll do so.

Mart666: Your column has made me understand why people like to read those neo-fascist rants in the tabloids. I never could understand the pleasure you could derive from simply reading someone who expresses what you think. Keep up the righteous battle, Julie.

JB: I hope you are sincere, because if so I find your letter very vivifying and encouraging. Did you really have to throw in the neo-fascist reference, though?

Jhow: In the rather dull landscape of British journalism you are an exception. I wonder if any kind of pressure is put on you by your editors.

JB: I do feel VERY lucky to be able to write what I want, though it's not for lack of TRYING on the part of certain Guardian readers to try and get me BANNED if I mention SUICIDE or SERBIA or anything other than pop music and make-up.

BffyStrglv: Do you, in your wildest dreams, or even during REM sleep, believe that your opinions, or mode of expressing them, would have been tolerated in the much loved and drooled over ex-USSR? Eh?

JB: People ALWAYS say this: "Oh, you'd have got shot if you'd lived in the USSR!" NO I WOULDN'T! Because when the cause is right, I can be VERY OBEDIENT. Lots of great writers, such as Ilya Ehrenberg, were good servants of the regime AND REWARDED VERY HANDSOMELY, THANK YOU! With shopping expeditions and dachas on the Black Sea.

Factotum: I recall you saying that you wouldn't exploit your father's memory by writing about him. Why then do you persist in doing so?

JB: Sometimes I just can't think about anything else and come over all teary.

Jude19: After I read your "nipple police" article I gave up breastfeeding promptly. And I've gone back to work now – full time – shock!! Thanks.

JB: Good for you, girl! I'm sure your infant will thank you, and be proud to have such an affluent mother with a nice figure. DEAR FANS AND DETRACTORS: I have a hot date with a cold man and must be off to wax my feet. JULIE XXX •

Letters

19 November 1999

Re the Julie goes online column (November 17): it was a parody, wasn't it?
Antony Shepherd
Croydon, Surrey

Sixty per cent of "straight" men aren't gay – they just claim they are when propositioned by Julie Burchill.
Tom Winchester
Greenford, Middx

The plural of clitoris is clitores, not clitori.
Nick Zair
Bristol

I'm not sure about the plural of clitoris, but I do know the singular of fatwa (Letters, November 17) is fatwa with a final long vowel.
Prof G Rex Smith
Dyserth, Denbigshire

20 November 1999

I think Nick Zair is wrong. Clitoris in Greek grammar (as in life) is feminine. Its plural would be clitorides, admittedly a bit of a mouthful.
Paul Hartmann
Otley, West Yorkshire
guycroft@clara.co.uk

I can never find the plural of clitoris.
Tom Freeman
Sheffield
PIP99TAF@sheffield.ac.uk

It strikes me that one must have an interesting lifestyle if one has occasion to use the plural of clitoris.
The Rev Tony Bell
Glapwell, Chesterfield
tonybell@glapwell.force9.co.uk

23 Nove mber1999

Paul Hartmann is right to say the plural of clitoris is clitorides in Greek.
The question, for those of us fortunate to need to know, is what's the plural in
English? Surely it's clitorise, just as we use irises not the Greek plural irides
    Peter Mackridge
    Oxford

Re Paul Hartmann's helpful note that the Greek plural of clitoris is "…a bit of a
mouthful". He's obviously a cunning linguist.
    Jim Moon
    Bristol

Given the interest of male writers in the plural of clitoris, women everywhere will no
doubt be delighted that men can at least locate it in the dictionary.
    Annily Campbell
    Sutton Coldfield
    annimike@usa.net

25 November 1999

Annily Campbell is mistaken. If men knew where to find clitoris in the dictionary
they'd know what the plural was. If we knew where to find it anywhere else, it
wouldn't be lumbered with an ancient Greek name.
    Jim Brooke
    Witham, Essex
    Jim_Brooke@compuserve.com

After constulting with my women friends (proud possessors of several fine
clitori – one each), we declare proudly that we are members of the Clitorati.
HQ near Maidenhead.
    Ann Nicholls
    Norwich

Can anyone think of a name for the proposed Fuqin long tunnel (Chinese show
tunnel vision for the 21st century, November 24)?
    Tony Peace
    Birmingham

27 November 1999

I note the clitorati letter signs off with the schoolboy code word Norwich:
Nickers Off Ready When I Come Home.
   Rob Bartholomew
   Andover, Hants

I am appalled you published sniggering obscenities this week. The Guardian
is worse thant the tabloids in its desperation to get a few laughs by printing filth.
   John Parham
   Bristol

Art beat

....

23 February 2000

Fiachra Gibbons

Effing is off, rules theatre computer

t is the theatre which likes to call a spade an effing spade, which has fearlessly fought censorship for a century, and where no taboo is ever safe. But the Royal Court, which defied the lord chamberlain in the 60s, and where provoking moral outrage is almost a point of honour, has finally been brought to book – by its own computers.

Expletives are immediately deleted every time a piece of gritty, full-blooded dialogue is typed into its new system. Even furious staff emails complaining about the computer's censorious ways have lost their more colourful turns of phrase.

"It's hilarious," said literary manager Graham Whybrow. "It's just bizarre that the theatre that brought the world Shopping And Fucking, that campaigned successfully to stop the lord chamberlain's vetting of plays, and that has championed playwrights from Edward Bond to Sarah Kane should be pulled up by its own computers like this."

The Royal Court's history of profanity is long and glorious. Sir John Gielgud is believed to have uttered the first perfectly pronounced "fuck" on a British stage in its production of Veterans in 1972.

Staff realised something was amiss last week when they moved back into the theatre's Sloane Square headquarters in central London after a £26m refurbishment.

The preferences for their new Microsoft system, which automatically "corrects" swear words, and which was designed to curb abuse and harassment by email in American offices, were set centrally by the theatre's computer department. They are now hastily freeing the boundaries again.

Last night hundreds of actors, writers and celebrities turned up for the first of the theatre's two-night reopening celebrations. Royal Court legends Harold Pinter, Arnold Wesker and Michael Frayn were in the audience to see Conor McPherson's new play about an alcoholic undertaker, Dublin Carol, which features a healthy quota of expletives. ∎

Letter

24 February 2000

You're effing wrong

Sorry, but the first perfectly pronounced "fuck" on a British stage was not by Sir John Gielgud in 1972 (Effing is off, rules theatre computer, February 23). He was preceded by Gerald James as William Blake in my play Tyger, presented by the National Theatre at the New Theatre in London on July 20 1971 (which also included probably the first on-stage use of clitoris). Beautifully delivered, with a Welsh inflection, the immortal line was: "If you can't beat 'em – fuck 'em!" I offer this, free of copyright, as a slogan for Ken's mayoral campaign.

Adrian Mitchell •

15 April 2000

Michael Billington
Crowning glory

Comparisons, says Dogberry, are odorous. They are also sometimes inevitable. And when you see a pair of kings in a fortnight – Richard II at the Gainsborough Studios in Shoreditch, east London and at The Other Place in Stratford-upon-Avon – it's difficult not to start ruminating on acting, politics, Shakespeare and even the state of England itself.

Space, of course, is a determining factor on performance, something critics rarely acknowledge. In opening up a former film studio and Edwardian power station for the Almeida's Gainsborough Studios Richard, Jonathan Kent and his team have come across a magnificent ruin: one in which the walls are not so much distressed as in a very bad way. But, though we gaze in awe at this dilapidated industrial cathedral, its sheer scale sometimes leads the actors towards anonymous rhetoric. Cut to Stratford where Steven Pimlott is staging Richard II in an intimate 200-seater. The great advantage is that the actors can converse rather than bellow: the problem is, the production is sold out. Small may be beautiful. It is also, by definition, exclusive.

Acting areas dictate style. They also explain some of the key differences between Ralph Fiennes's Shoreditch Richard and Samuel West's Stratford one. Fiennes has to use expressive body language and an extensive vocal palette to get his points across: West can afford to be quietly sardonic. But what fascinates me is how both strenuously avoid lyricism and sympathy. Richard always used to be seen as irresponsible in the first half and elegiac in the second. But such is our modern cynicism about kingship that neither actor craves our indulgence. You can't help but feel for the deposed, humiliated Richard. But both Fiennes and West imply that Shakespeare's hero is as much imprisoned by monarchy as by literal incarceration.

The real difference, however, lies in the directors' approaches to the play. For Kent, politics seem marginal: for Pimlott, you feel, they are the main reason for doing the work. And what hit me like a thunderclap is that the real key to Richard II lies in how you interpret Bolingbroke: the man who seizes the throne. In the old days you cast your smooth actor as Richard, your hairy one as Bolingbroke. It was John Barton who shattered the stereotype in 1973 by having Ian Richardson and Richard Pasco alternate the two roles – suddenly they became a mirror image of each other. Deborah Warner picked up on the idea in her 90s National Theatre production by suggesting a strange sibling kinship between Fiona Shaw's Richard and David Threlfall's usurper.

What is clear is that both are awoken to the isolation and fragility of power. Richard is unseated by Bolingbroke – the latter discovers that illegality opens the door to rebellion. But Pimlott takes this much further. West's Richard is a heedless tyrant, David Troughton's Bolingbroke is a purposeful one. What both have is the absolutist's ability to hide behind the sanctity of God and nationhood. In the Westminster deposition scene West, quite literally, wraps himself in the national flag. Troughton meanwhile, appealing to a divine right he himself has shattered, at one point asks the audience to rise in prayer. This brilliantly pins down the tendency of dictators, and even democratic politicians, to cloak themselves in convenient abstractions – a point Pinter has tirelessly made in his recent political plays.

Shakespeare's history plays are not just about the Tudor myth: they are actually about the daily practice of power. In that sense, they are the greatest political plays ever written. What you can't do today is ignore their ramification s. I would not claim Kent does that at Shoreditch. He reflects our scepticism about monarchy, and in David Burke's John of Gaunt and Oliver Ford Davies's Duke of York he depicts the extremes of passion and vacillation.

But his failure lies in leaving Bolingbroke an enigma. What on earth is Linus Roache up to? Is he suggesting Bolingbroke returns from exile simply to claim his lands? Or does his quietude imply he is a crafty opportunist hoping the crown will fall into his lap? The fact is we simply never know. Having gained power, this Bolingbroke also never seems to exercise it. He casually condemns Richard's favourites to death. Troughton personally puts a bullet through their brains.

Audiences, I suspect, are drawn to Rich ard II by the prospect of a star performance – they certainly get that in spades from the richly expressive Fiennes. The reality is, however, that it is Bolingbroke who motors the play from the initial appeal against Mowbray to the final remorse over Richard's death. Put Bolingbroke at the centre, as they do at Stratford, and you have a profoundly political work. Make Richard the spotlit focus, as they do in Shoreditch, and you have the lesser form of tragedy. ∎

9 October 1999

Birthdays

Don McCullin, 64 today, has been hanging around for an assignment for nearly 20 years, ever since Murdoch's Sunday Times decided its readers didn't need truth-telling photo-journalism any more. He quit after six months of pacing the office in his safari suit – with passport ready in top pocket – and the ad agencies used his gritty realism for campaigns for, among other things, the police. Bad move; he got a lot of criticism for going over to the other side, though, as he says, he had to eat.

Friends say he is too honest for his own good, and certainly McCullin has a post-interview habit of regretting how much he has revealed about his – apparently bleak – private life. He still spends hours in the darkroom in Somerset, alone with the ghosts hiding in his negatives, but his work still shines: his recent book on India is awash with timeless images which could have illustrated the Bible. McCullin spends relatively little time with his wife, the American aerial photographer Marylin Bridges; she hates Somerset, he hates Americans. He keeps fit by walking the local hills – and obsessively doing the housework. •

25 September 1999

Gordon Burn
Walking the plank

"Solitary studio practice" is a term that has been bandied about a lot in recent years in connection with young British artists. Solitary studio practice is some-thing that the hard-drinking, hard-drugging, up-all-night, who-pushed-your-button? YBAs just don't do. Angst has never been their thing. In a work mode they have a tendency to be cool, unexpressive, emotionally disengaged. Warhol's children, expressing complete boredom for aesthetics as we know it.

As the world and his granny must be aware by now, Sarah and Tracey and Abbie and Angus and Mat and Sam and the rest play and work mob-handed, giving it large in the bar at St John in Clerkenwell, pissing it up further along the street at Vic Naylor's or wherever, and staying at all times full-on. That's full-on. Yeeeeaaarrghh!

It so happens that John Hoyland lives on the other side of Charterhouse Square from the falling-down places of recent legend, and solitary studio practice is something he knows all about. Just after six most mornings, when the lights in the meat market are being diluted by the dawn and the art world's gilded girls and boys are trying to decide whether to call it a night or move it all on, Hoyland is rolling out of bed to start work.

Twenty years ago he bought a large unit in a former hat factory on the square, over-looking Bart's hospital and tantalisingly near to the pubs that open in the middle of the night for the Smithfield butchers and market workers. He turned the back part of the space, with a view of the railway lines going into the Barbican station, into a studio. And it is there that most pre-dawns will find him preparing canvases or slinging the old chromatics on to monster canvases that he has laid horizontally on the floor. For years, his preferred working method has been to walk into the picture. He likes to loop and detonate paint straight out of the bottle and tube – getting the whole body behind a gesture; drawing from the shoulder. It's like Jackson Pollock made holes in cans so he could do an extended line. It's like that. He can squirt and spray, and it's like frozen energy when it dries. The speed and violence of the mark are all in there. The cult of Pollock seems to centre around photographs, not of his paintings but of him painting. And more than 50 years later, Hoyland is still at it.

It is excessively physical. He sweats. The stretchers are big and unwieldy. The ceiling is not that high. But he is drenched most of the time in panic sweats. He takes off his shoes and steps into the canvas when he wants to paint wet on wet. He sets up breeze-blocks and a plank and walks the plank over the painting, flinging dribbles and gouts of paint like a dervish. Feathering it like a parlour maid or van Gogh's Sower. A man in his 60s at six o'clock in the morning. Hey, geezer!

"I ought to have some sleek trolley cantilevered out, made out of core-ten steel, or bloody aluminium or something. Some hi-tech machine like a crane or something," he says, not sounding convinced. "A bridge. But I'm afraid it's just a plank that I got from the builders, when they were doing the scaffolding, that doesn't bend in the middle. You've got to be careful you don't fall into it. Trip and fall off the fucking plank."

A pair of boots standing on a shelf in the studio tell how long this has been Hoyland's life. A pair of 60s, high-zip dandy boots from Blades, lined in leather with block toes and rock'n'roll heels, the whole encrusted in acrylic. Museumised. A museum of himself. Painting in the studio is a job. It's different from the perfectly worthwhile jobs that people do. It's a different activity. But you do your job. "I go round picking up the canvas, so the silver iridescent's all moving around, and then I start throwing colour into it. Yellows, violets, oranges, into the wet. You know you want some kind of a rythmical break down there. And then I start picking it up and manip-ulating that. Letting that stuff all break up the flow. It's like trying to pull a fish. You can't just yank it out. You've got to let it run, find its own nature, and then gradually haul it in."

He says, "It's like being a god half of the time and a murderer the rest of the time. You're creating a universe in the studio. You're trying to make something new in the world one minute, and then you're cutting it up and lacerating it. You're tearing it. Sweating like a pig. Totally soaked. Painting is killer shit. It's kill or be killed. It is. Painting is a killer sport. That's why it's so nice to do craft kind of work sometimes. Like prints or glass or ceramics. Collaborations so you can talk and chat and have a laugh and listen to the radio. Whereas when you do painting anybody can come along and say, 'Well, you've led a completely worthless life.' And, hey, listen, they will. Oh, are you kidding?"

Hoyland's has been a heroic endeavour. During a 30-year period when painting has been at an all-time critical low, supplanted by photography, video, assemblage and installation, he has never let himself be dragged down or wavered for a second in his commitment. The Royal Academy show (opening next week) should establish him beyond doubt as one of the most gifted British artists of his generation and one of the best non- figurative painters still working anywhere.

As Paul Moorhouse, the curator of the new retrospective puts it, his paintings now look like irresistible icons for the cause of painting.

Hoyland's predicament is one that is common to all artists of his age. At 64, he isn't yet old enough to a be a grand old man, but he is no longer young enough to be regarded as a young turk. He spent the early years of the 90s without a dealer. The Tate hasn't bought a picture of his for more than 20 years. Although he added the Wollaston Award for most distinguished work in last year's Royal Academy Summer Exhibition to a long list of honours and prizes, it took the intervention of a long-time supporter, Sir Anthony Caro, to secure the Academy show for Hoyland, who has been an RA since 1983. He has known a fond disregard. A stasis. He has been a dweller in limbo-land. Hoyland decisively rejected Minimalism and Duchamp-inspired Conceptualism, where a favoured young painter such as Gary Hume, say, many years later embraced them. The result is that a painter who was once seen to be on the cutting edge of advanced art is now, thanks to the vicissitudes of fashion, relegated against his will to the ranks of the nay-sayers and cultural conservatives.

These circumstances have made Hoyland, with his super-tuned bullshit detector, an uncomfortable presence. He has earned himself – unfairly, his friends would say – an abrasive reputation. He can be irascible. He can also be rib-achingly, scurrilously funny. He is to the art one-liner what Les Dawson was to the mother-in-law joke. "They're like Sickert on Tizer," is his description of Frank Auerbach's "exercises in suburban expressionism": "With Frank, there's all that struggle and turmoil, and then he ends up having to put a cartoon face on top of the thick paint. A couple of dots for the eyes."

Francis Bacon's art is "far too illustrational. He might do a little seemingly free mark, but actually it's a little toss-off, and then a little air-brushing on it." Bacon and Lucian Freud are merely painters of "melodrama". "Drama is one thing. But melodrama is another. Like painting your mother naked with all her old veins and a rat on her tit. Or it might have been her shoulder. I mean, what kind of a life is this? People lying around with their bloody dicks hanging out." He describes an eminent contemporary as being "a big star of stage, screen and horseshit". Britain is "visually uncultivated, cultivation being fine as long as you stick to gardening, and you better keep it neat."

Hoyland didn't go to the Venice Biennale this year because he "didn't want to see any more videos made by Uruguayan transsexuals". "Do you want wooden or do you want wooden?" he says, holding open a catalogue of etchings that has arrived in the post. "Would you like it in teak or balsa?" "Those tossers in Art and Language. You know where their headquarters is? Leamington Spa. It's not Brooklyn."

"Have you heard about the man who once asked Picasso, 'What do you do if you run out of blue?' He said, 'I use red.'" Boom-boom.

Hoyland's outspokenness has always got him in trouble with the members of what he calls "the whispering classes" who are the chiefs of the art tribe. On the other hand, it was his candour and his refusal to mouth the usual pieties that brought him close to Barnett Newman and Mark Rothko and Robert Motherwell and other legends of the New York Abstract Expressionist scene, and made them his friends. "When I've had a few drinks, I tend to be rather honest," Hoyland says.

"And they liked that. I think Motherwell couldn't wait to go into the studio and talk. Basically, we had so much in common. He liked talking about cars and girls and art, which was the most important thing in his life. And of course when you're an intellectual, which he was, and you've got a heavy hangover and you come down to confront a blank canvas, you're no better equipped to paint than a non-intellectual who's got a hangover in front of a blank canvas. Because being an intellectual doesn't help you in painting. You can be overburdened with connoisseurship and intellectual ideas and too much exploring irrelevant things. Painting is of a different order. It's a different language."

Hoyland grew up in Sheffield. He's Yorkshire. And he puts his outspokenness down to that. His father was a tailor. "He never had his own business. He only worked for other people. I'm just like him, but earn more money." In the cave-like living room in Charterhouse Square, Kenneth Hoyland's face and hands shine out of a portrait that John did of his father when he was still a teenager. Outside the bathroom is an etching of Hoyland half-dragging, half-carrying his old man home from the boozer, something he did often.

He started at Sheffield Art School when he was 17, and arrived at the Royal Academy Schools in London five years later knowing nothing. "Nobody taught us about modern art, because modern art was taboo in England in those days. Matisse was dismissed by everybody at Sheffield as being a purely decorative, albeit 'pretty', painter. Picasso was tying a paintbrush to the donkey's tail and insulting the public. It was just regarded as a complete joke. We had to draw from the cast, and from models. I mean, plenty to draw. Like, lots of veins. You used to sit there and watch flesh being heated by the radiators. I always found models a bit mad, like demented housewives. People who really wanted to be exotic dancers but didn't have the figure for it, you know. But exotic dancers who were passionate about cricket. Nutters. With nothing remotely sexual about any of them. It was just so embarrassing. I used to draw down to the knee and think, 'Well, there's not much further to go; I'll be down to the ankle shortly.' It was a terrible drudgery. I hated it."

Hoyland started at the Academy Schools in 1956, the year the show Modern Painting In The US came to the Tate. This was followed in 1959 by the landmark exhibition of Abstract Expressionism, The New American Painting, full of giant, heroic works by Pollock, Rothko, Motherwell, de Kooning, Kline and Gorky. "Seeing those big Rothkos now, they're not that big. But we'd never seen anything that big. There was a kind of radiance, and the sheer inexplicable mystery of them. The uncompromising nature and the scale of ambition. It wasn't a difficult choice for me. Either go towards refinement, painting debutantes' eyelashes, or shiny horses' arses, which was always a surefire thing. Or get involved in the revolution of 20th-century art."

This part of the revolution involving the painters of the New York School had an orthodoxy and a script. Both were the work of the chief theorist of the Abstract Expressionist movement and its most energetic promoter, Clement Greenberg. Greenberg, who Hoyland would come to know, believed that art should be reduced to flat colour on a flat plane. The narrative or social content of the paintings should be nil. All that mattered was the surface interplay of colour and texture, space and shape, and the artist's ability to create a world instead of merely copying one. "Paintings are there to be experienced – they are events," Hoyland has said. "Paintings are not to be reasoned with, they are not to be understood; they are to be recognised. They are an equivalent of nature, not an illustration of it."

He was never part of Swinging London. He spent much of the 60s and 70s in New York. He liked the way Rothko and Newman were sober-suited. They wore watch-chains and overcoats. Newman in particular looked "a bit like the manager of a textile company down Broadway". They were intellectuals, but they didn't come on intellectual. Ad Reinhardt looked like a boxer. He always said, "Art's too serious to be taken seriously." Hoyland decided this was a good way to be. "I rather looked down on Pop art. I was a bit more Miles Davis and classical music. James Joyce and Murder In The Cathedral and Auden. This kind of stuff. Duke Ellington and Stan Kenton and the blues. I thought the Beatles were rubbish. I didn't even like Elvis Presley. I was very anti all that. You've only got to see a photograph of me in those days to tell, trying to be the young professor. Professor Piffle."

Throughout the 60s he made paintings that aimed for extremes of flatness, emptiness and bigness. The pigment was stained into the weave of the canvas rather than cluttering up the surface. In Greenbergian terms, they were very right-on. His main concern after 1970, though, was with building on the formal implications of his work to make it more expressive. The extremism of Newman had led to a cul-de-sac. It left nowhere for people to go except towards minimalism. Hoyland reached the point where he wanted more than formal disclosure. He wanted to let the world and emotional experience in. He wanted to re-complicate the surface of the picture without resorting to some kind of easy, illustrational solution.

He started to play around with free elements. The paint-handling became very loose. There was an increasing amount of dripping and dribbling and pouring, until he stopped using brushes altogether. Slowness tends to be associated with seriousness. Painters such as Frank Auerbach and Howard Hodgkin take years. And Hoyland was fantastically prodigious. He seemed to be knocking out works too fast. Fried Eggs with Purple Sausages. It was in Private Eye. "There's the rather puritan idea that somehow, through struggle, and worthiness, something good will come out. Something good comes out through vision. I mean, I've always said that Auerbach was a triumph of style over vision. It's so precious the whole thing. The sort of web that Frank has woven round himself. He's more serious about art, more serious about life, more moral. It just doesn't wash with me. So what?

"Picasso probably did five drawings a day. Completed works. And how long do you think some of those Matisses took? Some were long struggles. But you look at a Derain or a Matisse. Of course, they had their scraping-down times and their throwing work away. But a lot if it is just bomp-bomp-bomp-bomp-boom. And that's it. And it retains that freshness. William Scott always said don't fuss a painting. Never fuss a painting. This is an English disease, this fussing at work. 'I don't think that passage in the nose is quite right, Hoyland. You need perhaps a touch of green.' It's always: 'I don't think you've quite resolved that passage.' They make a big virtue in England of this struggle factor."

Struggle – the great existential dance of death – is the theme that Ron Kitaj believed linked Auerbach and the other School of London painters. School of London was the title Kitaj came up with in 1977 when he set out, with David Hockney, to promote a return to representations of the human figure. The campaign was aimed mainly at the conceptual work which at that time was filling the commercial galleries and art institutions. But Hoyland interpreted it as an act of general aggression.

"Calling for a return to the figure was a completely ridiculous thing to do. I mean, if people want to paint the figure for personal reasons that's one thing. But a manifesto, saying art's all gone wrong because it's left the figure, is ridiculous. I mean, it's a real kind of Luddite thing which appeals to the most reactionary, revisionist minds. That's why it appealed in this country so powerfully. Everyone said, 'Oh thank God, we're going back to real art.'"

Seven years later, in 1994, Kitaj was given a retrospective at the Tate. His experience became an object lesson in the high-risk nature of the kind of enterprise on which Hoyland is now embarked. The critical mauling he suffered caused Kitaj to return to the US after 30 years living in London. He even blamed the critics for the death of his wife.

"Kitaj had always been so feather-bedded by everybody," Hoyland says. "The friend of the great and the good. Oxford dons. He'd always insert little meaningful passages into his work and titles that referred to literature and culture. He was always talking about Wittgenstein. A big house in Chelsea and beautiful children and a wonderful library. I mean, he lived a very privileged, cosseted kind of life. He didn't teach in art schools for years, and have to go to Croydon on the train. And South Norwood, even worse. I was the original Norwood junky. So I think he was living in a bit of a fool's paradise. Always treated different, even by the Academy. They all treated him reverentially. And when somebody suddenly comes along and says, 'Hey, wait a minute – that is not all it's been cracked up to be', then it just blew him away. Andrew Graham-Dixon [of the Independent] was the main one, but a lot of English writers are very flaky, anyway. They don't know what they think, so they'd go along with it."

John Hoyland. Brush-cut, tinted heavy glasses and a string bolo tie. A bit fly for somebody about to pick up his pensioners' bus pass next month. Just because he's paranoid doesn't mean they're not out to get him. He knows a lot of people are waiting to see him take a slapping. See him place the breeze blocks. See him walk the plank. Hey, grandad! See him step lightly in the high-zip dandy boots when he reaches the other side. •

John Hoyland at the Royal Academy, September 30 to October 31.

....

10 December 1999

Andrew Clements
Hector's nous

Colin Davis has been a champion of Berlioz for over 40 years now. Yet no one who was lucky enough to hear the start of his Berlioz Odyssey, at the Barbican last Sunday, could doubt that the conductor's crusading zeal on behalf of the French composer burns as fiercely as ever.

From the opening bar of the overture to Berlioz's first opera Benvenuto Cellini, Davis was clearly enjoying himself, wonderfully relaxed and natural in the way he phrased the music, and able to bring to it an energy and freshness that seemed as if he and the audience were discovering its beauties for the first time.

Now, with the London Symphony Orchestra, Davis is getting the chance to celebrate that passion. Over the next year he will conduct all of Berlioz's operatic, dramatic and symphonic works at the Barbican, ending up next December with concert performances of his masterpiece, The Trojans. "No one has attempted to do such a damn fool thing as this, which is to review all the major works in a single span," says Davis, "but I think he deserves it."

Davis discovered Berlioz long before he became a conductor. As a fledgling clarinettist in the late 1940s, he attended the Bryanston summer school, where he played in the second part of The Childhood of Christ under the great French conductor Roger Desormière. "I had never heard melodies like this in my life. I thought, 'Whatever this is, it's so beautiful,' and that's where it all started".

At that time the composer was just a name in the music history books, which were full of wild assertions about the impossibility of performing his major scores. But when Davis made the transition to conducting himself, he began to prove the textbooks wrong, putting on pioneering concert performances of the operas with Chelsea Opera Group, and doing the dramatic symphony Romeo and Juliet with the LSO in 1964. The record company Philips agreed to record the orchestral works, and later the operas too, after Davis had conducted productions of Benvenuto Cellini and The Trojans at Covent Garden.

"It was a great adventure then," he says, "but now it's different. You are in orbit around these pieces, so they never look the same. My enthusiasm for Haydn and Mozart hasn't diminished, nor for Berlioz. There's something so profoundly touching about his personality; there are passages in The Trojans that are as genuine and as true as anything Mozart wrote."

Yet still Berlioz hasn't won universal recognition as a great composer and one of the 19th century's true originals, and Germany in particular is still suspicious of him, even though, when he was chief conductor of the Bavarian Radio Symphony, Davis regularly included his pieces, most of which were entirely new to the orchestra. Perhaps his stance in direct opposition to the Austro-German tradition still counts against him.

"He was the first new-laid egg of romanticism," says Davis. "Imagine the leap from 1827, the year of Beethoven's death, to 1830, when the Fantastic symphony was performed; it must have opened a completely new door. It wasn't taken up, because the composers in the Austro-German tradition were still struggling with the legacy of Haydn, Mozart and Beethoven – they were under the shadow of those intolerable experts.

"Weber was an original, but he didn't have the stature, the imagination and the literary background of Berlioz, and the German romantics just didn't go that way. Mendelssohn was more mature than Mozart at the age of 17, but what could he do with the classical language that hadn't been done by Beethoven? Unless you were a really wild bloke like Berlioz you were never going to break through. But because he was independent of the academic tradition he could do it: he came from outside, he didn't have composing lessons as a kid, but that was an advantage because he wanted to create a new kind of music with his own freedom."

Davis doesn't think that Berlioz was ever standing back from the literature that so often inspired his work. But he believed passionately in its force and the expressive power of its intimate association with the music it generated. "I don't think it's commentary – the love scene from Romeo and Juliet isn't commentary. But unless you know the play you won't understand it, and it's only when you read the memoirs of Benvenuto Cellini that you understand why he appealed to Berlioz; for Berlioz he was an independent, crazy man.

"Berlioz personalises everything. When Dido is saying farewell in The Trojans, Berlioz is saying farewell too; like Mozart, he is on everybody's side, he makes no judgments. He's trying to break through to another world where you are not fettered by convention. He was a very decent man, paid all his debts, a good citizen; but when it came to artistic creation he wanted that kind of freedom that he found most of all in Shakespeare."

If literature was one spring board of his imagination, then the operas of Gluck were another. Gluck's crusade in his reform operas was to clean up the form, to rid it of all "the idiotic decoration", as Davis puts it, and try to get back to simple genuine feeling. "That was what attracted Berlioz; Gluck's ability to spin wonderful melodies appealed to him because of this purity. He believed that melody was the carrier of poetic feeling, that harmony was not the point. When Berlioz uses wild harmonies it's for some diabolical reason or other, to create a disruptive force, not for idealised passion."

It has been easy for academic pedants to criticise Berlioz for his failures, for those moments when his creative vision seemed to have exceeded his musical command. Although, as Davis observes, "The point is, do we get a sufficient amount of pleasure from his works or don't we? I for one get an enormous amount of pleasure from his tactics."

He maintains too that, though he didn't have the natural fluency of a Mozart or a Mendelssohn, Berlioz was a born composer – not someone, like Tippett or Bruckner for instance, who had to learn the craft the hard way. "Berlioz did have an immense gift for music, otherwise he wouldn't have bothered, for it gave him so much unhappiness. He did earn his living writing about music, but what he really wanted to do was compose.

"The force of his imagination was principally concentrated in his music; though his books are wonderful, he didn't write anything that can be compared with the composition of The Trojans, which proves to me beyond all doubt that he was a born composer. By the time he got to The Trojans he had stopped experimenting and knew exactly what he could do within the musical framework that he had created for himself."

But it's the idealism of Berlioz, the sheer persistence of his attempts to realise his visions in the concert hall and on the stage, that makes his music and his personality so endearing. "What are we doing with music?" asks Davis. "We are trying to get something that will balance the encroaching threat of reality. Art is transcendent, but it's also a reminder that the idealists, like Berlioz, are the only people who do any good in this world and they are not to be laughed at." •

....

28 March 2000

Matthew Engel

It's titwillow, titwillow, for hours on end

The Mike Leigh film Topsy-Turvy yesterday won the Oscars for makeup and costume; which is roughly equivalent to my own honour at the British Press Awards last week; for Most Creative Use of Semi-colons In a Column of 832 Words or Under. The bad news for Mr Leigh is that he has received only a booby prize at the ceremony organised by CANWEGOHOME (The Campaign for Naming, Waging war on, Execrating and Generally Opposing Hopelessly Overlong Movies, Etc).

As you may know, Topsy-Turvy is about Gilbert and Sullivan, an unexpected subject for a director who made his reputation dealing with the nuances of modern life. Unfortunately, the film lasts two hours 40 minutes, which shows no understanding of modern life whatever. Did Mr Leigh know or care that I was looking forward to a nice Thai meal afterwards? Does he know anything about babysitters' bedtimes? British films are normally more trustworthy than US or foreign films in these matters: I've always assumed there was a national celluloid shortage. In this case, there was a huge editable rehearsal scene in the middle, of which I would provide a more detailed critique had I not taken the chance of a little zizz.

Nonetheless, there were real delights in this film. One was the sight of the actor playing Gilbert's father: Charles Simon, who is of an age to make Sir John Gielgud seem like a juvenile lead. Mr Simon used to play Dr James Dale in the old-time radio soap opera The Dales. More than 30 years ago the late Jessie Matthews regularly confided to Home Service listeners: "I'm worried about Jim." Well, she needn't have been.

The most important delight is that Topsy-Turvy will do a great deal to remove the stain on Gilbert and Sullivan that has made them so deeply unhip. Their very names have reeked for years of suburban, light operatic societies. G and S, one has always felt, is what Auntie Madge would enjoy, if indeed one had an Auntie Madge.

Even Sullivan didn't think much of being part of G and S. He was (and this is crucial to the film) desperate to escape from all the comic taradiddle and be taken seriously as a composer. The film is not unsympathetic to this fancy, as was establishment opinion at the time: Sullivan got knighted more than two decades before Gilbert did. But the world is always full of gifted musicians who think they're Mozart. There has never been a lyricist quite like Gilbert. He was the most quotable writer since Shakespeare ("I've got a little list", "I am the very model of a modern major-general", "Lord High Everything-Else"), but much funnier, and wonderfully evocative too:

"Is it weakness of intellect, birdie, I cried?
Or a rather tough worm in your little inside?
With a shake of his poor little head, he replied
Oh, willow, titwillow, titwillow."

Of course, the music's just right. But I reckon Gilbert and Bloggs would have stood more chance than Bloggs and Sullivan. Anyway, it's good to have this stuff back in fashion. The shame is that, even at almost three hours, Topsy-Turvy missed so much. For a start (unless it happened when I nodded) no one mentioned the carpet. To be sure, the carpet incident didn't happen in the film's timescale, but when has that bothered a film-maker? There were lots of reasons for Gilbert and Sullivan to split up: Gilbert's bitterness over the knighthood; Sullivan's pretensions; Gilbert's bad temper; and the sheer hell of artistic collaboration, an arrangement that always contains the disadvantages of marriage without the compensations.

In 1890 Gilbert discovered that the expenses for The Gondoliers – which, under the writers' deal with the D'Oyly Carte company, they had to pay – came to £4,500. This included £500 for a new theatre carpet. Gilbert wrote at tedious length to Carte complaining. To his astonishment, Sullivan sided with Carte. There followed a furious confrontation. They hardly spoke for two years, and even when an uneasy peace broke out, never again produced anything worth a light.

It was a shame too that there was no room for Charles Simon to draw out the real-life irascible splendour of Gilbert senior, a doctor who turned to writing in middle life, and never quite acquired the writer's usual phlegmatic fatalism about criticism. He once turned up at the offices of a magazine: "I wish to see the editor of the Saturday Review." "On what business, sir?" "To thrash him."

G and S is a rich, rich seam, both for biography and for a great deal more performance. With no copyright problem any more, it's puzzling that the West End is so uninterested. There's room for another Mike Leigh too. But do us a favour, please: no more than two hours at a time. Thank you. ∎

29 March 2000

Jonathan Freedland
Oscar gets serious

O f course, the most fun are the dresses – backless, strapless and shameless – and the rictus smiles of the nominees, forced to cheer when they lose and clap when they want to cry. Usually there is an extra treat when a winner descends into Gwyneth Paltrow blub or Tom Hanks gush and we can see our own toes curl, live and exclusive at home. Judged on these grounds, this year's Oscars have been a sore disappointment. Cher did not appear in her underwear; Liz Hurley was fully clothed. Kevin Spacey did not sob dry, thespian tears; Sam Mendes did not declare himself "King of the World!"

As a showbiz event the Academy Awards may have been a let down (at least to the handful of Sky Premier viewers able to watch it), but that should not detract from what happened. For this year Hollywood confounded the critics who dismiss it as a mere junk factory, defied those who repeat the dread charge of "dumbing down" – and produced a clutch of substantial, thoughtful films. Those who see the sound stages of California as the propaganda arm of US imperialism ought to think again, too. Far from serving as a glorified advertising agency for the American way, the moviemen have taken pleasure in exposing the darker, uglier aspects of the great republic. Hollywood is getting serious – and, far from blushing at the prospect, Oscar has stood and applauded.

Just look at the field for best picture. The winner, American Beauty, is a slick, elegantly-played probe into the dysfunctional reality of apple-pie suburbia. Where once Hollywood might have exported picture-postcard images of domestic life – think Doris Day and Donna Reed – now it lays bare the adulterous, dope-smoking, disintegrating truth. American Beauty shows it all: mid-life crisis and repressed homosexuality, male redundancy and female neurosis, under-age lust and all-too-easy violence. It's no advert for America, and yet its writer, stars and director stand knee-deep in rose petals tossed by their peers.

The movies it beat to first place are no less lacerating. The Insider is a detailed, angry attack on corporate capitalism – specifically, the tobacco industry and the television business which bows to it. The Cider House Rules weighs in on abortion and child abuse; The Green Mile squares up to racism and the death penalty. Even The Sixth Sense, the most conventionally commercial of the five nominees – all of which did well at the box office – is an unexpectedly sensitive film. No wonder the New York Times ran its assessment of the Oscar field for 2000 under the headline: "The US needs more Prozac".

Is that what explains this sudden, self-critical gaze in the Hollywood mirror? Are Americans so depressed that all they want to see at the movies are sadness, estrangement and pain? History suggests the very opposite might be true.

Flick through the Oscar record books and you soon spot a pattern. When America is in the doldrums, it yearns for escape and finds it in the cinema. In the teeth of the depression, Americans queued up for Busby Berkeley's chorus-girl choreography and the singalong fantasy of the MGM musical. They did not want realism: they had enough of that at home. During the second world war, they longed for laughs (Going My Way, starring Bing Crosby, was a rare comedy winner of best picture) or romance: Casablanca took the prize in 1943. In the chilly years of the cold war, there was comfort to be had from Around the World in Eighty Days or An American in Paris. A decade later, after the shock of John F Kennedy's assassination, Americans needed more diversion: top honours in the mid-60s went to My Fair Lady and The Sound of Music. That seems to be the rhythm: Oliver! cheering folks up during Vietnam, Rocky pepping the spirits after Watergate.

So much for the years of famine. In good times, America seems to lose its need for sweets, allowing its storytellers to deal in harsher truths. In the post-1945 rush, when a war had been won and America was supremely confident, Hollywood did not revel in jingoism and cheerleading pride. Instead it fretted over alcoholism, the abandonment of war veterans and homegrown anti-semitism in The Lost Weekend, The Best Years of Our Lives and Gentleman's Agreement respectively (winners for 1945, 46 and 47). At the height of the mid-80s boom, when America was flush, it finally felt ready to watch a tough movie about Vietnam – with Oscar nodding to Oliver Stone's Platoon in 1986.

The rule seems to hold good even now. As the US enjoys its longest-ever period of unbroken prosperity, Americans forked out a record $7.5bn last year in movie tickets – to stare at an unflattering reflection of themselves. They have enough money in their pockets to sustain an assault on consumer culture like Fight Club. They have enough food on the table to watch the unravelling, lost families of Magnolia or Tumbleweeds. When the real world is light enough, people can take a glimpse of darkness – in the dark of the cinema.

But it is not just a matter of economics. What the studio executives have understood, the politicians have, too: in times of wealth, people yearn for something more. When their material needs are met, they start to wonder about the rest of their lives. That is why much of the campaign talk in this year's presidential race is of an America that knows it has material value, but worries about its values. "We know we are wealthy," muse the candidates, "but are we healthy?" It is in this terrain – values – that Al Gore and George W Bush will slug it out until November. Working on the assumption that the economy is more or less taken care of, they will pose the same questions that Hollywood has been asking in its latest crop of movies. Is the American family breaking apart? Is abortion sometimes the only morally just option? Is the law powerless in the face of the tobacco companies?

Perhaps we shouldn't get too carried away. Philip Dodd, the shrewd culture-watcher at the Institute of Contemporary Arts, thinks Hollywood is still Hollywood, not yet an academy of risk-taking inquiry. It rewarded American Beauty because it looked edgy, when in fact its chief targets live safely outside Hollywood's backyard – chief among them a militaristic redneck, a traditional Hollywood hate-figure. The Cider House Rules is similarly safe, says Dodd; as an implicit attack on the anti-abortion Christian right, it was bound to go down well in liberal LA. Whereas The Insider, which works as a critique of any business – including Hollywood – was too close for comfort: it walked away Oscar-less on Sunday.

Still, even if the Academy has its misgivings about movies of substance, audiences have not. They have flocked to these films, and to others like The Matrix and Being John Malkovich, which dare grapple with 21st century questions of virtual reality and altered consciousness. They are proof that, in these days of material well-being, our anxieties do not end. Our leaders need to hear that concern; perhaps they should get out more – starting with a trip to the movies. •

11 May 2000

James Fenton

This turbine hall, these galleries of light
Are freighted with a purpose and a power.
This bridge is like a contract, and this tower
Evidence of a legacy, a right

Massive with possibility they stand
Open to such surprise as may exist
Deep in the pulse, the chambers of the heart
Exacting fresh precision from the hand,
Risk in the brush, resilience in the wrist,
New thoughts to paint, new passions to impart. •

12 May 2000

Maev Kennedy
Tate and style

Thereerer was a new star on the London skyline last night: Britain's powerhouse of art, Tate Modern. The Queen, accustomed to higher ceilings than the rest of us, cast one incurious glance upwards and then looked straight ahead when she arrived to open what some see as the most important arts building of this and the last century.

Instant neck strain hit the hundreds of other guests, as they walked through the glass doors and were awed by the sheer scale of t he Turbine Hall, the no-longer-beating heart of the building, a single astounding space 152 metres (500ft) long, 30 metres high and 23 metres wide.

The hall dwarfed even the opening installation, the three rusting towers by Louise Bourgeois, each the size of a tall house. The 82 galleries stacked up along the side wall, stuffed with Picassos, Dalis, Warhols, Matisses and one huge wall of Gilbert and George, will allow half the entire collection to be displayed at any time, and still leave acres of space for temporary exhibitions.

The £134m transformation of Sir Giles Gilbert Scott's 1940s power station, by Swiss architects Herzog & de Meuron, has already been hailed by critics as putting London back, at a stroke, in the superleague of the international contemporary art world, up there with the Museum of Modern Art in New York and the Guggenheim in Bilbao.

"Big," said Simon Thurley, director of the Museum of London, enviously. "Very big," said Robert Anderson, director of the British Museum. Charles Saumarez-Smith consoled himself that he has a bigger escalator in his new wing at the National Portrait Gallery, "but it's the only thing I do have that's bigger".

The Queen must have felt quite ill at ease: there was no smell of wet paint whatsoever. Tate Modern was not only ready but, a thing almost unprecedented in the current slew of huge Lottery-funded arts openings, completely finished.

The most nervous man in the building was not director Lars Nittve but John Wallace of the London Sinfonietta, who had to play the first piercing painfully exposed trumpet notes of Sir Harrison Birtwistle's special composition, Seventeen Tate Riffs. The orchestra members first saw the music late on Wednesday night. "Hot from the press, it was. There was a bit of a sharp intake of breath," Mr Wallace recalled. "Very Harry. Big, loud and fast. Quite tricky."

Like every aspect of the opening, the performance proved note perfect.

The streets outside were peppered with police officers, reportedly anxious about the threat of anarchist protests. In the unrelenting rain there wasn't so much as a disgruntled art student. The only clash was between the Queen's mint green outfit and the lime green name board under which she stood for the opening ceremony.

Even Gerald Kaufman MP, the dreaded head of the Commons arts and media select committee, scourge of over-ambitious Lottery projects, smiled a thin wintry smile of approval. "I am only a scourge of ill-spent huge sums of public money," he said.

Tate chairman David Verey recalled that in 1962 the Queen had visited the same building, when it was a power station lighting all of London's south bank. "This building, in its new guise, will generate no less power – and light – than it did in its old role," he said.

The Queen, not noted for her interest in modern art, was led on a galleries tour which incorporated two living artists. Bridget Riley, whose op-art abstract spirals became icons of swinging London in the 1960s, said: "I think the Queen was a bit tentative. This must be a challenge for her, as it is for most people. How could she be any less bewildered than a member of the public?" The Queen also met the sculptor Sir Antony Caro, on whom she conferred the Order of Merit two days ago.

The sculptor Antony Gormley, creator of the Angel of the North, is represented in the collection by three iron figures based on casts from his own body. Wilfred Cass, the founder of Sculpture at Goodwood park, looked with raised eyebrow at one of the figures, which has an imposing erection: "Boasting a bit, I think." Mr Gormley remembers the taking of the cast as an entirely pleasurable experience.

He was fervent about the impact of Tate Modern and the symbolic importance of the bridge, designed by Sir Antony, which will bring Bankside, St Paul's and the City a pedestrian's stroll apart. "This is the beginning of something enormous in British art, a re-ordering, a great tempest of cultural energy which will blow apart all the old certainties, all the traditional hierarchy of law and money and God."

Councillor Nick Dolezal, is chairman of the regeneration and environment committee at Southwark Council. The council, representing one of the most concentrated areas of urban poverty in Britain, somehow found the £2.5m five years ago for the international architectural competition which resulted in yesterday's event. He has already seen the transformation of the once-blighted streets around the rotting hulk of the power station.

"I'm not pleased, I'm ecstatic," he said yesterday, scampering from gallery to gallery. "I feel like a child who's got his hand into the sweet jar." •

10 May 2000

Martin Kettle

The oldest singer in town

When the Three Tenors all attend a concert, but only as part of the audience, then you know that something special is going on. And indeed, ever since the word got out that the revered tenor Carlo Bergonzi planned to sing his first and only performance of Verdi's Otello in New York at the age of 75 this month, seats for the Carnegie Hall event have been opera's hottest ticket of the year.

It seemed incredible that a singer who quit the operatic stage more than a decade ago and who is at an age where even the most carefully preserved voice is a shadow of its former glory could still have the drive and the resources to undertake one of the most demanding roles in the operatic repertoire for the first time. Yet Bergonzi never did anything lightly. Throughout a career that began nearly 50 years ago, he was always disciplined, preserving an unequalled vocal technique by not straying beyond his range, which was mainly Verdi. If anyone could do a first Otello at 75, then perhaps he could.

A few months ago, the word from Milan was that the incredible was happening. Bergonzi was deep in study of the score. He had even gone back to Verdi's villa near Parma to study the composer's own manuscript. Tentative enquiries from New York as to whether the great singer would prefer to sing the role transposed down – as even Placido Domingo now does – were met with a disdainful reply that Bergonzi intended to do the role "tutto in tona".

Reports from the dress rehearsal increased the expectations. "Bergonzi is thrilling," the conductor Eve Queler reported to the press. "To think that this man could accomplish this at 75 is indeed a miracle," said New York opera buff Ed Rosen.

That afternoon, straight after the rehearsal, I spoke to Bergonzi in his hotel overlooking Central Park. He oozed charm, discoursing authoritatively on Verdi and the tenor voice, breaking into song, in that long-remembered voice, to make a point.

"I accepted the challenge voluntarily, with happiness and joy," he said of Otello. "After the rehearsal, many of the orchestra players said to me, 'Today we heard the Otello of Verdi for the first time.' That is all I want. All that I want is to do the best that I can and leave this as a last memory of a great career."

Not surprisingly, the atmosphere at Carnegie Hall on the night of the concert was electric. Ticketless opera fans milled around on 57th Street hoping for returns. The hall was packed. The great ones were there for the occasion. Pavarotti, Domingo and Carreras sat together in a box, drawing all eyes. James Levine arrived just as the doors were closing.

As Queler launched her Opera Orchestra of New York into Otello's stormy opening, expectations could not have been higher. The side door opened and, to a smattering of excited applause, the familiar portly figure entered, marched to the front of the stage and delivered the Esultate, perhaps the most famous opening lines in the tenor repertoire.

It was immediately apparent that there was something wrong. A grainy tone in the voice inhibited everything. Bergonzi strained audibly in an unsuccessful attempt to reach the high A that caps the triumphant entry phrase. As he walked off the stage again, one wondered what he must be saying under his breath.

This underlying tension – so different from the glory days – lasted throughout act one. Bergonzi seemed in permanent danger of singing slightly flat, and would cup his left hand to his ear to help him stabilise any projected or exposed tone. The love duet, even with Kallen Esperian at her best, was strangely subdued. You could feel the audience willing him on, but maybe the expectations had made him too nervous.

In retrospect, people said at the evening's end, maybe Bergonzi should have called it a day at that point, should have made his own announcement that he had tried, should have acknowledged that it was not working, and craved the audience's understanding for a situation they would have been only too willing to understand, however great their disappointment.

But Bergonzi pressed on. Perhaps he felt that he owed it to himself, perhaps to the public. Perhaps he felt that he could sing his way through his difficulties and reclaim the old authority as the opera developed.

If so, it was not to be. There was, though, one truly wonderful moment, where technique and musicianship came together in a passage of great vocal art. In the Ora e per sempre addio ("now and forever farewell"), Otello begins to understand that his glories are behind him. Normally, in defiance of the score, Otellos tend to go stentorian here. Not Bergonzi. As he told me beforehand, this passage is reflective. Verdi wrote it to be sung mostly softly, with a covered tone, rather than the big open sound that most tenors adopt.

As the emotional temperature rose through act two, with Alberto Gazale an increasingly imposing Iago, Bergonzi seemed to struggle more and more. He was using his great art to try to conceal his difficulties, not illuminate his insights. Anything exposed was a high-wire act, and too often he slipped from the wire. By the end of act two, he looked an old man.

When an official came on to the platform at the start of act three, we all knew what she was about to say. "Mr Bergonzi is indisposed and will not continue his performance." Antonio Barasorda stood in, and did a good job in difficult circumstances.

And so Carlo Bergonzi's great operatic career came to a sad, humbled end. The Bergonzi Otello was a grand dream, but it was not to be. The miracle of the ageless tenor did not happen. Only those who were at the dress rehearsal know how he sang Dio mi potevi, or the death scene. But at least, and perhaps appropriately, some of us also have the memory of his singing of Ora e per sempre addio. ∎

12 November 1999

Bel Littlejohn
Bloomin' Bloomsbury

They're back: Vanessa, Roger, Vita, Duncan, Lytton, Quentin and dearest, darling Virginia. The Tate Gallery, which only last month climbed a peak of postwar art with its extraordinary Emin masterwork, has suddenly plunged right back to rock bottom with The Art of Bloomsbury. "Pass the scones, Virginia – and may I pour you a little more jasmine tea? Lytton made the sponge himself. Light as a feather! Serviette, Vita?"

Is this really the cut-and-thrust of true artists, grappling with the great issues of life and death? Of course it's bloody not. It's the idle chit-chat of the pampered and the well-heeled, more interested in who's pouring the tea than in anything approaching post-Lacanian theory.

Pardon me while I puke.

I suppose it was all my fault. I should never have gone to see Tracey Emin's painful, utterly devastating Bed before dropping in on the Bloomsbury exhibition. As in all great art, you see new things in that Bed every time you visit it.

This time I spotted a used Kleenex, seven crumbs – all from the same piece of toast, yes, but still grotesquely isolated, each one of them horribly alone in its scorched breadiness – and a half-eaten Kellogg's Pop-Tart, strawberry flavour from the smell of it, none of which I had noticed before. Tracey Emin, Artist. Fucked-up, maybe. Tucked-up, never.

But my eyes returned again, as they always do, to the used condom just to the left of the second-largest wine stain. How many potential baby Emins did it contain, all now staring out in supplication from their latex prison? A million? Ten million? Fifty billion? Twenty hundred million zillion quillion tillion? And how many of these Turner-nominated spermatozoa would themselves have produced leading British artists for the next millennium and beyond?

Even if, say, just one in a hundred of them had inherited a fifth of Tracey's talent, this would still mean a bare minimum of at least 500,000 Turner Prizewinners, and in 25 years the new Tate would be full to bursting with enough unmade beds, messy stair carpets, stained tea-towels and soggy toilet rolls to carry Britain kicking and scream-ing into the 22nd century.

A sobering thought. But that's Tracey Emin for you. She makes you think and think. And, having thunk, she makes you think some more.

So I need hardly tell you why The Art of Bloomsbury proved such a dreadful anti-climax. Think paintings, normal-sized, hanging, as per bloody usual, on walls. Think still lifes, think nudes, think – yawn! – landscapes, think all those dreary things painters were forced to paint before the welcome advent of conceptual art. Think all those weary, over-used colours – reds, greens, yellows, blues – need I go on? Are you still awake? Well, are you?

This is what the Bloomsberries serve up, time and time again. "More landscape, Vita? A touch more jug-and-apple for you, dearest Lytton?" You can imagine the oh-so-charming conversations that took place on the well-manicured lawns of their double-barrelled stately homes, while all around them low-paid servants doffed their moth-eaten caps and curtsied on bended knees as their babies perished in below-stairs rooms from neglect and malnutrition.

The current exhibition is the last gasp of a gilded age that produced nothing worthwhile. Did Damien Hirst come out of Bloomsbury? No he did not.

Were Gilbert and George ever invited to – God help us – Garsington in order to display their thoughtful 1994 canvas "Shitty Y-Fronts For All" at one of Lady Ottoline Morrell's too, too civilised afternoon soirées? Not bloody likely they weren't. And even if they had been, they would not have accepted.

Unlike all those Bloomsbury toffs and twitterers, they've got too much art bubbling up in them to be able to afford to take time off for tea with Vanessa Bell and co. With the mythical British talent for diplomacy, compromise and colonisation, not to mention the slave trade, the Irish famine and the Highland clearances, Bloomsbury and its toffee-nosed chums succeeded in stifling all creative talent in these God-forsaken islands for the past 70-odd years.

Why bother with Bloomsbury then, one might ask? The offices of my own public relations company, Bel and Frendz, are decorated with 57 Penises by Sarah Lucas, and we've already put in a sealed bid for Tracey Emin's Bed, which we're hoping to have instead of the present settee in the Client Waiting Room by the end of December. This is now. That was then.

'Nuff said. •

28 December 1999
Adrian Searle
Brush hour

I t's over. We're through with 20th century art, even if it hasn't yet finished with us. I see 1900, Art at the Crossroads in the wings, about to fill the Royal Academy in a few weeks' time. Better start queuing right away. Do we queue in the year 2000? It is supposedly good to suffer for art, though we could just visit the website, the hands-off, stain-free, virtual art-like experience and be done with it.

"When Modern Art Challenged the Establishment" reads the subtitle. The dread word "challenge" may have meant something a century ago; now it is an oxymoron.

Challenging convention has become so, well, conventional. Maybe painting will make a comeback again this year. We had Monet and Van Dyck at the Royal Academy, Pollock at the Tate, Ingres and Rembrandt at the National Gallery and Gary Hume in the British Pavilion at the Venice Biennale in 1999. He's now on at the Whitechapel art gallery, a much better installed show than at Venice.

Almost everyone seems to like Gary Hume; I like him. His paintings have a timeless yet pop-like, futuristic feel. They're hard and shiny, but very lyrical paintings, with birds and children and angels in them. Even when they are fiercely abstract, he imagines them as the world seen through the eyes of a bird, or as a song in the throat, waiting to be sung. I think Patrick Heron, who died this year, would have liked them.

One thing that connects the two artists is that they shunned all the angst and turmoil and testosterone that made Jackson Pollock's mythic reputation. It is the mythical Pollock – the self-doubting, tormented, all-American existential hero – that people fell over themselves to see at the Tate in 1999. They got the backwoods mumbling drunken Jungian all right, the child of Picasso with the jangling Oedipus complex, but they also saw Pollock the dancer, the grace-under-pressure painter whose finest works have your eyes swimming in their liquid interstellar spaces.

Usefully, there was a concurrent show of Henri Michaux at the Whitechapel. Interest in Michaux is growing and I note that the diabolic and terrifying Diamanda Galas sang one of Michaux's poems at a concert in London this month.

We queued for Monet too. I feel I've seen enough late Monet to last me a lifetime of vaporous dawns and hushed, limpid evenings, such was the excess of publicity that accompanied the show. There was something odd, too, about the idea of visiting the Monet show at 5am, when the Royal Academy extended its opening hours round the clock, just like Sainsbury's. I guess the allure was much like staying up all night to go tench fishing at dawn on some lily-padded pond. I'll be doing that again next year, and I might even think of Monet for a moment or two while I'm at it.

Rembrandt wasn't someone I'd want to look at in the graveyard hours, although it always feels like the middle of the night in the Sainsbury wing at the National Gallery. Rembrandt by Himself was a majesterial, dark show, and gave us the man in full. But you got a faceful of everyone else who was trying to look as well. Looking at Rembrandt involves a kind of confrontation that the jostle of a large audience makes almost impossible. Coming out, everyone looked like the paintings: pouchy-eyed, slump-faced and badly impastoed. I knew how they felt.

There were more nocturnal shenanigans in Martin Maloney's paintings of men having sex outdoors and in louche gay clubs, on show in Charles Saatchi's new neurotic realism putsch. This was a package, rather than a movement, and I'm yet to hear an artist say "Hi! I'm a new neurotic realist!", although there are some miserable characters out there now calling themselves Stuckists. I have no idea what it means, much less do I care. I think they're an offshoot of the There's a Conspiracy Against Me, Sincerely Expressionist school.

I sat at home in London, doing a live phone-in on New York public radio. "Hi, this is Moira from Queens. Does Chris Ofili have a big following among the exiled Nigerian community in London?" "Is his work some kind of heavy voodoo thing?" asked Carl, on his cellphone, stuck in heavy mid-town traffic. Here I was in London talking to people who hadn't even bothered to go and see Ofili's painting in Saatchi's Sensation! show, now at the Brooklyn museum. But then mayor Giuliani never went to see it either. The show was going to rumble on into the new millennium, ending its tour in Australia, but after the New York debacle in which the mayor tried to close the show and rescind the museum's grant, the uncharacteristically querulous Australians got cold feet and dropped it.

Storm in a teacup? Art storms usually are, or bedroom farce in the case of Tracey Emin's Turner prize show. Chinese artists jumped on her bed and a woman came up from the west country with a chambermaid's kit and rubber gloves to tidy up the mess. This I liked. Germaine Greer said on telly that "This was the bed where Judith cut off the head of Holofernes, this is the bed where the Rokeby Venus lay... it's formally perfect from every angle." Of course it's formally perfect. It is a bed. That is its form. Its very beddishness is what strikes you, whichever way you look at it. It didn't win, and Emin stood on the steps of the Tate and announced to a media crew that the real tragedy of not winning the prize was that she would have given the money to the Turkish earthquake victims. So it is the jury's fault and my fault and everyone else's fault that the homeless Turks are spending another night, bedless in the howling wind and snow.

Steve McQueen won the Turner prize, announcing that the impact of the award probably wouldn't hit him till he was back home in Amsterdam, doing a spot of hoovering. The very next day Hoover sent their latest model round to McQueen as a congratulatory gift. No sooner was the prize announced than speculation about next year's line-up began. Martin Creed, the Chapman brothers, Fiona Banner and a second chance for Mark Wallinger are already being talked about. Wallinger's Ecce Homo is undoubtedly the public artwork of the year, although Creed's blue neon sign, reading Everything Is Going To Be Alright, on the pediment of some dilapidated arches in Hackney, is good, and popular with the locals.

Unlike Antony Gormley's Millennium Man (sorry, Quantum Cloud) at Greenwich, Wallinger's sculpture didn't take an army of boffins, civil engineers and steel erectors to construct, nor did he have to get permission from air traffic control to illuminate it. A few blokes in a shed near High Wycombe (a group of extremely able technicians in a greenfield site workshop) helped Wallinger realise his life-size Christ figure for the vacant plinth in Trafalgar Square. This modest figure is soon to be replaced by a work by Bill Woodrow, but Ecce Homo has already managed to melt into the cityscape, which seems entirely appropriate, 2,000 years on. Wallinger's Christ, although wearing only a loincloth and a barbed-wire crown of thorns, his hands tied behind his back, is a static everyman, perched on the brink of his plinth. I hope he makes it through millennium night without being moved on. •

18 December 1999

AC Grayling
The last word on Art

A survey published this week found that most teenagers dislike museums, art galleries and the theatre. They think such places boring, and associate them with "rich old people". The survey concludes that if homes of the arts offered more cafes and leisure activities, and if performances were shorter, teenagers might be more inclined to go.

With luck, no one will take any notice of this survey. It says nothing new, for things have always been thus. If galleries and theatres start trying to attract teenagers, they will fail, while at the same time alienating their natural constituencies. The arts have always been, and always will be, avocations for minorities. "Art teaches nothing, except the significance of life," said Henry Miller; and most people never get to the second half of the sentence.

The good news is that as populations increase, so do the numbers in minorities. As a result, more people than ever before in history now enjoy the arts. Exhibitions are crowded, concerts fully booked. And therefore more people discover the richness of pleasure and insight that the arts give. "Thanks to art," said Proust, "instead of seeing one world, our own, we see it multiplied, and as many original artists as there are, so many worlds are at our disposal."

Philistinism is not universal among teenagers, but it is a professional phase with many. Their supposed contempt for the arts is not really about the arts, but about themselves: they are not always ready for what the arts offer. Some come to feel the need for more content, more juice in things, and that is when the arts invite them. "Art comes to you proposing frankly to give nothing but the highest quality to your moments as they pass," said Pater; once accepted, that invitation can never thereafter be refused.

Pieties, unlike clichés, carry no guarantee of truth: but there is a familiar one about the arts which does. It is that when a thoughtful and receptive sensibility engages with the arts, it is nourished by them, and learns from them, not least how to be discerning: "It is only the dullness of the eye that makes any two things seem alike," Pater also says, and the idea of the uniqueness and particularity of things carries over from a painting or a moment of dance to a moral circumstance or an individual's suffering. In that way art civilises too, because it is, as Shaw says, the mirror for souls.

Perhaps the young find it hard to appreciate the arts because the arts are themselves always youthful. "Art is never didactic, does not take kindly to facts, is helpless to grapple with theories, and is killed outright by a sermon," said Agnes Repplier, and she could have put "youth" for "art" at the sentence's head.

Many mistakenly think that art must be approached in one's mental Sunday best; that it lacks laughs; that it changes nothing. The opposite is true, and those who discover this fact are infinitely the richer for it. •

Take me to your leader writer

21 February 2000

Là ci darem la mano

The trouble with critics who lay into "popular culture" – such as schools chief Chris Woodhead the other day – is that classic culture is not exactly replete with uplift and correct behaviour. Take opera. The canon revels in blasphemy (Tannhäuser), incest (Valkyrie), torture (Turandot) and child abuse (Peter Grimes); there is devil worship (Mcfistofele), sex with ghosts (Flying Dutchman), fairies (Rusalka) and goddesses (Pearl Fishers). By comparison modern opera – aliens, fellatio and the murder of disabled people – is tame.

But now, it seems, a truly offensive scenario is being adapted in which a teacher makes love to a pupil. This is the subject of a Glyndebourne collaboration in a series designed to appeal to a young audience. Could the plot have been inspired by the suggestion that once upon a time the chief inspector of schools himself was involved in a not dissimilar set of events? Ofsted's reaction yesterday was churlish. It is a rare honour to become a librettist's inspiration in your own lifetime. To that illustrious roster Bluebeard, King Herod, Don Giovanni, Count Almaviva, Fafner and Pinkerton may now be added the name... Woodhead. •

26 February 2000

Labour's monument

We cannot help but take pleasure in the Labour party's 100th birthday this weekend – and not only because the party was founded just around the corner from our current headquarters, at the Methodist Memorial Hall in Farringdon Street, central London. Our pleasure also springs from the fact that throughout Labour's century we have stood as a candid, often awkward, friend, endorsing the party directly or indirectly in almost every election it has fought. Its history is part of our own. Tomorrow's anniversary of that very first meeting of trade unionists, activists and socialist societies – eventually producing the Labour Representation Committee – provides an apt moment to reflect on Labour's past and to wonder about its future.

A view that was once merely fashionable, but which has now graduated into conventional wisdom, declares that this birthday might not be a cause for celebration at all. Roy Jenkins, once a deputy leader of the party, has led the way in arguing that the tragedy of 20th century British politics was the division of the liberal left into two parties, one Labour, the other Liberal. If these progressive forces had only been united, runs the argument, then we might not have had to live through seven decades of

Conservative or Conservative-dominated rule. Thanks to that division, Labour has governed for no more than 24 of the last 100 years. Tony Blair himself is an advocate of this view of history: indeed, it forms the rationale behind his beloved "project" of ever-closer cooperation with the Liberal Democrats. Mr Blair urges a reunion of the liberal left, to ensure that if the 20th century belonged to the Conservatives, then the 21st ought to be in the hands of the progressives.

There is some appeal in this argument, not least the compelling evidence of the numbers. Still, despite our century-long advocacy of accommodation between the Labour and Liberal parties, we cannot agree with it completely. Lest we forget, it was Labour which built the modern welfare state – including a national health service and pensions system – oversaw the peaceful end of the British empire, constructed the open university and presided over a decade of social progress, with liberalising legislation in the 1960s on abortion, sexuality, the death penalty and equal pay. No party with a proud record like that should be asked to regard its own existence as a mistake. On the contrary, if the brute reality of our first past the post electoral system means there was only room for one progressive party, it would surely have been the Liberals who had to leave the stage – not Labour. Liberals cannot, with any conviction, claim they would have notched up that same catalogue of achievement. It took the Labour party.

A tougher argument is the one about the present and future. The party of Tony Blair faces problems that would have baffled its predecessors. For one thing, devolution has moulded an unfamiliar landscape. There are now at least three distinct political battle-fields in Britain: Scotland, Wales and the UK-wide parliament in Westminster. Labour is the only party which is a lead player on all three grounds – taking on the national-ists on the first two, and the Conservatives on the third. Labour's dominance in all these different arenas leaves a problem: how can a party tailor different messages for these increasingly distinct political entities yet still remain a single, coherent UK-wide party? Can Labour continue to speak a language that appeals to Edinburgh and Cardiff while simultaneously reaching the voters of middle England, the people who decide general elections at Westminster? Can it have one transport policy for the coun-try and another for London, if that's what it takes to win a London-wide election? This is an existential challenge to Labour far more than to the Conservatives – who have all but given up on being a UK-wide party. It is Labour which needs to crack this riddle.

The party's second problem is related. Labour's great modern achievement is to have transcended its original status as a sectional vehicle for one class. The Blairite Labour party is a home fit for millionaires and business leaders now; no longer the ragged-trousered comrades who gathered on Farringdon Street. This counts, in part, as a testament to Labour's own achievement: its expansion of higher education led to the creation of a vast, new middle class and the eventual blurring of the old class hierar-chies. But it also leaves Labour with a conundrum. How can Labour be the party of David Sainsbury and Bob Ayling – and simultaneously keep hold of its loyalists in the heartlands, the men and women typified by the former minister, Peter Kilfoyle, who resigned over what he regards as the excessive attention lavished on affluent middle

England? The prime minister says he's "not interested" in the tired old language of class. But that is too easy. Labour needs to find a way to stay true to its roots, even as it stretches and grows, touching areas that were once deemed out of reach. These concerns need not be sources of angst. On the contrary, they are problems that come from success, rather than failure. After 100 years there is much to celebrate. Labour can wish itself a very happy birthday. •

19 November 1999

A pother of pedants

Some Tory MPs think the Queen needs to wash her mouth out. Not only, they say, did Tony Blair force into it a string of unjustified boasts about Labour's record and future intentions, turning the Gracious Speech into a party political broadcast; even worse, he caused her – sensitive souls should look away at this point – to split an infinitive, in speaking of laws which would make it an offence "to racially discriminate". Nor is her majesty the only offender. P O'Neill has done the same thing. O'Neill is the name under which the IRA traditionally issues its statements. The one he put out this week said the IRA was now willing "to further enhance the peace process" – a solecism duly denounced in yesterday's Telegraph.

It seems that the forces of conservatism have not been keeping up with the game. Had they done so, they would have known that the splitting of infinitives now has the sanction of most good grammarians. Fowler, the nearest thing they have to a bible, withdrew its ban on the practice decades ago. Last year Oxford University Press published a new dictionary in which split infinitives were not just condoned but encouraged. The rule in these matters ought to be this: the form which serves the reader or listener best is the one you should go for. (Or, if Tory MPs prefer, the form for which one should go is that which serves best the reader or listener.) Language should be a flexible servant, not a Draconian master. True, some thought they detected the faintest moue of displeasure on her majesty's face when she came to the words complained of. Maybe she had not been consulted; and it is, after all, the Queen's English. But it is only the Queen's English in the largely fictional sense that the speech from the throne is called the Queen's speech, though everyone knows it is really Tony Blair speaking. When our elected prime minister decides to boldly dump old-fashioned linguistic practices, then that, nowadays, is effectively the end of the matter. •

8 March 2000

The policy isn't working

Nearly 10 years on, Saddam Hussein is finally winning the Gulf war. Western and Arab opinion, once united in condemning and reversing his 1990 invasion of Kuwait, now affords little support for the US-controlled, UN-directed sanctions regime subsequently imposed on Iraq.

The American and British governments find themselves almost alone in defending a policy held responsible for high infant mortality, the deaths of tens of thousands of children and elderly people and, more generally, for the impoverishment of most of Iraq's 23m people. The sanctions are officially justified as the primary means of enforcing security council resolutions, particularly the demand that Iraq scrap its nuclear, chemical and biological weapons programmes. But the inspections remain incomplete after the UN team withdrew from Baghdad in Decembe r, 1998. An ensuing, large-scale Anglo-American attack failed to persuade Saddam to change course. Despite a new UN resolution, the inspectors have still not returned. Meanwhile, the continuing US and British air strikes in the northern and southern no-fly zones – there have been 16 so far this year – have become a paradoxical symbol of allied impotence. Like the victims of sanctions, they are mercilessly exploited by Saddam's propagandists.

Ten years on, Saddam's envoys have succeeded in destroying the security council consensus. France has joined permanent members Russia and China in undermining Anglo-American policy. Iraq is also making steady advances in its return to the Arab and regional fold. Last month it signed a trade deal with Turkey. A Syrian interests section has opened in Baghdad and there is talk of reopening the Iraqi-Syrian oil pipeline shut since 1982. Leading Jordanians launch a pan-Arab campaign to normalise relations; this week, Baghdad's representatives will attend an Arab League meeting in Beirut. Meanwhile, the open flouting of the sanctions regime proceeds apace. Supplies, licit and illicit, for Iraq's elite flow across the land borders. Turkey is said to be illegally importing 1.1m barrels of Iraqi oil. US naval commanders in the Gulf report a sharp increase in Iraqi oil smuggling, facilitated by the Russians and the Iranians. Rising oil prices are another uncomfortable indicator of Saddam's returning strength: Iraq, after all, has the world's largest proven crude reserves after Saudi Arabia. Saddam hopes to wield this power with a vengeance one day. Some believe Washington's true purpose is to deny him this weapon; it represents a threat far more fearsome than any souped-up Scud.

Saddam's success is also one of survival, measured against the west's premature victory declaration in 1991 and its fierce but now waning determination to depose him. The Clinton administration's attempts to mobilise Iraqi opposition groups, and the CIA's covert efforts to overthrow the Iraqi leader, have at best been half-hearted. The US now seems to have almost given up trying. In a broader sense, the policy of "dual containment" of both Iraq and Iran has unravelled. Despite continuing tough posturing from its ambassador, Richard Holbrooke, the US has lost the argument at the UN.

The latest resolution proposes progressively to ease sanctions after weapons inspections are satisfactorily resumed for an initial 120 days. Iraq's flat refusal to accept these conditions would at one time have quickly been squashed. Now most countries seem to sympathise with Baghdad. The new chief weapons inspector, Hans Blix, may make a difference. But while technically successful, the inspection process remains a political minefield. Meanwhile, the recent resignation of Hans von Sponeck, over the inadequacy of the UN's oil-for-food programme for which he was responsible, marked a new low. In vain do US and British officials insist that it is Saddam who is responsible for his people's agony. The finger of blame is pointed at them.

Ten years on, the struggle with Saddam has indeed become the mother of all battles. But it is clear that, infinitely difficult though it is, one more big push to cut a sanctions-inspections deal with Iraq is required. It is true that the unstated purpose of sanctions was to punish, isolate, and ultimately bring down Saddam. This policy has utterly and demonstrably failed. The human cost has been, and is, horrendous. Few believe it is morally justifiable. Even fewer believe it will ever work. But it is also true that an abandonment of the attempt to deny Iraq its weapons of mass destruction would be grossly irresponsible, surrendering the little leverage the outside world still has. It would ensure that Saddam, sooner or later, could again threaten his neighbours and perhaps western Europe. It would be a gamble with the security not only of the Middle East but of any part of the world where "rogue" dictators roam. To drop sanctions without conditions or fulfilment of security council resolutions, as Baghdad insists, would be to shatter the credibility of the UN and the ethos which has underpinned intervention elsewhere. And it would triumphantly secure Saddam at home, guaranteeing perhaps an even more iniquitous oppression of Kurds, Shia, and others who oppose him. His claims that there are no more weapons to find simply cannot be taken at face value. For Saddam is a murderous, reckless man , in all probability a psychopath, who cares nothing for others. Amid all the misery, that must not be forgotten.

So: one more big push, one more effort to find a way. Suspend the non-military sanctions now; have the inspectors return simultaneously; maintain the no-fly zones; watch carefully for dual-use technology imports; then press hard at the end, say, of a six-month trial period, for a settlement that will last. It is possible that Saddam, sensing victory, will reject even this. But we must try. It is time, finally, to end this war. For at present, we have the worst of all worlds. Saddam advances steadily and by stealth, the UN is discredited, the west divided – and the suffering goes on. •

15 October 1999

Cold comfort

We are a family, and we behave like a family – Michael Ancram, Conservative party chairman, on the eve of conference. It was the last and dreariest day of September. Ravaged sheep trembled as the gales tore through their folds as cruelly as Chelsea strikers through a Manchester United defence. As she approached the ruined house, where tattered curtains fluttered at shattered casements, the young social worker shuddered. A crone emerged from the shadows. "Is this Cold Comfort Farm?" the young woman asked. "I have to visit a dysfunctional family here. I think the name may be Starkadder."

"Starkadders?" the old woman cackled. "They be dead and gone a murrain of twelvemonths since. No, there's folks in there now that makes the Starkadders look like something out of Hello magazine. Come and see." The door swung loose on its hinges. Inside was a scene for which years of training had never prepared her. In the centre of the kitchen a figure in glasses was scratching away on a slate. "She must be destroyed" he was muttering. "She has lost the knack of keeping the two sides of her personality bolted together." "Writing his memoirs" the aged spectre explained. From a corner cupboard the social worker could hear a hissing of "traitress!" "That's old uncle Ted" vouchsafed the harridan. "They try to keep him out of the way, but they never succeed." Before a dying fire, a nurse was shovelling lumps of glup from a vat marked "Common Sense" into a small bald infant. "T'es Wee Willie" the old witch confided.

"But this is terrible!" the social worker exclaimed. "Whatever has brought them to this?" "Some say" the old woman whispered "t'es all the fault of Aunt Maggie Doom. You'll hear her shouts from the woodshed. She thinks she's seen something nasty in there. T'others think the nasty thing in the woodshed is her... And this isn't them at their worst, mind'ee. Just you wait till they get to Blackpool." •

The sex war

....

16 October 1999

Julie Burchill

'Suicide is a side-effect of affluence. You didn't get many suicides in Jarrow in the 30s'

Was I the only person cynical enough to think that a good catchline for the recently launched football initiative against young male suicide might have been "Don't take it out on yourselves, lads – punch a woman!"?

Last month, a survey found that more than half the young men questioned thought that hitting a woman was acceptable under certain circumstances; many people were shocked by these findings but, considering the diet of rap music and women-assaulting footballers that most teenage boys grow up on, I was rather surprised that so many young men still clung to such quaint concepts of chivalry as not beating up women.

Not a peep was heard from the great and the good of football on this subject, however. It's amazing, isn't it? Not a Sunday goes by when some ball-kicking scumbag isn't revealed in the tabloids as having beaten up his wife/girlfriend/a woman in a bar – between bouts of sex with girl-children, that is. Top of the league is the heroic Stan Collymore, with a grand total of three attacks on women. Give that man a medal!

But then, just when you thought romance was dead, here's Dean Holdsworth, who invariably keeps his fists for the face of his loyal wife, Samantha. After all, as that lovable rogue George Best once said, "I think we've all given the wife a smack once in a while."

It is interesting to note that the current hate figure of football among fans and media alike is David Beckham – for the truly unforgivable crime of being devoted to his wife, and sometimes deferring to her on the grounds of her superior intelligence and worldliness. If he blacked her Posh eye for her, he'd be a hero again.

Is there any initiative from football to tackle this problem? Not a sniff. Do they have daughters, the football managers who consistently refuse to punish players who attack women or have sex with underage girls? Or do they by some miracle of modern science sire only boys, who will never know what it is like to be attacked in your own home, your own little love nest with the pink-and-blue toothbrushes, by a snarling maniac who has promised in front of a roomful of people to love, honour and cherish you until death you do part?

Well, if the men who manage football think that 545 under-24 male suicides a year is a more frightening statistic than two women killed each week – and hundreds of thousands injured every year – by the men they live with, then they must be even stupider than they look; though it's hard to imagine, I know. But I can't help feeling they're on very dodgy ground, taking on the young male suicide thing. For a start, it's a phony panic, catering to that lowest of modern male desires – to be a victim – for if we are to use the desire for death as a barometer of stress and misery levels among young people, then surely the fact that vastly more young women attempt suicide must mean that young women are still under far more pressure than young men. (Anorexia and bulimia, the scenic-route suicides, are still something like three-quarters female.)

That young men succeed in suicide more often than girls isn't really the point. Indeed, the more callous among us would say that it was quite nice for young men finally to find something that they're better at than girls. Then there is the uncomfortable fact that modern football, with the vast amounts of money and hero-worship involved, is hardly a comfort to young men anxious about their ability to carve out a niche in the world. With the emphasis on winning at all costs and making it by the age of 25, millions of young men are faced every day with the proof that they just couldn't measure up to the one thing they really wanted to achieve.

Football is all about emotional incontinence and blind devotion; it is as camp and overblown as a Bette Davis film, and hardly the best thing to dangle in front of young men who are already punch-drunk with hormones and hysteria. What does it feel like, waking up on a freezing morning to go to your minimum-wage job, and seeing those golden boys on the front of the tabloids earning £1,000 an hour and sleeping with beautiful young household faces? It's enough to make you suicidal.

No one is "in favour" of suicide, but when we interfere with people's right to take their own lives, we are on very dangerous ground. The level of pain that must have been reached to make suicide an option must be unbelievable. Perhaps all it behoves any of us to do at that point is to make the death as comfortable as possible. (Teenage suicide is like teenage sex: if you don't let them do it at home, they'll go out and do it somewhere nasty and dangerous.) And suicide, like car theft, is a side-effect of peace and affluence. You didn't get many suicides in Jarrow in the 30s, and until recently it was all but unknown in Northern Ireland. It really is one of those problems with no solution.

The last time I suggested that suicides should be left to get on with it, I received a small number of letters from people whose sons had killed themselves. All of them demanded an apology. I'd advise them this time to save their stamps because, you see, I don't care. I don't care because most nights of the week I still dream of my dad, who I saw waste away almost to nothing, eaten alive by the tumours that were his retirement gift for working with asbestos. Every day, as his legs went, as his sight went, my dad would declare that tomorrow he would be taking the dog out; he clung to life like a dog playing tug-of-war for the biggest, juiciest raw steak in the world.

To ask me to feel sympathy with suicides after witnessing this is, I suggest, just as unfeeling and ignorant as my callousness must appear to you – like asking a starving African to sympathise with an anorexic. In a society still beset with the most vicious social deprivation and rampant cruelty to the very young, the very old and the very weak, the voluntary exits of a few hundred able-bodied young men each year are best dealt with as private tragedies rather than a public concern. Let them go. •

25 February 2000

Leanda de Lisle
Boys will always be joys to me

One of the great questions of the age is: what is the point of men? We are told that boys do worse than girls at school, have poorer communication skills so are less well equipped for today's employment market and play an increasingly insignificant role in the process of reproduction. The suggestion is that they are almost redundant. But this is nonsense. It is obvious that men are the superior sex. They are more clever, more charming, more affectionate and more attractive.

As a child I wasn't prepared to accept what was, in those days, the commonly held view that men were more intelligent than women. But then, as a teenager, I learnt that boys think about sex once every three seconds. I thought about sex myself – particularly in libraries, for some reason. But I had to wait for my reveries to pass before I could attempt to absorb Chadwick's Sanitation Report.

Anyone who could think about sex every three seconds and pass exams must, I realised, be very clever indeed – a fact that was driven home when I arrived at university. For there I discovered something else that clearly indicated that men are brainier than women.

Only female undergraduates took lecture notes. This, it soon became obvious, was something to be despised. It apparently demonstrated that women were plodders who attempted to compensate for their lack of male genius by sucking up to teacher – something which the current generation of secondary school pupils has done nothing to dispel.

If I read once more that school girls read more than boys, study harder and have a better relationship with their teachers, I will begin to despair at us ever achieving sexual equality. Today's girls should do their bit, as I did mine. Determined to demonstrate that not all university girls were sickening goody goodies, I rarely went to lectures at all.

However, sadly, when it came to my final exams I was overcome by what was doubtless a hormone-fuelled terror of getting a third class degree. Only men were considered exciting and sparkling enough to do either extremely well, or extremely badly.

I asked groups of friends if I could photocopy their notes and a boy agreed. It turned out that he had, for the past three years, simply pretended not to be doing much work. This, was, of course, part and parcel of his charm. An art at which men excel. The recent scientific survey that purported to prove that women are more charming than men, in fact proved the opposite. For the charm that can be illustrated in graphs and pie charts after a few interviews isn't charming at all.

Real charm is both a tool of ambition and a mask to disguise its face. Once spotted it is perceived as a threat and becomes useless.

My charming friend was as generous with his notes as he was silent on the subject of his exam results. He may have got a starred first or a pass degree. One didn't like to ask, but I note that he seems to have done extremely well since.

These days I have the academic careers of three sons to think about. I read their school reports with pride and, I admit, intermittent panic, as is to be expected from a mere mother.

But they are a reminder, too, that affection is a very male attribute. Little girls are quite self-contained when compared to little boys, who demand a lot of hugs, particularly after fisticuffs. When they grow up, it is much the same story. Happily sons stay with their mothers for longer than daughters do, so mine may remain with me for some time. But one day they will doubtless move in with a partner.

I am aware of the well worn phrase: "All men are bastards". But it simply isn't true. They only leave a woman if another woman is taking them in. Women, on the other hand, just go off to find a new life, as often as not, taking their children with them far away. What kind of bastard does that? Not a very attractive one, that is for sure.

But then, I don't think women are very attractive. At best they are horribly smooth-faced, at worst they have breasts.

It is amazes that lipstick lesbianism has become as fashionable as it has. Besides a woman's – one can only say "feminine" – appearance, women can do absolutely nothing to you that a man can't do. What is the point? Male homosexuality – now that I can understand. A woman would be almost useless to a gay man.

Gay or straight, chaps come first. ∎

· ·

10 September 1999

Bel Littlejohn
Men, you're miserable

Drained just isn't the word. It's been an experience. In fact I've never felt so drained. It makes me wish I'd been on a journalist draining scheme, just so I'd know how to cope.

I'm talking, of course, about my new book, Half-Cocked: Men In Crisis. For the past seven years, I have been talking to all kinds of men. Tall men. Short men. Medium-sized men. Men who wear neckties. Men in open-necked collars. I was even introduced to one man, in an alley off Brooklyn, who was wearing a cravat. I have been talking to men with one eye. Men with two eyes. Men in trainers. Men in shoes. Men in sandals. Famous men with two eyes but without trainers. Unknown men with sandals but with only one eye. The lot. And I've been asking them a simple question they've never, ever been asked before: Why do you feel so very, very angry and miserable – is it because, deep down, you are so utterly worthless?

No one had ever taken the trouble to ask men that question before. What I found on what I call my Listening Tour was a feeling of supreme irrelevance among them. "Why do you feel so totally irrelevant?" I would say, before adding "Next, please!" By the way they'd slouch out of the station, I'd intuit a profound sense of anger and disaffection, as though they were feeling ignored by a society that had once primed them to feel important.

We have changed fundamentally from a society that produced a fundamentally changing culture to a society that produced a culture of fundamental change. The difference, I discovered, was fundamental. And what of the men who were left behind? To understand what all men really thought, I made it my mission to talk to some of the most fundamentally stupid men still alive on this planet.

To find out what modern man really thought of women, I listened to what half a dozen serial rapists from a high-security prison in Colorado had to tell me. And to find out what modern man really thought about concepts such as the uses of structuralism in a post-modernist age, I turned to leading Hollywood movie star, Keanu Reeves, with whom I enjoyed an exclusive 10-minute interview.

I even managed to locate an educationally sub-normal 310lb kleptomaniac from Nebraska to advise me on the limits of changing concepts of masculinity within the context of local communities in decline. Only by uncovering the dashed hopes and expectations within the most fundamentally daft men in the world would I be able to come to terms with the full severity of the crisis facing modern man.

Unlike his daft father, today's daft man grew up without any sense of pride. Where his father might once have marched off proudly to die in a war that had not yet been scheduled, today's daft man had to be content with falling flat on his face after an accident arising from a genetically modified banana skin. Today's man wears a baseball cap the wrong way round.

He sings the latest Sloopy Doggy Dog number to himself without really understanding the lyrics. He is unemployable because he has lost all sense of self esteem, resulting from wearing trousers many sizes too big for him. His fingernails are rarely clean. And in the basement of his modest, clapboard house, situated just off the main street in an unassuming mid-American town there lie three partially-charred, semi-clad corpses.

They have been there three months now, the victims of modern man's unquenchable desire to regain his domination over his environment. I initially uncovered this horrifying trend by visiting death row and talking to a man who is widely regarded as the most unpleasant human being in Montana.

It's crucial for society not simply to denounce but to figure out what the hell's going on. Men speak with their mouths full. They kick stones in the street. They challenge old ladies to arm-wrestling competitions on the top of double-decker buses – and then leap off without paying their fares. Why are men like this? Or – to put it another way – this like men are why?

It all goes back to space travel. When I talked with men who grew up in the shadow of space travel, they all heard me tell them the same thing. For them, space was a bitter disappointment. Despite all their masculine hopes, the moon had turned out to be a depressing environment, approachable only by cramped and noisy rocket, and with no male infrastructure to speak of: there was no baseball park on the moon, for instance, and little or no opportunity for date-rape or male bonding.

Once again, the male felt betrayed – and it is to his deep sense of disillusion that I shall return next week. •

31 January 2000

Peter Preston

My daughter is just fine

Tolerance. It's an excellently soothing word; one used almost promiscuously by politicians, leader writers and churchmen intent on spreading a little even-handed balm. For who, pray, seeks an intolerant society? We all need tolerance, oodles of tolerance. But what the hell do we mean by it?

The most relevant text, for the moment, flows fresh from the pen of the Chief Rabbi – and inevitably concerns that great test of sexual tolerance called section 28. So Dr Jonathan Sacks climbs gingerly up on the tightrope already swaying under the weight of Cardinal Winning, Archbishop Carey, the editors of the Sun and the Daily Mail, and the boss of Stagecoach buses.

"I can never forget, as a Jew, that homosexuals were sent to Auschwitz just as Jews were. Therefore, if our society has become more tolerant, that is a good thing," says Dr Sacks. So that's all right, then? It wouldn't be a "good thing" to send gays to the gas chamber.

"However" – there is always a however – "the current proposal (to repeal section 28) is based on a fundamental confusion between tolerance and moral judgment. Tolerance means treating with respect people whose positions are fundamentally different from your own. It does not mean regarding those views as equally valid."

Here, essentially, the Chief Rabbi echoes Cantuar. "I condemn totally prejudice against anyone on the basis of sexual orientation. But I also resist placing homosexual relationships on an equal footing with marriage as the proper context for sexual intimacy," in the Carey version. Sacks does not, to be fair, go the Winning way and talk of "perversion" – let alone about an "active and militant lobby" mustering its forces "all over Europe" to threaten "the Christian family". Tolerance has its boundaries.

But now the phone rings. It's one of our daughters and she's pretty upset. She wants to talk about tolerance, too.

We have two daughters. They are identical twins, born 10 minutes apart. Suckled at the same breast, tended side by side in adjacent cots. They grew up together, played together, made friends together. They went to the same schools and achieved the same spread of results in (mostly) the same subjects. They played the same games and sang the same songs. They are, even today, difficult for strangers to tell apart when they dress alike. Two peas from the same pod. Same genes; same everything. One is gay and one is not.

"How interesting!" the occasional child psychologist will say at the occasional dinner party. It must have been nurture, not nature. Well, perhaps; but don't ask me how that came to pass. They were loved and cherished equally in the most natural sense; brought up without a flicker of difference between them that I can recall. They remain their own best friends.

It is my elder (gay) daughter who calls. She's listening to another radio debate about section 28 and the familiar liberal defences being trotted out there are just so feeble. A "tolerant" society? An excuse for not thinking, for the denial of human identity.

And that, of course, is right when you pause over her distress. Right from where she sits – and right for us, the witnesses who never seem to get called when the tide of purse-lipped toleration starts running again, the parents of gay children we respect and love.

When our twins are home for a family birthday party, what do we say? Do we echo the Chief Rabbi and affirm that one daughter, happily married with a baby, is secure in "moral judgment" because she has not "abandoned a moral code shared by virtu-ally all the world's great religions" – whilst her identical twin, has suffered a "moral confusion" which renders her existence somehow less "valid"? Deserving of "toler-ance" but not of equality?

Do we sing along with the Archbishop of Canterbury and "resist placing homo-sexual relationships on an equal footing with marriage as the proper context for sexual intimacy"? Welcome to the C of E premiership and the depths of its first division. One sister has a loving husband, the other a loving partner. Both are family. What on earth, in the human terms which are the only terms that matter, is George Carey wittering on about? How would he draw his lines in our home at Christmas?

Section 28's language speaks, coldly, for itself. "A local authority shall not (a) inten-tionally promote homosexuality or publish material with the intention of promoting homosexuality; and (b) promote the teaching in any maintained school of the accept-ability of homosexuality as a pretended family relationship."

You can, I'm afraid, hear the likes of Cardinal Winning mouthing such phrases, building them into a bulwark against repeal. "Cast your minds back to the dark days of the second world war," he declaims. "In place of the bombs of 50 years ago, you find yourselves bombarded with images, values and ideas which are utterly alien."

But what is the "promotion" of such values? And what is a "pretended family rela-tionship?" My daughter – troubled and uncertain from the age of 13 on – found noth-ing to help or to guide her at school: merely an RE teacher the cardinal would have embraced. She did not, to our subsequent chagrin, confide in her parents until her mind was clear. She had damn all in the way of information, let alone the illusion of town hall propaganda. She was left alone to struggle through the most difficult years.

Where is there the least hint of Christianity in that? When did Christ – abandoning any mention of love – inveigh against "pretended family relationships" (which the Daily Mail, for its own reasons, defines as an "equal alternative to marriage")? Why does it sometimes seem that Robert Mugabe must be the natural leader of this panic-stricken crusade?

The repeal of section 28 won't transform society. There will still be vicious playground bullying of the kind copiously documented by teachers themselves. There will still be prejudice and fear. Bits of law do not, in themselves, change our world. But the fight, for all that, has a momentous symbolism attached. It forces every one of us to look into ourselves and decide what's right. It allows no political weaselings. No hiding place.

My daughter isn't some notional stereotype invented to scare elderly cardinals. Nor is she a visitor from an alien place. She is like millions more in the world around – and we, in turn, are like millions of other parents. This is our flesh and blood; part of us, a reflection of us. We don't have to say she's equal. She IS equal. And no drizzle of incomprehension, no fear fostered in ignorance, no puny section, can alter that. It isn't tolerance we need. It is knowing what makes our hearts beat. •

Honi soit qui mal y pense

12 June 2000

Catherine Bennett
The appeal of Camilla

Private. Intensely private. That, for a very long time, was as much as we were told about Camilla Parker-Bowles. True, the woman had more reason than most to be private, but love of privacy, her friends insisted, would have been a Parker-Bowles quality even if she hadn't got involved in a 25-year affair with her future sovereign and endured having their intensely private smutty telephone call transcribed as entertainment for the masses.

Since she was so private, not being officially acknowledged or generally liked seemed to suit Camilla just fine. "She is without personal ambition," revealed Ingrid Seward, one of her supporters, "and insists she will always be happier pruning the roses than planting them." "Camilla becomes nervous when the spotlight turns on her," said fellow sympathiser Stuart Higgins, a former editor of the Sun.

All she wanted, her friends said, was to be with Charles. "She's a very private person – I can't see her cutting ribbons," Patti Palmer-Tomkinson, a friend of the couple, told the New Yorker in 1997. "I've never heard them mention marriage. While they've got each other in private it's their romance; it belongs to them."

That summer, when everyone still expected the Diana v Camilla story to run for ever, a love of privacy was starting to look like rather an attractive quality. While the princess pranced around the Mediterranean in high-cut swimsuits, public opinion began to soften towards Camilla. It may even have helped when Diana's new boon companion, Mohamed al Fayed, whose son would become her lover, gave a press conference in which he boasted about their intimacy and declared that "Camilla's like something from a Dracula film compared with Diana, who is so full of life". In July 1997, just before her 50th birthday, 68% of those polled for the Daily Mirror said Charles should be free to marry Camilla. William Hill cut the odds of the couple marrying before the turn of the century from 6-1 to 3-1. Two months later, Diana was dead.

As Diana worshippers clamoured for vengeance, Camilla returned to her privacy. In fact, as reported by the kindly Higgins, she "temporarily vanished from view while she supported Prince Charles, giving him hope for the future". Business as usual, really. When she came to vulgar notice in 1992, with the publication of extracts from Andrew Morton's Diana: Her True Story, Camilla had been avoiding public notice and giving Prince Charles hope for the future for a good decade or two already.

The press only caught on when Morton transcribed Diana's charge that Camilla had haunted her marriage since her honeymoon, with the implication that the affair with Charles had resumed, and was now callously conducted in full view of staff, neighbours and friends. The day the extracts appeared, Camilla's home fell under siege. "It's fiction, it's fiction," said a helpless Andrew Parker-Bowles.

According to the rushed biographies that followed, Camilla Shand, the scantily educated daughter of a master of foxhounds, and great grand-daughter of Alice Keppel, mistress of Edward VII, had instantly appealed to Prince Charles when they met in 1972. Although not, as they say, photogenic, Camilla is reputed to have had many other charms, "animal magnetism" foremost among them. And crucially, as Jonathan Dimbleby recorded in his hagiography, "she was convulsed by the Goons".

Royal-watching mythology has it that, on their first encounter, Camilla propositioned Charles thus: "My great-grandmother and your great-great-grandfather were lovers. So how about it?" The animal magnetism did its bit. "It finally made him a man," one of Camilla's "friends" told Christopher Wilson, the author of A Greater Love, Charles and Camilla.

Which makes it all the more ungrateful that the newly virile Prince Charles promptly embarked on an eight-month cruise aboard HMS Minerva. By the time he returned, Camilla had married a cavalry officer called Andrew Parker-Bowles, a match that appeared, at the time, to have been made in animal magnetism heaven.

So the royal dalliance was put on hold. But after the Parker-Bowleses had had their two children, Camilla and Charles's feelings would no longer be denied. "To most of the population," Christopher Wilson remarks, "theirs was a passion which simply did not exist. But a privileged few were witness to an astonishing display of the almost animal attraction that the two now had for each other." At the Cirencester Polo Club Ball, he reports, the pair were seen "kissing each other, French kissing, dance after dance". On another occasion, a "trusted friend" reported, the heir to the throne was unable to resist the attractions of Camilla's favourite dress: "Charles took one look at it, plunged his hands down the front and grabbed her breasts. In mixed company, that is not the done thing." Indeed not.

Charles bought a new house, Highgrove, because it was close to Bolehyde Manor, the recently acquired seat of the Parker-Bowleses, and the magnetic twosome, now nicely settled, set about procuring the prince an official wife.

Once Diana had been installed, the affair temporarily ceased, only to be reignited as the royal marriage disintegrated. "Camilla was normal," contends Christopher Wilson. "She was grown up. She was womanly, with voluptuous curves, not a bag of bones. She was sexually adventurous. And she was, in all truth, a very nice woman." Who could ask for more?

As Charles later pointed out in a television interview, his marriage had "irretrievably broken down" by the time he and Camilla resumed extra-marital proceedings. Andrew Parker-Bowles was allegedly happy to try his luck elsewhere. Diana was enjoying riding lessons with James Hewitt. There was nothing – unless you count the princes and the Parker-Bowleses' children, and, perhaps, Charles's future as Defender of the Faith – to stand in the path of true love. Had Diana not told Morton about the arrangement, it might have gone on for years, even become the done thing. But in December 1992, six months after Morton's revelations, John Major announced a royal separation. Outside her house, Camilla gave a statement: "If something has gone wrong I'm very sorry for them," she said. "But I know nothing more than the average person in the street. I only know what I see on television."

Her fib was exposed just a few weeks later when newspapers published a taped conversation between the Prince and Mrs Parker-Bowles. Camilla was not, it made clear, "an average person in the street". Unless, that is, average persons in the street are in the habit of calling Charles at midnight, and telling him they miss him desperately, desperately, desperately. There was more. Loyal subjects were touched by a section in which the faithful Bowles beseeched the Prince to let her see his latest speech. Most of the tape, however, comprised complicated arrangements for future assignations and lustful declarations. Camilla: "I need you all the week, all the time." Charles: "Oh, God, I'll just live inside your trousers or something." It was suggested, to their shared amusement, that Charles be reincarnated as a Tampax. So this was what animal magnetism sounded like.

At the time, the tape seemed to constitute a blow from which the royal family – and Charles in particular – would never recover. How, after this, would the prince ever dare to lecture his subjects on aesthetics, on the English language, on spirituality? But the damage to the prince's reputation was short-lived. Within months of what could have been eternal disgrace, Prince Charles was droning away like 10 men, as if nothing had happened, on everything from the horrors of modern architecture to his role as "Defender of the Divine".

In fact, those who wish the royal family would keep their opinions to themselves owe a debt of gratitude to Camilla Parker-Bowles. One might go further. Until the dreadful day earlier this month when Camilla was formally conversed with by the Queen, she was the model royal: shy, opinion-free, almost invisible. If she has opinions on GM foods, she is to be congratulated on not sharing them with us. If she cares, like her boyfriend, about Shakespeare, Islam and organic carrots, she has done the decent thing of never mentioning it. It was too good too last. Sooner or later, Camilla would have to become a role model, like her ghastly future in-laws. Not long after Diana's death, Charles's spivs got to work. Camilla was seen out and about, she was reputed to be tolerated by the young princes, and now, less than three years since she seemed to be doomed to life as a Chippenham-based anchoress, Camilla is inches away from public acceptability. The archbishop of Canterbury offers consolation over tea. She entertains Scottish prelates with her prince. Last week 68% of Mirror readers said she and Charles should marry. William Hill's odds on the pair getting hitched within a year have dropped to 6-4. Tabloids that would once have rejoiced to see her hung, drawn and quartered now scream, "Marry her!"

If nothing is done, it is only a matter of time before Charles's privacy-loving helpmeet is up there beside him, planting trees, cutting ribbons, and preaching the joys of Islam, or reed-bed sanitation units, or whatever her partner's latest hobby happens to be. For however earthy, independent and sensible Camilla may be in other respects, when it comes to the massive folly of worshipping a twerp like Charles, she is peerless. Remember her "great achievement"? "Your great achievement is to love me," Charles said, unbelievably, on that tape. And even more unbelievably, Camilla took it as a compliment. If only we could attribute it to her Goonish sense of humour. •

21 March 2000

Leanda de Lisle
The king and I

Would the Queen be more popular with Australians if she chowed down with them at barbecues? Matthew Engel in this newspaper certainly suggested recently that "ordinary guy", King Harald of Norway, could teach her a "thing or two".

However, in my experience an ordinary royal is an oxymoron. They may ride bicycles, but they are always on pedestals – and they look to each other, not for lessons, but for a safety net when they fall off them. I studied with interest the Guardian's photograph of the previous King of Norway – Olav V – travelling on a tram. It was taken about a year before he came to lunch at my parent's terraced house in London.

It was an event that proved about as "ordinary" as a Martian landing. I was 14, an age when you are desperate to blend in with your peers. This proved difficult when, in the middle of a class, my teacher announced, "Leanda is now going off for lunch with a king. " I concentrated very hard on piling up my exercise books as one of those peers goaded, "I didn't know you knew any kings, Leanda."

Indeed I hadn't made friends with any kings down at the local Wimpy Bar. However, from what I'd heard, my father had almost grown up with the Norwegian royal family. They had lived in his parents' house in Berkshire for much of the second world war. I didn't wonder at the time why this should be, since there is no accounting for the behaviour of one's parents or grandparents. Nevertheless, I did worry what our neighbours and the regulars in our street's five pubs, would make of the Rolls-Royce that drew up outside our front door.

The area we lived in – Brook Green in west London – is now so chic that it is difficult to believe that it was working class until less than 20 years ago. But it was so, and there were few cars there besides my parents' old Ford Cortina.

The image of the king's impossibly big, curvaceous and shiny Rolls-Royce still stays with me. When it arrived, it looked like a patent leather clad duchess parked on the dusty curb. On its bonnet a flag fluttered in the breeze. Clearly King Olav V had decided against visiting us incognito.

Why was he coming to visit? My great-uncle, Sir Cecil Dormer had been the British minister in Norway when the Nazis invaded in 1940. He persuaded King Haakon VII, together with the then Crown Prince Olav and the entire Norwegian cabinet to flee on the HMS Devonshire.

While at sea, the Devonshire received a message. The aircraft carrier Glorious and two escort destroyers, had come under German attack. The signal was ignored. The official story is that it had been too garbled for the captain, Admiral Cunningham, to make sense of. However witnesses have since said that it was perfectly clear. Not long after, Glorious and her escorts sank. There were 900 men who went into the water, but the Devonshire kept to her course and maintained radio silence. Three days later a passing Norwegian trawler rescued a mere 41 survivors.

I expect the lunches Admiral Cunningham attended at my grandparents' house were rather different from the one I served for the Norwegian king, squeezing my way around the chairs in our tiny London dining room.

However my father remembered the etiquette: he told me that I must not eat after the king had finished his food. Unfortunately by the time I'd sat down after serving each course, the king had had his fill and I was left staring forlornly at my plate.

The meal then concluded with him falling asleep. He appeared to be very old. It seems strange to me that his life might once have meant as much as that of 900 young men.

However, the lives of the Norwegian royal family were important not only to the British government, for whom they had propaganda value, but to George VI. Saving his uncle-in-law and first cousin might have helped expunge the memory of other royal cousins who had needed his family's help, but were left to die.

For both the British and Norwegian royal families, the other battleship that never came was the one that failed to rescue the Tsar and his family after 1917. King Haakon said to my grandparents that he offered to send a battleship for the Tsar, but George V, his brother-in-law, had told him not to bother: he would do so himself.

Documents about the 1917-18 imprisonment of the imperial family have been removed from the British royal archives. However, George V's campaign to refuse the Tsar asylum is well recorded. My grandparents always said King Haakon never forgave him for the Tsar's subsequent death. In 1940, King Haakon and Crown Prince Olav were not to be allowed to suffer the same fate. •

12 June 2000

Simon Hattenstone

So what exactly do you do for a living, ma'am?

Thursday, 25 May

MEDICAL SIMULATION CENTRE, ST BARTHOLOMEW'S HOSPITAL

"Could you brush away the water?" says the senior anaesthetist. "I'm worried about the little depression collecting in the pavement." The hospital cleaner scrubs for all he's worth. Which, in money terms, isn't much. As the Bentley rolls through the front entrance, he vanishes to order.

"They're almost here," shouts an excitable doctor.

"Just as well. I'm freezing," says another senior bod, with a seditious rub of his hands.

We are waiting in two lines at the King George V entrance. One line is for the anaes-thetists. The other sad, diminished line is for the journalists – the Press Association's royal correspondent, his photographer, and me. The Princess Royal doesn't like the hack pack. Never has done.

In 1962, when she was 12, Anne was on holiday and took an introverted turn for the worse. "Princess upset by overexuberance of French photographers" read one head-line. The media may have been a less ferocious beast in those days, but as far as Anne was concerned it was still very much a beast. Every incident in her life was dutifully reported. In January 1964, we learned that "Princess Anne joined with other local youngsters in a paper chase on ponies in Sandringham woods". A year later "Princess Anne stayed indoors at Valduz castle with a slight cold".

It has to be said that the hack pack has never cared much for Anne, either. As a young woman she was considered aloof, abrupt, staid. As a woman approaching 50, she is respected as the hardest-working royal – close on 500 official engagements in Britain last year. Respected, but hardly liked.

The Guardian has put in a request to Buckingham Palace. We'd like to follow Anne for two or three days, snatch a few words between openings. Felicity Murdo-Smith, her PA, takes a week to reach a decision. No way. Perhaps I could observe her at the British Knitting and Clothing Export Council where, as president, she will attend the AGM? Felicity says that's up to the knitters. Sorry, say the knitters, private do. What about the preview of Christie's sporting art sale which she will attend as president of the Animal Health Trust? 'Fraid not, says Christie's; private. Surely the Worshipful Company of Farmers will allow me to attend lunch with Anne, their Junior Warden? Maybe not, but they promise to send on all the bumf.

Despair is setting in when St Bartholomew's say they'd be delighted to entertain me. Of course there's no chance of talking to Anne, but they're happy to let me share a room with her as she opens the simulation centre.

Anne steps out of the Bentley, a vision in yellow. We follow her past the Queen Elizabeth II wing. It must be strange, forever shadowing your heritage; there's Mum, Great Granddad, Great-Great-Great-Grandma. Every stop is punctuated by hand-shakes. Actually, only Anne shakes hands; the dignitaries are shaking a black glove. I ask Peter Archer, the Press Association's royal correspondent, whether she wears gloves because she doesn't want to be polluted by the masses. No, he says – if you had to shake as many hands as she does, your digits would get sore. He says the Queen goes through a pair a day. In his six years on the job, Anne has never uttered a word to Peter. Diana, of course, would often stroll over for a chat, and since her death Charles has learned to do the same. Anne's way of acknowledging him is to walk past, head buried in her chest. He admires her for it, says she is her father's daughter: no-nonsense, businesslike. What, though, is her business?

Anne became president of the Save the Children Fund at 19. Now she is patron of 222 organisations. She has said that her role is to make the most of her position; to burst into the offices of corporate bosses, grab them by the ears and demand what they can do for her starving children.

A handful of prize-winners are invited to shake Anne's glove. "How long have you been here?" she asks. Whenever Anne asks a question, she bounces on her feet. As she listens she clenches and unclenches her hand behind her back. Maybe the gloves irritate her.

The ceremony climaxes with the unveiling of a plaque. Anne draws back the curtain. "The Medical Simulation Centre, opened by HRH the Princess Royal, 25th May 2000." She stands to the side, proofreads and nods.

A crowd of patients has gathered in the drizzle to wave her off. Some are in pyjamas, and one has a drip attached. She doesn't seem to have seen them. They disperse, walk back to their wards, say it would have been nice if she'd waved back.

Friday, 26 May
QUEEN ANNE'S SCHOOL, READING

The palace laughs when I ask to attend the European Forum for Victim Services reception at Windsor Castle. But not even Felicity can banish me from the opening of the sports centre at Queen Anne's School. A sporting day for a sporting woman. In 1971 she won the European three-day event at Burghley. That year she was named Britain's sportswoman of the year, and was the subject of a series of profiles. Anne didn't fit an easy stereotype. Some said she was sullen, peeved that she wasn't going to be queen. Others said she was happy to be a maverick from the Hemingway school of adventurers.

On the train, I jot down questions, just in case. Which event has meant most to her in the past week? Does she ever wish she had a normal job? Does she prefer to be called Your Royal Highness, or Ma'am, or Annie? Are any of her friends republicans?

On the few occasions she does grant interviews, it is to advance her own agenda. Last week she talked to trade magazine The Grocer to say that GM foods are quite groovy, actually, and put one over on her elder brother. Interviewees have to submit questions beforehand, and the sheet is returned with all but the anodyne lashed out.

Queen Anne's is a girls' public school, £12,500 a year. After years of planning, the day has turned into a disaster. It's pissing down. The fireworks are cancelled; the parents, cooped up in the library, are trying to make the best of it. "This is bad luck for them. Dreadful. Every time I put on my boots the heavens open," says one man, flicking the rain from his face.

The sports centre is magnificent. In the gym, 14 girls are engaged in an abdominal workout. Anne is 15 minutes late, and by the time she arrives, they are exhausted. We move off to the basketball court, lacrosse, aerobics, the rockery. Anne occasionally pauses to ask that question: "How long have you been at this school?"

As Anne talks to the children, she bounces on her heels, clenching and unclenching her gloved hands. Many people say she can be funny and spiky and irreverent, yet she is loth to show it in public. As if it were beneath her dignity. As well as the horses, she's a fine lacrosse player, a crack shot on the shooting range. She once broke Patrick

Lichfield's lap record on his private speedway circuit. How can she watch those girls chucking basketballs and not ask for a shot? Perhaps she worries that the girls will go home and say: "I met Princess Anne and she was a right good laugh."

I'm within hugging distance of her. Just as my mouth opens for the first question, a discreet security man ushers me back towards the stairs.

Anne starts her speech with a joke. "May I point out that the Princess Royal who visited here in 1929 was not me." She congratulates the school for the sports centre, then draws back the velvet curtain. The plaque tells her what she has just done. She stands to the side, reads and nods her approval.

"What's the point of her coming here?" says 18-year-old Rowena Barber. "If she was coming to raise some money, maybe. But she isn't." Her friend, Catherine Davison, agrees. "If this was a state school, fair enough. A visit from royalty could show them they are valued. But feeling undervalued isn't a problem here."

The two head girls are giving Anne an upbeat send-off. "Three cheers for the prin..." They stop, realising they have botched the protocol, and start again. "Three cheers for Her Royal Highness. Hip hip, hoorah!"

A rope divides the princess and sporting volunteers from the mass of pupils. Row after row bend an ear to listen. After her speech, she shakes gloves with the headmistress and leaves without a glance in their direction. Anne looks like she needs a good ironing.

Wednesday, 31 May
HAMMERSMITH AND FULHAM CARERS' CENTRE
Felicity gets quite unpleasant when I suggest asking Anne a few questions about her work with carers. "No, no, no! " she says. "I've already told your colleague you can't interview her. No! " I tell Felicity she is not allowing us to see the princess in her best light.

The carers' centre is a place where all ages come for respite – some look after elderly partners, some are kids looking after their families. A photographer in the waiting room is complaining about his treatment. "The policeman on the door said, 'How do I know you're a photographer?' and I said, 'Because I've got a press card that says photographer, issued by the Metropolitan police.'"

I ask the administrator how long they've been preparing for the big day. "Oh, months," she says. "It's been murder! We've had the whole of the outside painted, and that was just the start." It reminds me of the time when Rajiv Gandhi was visiting a rainy suburb of Delhi, and the local authority had the pavements raised for him.

In the corner, Albert the clown is teaching the children circus skills. Daniel Meekings is balancing on an iron globe. He's seven, the youngest carer at the centre, and looks after his deaf sister. Does he know who Anne is? He spreads his hand in baffled awe. "Her family rules the country."

It's four days since I last saw Anne. In the meantime she's changed her gloves and attended the Army Families Federation Conference and the commemoration of the new roof of the choir of Paisley Abbey in Scotland. She seems more animated today, and praises the kids' homework club. "It's not eashy to conshentrate on school. Care is about creating time for yourshelves." It's taken me a week to realise who that deep, slurred voice reminds me of: Bill Deedes. A girl presents her with a bouquet. It looks the same as the last one. What does she do with them all? Does she like flowers?

She smiles at a little girl and for a second I think she's going to swoop her up and drop a big sloppy kiss on her cheek. Instead, she bounces on her feet, flexes her hand and asks how long she has been coming to the centre. The trouble is that Anne refuses to acknowledge she is in the PR business – PR for her charities and, these days, PR for her family. The only way she can measure herself is by the money raised for her causes. And there is nothing the hospital or the public school or the carers' centre would like more than a soft-focus newspaper picture of a sunny princess fighting their corner.

A while ago, Anne was interviewed about her work for Save the Children. The interviewer, desperate for colour, asked for one memory that stood out, one anecdote. She refused to provide it, implying that it would be invidious. But perhaps it all begins to merge. Perhaps, like many of us, she lives a Groundhog Day existence. She was once asked what she would have done if she'd not been a princess. She said she'd like to have been a long-distance lorry driver.

It's time to leave. Another day's work done. The plaque is unveiled. She opens the velvet curtain. "To commemorate the visit of her Royal Highness the Princess Royal to the Hammersmith and Fulham Carers' Centre on Wednesday 31st May 2000." She stands to the side, reads, and nods her approval. "Smashing," she says. •

* * *

13 May 2000

Saira Shah
Plain tales from the hills

Princess Diana glides closer to her faithful retainer James Hewitt and begs him to give her the affection that her playboy husband Charles cannot. Hewitt, resplendent in naval uniform, is moved. Heavy black liner accentuates the torment in his eyes and his breast quivers. "No Diana!" he protests. Violins in the orchestra pit strike up. Under a shaky chandelier, the loyal lover embraces his beloved. The couple clinch. The audience goes wild.

This is not a made-for-TV dramatisation of the life of a late member of the British royal family. It is a theatrical event that has enraptured villagers in one of India's remotest regions. The Diana myth has, in just a few months, transformed the seemingly doomed fortunes of a five-century old travelling theatre tradition in Assam. Many in the audience have never heard of Diana, but the theatre group claims her story has an important message about marital fidelity for the humblest villager.

"Princess Diana's story is a morality play," says Mukib Ahmed, who plays Prince Charles. "Even in Assam we have cases of husbands who are unfaithful to their wives. In Diana's case, it ended in tragedy. We can learn from her life."

The travelling theatre began with the efforts of a 15th century moralist and religious reformer, Shankar Deb, to educate the Assamese away from the brutal practices of Tantric Hinduism. In a new book, To The Elephant's Graveyard, Tarquin Hall describes a popular method of divination: examining a nine-month foetus cut from the body of its mother. Appalled, Shankar Deb founded Vashnavite Hinduism, prevalent in Assam to this day.

To spread his new values of decency and uprightness, his followers travelled from village to village performing yatra, morality plays. In an area starved for entertainment, these soon became immensely popular. Today, the painted lorries heralding the troupe's arrival are greeted rapturously by villagers. Daily chores cease, and an impromptu four-day carnival begins. Stalls selling sweetmeats and snacks spring up. Village youths lounge outside the tent on their motorcycles, hoping some of the glamour of theatre will be sprinkled on them. As dusk falls, the entire community converges upon the theatre. Many have walked for miles. The bamboo stage is enormous and the tent seats 2,000. There is a portable generator so plays may be performed in villages with no electricity.

It is an expensive business. There are about 100 people in the troupe, including cast, costume and make-up personnel, a full orchestra, engineers and cooks. Travelling theatre has survived because Assam's remoteness meant little competition. The region has largely resisted the lure of Bollywood films in Hindi. But the recent growth of cinema in Assamese is a greater threat. So large is the appetite for these films, with their lurid plots featuring sex and violence, that fights for tickets have exploded outside the mobile cinemas that tour the villages.

The Abahan Theatrical group decided to fight back by staging blockbusters with an added moral dimension. Its first experiment last year was a production of Titanic, based on the plot of James Cameron's film. It was a success, and this year the group launched into its most ambitious project, a locally-scripted version of the life and death of Diana. The play is an unlikely triumph, with distance lending an intriguing cultural twist. A team of researchers sifted through contemporary writing about the late princess, including biographies and back copies of Hello! magazine.

The challenges are amazing. "I have seen still pictures of Camilla," says Likuma Sharma, who plays the woman referred to in the play as Camilla Parker-Bowels, "but I have never had a chance to see film or video of her. That is very important for an actress to get a chance to see how she talks, how she moves. I had to guess all that and I have managed very well."

Details are slightly askew. Charles is glamorous, given to disco dancing. Likuma, who once played basketball for Assam, portrays Camilla as a young nymph. Diana is a poor girl from a humble family and James Hewitt is the unlikely hero. The Queen and her press officer meet outside the gates of Buckingham Palace, where the Queen laments Diana's lack of breeding, intending to have the girl live in the palace where she can be taught etiquette. The press officer suggests that she be dispatched to Kensington Palace instead, where Hewitt can mould her into a member of the family.

On the deck of the royal yacht Britannia, Diana bemoans that they have passed "Gibraltar, Sicily, the Suez Canal and Algeria" and yet still the press follow: as indeed they do, bobbing in a rowing boat on the muslin sea. Charles, meanwhile, openly consorts with Camilla. The day after his wedding to Diana he gives his mistress a necklace proclaiming: "Diana may be Princess of Buckingham Palace, but you are Queen of my heart."

The production is remarkable for its meticulous detail: the props include a Mercedes, motorcycles for the paparazzi, a helicopter that flies around the stage and a scale model of Britannia. The finale is the crash in the Paris underpass. "I've never seen pictures of the accident, but I'd heard about it," said Rajen Shah, technical engineer in charge of sets. "I thought surely we could re-create it. I hope I haven't made any mistakes."

The director refused to stage the play until he had searched Assam for the perfect Diana lookalike. The brunette, buxom Jubilee Rajkumari (she adopted the name Jubilee in honour of the part) bears little similarity to Diana, but on stage, with white makeup, her sideways glance under lowered lashes seemed oddly familiar.

The production is two and a half hours long and, even to non-Assamese speakers, absorbing. Dialogue is interspersed with musical numbers and farce, such as the scene in which Diana is smuggled out of Buckingham Palace gates in a black Islamic veil, or when the paparazzi bribe Palace guards for an interview.

Not all critics approve of it. "The ancient art of yatra has been trivialised by the adoption of western themes, such as Titanic and Diana," the Indian film actress Moon Moon Sen says. "It may allow the theatre to survive, but the religious art itself is dead." The play shows how, less than three years after her death, Diana is a legend, with the power of myth even for the villagers of Assam, most of them tea-growers. One man queuing patiently for tickets to the show says: "I earn 10,000 rupees a month. One ticket costs 1,000 rupees, so to afford tickets for all my family, I had to save for many weeks. But we all want to learn about Princess Diana. She cared about the common people. She is like Mother Teresa."

The play's success has guaranteed the Abahan group's immediate survival, and prolonged the art form into the 21st century. There is even talk of bringing the production to Britain. The company is already planning next year's play, based on the recent hijacking of the Indian Airlines jumbo jet by Kashmiri separatists. •

Photo opportunity

The days when Guardian colour was only in the words of reporters have gone for good. Now photographers file brilliant colour pictures from all over the world, but the impact of the occasional photo demonstrates that black and white can have its own colour value.

Children among the 250,000 homeless people after the floods in Mozambique (see page 41).

PHOTOGRAPH: MARTIN GODWIN

Above: End of the peer show – Lord Monk Bretton at Westminster
after not becoming one of the Lords' chosen (see page 55).
PHOTOGRAPH: JOHN STILLWELL

Opposite top: Spad — signal passed at danger — became a homely acronym
for a disastrous common practice after the Paddington rail disaster.
PHOTOGRAPH: FRANK BARON

Opposite bottom: Probationary santas prepare for training in Mile End, London.
PHOTOGRAPH MARTIN GODWIN

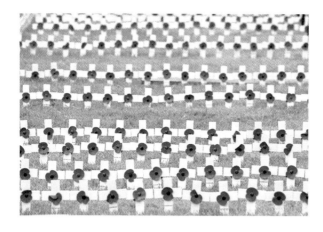

Left: Cutting the cost of remembering with plastic instead of wooden Remembrance Day crosses at Westminster Abbey

PHOTOGRAPH: BRIAN HARRIS

Below: Welding a Vosper Thornycroft trimaran warship into sea shape in Southampton.

PHOTOGRAPH: ROGER BAMBER

Above: Time runs out for Carnforth station,
where Brief Encounter was filmed (see page 63).

PHOTOGRAPH: DON McPHEE

Below: Celia Johnson and Trevor Howard in Britain's
favourite weepie, Brief Encounter (see page 63)

Above: Long way go see: Ullswater is Britain's
foremost attraction for Japanese tourists
PHOTOGRAPH: DON McPHEE

Opposite: Beefing up production as British farmers
intensify precautions against BSE.
PHOTOGRAPH: MURDO MacLEOD

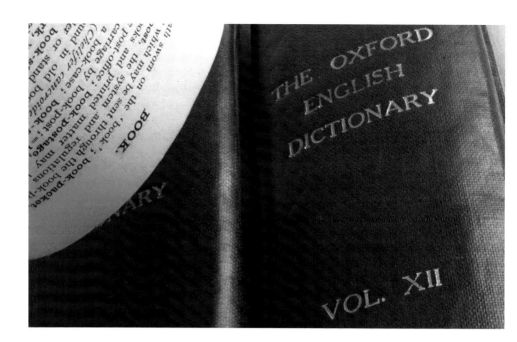

Top: End of the run? The online edition may kill off the hard copy (see page 81)

PHOTOGRAPH: ROGER TOOTH

Opposite: The year when doing something good beat doing something that seemed a good idea at the time. Sir Nicholas Serota's Tate Modern scooped as the Millennium Dome drew derision (see pages 107 and 108).

PHOTOGRAPH: EAMONN McCABE

Bottom: All lit up and nowhere to go (see page 173)

PHOTOGRAPH: GRAHAM TURNER

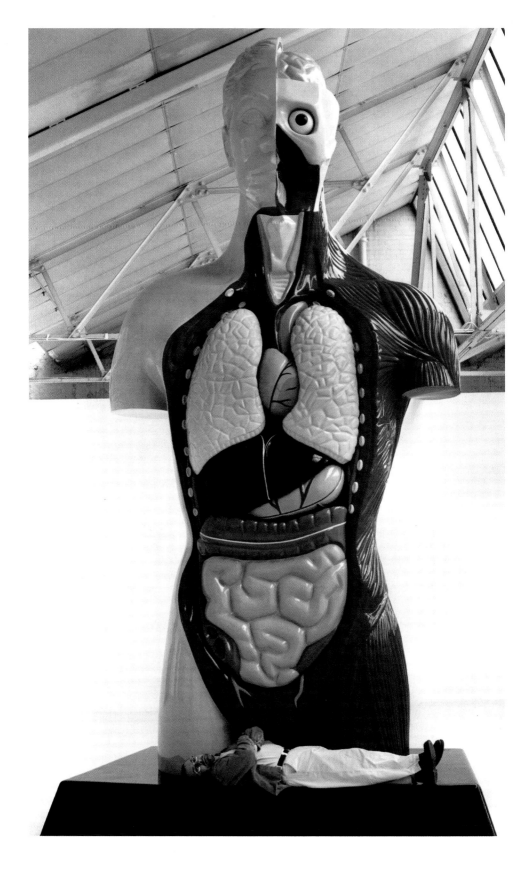

Above: Bridget Riley at work: she gets a gallery at the
Tate Modern for stripes stretching from the 60s.
PHOTOGRAPH: EAMONN McCABE

Opposite: A laid back Damien Hirst with
his sculpture Hymn, inspired by an educational toy
to whose maker the artist paid compensation to avoid legal action.
PHOTOGRAPH: EAMONN McCABE

Top: On yer Beijing bike: Chinese artists at the
Institute of Contemporary Arts in London with a show
constituting a demonstration against censorship.
PHOTOGRAPH: MARTIN ARGLES

Bottom: Royal College of Art students put 2,002 works on sale to raise funds.
PHOTOGRAPH: SEAN SMITH

Opposite: Edinburgh burning its Viking boats during a week-long millennium clebration.
PHOTOGRAPH: MURDO MacLEOD

Above: Sir Garfield Sobers, of little Barbados and the wide universe (see page 265).

PHOTOGRAPH: JANE BOWN

Opposite: Taking off in the 125cc class in the British motocross championships at Canada Heights in Kent.

PHOTOGRAPH: TOM JENKINS

Below: Alastair Hetherington, a great Guardian editor and fell walker, died aged 79 (see page 281)

Ian Dury, rock musician, bawdy humourist, wit,
music hall philosopher, died aged 57 (see page 276).

PHOTOGRAPH: EAMONN McCABE

Here and there

6 March 2000

Nick Davies
The great divide

Today is speech day at Roedean College. The string orchestra plays Mozart as the parents gather in the centenary hall. They have come to hear the report on the state of the school, to join the applause for the retiring staff and to watch the three head girls deliver their review of the year, but most of all, these mothers and fathers have come to salute the achievements of their children.

The headteacher, Patricia Metham, calls the girls up one by one, announcing their awards and their prizes and their exam results. "Irina Allport, eight and a half passes at GCSE. Leonara Bowen, nine and a half passes. Angelica Chan, 11 passes." The applause drenches the hall.

Mrs Metham says the school's results are the best in Sussex and place Roedean high in the first division of league tables. And the future? "For those at Roedean," she declares, "it need hold no terrors."

Down the grassy hill, on the far side of the Roedean playing fields, on this October Saturday it is just another morning on the Whitehawk estate – lads belting a football around East Brighton park, dogs sniffing at the dustbins. Whitehawk is a sprawl of terraced red-brick houses, home to something like 11,000 people, most of them white, many of them out of work. Whitehawk is the poorest estate in Brighton and one of the poorest 10% in the country.

While Patricia Metham is celebrating success, another headteacher is having a very different experience. Libby Coleman spent three long years as the headteacher of Stanley Deason comprehensive school on the Whitehawk estate and now she sits at home, less than a mile away, staring out at the sea and looking back over those years that began with so much hope when she had no idea – really, none at all – that by the time she left, her career as a head, her health and the school would all be in ruins.

This is the story of two women. In many ways, they are quite separate – the secure and confident head of the famous old private school where almost every pupil scores at least five top grades at GCSE, and the rueful and defeated head of the state school where only 10% of the children could achieve the same marks.

The two women have never met. The strip of land between Roedean and Whitehawk marks the most notorious division in British society. And yet, for all this separation, the women have this in common: that after several decades in teaching they know what makes schools tick.

A few weeks before Roedean's speech day, Tony Blair appeared on Channel 4 news and talked about this same division. He made clear how passionately he wants state schools to match the results of their private counterparts. You can see why. There are 550,000 children in private schools. They count for a mere 7% of the pupil population and yet provide more than 20% of those who make it to university and nearly 50% of those who go to Oxford and Cambridge. A Financial Times survey of A-level results last year revealed that all but 13 of the top 100 schools were in the private sector. In the private schools 80% of pupils pass five or more GCSEs at grades A-C; in the state schools only 43% reach the same standard.

Why is this happening? In government circles, the answer has been agreed for years: teachers in state schools fail to do their job properly. The analysis is alarming: over a period of 30 years, beginning in the 60s, the quest for excellence was undermined by an obsession with equality; student teachers were injected with a theory of child-centred learning that poisoned the heart of pedagogy, allowing the pupil to dictate the pace and direction of teaching; discipline and effort were banned from classrooms where no child might now be accused of failure; whole-class instruction gave way to groups of children ambling along; criticism was replaced by consolation, and achievement was subverted by a poverty of expectation.

By contrast, according to this view, the private schools were innoculated from this progressive disease by their tradition of competitive achievement.

This perspective was born on the right as a rebuttal to the comprehensive movement. It was expressed with clarity by the former Tory education minister, George Walden, in his book, We Should Know Better: "The idea that every child can advance at his or her pace by informal, non-competitive techniques that favour spontaneity over effort is a beautiful dream which, lodged in impressionable minds and given scientific status, becomes unconscious dogma. In reality, it leads to overstressed teachers, low aspirations for the gifted and ungifted alike, bored or disaffected pupils, and an enormous waste of time and money. The contrast with the private sector needs little emphasis."

Rightwing journalists pursued the same critique with passion and found that, in opposition, Tony Blair's Labour party had joined their crusade. It is now close to the heart of New Labour's approach to education to see private schools not as an enemy to be abolished, but as a partner to be emulated – as "a benchmark of best practice". In the three months before Roedean's speech day, both the head of Ofsted, Chris Woodhead, and the minister for school standards, Estelle Morris, spoke at conferences of private headteachers, stressing admiration for their work. Since May 1997 the government has invested £1.6m in bridge-building schemes to allow state-school pupils to enjoy the techniques of private-school teaching.

It is explicit in this analysis that the strength of private schools is not to be explained by their intake of highly motivated children from affluent families, compared with the deprived and demotivated children in some state schools – in the government's words, "poverty is no excuse". Nor is it to be explained by the extra resources or smaller class sizes in private schools, as Mr Woodhead has explained repeatedly, pointing instead to "a toxic mix of educational beliefs and mismanagement". As the department for education recently told the Guardian: "The quality of teaching is the main thing."

Libby Coleman was full of hope when she arrived at Whitehawk. It was January 1995. She had already been a head for 10 years, first in Northampton and then in Barnet, and she had done well – and yet she wanted something different. In both her schools, she had seen deprived children struggling to make the grade and she believed she could help them, that poverty was no reason for failure.

She was excited by all the new ideas that were bubbling out of the political world – literacy hours, numeracy hours, mentors, beacon schools – and so she had decided to move to a school that was really struggling and to try to use these ideas to turn it around.

Stanley Deason was struggling with poverty. Ms Coleman was struck by two things: some 45% of its pupils were poor enough to claim free school meals, and almost all of them were white. There were no aspiring immigrants here, pushing their children to succeed. These were second- and third-generation long-term unemployed. By the time the children reached Stanley Deason many of them had fallen way behind. Among the year seven children she found only 10% had a reading age of 11. And the attendance was terrible. On average, each morning, only 72% of pupils were turning up. By the afternoon, even more had faded away.

Ms Coleman was undaunted. She could do it, she was sure. As the weeks passed, she found the kids had a wildness in them. There were children who reeked of lighter fluid: they had soaked their shirts in the stuff and hooked them over their faces to suck in the fumes. One boy had started working as a prostitute down on the Brighton waterfront: as far as Ms Coleman could find out, he had originally been seduced by his stepfather who had tried to cash in by taking the lad to Amsterdam to sell him in the brothels there.

Then she was dealing with a lovely, bright girl who had the intelligence to reach the top level in her Sats tests but she wouldn't speak. Not a sound. Ms Coleman had come across such muteness before – it is often a sign of abuse. But she was told there was hardly any point pursuing it: there was so much sexual abuse on Whitehawk that unless you had real evidence no one was going to try to prove it.

In Whitehawk, she learned, the apparently simple could rapidly become bizarre and frightening. She was asked to find a place for a 14-year-old boy who had been expelled from another school. As soon as she met him she could see he had good in him but, within days, the boy was abducted from the estate by three men who drove him to some woods and raped him. She had the boy and his mother in afterwards to talk about it, but the mother was incoherent with tears and the boy attacked her. There was nothing she could do. He ended up in a locked ward.

The parents were as troubled as the children. She held an open day for new parents but a group of them turned on a young mother who had been a pupil there with them years ago and started bullying her, just as they had done as children. Some parents disappeared; one ran off to London with her pimp, leaving her boy with his blind grandmother.

Still, this was why she had come here, to help kids in this kind of trouble. She was sure she would be all right. But if there was a problem that worried her it was in the staffroom. From the first she had been warned she was in trouble. The vice-chairman of the governors, a man called Robert Metcalfe, universally known as "Met", was apparently dead set against her. Having retired as the school's deputy head, he seemed to look upon the place as his personal fiefdom. He had backed another candidate for head and lost. Now he was telling anyone who would listen that this Coleman woman was no bloody good. She was warned that Met had several friends in the staffroom who were sewing the seeds of dissent. They were saying she would be out in less than six months.

Patricia Metham's study is a peaceful place. There is a group of wicker chairs in front of the fireplace, a Persian rug, a collection of sculpted hands, a computer, a printer, a teddy bear, a neat and tidy desk and a picture window looking down over the playing fields to the sea. Mrs Metham is intelligent, forceful and clear in her thinking. First of all, she is clear that Roedean is not the private school of familiar cliche, all fresh air and hockey sticks. It is a place of academic excellence but, more than that, she says, it is a place of breadth, which prizes drama and dance and sport and music. Even more than that, she wants it to be a place for free thinkers. She was rather proud to find one of her old girls leading a rent strike at Oxford last year. "Intelligent independence" is her mantra.

It may be for this reason that although she knows what ministers and conservative journalists say about private schools such as hers, she does not agree with them. Not at all.

Teaching technique comes into their success, but her explanation has almost nothing in common with the government's analysis. It is built, first of all, on a simple foundation: the intake of children. "Those schools that dominate the league tables choose to be, and can afford to be, highly selective," she says. Every pupil who wants to enter Roedean sits an exam. The 11-year-olds who enter the school are among the brightest and the best.

Roedean puts its year seven pupils through cognitive ability tests. Last year not a single child was below the national average for non-verbal or quantitative skills. And all of them could read.

Mrs Metham goes further. It is not just that these children have their academic engines running when they reach the school, but they tend to be from homes that have impressed on them the need to take education seriously. "On the whole, we have highly motivated pupils and highly motivated parents."

This is the most important part of the story – the intake of able children from supportive families – but it is by no means the end of the explanation. Three years ago the London School of Economics produced a study that compared the educational achievements of students who went to private schools on the Tories' assisted places scheme with the achievements of those who had turned down such places.

The LSE checked the verbal and non-verbal reasoning scores of the two groups and confirmed that the two sets of students were similarly able. And yet by the time they came to take their A-levels the group who had opted for the private schools had clearly pulled ahead. First, they had sat more exams and second, they had scored better results.

Translated into A-level grades, the children who went through the private schools were achieving between one and a half and three grades higher than their equivalents who had stayed in the state sector.

The intake of children is clearly important but equally clearly, as a mass of educational research has shown, schools make a difference. The successful private schools are selecting talent. But they are also developing it.

On the Whitehawk estate, life at Stanley Deason was sometimes like being inside a threshing machine, as one incident crashed down on the tail of another. One moment there was a neighbouring school on the phone complaining that two Whitehawk girls had been down there with razor knives, trying to cut up a girl for flirting with one of their boyfriends. The next, a boy kicked out a water pipe and flooded the library below. Someone started a fire in the toilets. And then Ofsted said it wanted to inspect the place.

Still, Ms Coleman knew what she wanted. She was just not so sure if she could pay for it. Early on she had discovered that the school roll was carrying "ghost children" – at least 30 kids whose names were being ticked off on class registers, who were being funded by the local education authority, and who were essentially fictitious. Either they had been at the school but left long ago or else, so far as she could tell, they had never existed. She called her union. It was fraud, she was told, and she could go to prison. So she called the LEA and told them about it. The ghosts were exorcised from the roll and the school lost about £40,000 out of its annual budget.

At first Ms Coleman thought she could live with the loss. Miraculously, the school had managed to store up £80,000 in its reserves. Except that the money was nowhere to be found. She called in two sets of auditors in search of the cash, but it was not there.

She wanted more teachers. There was no chance of that: the whole LEA was being told to expect a cut across the board. She wanted to buy a computer program called Success Maker for the year seven children to work with on their own, stretching each child to an appropriate level. But there was no money for that. In fact, there was no money for computers and the only ones the school had were too old to take software that used Windows.

She tried to tackle the truants, calling the parents and posting attendance figures on the noticeboard. She thought it would help to give prizes for the class with the best attendance and for three pupils who most improved their attendance so she paid for the prizes herself.

The whole school was struggling to drag itself forward and she could see the stress pumping through her staff. There were teachers who simply lost it and sobbed or climbed up on chairs and started yelling at the children. She saw one teacher screaming at a boy: "You're useless, you're completely worthless." She did not know what was more upsetting – to see a teacher reduced to such hysteria or to see a child's self-respect so battered. In any case, she went off to the toilets to be sick.

There were several staff off ill. An English teacher had died and everyone said it was stress. Another had simply disappeared. There were several who developed serious illnesses: cancer of the kidney, cancer of the colon. One of the art teachers had a breakdown, the head of maths left in tears, the new science teacher cracked up and took six months off.

Only the most talented teachers could thrive against these odds. There were others who limped along, with no help or support, constantly calling in sick, forcing the school to hire supply teachers.

And then there were those who, Ms Coleman believed, should never have gone near a classroom, teachers who treated children with contempt, who were glad when they stayed away because it made life easier and who were quite happy to manhandle them.

She wanted to get rid of these really bad ones but she couldn't. It was not just that the law created a 12-month obstacle course to dismissal, policed at every stage by unions that would jump on the tiniest procedural fault, but, worse than that, she would need the support of the governors and most of the really bad teachers were also allies of Met Metcalfe, now making no secret of his desire to oust her.

Soon, she was fighting a cold war against this group of teachers. From time to time, she would discipline a teacher for manhandling a student and there would be a storm of whispers in the staffroom. Teachers who had no time for Met and his gang of troublemakers began to worry that Ms Coleman was creating a culture where children were encouraged to dish dirt on teachers, true or not. Some began to say it was her fault they were suffering such stress, because she was so quick to criticise.

Several times she went to her desk to find that someone had been through her papers. She began to take sensitive work home. As she identified problems, she found her working day stretching from eight in the morning until late at night, spilling over the weekend. Every solution seemed to spawn another problem: there were teachers who were furious when she succeeded in steering the most unruly pupils back into their classrooms. Soon, the tide of tension was reaching her, too.

She had a lurking feeling of sickness. She found she was grinding her front teeth almost all the time, she realised that her neck and shoulders were constantly tight; in fact the tension ran all the way up around her skull and into her forehead. She was smoking more and more – up to 30 a day – and she was having trouble sleeping.

Sometimes in the evening she would drink whisky to force the tiredness upon her, but then she would wake in the small hours and wander around the house, smoking and squeezing her hands. She realised just how bad she was becoming when a girl refused to come to school because she had been gang-raped – several of the boys who attacked her were in her class. The police seemed unable to do anything, and Ms Coleman could not see a solution in the classroom. So the girl left. But what really shocked the head was the realisation that her sadness for the girl had been quickly supplanted by quite a different feeling: dismay that she would lose the couple of thousand pounds' funding that went with the student. She was getting chest pains, too. But there was no time to worry about any of that. Ofsted was on the way.

By the time the inspectors arrived, in May 1996, she had been running the school for 15 months. Things had improved a little, but not enough. The Ofsted team did a good job. They told Ms Coleman what she already knew: not enough children were coming to school; too many were failing exams; the school was in deficit and was going to have to make cuts to stay alive. Privately, one of them told her, they had never come across such treachery in the staffroom.

The Ofsted inspectors offered their own version of support, but it was not one she welcomed. They suggested the school should be put into "special measures". They said it would help: the LEA would have to give more support, she could get a better budget, the staff would have to work together to keep the school open. But Ms Coleman was worried. She knew special measures could be a poisoned chalice: the school would be branded a failure and the few remaining middle-class families would run, taking precious money with them. If she was really unlucky, the best staff would start fleeing, too. And this was all the help on offer.

She went home, too exhausted to think. It was half term and she believed she was dying, she could not speak, she could only shuffle, and she stayed cocooned in fatigue, wondering whether she might be rescued by death. In the car on her way back after the break she felt one side of her body go dead. She looked in the rearview mirror and saw that her face was bloodless, her lips were grey. She managed to drive to the hospital where she was told there was nothing wrong, at least not physically.

Patricia Metham is proud to show you her school: the chapel with the neo-classical ceiling and the Byzantine marble; through the quiet cloisters to the renaissance garden; into the language labs; the science labs; and then the network of libraries containing 20,000 books, a collection of videos and CDs, and 25 computers linked to the internet.

Here is the Roedean theatre; the dance studio; the art studio, the design technology suite where some of the sixth-form girls have been stripping down an old Austin; the six indoor netball courts, two indoor cricket nets, one indoor hockey pitch, the gym and full-sized indoor pool.

It is no secret why a private school may do more for its children than a state school. Money. "If the government want state schools to offer what we offer, they are going to have to spend on each child something much closer to the fees that our parents pay," Mrs Metham says. Roedean is paid £10,260 a year for a day girl, roughly five times the amount a school like Whitehawk is given for each pupil.

Money shows not only in physical resources but at the heart of the school's business, where the teacher meets the child. The biggest classes may have 20 girls, usually a highly motivated group of the same standard, but for those who are not so confident or who are approaching big exams, classes are much smaller, sometimes as small as three. The pupil-staff ratio across the school is 8:1. And, although Mrs Metham and her staff may work hard, they are not collapsing under stress and illness.

If Patricia Metham is right – that this combination of a bright intake and adequate resources is the real foundation of her school's success – there is nevertheless more to her account. There is a third factor that finally defines the division between these two educational worlds.

Libby Coleman knew her school was one step away from closure. She turned to the authorities for help, but the education department took five months to authorise her action plan; the LEA was being broken up, Ofsted was supposed to come back each term but disappeared for a year. She was alone. Worse, the announcement of special measures was driving families away; that meant the budget was being cut and the governors were looking for redundancies. The staffroom was a snakepit of dissent and depression. As a result of the special measures every teacher's job was now threatened. Met's allies were constantly whispering against her – the person who would decide their future – and she knew others were blaming her for failing to protect them, for raising their hopes in the first place.

She poured out ideas: catch-up lessons for poor attenders, a welfare officer for the lower school, work experience for older children, CCTV to stop vandals, a working party on staff absence, mentors for year 10 pupils, teachers to visit other schools, new homework programmes, shorter lessons, more lessons. But she was trapped by a lack of funds and lack of support. The staff were demanding that some of the most difficult children be excluded but the rules of special measures forbade it. Ms Coleman had identified the staff who ought to go but she could not get rid of them because no good teacher was going to replace them. The students started to roam wild in the corridors; she sent patrols of teachers with pagers and walkie-talkies to hold the line against chaos.

Eventually, in mid-1997, more than a year after Ofsted's visit, HM inspectors came by and said things were improving, and the new Brighton and Hove authority came up with some money for a senior teacher and the Success Maker software. That September the school was relaunched with a new name, Marina High, and it became the first secondary school in the country to introduce a literacy hour. Met's term on the governing body came to an end. Ms Coleman began to think things might be all right.

But she soon began to see that there were too many holes in the boat. The students had had a riotous summer, burning out half a dozen police cars on the estate. The police said some were working for a drugs syndicate that had moved down from Glasgow. The few new teachers were drowning in classroom disorder. One walked out for good. She decided to bring in a counsellor to help with some of the wilder children.

He arrived to find workers removing her study door (someone had smashed a fist through it) and Ms Coleman tried to explain that she had lost her sixth girl that year, pregnant; that a 17-year-old former student had just been murdered on the rubbish tip next to the school; that the brother of one student had just been accused of helping to murder the father of another; that a boy had just been run down on the crossing outside the school; that she herself had just had her purse stolen by a year eight girl who had evidently given it to her older sister, and that the older sister, a prostitute, had used her credit cards, and the police had traced her to a flat where they had found her dead from

Here and there

a heroin overdose along with her boyfriend, and so now the year eight girl had been taken into care and it was her friends who were upset and needed counselling. The counsellor said he would have to see what he could do.

In November HM inspectors came back, saw a rotten collection of lessons and narrowly escaped disaster when someone threw firecrackers at them in a crowded corridor. In December the LEA warned Ms Coleman that the school would close if there was not dramatic change. She spent Christmas in a fog of defeat. She had seen a psychiatrist to try to release her stress but now carried so much tension in her shoulders and neck that her jaw locked tight and she lost the ability to speak.

Within weeks of the new term beginning she knew she was hurtling towards disaster. In a single week children made two serious allegations of assault against staff. She followed procedure and suspended both teachers while she investigated. The staffroom went berserk and, when she reported that both allegations were groundless, the news only increased the teachers' irritation. The education department and the LEA and Ofsted and HM inspectors were all demanding results and the more Ms Coleman passed on the pressure to the staff, the more they hated her. Some wrote an anonymous letter to the LEA saying the school was in chaos and the headteacher was mad; the former governor, Met Metcalfe, phoned and demanded that the LEA sack her.

In February 1998 the education department paid a lightning visit to the school and did not like what it saw. HM inspectors were due back and, shortly before they arrived, Ms Coleman went to the LEA and told it she could not go on. It agreed to let her go with a decent package if she would stay for the visit. The inspectors came and shook their heads and took Ms Coleman aside to tell her she had done her best, and reported that the school was still failing. It was Ms Coleman's last day. She felt mad with fatigue and maybe relief, almost speechless with lockjaw. She went for one last walk through the school, leaning on the arm of a visiting deputy head. A year eight girl saw her. "Are you pissed, miss?" she asked. "No, darling – just very tired." The next day, she resigned. She was 52 and she would never teach again.

When she was talking to the parents at Roedean's speech day, Patricia Metham warned her audience: "It's not easy being a teacher these days. What other profession is so beset by 'experts' who haven't ever done the job themselves and who wouldn't last five minutes in a real school? Having in the distant past been a pupil is felt by too many to be qualification enough to dictate terms to those who are trained and experienced professionals."

Nobody dictates terms to the teachers in Roedean. They are not answerable to David Blunkett, the education secretary, or his department or the LEA or Ofsted. They are not bound by the national curriculum or Sats or special measures or any of the superstructure of supervision that has settled over the state schools. And that is the third factor in Roedean's success: freedom to teach as its staff think best.

"All teachers in the maintained sector have been constrained by the same rather rigid bureaucracy and requirements," Mrs Metham says. "If you talk to people who have had a really good educational experience, nine times out of 10 they will tell you about the charismatic teacher who stimulated an interest in a subject, an idiosyncratic person who knew enough about pacing and matching, understanding what was required. At independent schools, teachers are highly accountable – to the headteacher and to the parents – but how they get their results and what they do in the classroom or in a department, the judgment is left to them." •

22 June 2000

Catherine Bennett
Best at self loathing

Ashamed to be British? In this season of self-loathing how refreshing to fall upon the headlines, a few days ago: "We're champions of Europe ... at nookie", and "Land of red-hot lovers". "Britons are good at sex," announced the Daily Mirror, a fact confirmed by the Daily Mail: "the British are the sex machines of Europe".

Tabloid exultation had been inspired by a forthcoming book, the Penguin Atlas of Human Sexual Behaviour, in which a British sex act is reported to last 21 minutes, as opposed to 14 in Italy. Rejoice! Upon examination, however, the British claims to prowess dwindled almost to nothing. The title for most protracted love-making actually goes to the Brazilians (over 30 minutes), while the frequency cup goes to the French, who make love an average of 130 times a year. The Americans triumph over the British in both frequency and endurance. The one sexual arena in which we have truly achieved world domination is unmarried teenage pregnancy.

Still, considering the current scale of our national indignities, what is one further failure? Compared with the embarrassment of sharing the same nationality as English football supporters, as most of us do, further evidence of sexual mediocrity is no more than a pinprick. Every week, almost every day, we wake to fresh testimonials of uselessness and depravity. Earlier this week, while commentators were still brooding about the nature of a country that spawns the most repulsive fans in Europe, it was separately announced that Britain's unemployment benefits are "some of the least generous in Europe", and that the NHS is now ranked 18th in the world.

Looking on the bright side, 18th sounds a bit better than "worst", which is how this country is increasingly described, in comparisons of all kinds. Sometimes, as in kissing, asthma, social inequality and the smelliness of our homes, we manage to come among the worst in the whole world. More routinely, the statistics perhaps being more readily available, we are placed worst in the EU, or Europe.

In recent months Britain has been ranked the worst, or almost worst in Europe for heart disease, pay inequality, fertility treatment, killing children with cars, divorce rates, and – hardly a surprise this – our "traditional cooking". A disturbingly high number of those polled in this pan-European study, believed our pre-eminent national dish was jelly. Then again, maybe it is jelly. Our workers, says a recent international study, are the most disgruntled and have the lowest opinion of their management.

This is scarcely surprising, as British employees are also said to work the longest hours, for less pay and fewer holidays and rights than anywhere else in Europe. According to Steve Biddulph, the child psychologist, Britain is also the "worst place in Europe" to bring up children – partly because British parents pay the highest childcare costs in Europe. All of which may account for the astonishing achievement of British children themselves, of being worst at virtually everything that can be imagined.

In no particular order, British children are the laziest in Europe, with the worst health in Europe (on a par with Albania), they watch the most television and have been described as the most "socially irresponsible". This is because they take more illegal drugs, have more unwanted pregnancies and abortions, and are more likely to develop sexually transmitted diseases and smoking and drink-related problems than any other children in Europe. It's with some justification that one report concluded "teenagers from the British Isles take themselves less seriously than those in the rest of Europe". They do, however, find time to be "the greediest and most selfish in Europe", being interested only in getting rich.

There is no reason, of course, to privilege any of these findings over the anecdotal. When it comes to diagnosing the sickness of being British today, everyone will have her own measure of terminal ghastliness: our indulgent fascination with road rage; the plague of columnists; Tony Blair's glottal stops; Carole Vorderman on Shakespeare; "Lord" Puttnam's "education Oscars"; the transformation of BBC2 into a snooker channel; the current summer of sport to which we have all, willy nilly, been sentenced.

Boorishness on this scale seems to go beyond party politics, which may explain why a preoccupation with the awfulness of being British now unites, however fleetingly, commentators from the Sun and the Guardian, the Mail and the Independent. Obviously, explanations vary. Who is to blame for our abject yobbery? Why, declares the Sun's Richard Littlejohn, "the wrongheaded policies promoted by Joan Bakewell's generation". Indeed, agrees the Mail's David Thomas, "the blame lies squarely at the feet of those politicians and liberal intellectuals who have, for the past 40 years, mocked the very idea of responsible behaviour as irredeemably old-fashioned and elitist". Hugo Young? "Margaret Thatcher, the mother of materialistic individualism, legitimised macho yobbery. Excessive liberalism made its contribution ..."

But let's suppose the causes of British decline were, indeed, a cocktail of equal parts brutal Thatcherism to idiot liberalism, with a smidgin of old-fashioned class poison thrown in for good measure; the analysis seems to take us no closer to a solution, or reversal. What can be done? Nothing, seems to be the despairing consensus. No political party can re-educate a generation taught to celebrate its own, affluent ignorance, let alone salvage its benighted children. The only way is down.

Except, of course, in self-loathing. When Penguin gets round to publishing an Atlas of Self-flagellation, the British will undoubtedly come top: for frequency, longevity and, most of all, accuracy.

TO TAN OR NOT TO TAN, THAT IS THE QUESTION

As the sunshine grew hotter last weekend, the Sunday Times's Style section issued a timely warning against going out and lying in it. "Despite 20 years of media coverage about the dangers of sunbathing, the British resolutely remain a nation of sun-worshippers," admonished an article which questioned the degree of protection purportedly offered by suntan creams. The previous few days had offered ample proof of this observation as the British tore off their clothes and strove to achieve the maximum possible sun damage in the shortest possible time. But who can be surprised by such folly? Not, surely, the Sunday Times, which announced its Sun Special with a photograph of a model's fiercely cooked epidermis and the the the coverline: "Looking Hot: 7-page special on the best ways to get brown and beautiful."

We have become accustomed to a certain lack of conviction in women's magazines which routinely preface their scorching tips with warnings about wrinkles and skin cancer, but few of these publications can ever have rivalled, for brazen indecisiveness, the Sunday Times's Sun Special. "Apply a high-factor cream regularly, limit your sun exposure, and cover up between the hours of 11am and 3pm," it began, responsibly. On the same page, a cheerful little box retorted: "The sun isn't all bad though ... It gives us a psychological boost." The paper's alternative health correspondent seemed equally torn, suggesting on the one hand that pills made of carrot juice and "oligomeric proan-thocyanidins" can "protect skin from burning", while simultaneously reminding readers that "the best way to avoid burning is to expose your skin to the sun for no more than 20 minutes a day ..."

Confused? It got worse. "Nothing looks healthier, or sexier, than deep terracotta limbs, especially with the new, ultra-short skirt lengths. But lying on the beach is the easy part," began a piece on how to achieve "tan longevity", ie, "preventing the horror of peeling".

"Yes, the man with a tan is back", proclaimed another article, "when you take into account that it makes eyes look brighter and the teeth whiter – wouldn't you go for the bronzed look?" Even if, as an earlier page calmly states, "there is a clear link between malignant skin cancer and time spent outdoors"? For all its torment about ineffective sun-screens, the Sunday Times Sun Special made it clear that anyone who wants to look beautiful this year should be prepared to pay the ultimate price. Let's pray those carrot pills really work. •

14 October 1999

Owen Boycott
@Murmansk

Captain Stanislav Schmidt has been waiting four months to put to sea. His nuclear-powered ice-breaker, which can force a passage through the frozen Arctic, is short of only two essentials – enriched uranium fuel rods and the means to pay for them.

From the bridge of the Sovetskiy Soyuz, tied up alongside the Atomflot quay at Murmansk, he surveys the broad, windswept fiord stretching down towards the Barents Sea. To the west, a wilderness of stunted birch trees fringes the water's edge. On either side of the main channel, the up-ended hulls of semi-scuppered vessels poke up above the waves. In docks along the eastern shore of the port, ships of Russia's Northern Fleet – slate blue aircraft carriers, camouflaged hospital ships and anti-submarine frigates – are laid up, immobile.

Schmidt and his crew are fastened to the harbour's jetty by his country's crippled economy as firmly as if they were wedged in the pack-ice between towering glaciers. Perhaps it will be another year before they can cast off, he admits.

A veteran seafarer, Schmidt has spent 23 years working his way up the ranks. Now 51, and with a line of glinting medals on his chest, he is proud of his ship and its two, 170 megawatt nuclear reactors. Unlocking a sealed door to the bridge, he boasts that it has three times the power of a conventional, diesel ice-breaker. On voyages to remote Siberian destinations, where it cuts a path through ice floes for following supply ships, the Sovetskiy Soyuz – or Soviet Union – can reach a maximum speed of 21 knots in "easy ice". In ice more than 2m thick, the vessel's reinforced bow can push its way forward at a steady speed of three knots. "If the ice doesn't move, you reverse back and charge again," he grins.

Such a single-minded philosophy is unlikely to break the log-jam of Russia's economic woes. Like the navy, the Murmansk Shipping Company, which operates the country's fleet of eight nuclear-powered ice-breakers and one nuclear container ship, is desperately short of funds. Warmed by the fading ripples of the Gulf stream flowing around the tip of northern Norway, Murmansk, well inside the Arctic circle, is normally the only northern Russian port free of ice all year round. Last year, however, temperatures on the Kola peninsula plummeted to -42°C , coating the harbour with ice. From late November to late January, the sun never rises above the horizon.

A Russian ice-breaker is an imposing but friendly-looking vessel. Its black hull is emblazoned with an atomic motif: two particles whizzing around a nucleus. The tall, orange superstructure, studded with portholes, suggests a cross-channel ferry. The logo of a polar bear, painted on its funnel, is reminiscent of a Fox's Glacier Mint. First launched in 1959, nuclear ice-breakers have, however, alarmed Norway and other western neighbours because of their practice of dumping spent radioactive fuel in the Barents Sea.

Half a mile down the fiord an elderly storage ship, the Lepse, swings at anchor with a cargo of fuel rods mangled in an accident and waits for someone to devise a means of rendering it harmless.

But on board the Sovetskiy Soyuz all is shipshape. There are clean corridors, waxed lino floors and polished handrails. Inside the control room, the twin reactors can be glimpsed through triple layers of glass. Pressurised tubes and spirals of wire twist down to the metal storage vessels on top of the reactors. The ship is only 10 years old: constructed in Finland, its reactors installed in what was at the time still Leningrad.

Ashore in the main hall of Atomflot's headquarters, time is ticking away towards winter. Three other nuclear ice-breakers are working the Arctic routes this month. What Schmidt is hoping for is a party of wealthy western tourists. In the past he has carried up to 100 passengers, mainly Americans paying $25,000 a head, for two-week trips to the North Pole. •

....

14 December 1999

Duncan Campbell
Jackrabbit's last raid

On June 9 last summer, Susan Musgrave wrote a poem which began with the image of her parents driving the family round the "ritzy districts" of town at Christmas to see the lights on the houses and the trees. "My dad would always take this detour by the orphanage to show us all the kids who didn't have anything," she says, sitting by the log fire in the Deep Cove restaurant not far from her home on Vancouver Island's Saanich Peninsula. "It was a quintessentially lonely poem."

When she finished it, she discovered a message on her answering machine – the first hint, she says, "that something was wrong". What was wrong was that her husband, Stephen Reid, had been arrested for bank robbery and the attempted murder of a policeman. Later this month, he will be sentenced. Reid's lawyer acknowledges that he must expect a "double digit" sentence.

If Reid is Canada's best-known bank robber, Susan Musgrave is its most charismatic poet. Once, they were a fêted couple, the subject of an affectionate CBC television portrait, The Poet and the Bandit, only last year. For the past decade or so, Reid has enjoyed a kind of redemptive celebrity status: someone who had emerged from a life of crime and a long prison term to begin a successful creative life as a writer, a happy new marriage and contented fatherhood.

Born in the small town of Massey, Ontario, nearly 50 years ago, Reid was one of the brightest boys in his class, and a fine athlete. However, in circumstances he is still unwilling to discuss, at 13 he started taking heroin and dropped out of school three years later to hitch-hike west to Vancouver. There he picked up his first convictions for marijuana possession and shoplifting. He moved on to robbery and, in 1971, was jailed for 10 years in Ontario.

After an early parole in 1974, he took part in one of Canada's most famous robberies: the heist of five gold bars from the Air Canada depot at Ottawa airport. With two accomplices, Paddy Mitchell and Lionel Wright, Reid formed what became known as the Stopwatch Gang, a trio of bank robbers who made a point of carrying out their heists in 90 seconds flat, timed by the watch hanging round Reid's neck. He went armed and was shot three times: once by police, once by a friend and once through his own clumsiness.

The long roll of robberies – the three were credited with stealing more than $2m – ended when Reid was captured in 1980 at a hideout in Arizona, where he was learning how to fly. Wings clipped, he was jailed for the next 16 years, spending the early part of his sentence in the grim Marion prison in Illinois. All three took part in dramatic escapes.

Mitchell is now in jail doing one of those multi-decade, unforgiving American sentences in Mississippi. Wright, who always counted the proceeds of the robberies meticulously to the last $10 bill on a motel bed, is now a successful and mild-mannered accountant, writing the payroll cheques for Corrections Canada, the national prisons department.

In prison, meanwhile, Reid had started writing poetry and fiction. Susan Musgrave, already well-known as one of Canada's most-published poets, was writer in residence at the University of Waterloo, near Toronto, when she was given a manuscript of 90 pages called Jackrabbit Parole (prison slang for escaping) by a criminologist colleague in 1983.

"I didn't fall in love with the idea of a glamorous bank robber; I didn't fall in love with a heroin addict," she says. "I fell in love with words, which is what I always fall in love with: anyone who can write." From the first page, she was hooked, and sent the book to her publisher, Bantam Seal, who responded speedily.

Born in California to British-Irish stock and raised on Vancouver Island, Musgrave was and is both a beauty and a frank, free-spirited soul who burst into the public consciousness in 1970 with her first collection of poems, Songs of the Sea-witch. Her life and loves – she was married to a successful barrister and then to one of his clients – have taken her to Cali in Colombia, and to Ireland.

Her poems are, in the understatement on the back of Things That Keep and Do Not Change, "dark, playful and edgy". She has now published 20 books, mainly poetry but also four children's books and two novels. In 1996 she won the CBC/Tilden Canadian literary Award for Poetry and has been shortlisted for other major literary awards. She was chair of the Writer's Union in Canada in 1996-7.

When she first saw Reid's manuscript, she was living with her daughter from her first marriage on Vancouver Island, the Brigadoonish 300-mile long outpost off the west coast of Canada. Its 600,000 inhabitants make their livings from shipping, fishing, logging, tourism and a bit of discreet marijuana-farming.

Having fallen for "Bobby", the main character in Jackrabbit Parole, she fell for the real thing when she met him in jail – and the couple married in 1986, the year both Reid and the book were released. Jackrabbit Parole became a bestseller, drawing plaudits from Canada's top critics for its rich, realist prose. It has, like the true account of his Stopwatch Gang days, attracted the interest of movie-makers. An option to film it has been bought.

On release, Reid became stepfather to Charlotte, now 17, and the father of Sophie, now 10, and the family lived an idyllic life on the Saanich Peninsula. Reid continued writing and taught others in workshops inside and outside prison, took part in restorative justice programmes with young offenders, joined the board of PEN International, and played old-timers' ice hockey for the local team.

But the jackrabbit had a monkey on its back: Reid had never quite kicked his heroin habit and, however much he might have tried to clean up, he never quite made it. He would be clean for a couple of years and then start shooting up again. When he added speedball cocktails, made up of heroin and cocaine, to his habit, Musgrave feared that an overdose was just around the corner.

"He did so much [heroin] that even veteran addicts would leave the room when he was shooting because they were convinced he was going to kill himself," says Musgrave. "Addiction is worse than a mistress. You can't call her up and have a chat about what she's doing to the family. It's stronger than any kind of love you can give. He described it to me once as this kind of hole that he could pour love into and nothing sticks. No matter how much people loved him, he still felt worthless. That's the shame of it.

"If anything, he overcompensated as a father; he would work doubly hard in the home. He'd go to Vancouver and come home with huge bouquets of flowers and we'd all be mad at him because what we really wanted was him; we didn't want presents. No woman wants the red rose from the guy who's been in the bar all night, she wants the guy.

"Many times I got fed up but it's like leaving a person who's sick, and I felt I couldn't just walk away. People would say, 'Why don't you just walk away?' but if he had cancer would they be saying that? I haven't been willing before to do any work for a relationship but this time it was different. It's not a huge sacrifice. I'm very happy with my life; my work is immensely satisfying; my kids are great, so what if I don't get sex for a few months? There are worse things."

For Reid, on June 9, there was nothing worse than being without heroin and cocaine. By the time he set off for the Royal Bank in Cook Street Village, he had already shot up in a petrol station. The robbery seemed doomed from the start. He went into the bank wearing a bizarre disguise: an Elvis mask and a policeman's uniform, complete with handcuffs. Musgrave had already noted with some puzzlement the arrival of the uniform and the handcuffs in the house and had wondered if he was having some kind of weird affair in town: "So in a way it was some kind of a relief when I found out what they were really for."

Initially, Reid and his accomplice (another man awaits trial) got away with $92,924. But, despite Reid's claim in his book that "real cops will seldom race to an in progress alarm", there was a hot pursuit. Reid was carrying a 12-gauge shotgun and a .44 Magnum. Eight shots were fired. Police Corporal Bill Trudeau was nearly hit as he followed on his motorcycle. Finally, Reid dumped the car and holed up in an elderly couple's apartment in nearby James Bay. Police surrounded the building and, after a five-hour stand-off, heard snores, broke in and found Reid passed out inside.

In Jackrabbit Parole, Bobby explains the essence of a successful robbery: "To do it right, to know just when, is part of a thing called drift sense – it's the juggling of time and events during this highwire balancing act." This time, Reid had fallen off the wire. His iconic status was punctured.

He pleaded guilty to the robbery and to confining the couple, but denied trying to kill Trudeau. His plea was not accepted by Judge Alan Filmer, who said that Reid's decision to use a Magnum was a clear sign of intent to do serious harm. Reid protested that he was not a killer but, wearing a neat blue blazer and leg-irons, accepted his guilt on the other counts with the words: "It's reckless, pathetic, crazy, stupid."

After his arrest, he wrote to his agent, Denise Bukowksi, about the response to his arrest from friends and people he did not know: "I don't want to sound like Sally Field or anything but the love from so many people, despite the things I did, is sort of affirming or something. I'll see you at the other end of this, if there is 'the other end of this'." Hosts of neighbours and friends gave character references for him. One neighbour, Paul Gardner, said that his image of Reid was of him walking his daughter to the school bus stop. An old FBI man, who had hunted him in the past, wrote to say he was sorry at the turn of events.

The police in Victoria and some of the local press take a less sanguine view and are unhappy that Reid is portrayed by some as the Sundance Kid. "A lot of people have made him into a hero because he's had a colourful past," said Dan Cottingham of Victoria police. "We don't think of him as a hero. We feel he is who he is." The local paper, the Times Colonist, wrote a leader headed: "Reid no glamour boy." Trudeau has been commended for his bravery.

The phone rings in the Deep Cove restaurant after the salmon has been cleared away. It is Reid calling from jail. The restaurant owner teases him that he hasn't even been sentenced, and his wife is already out with another man. On the phone, Reid is genial, expressing his gratitude to the people who gave character evidence for him in court last week. He is anxious to apologise and make reparation, through what is known in the Canadian judicial system as "healing justice", to the people who were frightened by the gunshots, to the staff in the bank, to the police. He knows that now is a bad time, with emotions still running high and one witness saying she would be fearful if he was ever released. There has been anger and dismay about the shootings in a quiet, polite city where people can't remember when anyone last shot at a policeman; and puzzlement that someone who seemed to have everything could throw it all away.

In Munro's bookshop in Victoria, Stephen Reid and Susan Musgrave are together, albeit on different shelves. Musgrave is in the poetry section. And Reid? The attendant looks on the biography shelves for a moment before she corrects herself: "Oh, of course, he's fiction, isn't he?"

Unfortunately for the man who seemed to have rewritten his own life with some success and courage, he is back in the true crime section. From inside jail, as he comes off heroin, he has to reflect on the fact that he will be unable to drive his family round the ritzy districts of Vancouver Island this Christmas Eve. It is a sobering thing. •

19 February 2000
Stephen Cook
Fool's paradise

"He was disappointed with the world, so he built his own – an absolute monarchy"
Mr Leland in *Citizen Kane* (1941)

It must have been a mixed blessing for the beautiful people of the 1930s to be invited for the weekend to San Simeon, William Randolph Hearst's grandiose castle on the Californian coast. You couldn't say no, for a start, because Hearst was big in Hollywood as well as newspapers and could break the career of anyone who crossed him.

Then there were all the restrictions: you couldn't bring your own maid, you weren't allowed as much as a cup of coffee in the guest rooms, and if you wanted to sleep with your boyfriend or girlfriend, forget it: Hearst co-habited with his mistress, the actress Marion Davies, but wouldn't let other unmarried couples share a room.

And so it went on. The pre-dinner drinks, according to David Niven, "flowed like glue". Anyone who managed to get drunk – Errol Flynn and Dorothy Parker were two lucky ones – would return to their rooms to find their bags packed and a car waiting to take them to the station.

"Life in this Hearstian empire," wrote the socialite Gloria Vanderbilt, " is lived according to the disciplinary measures laid down by its dictator."

There were a few dissidents, such as the guest who, when asked one morning if he wanted to ride, motor, shoot, golf, swim or play tennis, replied firmly: "Not if I can help it."

And it seems that when Hearst retired to his library to telegram instructions to his newspapers deep into the night, the more spirited guests would sneak off to the steamy, gold-tiled indoor pool for boozy parties.

Hearst indulged his every whim, and the eminent San Francisco architect Julia Morgan patiently went along with it all, year after year. The swimming pool was rebuilt three times, the foundations of the main house were moved at huge expense to make room for a bowling alley that was never built.

Davies and some of the women guests often did jigsaw puzzles in the Assembly Room after dinner, and on one occasion a skilled carpenter and painter were brought in to make a perfect replacement for a tiny lost piece. "Afterwards, nine chances out of 10, it was shoved in the wastepapaper basket," the carpenter commented later.

Nowadays, the hordes of mass tourism have taken the place of the beautiful people at Hearst Castle, but a whiff of the old man's authoritarianism lingers on. As you move across glittering terraces and through dim interiors, you're tailed by a dark man in mirrored sunglasses: just checking you're not lifting the marble statue of Galatea or tucking a prize rug under your arm.

The worst touch on our visit came when we went to a movie called Building The Dream, a sycophantic account of how Hearst came to create this great monument to extravagance and vanity. The flunkey with the task of switching it on declined to do so until the audience, like a kindergarten chorus, had said good morning to him in the approved manner: not if I can help it.

You learn, as you troop from room to room, that the 14th- and 15th-century Gothic ceilings came mainly from Spain, that the huge 400-year-old stone fireplace in the Assembly Room was made in Burgundy, that the four tapestries on the wall were woven from wool and silk in Flanders, that the 600-year-old choir stalls came from a Spanish monastery, that there are 155 Greek vases in the Gothic library.

The jumble becomes most absurd when you reach the coffee room and the adjoining billiard hall, where there are 1,700-year-old Roman mosaics close to a 15th-century Spanish ceiling, a 16th-century tapestry of a stag hunt from northern France, and the 1930s billiard tables. The loot of the world arrived here by the shipload. Often it was never unpacked, let alone looked at.

But one thing you won't find mentioned in the official guidebooks is the Orson Welles film, Citizen Kane, in which a super-rich newspaper magnate fails to achieve his political ambitions and tries to console himself by building a huge castle.

There was never any doubt that the character of Kane started with Hearst, who had twice failed to become mayor of New York and win the Democratic presidential nomination. The great man instructed his columnists to attack Welles and used his influence in Hollywood to try to block the film's distribution. It was, he claimed, "Communist inspired".

Welles issued a statement denying he was a Communist, praising the American political system and adding: "It is not necessarily unpatriotic to disagree with Mr Hearst."

But there were probably more differences than similarities between the fictional Charles Foster Kane and the real life William Randolph Hearst. In particular, the central device of the film – that Kane's psychological scar comes from his deprivation in early childhood of his beloved snowsled Rosebud – seems to have had very little to do with Hearst, who had never been deprived of anything. (The story that Rosebud was Hearst's pet name for Marion Davies's clitoris is widely regarded as a red herring.)

Film writer David Thomson argues in his book Rosebud that Kane's complicated, self-destructive character is closer to Welles himself than Hearst: "Some other resemblance developed behind the showy but superficial kinship of Kane and Hearst. In emotion and energy, Kane was based on Welles. No one who knew or has written about Hearst has ever reported such complex depths, such an air of the damned."

But the message that gives the film so much of its impact – the ultimate emptiness of power, wealth and ambition, and the limitations of the American dream – seems to hover in the air around Hearst Castle. The place is a triumph of money, willpower and acquisition, but all the time a little voice whispers: what on earth is it all for?

There are many beautiful things at the castle. The site is stunningly beautiful, 2,000ft above the Pacific on what Hearst liked to call La Cuesta Encantada, the Enchanted Hill. (The website refers to it as La Cuesta Encantada.) But as the tour bus takes you back down the winding road to the shoreline, through the grounds once inhabited by the 300 animals of his private zoo, it is hard to find any meaning in it all. •

14 March 2000
Michael Ellison
I don't feel defeated: I still seek justice

The first time Kadiatou Diallo visited New York it was for a carefree week with friends, driving around the city and exploring restaurants. The next occasion was to collect the body of her son, Amadou, an innocent and unarmed black man who had been shot dead by four white policemen.

"I just think, why did God choose me, why my son?" says Ms Diallo. She has not been assisted in her quest for an answer by the trial of the officers, which cleared them of all charges, from murdering the 22-year-old street trader down to reckless endangerment.

Since he was killed 13 months ago his name has become a byword for police brutality. His death is perhaps the most startling representation of what can happen when crime figures are driven down by official policies which funnel white fear and suspicion into the targeting of minorities.

In fact, the city is more than 60% non-white, though you would never know it if you spent most of your time below 96th street, in what Tom Wolfe described as the boutique of Manhattan.

Ms Diallo is talking in the 34th-floor offices of her lawyers, a block away from Wall Street, emblem of the economy that drives the unofficially segregated city.

A 40-year-old businesswoman from Africa, in a pistachio-coloured suit and black high-heels, her hair tied back in a bow, she is not an urban warrior. The details of, and motivation behind, the death of Amadou in the entrance to his apartment building have been disputed endlessly, but no one denies the dignity with which his mother has borne herself throughout the affair.

"It's not easy, I do it with prayers and by having faith," says Ms Diallo, a Muslim. "And my other children [two sons and a daughter, aged between 17 and 21] have given me a lot of moral support.

"In public maybe once or twice I have shown anger. But I am carrying the legacy of my son. Sometimes when I feel so sad I think of him in paradise. But people are looking through me at the image of my son. It's the first time we've had that kind of situation in my family.

"We have lots of support, all races and religions have come forward. Our purpose is to let the whole world know who he was and what kind of family he came from."

The police were looking for a rapist in the Bronx, one of the five boroughs of New York city, when they shot down Amadou. They thought he was reaching for a gun, when it was actually his wallet. They fired at him 41 times, 19 of the bullets hitting him.

Ms Diallo's hands move from a face that smiles more often than it might, and she sighs when asked about the trial verdicts. The case was moved 150 miles north to predominantly white Albany because it was decided that the officers would not get a fair hearing in the Bronx.

"I was shocked," she says. "I am a kind of person who does not try to seek something out of anger. But they had the opportunity of doing something better. This [the killing] could have happened to anyone. We expected to have something stronger than that from the case."

She is highly critical of the conduct of the prosecution. They kept saying the jury should put themselves in the shoes of the police. Amadou didn't come out in the trial. His side is also supposed to come out. But I don't feel defeated: we still seek justice," she says.

The justice department is considering a federal case against the policemen, a procedure used against the officers in the notorious beating of Rodney King in Los Angeles. Ms Diallo hopes that this will benefit both her family and the New York police department.

"That would be a way to help both sides. If they try to close the file and say this is over, these four men might go out and do it again," she says.

Ms Diallo has not allowed her grief to interfere with her purpose of securing justice for her son. Nor will she hear a word against Rev Al Sharpton, who marshalled the anger of the city after the death into a movement that put the case on the political map. "He's a very good man," she says. "Maybe he'll have a problem because he doesn't think twice when he sees something wrong, he just jumps in and helps."

Ms Diallo is aware of the accusation that the man hailed by some as a civil rights hero and by others as a charlatan has used her son's death to further his career. "If Rev Sharpton is mobilising people for the cause, people might criticise, but what I would say to them is: where were you when people came and helped our family?" she says firmly.

She has been away for close to a year from her job as a gold and bauxite mine manager, and believes that soon she might be dismissed. She has a very American attitude towards that possibility. "I'm not afraid of starting anew. I know I can make it, that's not a difficulty for me. What I have here is the most important thing. This is my son – that's more than anything for me. With an atrocity like that, you can't just turn the pages." •

2 February 2000

Jonathan Freedland
Wackos in white coats

The amateur psychology has been flowing fast and easy. In the pubs and on the radio, in the salons and in the broadsheets everyone's trying to crack the enigma of Harold Shipman. He's the serial murderer who wanted to play God, according to the Independent, the evil doc who relished "the power of life and death," says the Times.

He's a classic necrophile, says Brian Masters, veteran decoder of the world's darkest men. He felt "a perverted delight in the presence of death". The speculation is not all media-generated. Eavesdrop in the queue at the post office or the dry cleaners, and you'll hear it there, too. We all want to take a peek inside the mind of a man responsible for a death toll which could eventually, incredibly, stretch to four figures. And we all have enough familiarity with the basics of psychology – or at least the pop culture version of it – to hazard our own guess.

The current favourite is the mummy's boy theory. As every potted biography of Shipman has recalled, he was 17 when he witnessed his mother's death from cancer – watching as she sat in an armchair, watching as a doctor injected her with numbing doses of morphine. Perhaps the young Shipman felt so helpless at that scene, wonders media-shrink Oliver James, that the adult sought to repeat it, over and over – with himself recast in the powerful role, as the man with the needle. Maybe he was punishing his victims, predominantly older women, for enjoying the longevity denied his mother? Or perhaps he had been so stirred by that episode in 1963 that he enjoyed a surreal, quasi-sexual thrill in reliving it?

But there is a more intriguing relationship to examine here, one that says less about the psychology of Cheshire's Dr Death and more about the psychology of his patients.

For the awkward question raised by the bleak case of Harold Shipman may not dwell on his relationship with his mum – but on our relationship with those who heal us.

One clear fact emerges from the crates of evidence now prised open: that Shipman's killing spree could continue for as long as it did – perhaps a quarter of a century – solely because he wore the respectable spectacles of a doctor. The public inquiry announced yesterday by the health secretary will have to answer this aspect of the case, but already the belief is growing that Shipman's fellow doctors failed to see a killer in their midst – and refused to see the warning signs that now look so obvious. He was producing many more corpses than they were – between four and ten times the amount – and yet they closed ranks, like a trade union, protecting the reputation of one of their own. More than once the General Medical Council was asked to take action. More than once it refused.

More deeply, Shipman was allowed to kill thanks not only to the professional solidarity of the medical class – but to our stubborn faith in it. Several of Hyde's citizens said they feared ridicule if they dared challenge the town doctor, such was his standing within a small, traditional community. Doctors are archetypal authority figures, and Shipman exploited that fact to lethal effect: he could gain entry into people's homes and their trust, even when harm, pain and death were his objectives.

The sophisticated will want to see this deference as the antiquated preserve of the naive, the weak and the elderly: little old ladies bowing to the local medic as if to the witch doctors of yore. The rest of us are surely far too savvy for that. But we should not be too quick to congratulate ourselves.

In the 60s, a Yale University professor by the name of Stanley Milgram set out to test the limits of human deference. He was troubled by Adolf Eichmann's claim a few years earlier that, even though he had masterminded the Nazi destruction of the Jewish people, he "was only obeying orders". Milgram, a fine American patriot, was convinced that none of his countrymen would ever have obeyed such brutal orders, and he set out to prove it.

In an ingenious experiment, he persuaded volunteers to take part in a study on the effects of punishment on learning. One would be the "teacher", the other the "learner" – with the latter strapped into a chair with electrodes attached to his wrists. If the learner made a mistake in a series of simple memory tests, the teacher would zap him with a shock – jacking up the voltage with each wrong answer. What the first volunteer did not know was that the "learner" was actually an actor, and that the shocks were all fake.

Eventually the learner would be writhing in mock pain on the other side of the glass, crying out for mercy. In some experiments, he would complain of a potentially-fatal heart condition or, at 330 volts, pretend to fall silent, as if unconscious or dead.

But it was all to no avail. The volunteers, of all ages and across all social groups, repeatedly agreed to increase the voltage, no matter how loud the protests of their victim. Professor Milgram and his team were stunned by their results: fully 65% of their all-American sample were prepared to obey the most heinous orders, administering the maximum shock of 450 volts – even when such a blast was self-evidently lethal.

And here's the twist. Milgram's findings were highest when the "researcher" supervising the experiment wore a white coat. When he appeared in a regular suit, the obedience rates plummeted. People were deferring to the costume of the doctor-scientist, even to the extent of suspending their own consciences. If they protested, the researcher would merely say: "The experiment must continue." And so it would.

Milgram's Obedience To Authority was written to prove that it was not just Germans who submit to those with power and intellectual standing. It is a universal habit, as visible in a playground gang torturing a weakling on the instructions of a bully as it was in the Third Reich. Shipman's trick was to use that impulse for the facilitation of murder.

But we need not be resigned to it. Perhaps the elderly of Hyde had grown up doffing their caps to the local doc, but a new generation seems to be shaking off that deference. One of the blockbuster sites among American users of the internet is MD Web, aimed originally at physicians but used increasingly by patients. There and elsewhere punters can check out their symptoms alongside a vast reservoir of medical knowledge – and then challenge the diagnosis of their doctor. Now everyone who has a computer can get a second opinion, instantly. NHS Direct may eventually do something similar in Britain.

The result could be an eventual slipping of the white-coat halo. The debate over genetically-modified food has already exposed scientists as opinionated partisans, just like the rest of us. The Shipman case may do the same for the medical profession. The end of deference is not just a political trend. It relates to a more profound business too – causing death and taking lives. ∎

5 October 1999

Gary Younge
Stand in line

John Aspinall deserves justice. Last month three young black men robbed the millionaire zoo-owner and his wife and relieved them of a Cartier watch, an earring and a handbag. We will come back to Mr Aspinall later, but for the time being let us all agree that, unless it is inspired by hunger or abject poverty, taking things that do not belong to you is an awful thing to do and that the only way to deal with thieves is to make them first say sorry and then return the goods they have stolen.

There are only two ways someone in possession of stolen goods can get around this. The first is if they are never caught; the second is if they received the contraband without knowing it was stolen.

Given those basic moral precepts, the beginning of Black History month is as good a time as any to wonder why black people in this country are still waiting for an apology and reparations for slavery. A good 192 years after the trade in human bondage was abolished in Britain, enslavement remains one of the most peculiar taboos in the nation's psyche.

Yet the facts are clear. Britain, along with much of the rest of Europe and the Arab world, stole millions of pounds worth of labour, and later land, throughout the 17th and 18th centuries. There is no dispute about who did it. Slave trading was regarded as such a respectable profession at the time that the perpetrators did not have to be caught. They recorded their crimes in their ledgers and traded their stolen goods in broad daylight.

So their best defence is ignorance. This is actually quite convincing. When it comes to colonialism and slavery, British people know very little about their history. A Gallup poll last year found that around half the British public thought that America had never been a British colony.

When Clare Short rejected a request from Zimbabwe for additional aid to buy back land occupied by settlers under colonialism she replied: "We are a new government from diverse backgrounds, without links to former colonial interests. My own origins are Irish and, as you know we were colonised, not colonisers." The fact that she was elected by British voters to serve in a British government clearly passed her by.

As a result, the histories of the hundreds of thousands of men and women who were sold like cattle, their owners, and the economic forces which forged the relationship between slave owner and slave and enriched these shores, exist as though in a wilfully collective blind spot.

And without knowing about them, it is impossible to understand that while only a relatively small number of individuals may have inherited that wealth, Britain as whole benefited in many ways. The profits from slavery played a major role in funding the industrial revolution, in creating wealth for the four main high street banks and in building cities such as Liverpool, Bristol and Cardiff. But while ignorance might be a credible excuse, it is no defence.

White British people do not need to know all this so that they can feel bad about themselves. As Mr Aspinall will no doubt agree, if someone steals your Cartier watch it is not their sympathy you are after, it is the watch. They need to know this so that they can better know themselves.

This would first of all stop them making fools of themselves. In the lead letter to the Telegraph on Monday, Mr Aspinall said he "lays little blame on the Afro-Caribbean minority for their crimes", but saves his ire for Harold Macmillan who "invited them in the first place. . . there is nothing in their cultural experience to suggest they would take readily to our cherished way of life."

Mr Aspinall is clearly unaware that Afro-Caribbeans, not to mention Africans, Indians, Pakistanis and Bangladeshis, are not here by accident. In the words of Dr A Sivanandan, director of the Institute of Race Relations, we are here because you were there. A greater understanding of his own history would also teach Aspinall that taking things and running away is very much part of "the Anglo-Saxon way of life". Frankly there aren't enough Cartiers in the world to compensate for all the stuff the British stole.

But, more importantly, without acknowledging its past wrongs, Britain lacks the moral authority to lecture others on the domestic and international scene. Listening to Tony Blair talk about rights and responsibilities and Robin Cook advocate an ethical foreign policy, when they are the leaders of a country with such a brutal history of slavery, is a bit like Ronnie Biggs calling for more bobbies on the beat.

Mr Aspinall deserves justice. But he will have to stand in line. •

23 May 2000

Hugo Young
The folly built by our leaders that makes fools of us all

The Millennium Dome is out of sight. Down there in Greenwich, it's a long way from being in your face, even for most Londoners. For the nation, on whose children the prime minister once said the dome should confer "memories so strong that it gives them that abiding sense of purpose and unity that stays with them through the rest of their lives", it could be on another planet. But let memory speak, before the monster goes. It has been the most particular and incontestable folly of our time.

The physical distance assists the political amnesia. It's hard to find any politician who will talk about the dome now. Lord Falconer shuffles forward to mutter about an exit strategy, while Chris Smith is compelled, as a coda to the disaster the government set in train, to pour another £29m of lottery money down the Greenwich drain, the better to ensure that this exit, selling off the asset for a fraction of what was put into it, can duly happen. The announcement is as blithe as it is insulting. Otherwise, what's past is past, we're told. Time to move on. Time to talk about Tate Modern, an altogether superior monument built from the pockets of the poor who finance the lottery. The dome? Forget it.

This request I cannot meet. Somehow boredom wouldn't measure up. There was such grandeur here that slinking silently away would do an injustice to history. And history was the frame. Greenwich is the home of time, the government said. This was why Britain had a special duty to put on a millennial event that would lead the world and startle all who came from the ends of the earth to see it. The dome would "make a statement for the whole nation," said Mr Blair. It was the way for us "to take stock of ourselves". How, by that test, do we look?

The amount of lottery money consumed on the dome is closing in on £550m. Only half the expected audience have so far been willing to pay out of their own pockets for the experience. For this financial failure, they themselves, the British and global public, are to blame. Damn the punters, they inexplicably found better things to do. So the first thing we look, as a nation, is culpable. We let our prophets down. We didn't do what we were told.

But this was because we were not properly informed. The public is one scapegoat, the media are another. Asked a few awkward questions, Michael Heseltine, who can be called the dome's first begetter, was anticipating this before the money had been spent. "It's virtually impossible," he said, "to do anything in this country of any imagination without the media trying to vilify and ruin it." He was highlighting another national defect. We are apparently credulous in overlooking a brilliant creation just because a bunch of malign journalists tell us to. Or so the minister said. These are insignificant alibis for the truth. They spread the blame for the humiliating embarrassment the dome has become, so that we are all somehow guilty. Yet there has never been a project that grew so particularly and exclusively out of the preoccupations of the political class, irrespective of party, and the self-glorifying inanity in which its leaders are capable of collaborating as long as someone else pays.

The dome began as a Tory project, the last resounding belch of a dying regime. Promoted by the grandiloquent Heseltine and seized on by the cringing Mr Major, father of the lottery, it was supervised in the early stages by Virginia Bottomley and cheer-led by a variety of architects and propagandists with their own half-baked ideological, not to mention commercial, agenda for this way of proclaiming national greatness past and future – an assertion no other nation in the world felt that 2000 AD required it to make.

An additional rationale was proposed, concerning the renewal of poisoned land on the Greenwich peninsular. But it was never explained why this could be achieved only by the erection of a white elephant consuming, in all, £800m. History, and politics, were at the heart of it. Tories, when drawn into a discussion of their part, still contend that if a thousand years of history had remained the millennial motif, a triumph was guaranteed. It was New Labour's obsession with modernity, they say, that confused an otherwise flawless project.

But New Labour was on board before the Tories' fall. The consensus was all but sealed. Given the chance in May 1997 to act like a new regime, unneedful of hyperbole, Mr Blair decided he couldn't let the old, dead, corrupted one outflank him in nationalistic display, however pointless. Nobody ever answered the question about what the dome was for, except for that. Miles of verbiage and armies of consultants, up to the very millennial moment, addressed the question of content and purpose, but none was able to improve on Heseltine's best shot: "It's going to be quite wonderful but don't ask me how". They still can't. Made manifest before our eyes, the dome declared its irretrievable emptiness.

Many political projects turn out to be less than perfect. Most, indeed, can never hope to succeed in anything but a contingent and partial way. There are always more schools to build and patients to cure. For that reason the political rhetoric attaching to them is almost meant to be taken with a shovelful of salt. The level of pretension is understood to be an aspiration, the money available for its fulfilment is always inadequate. Blaming politicians for their failure is often a ritual that they can deflect with earnest remarks about the sincerity of their efforts. And besides, there's always another party, putting them to the question.

The dome is a different case. Normal lines of responsibility do not exist. It was built with funny money, for which nobody is accountable. The Treasury would never have countenanced tax money being used. No business could have defended such folly to its shareholders. Lottery money, falling outside either discipline, was made available as a plaything for egotistical wasters who invented a national purpose that did not exist. Not a little matter of a few million, either, but a donation of colossal magnitude, deployed by the same people who decided it should be handed out: people of all parties with their fingers in the trough of self-indulgence, leaving none with hands clean enough to do the ensuing scandal justice.

What one misses here is the faintest semblance of regret. No whisper have I heard, from the principals or their auxiliaries, that they may have been responsible for a mistake. Apology seems out of the question. When not whimpering a few resentful words that miss the point, they are silent. They're moving on. The dome was yesterday. Just another well-meaning blip in the awkward lives of politicians committed to national renewal. But it wasn't. It was an avoidable idiocy, which leaves Britain looking like a nation led astray by profligate, self- regarding philistines. •

7 March 2000

Roy Hattersley
Britain can't make it

I remember exactly the moment when the scales began to fall from my patriotic eyes. William H Brubeck, one of President Kennedy's special assistants for African Affairs, was talking about the failed attempt to rescue Patrice Lumumba from the Congo. "We should," he said, "have used Belgian paratroops. Most of them are tough Walloon ex-miners." Belgian paratroops? Tough Walloon miners? What, I asked, about the British, those indomitable south Yorkshire colliers who signed on for five years in the Coldstream Guards in preparation for a career in the Metropolitan Police? "We thought about the British," Brubeck told me. "But we decided that you would fuck it up."

My faith in the raw material remained – and remains to this day – unshaken. But it was not only on the Somme and in Gallipoli that the lions were led by donkeys. British paratroops sent to recapture the Falklands for the Empire were issued with such unsatisfactory boots that many of them bought better footwear from "outdoor adventure shops". One in three of the Clansman radios that British soldiers took to Kosovo could neither transmit nor receive messages. Many of our planes could not fly, at times, over low cloud cover, and then poor visibility prevented them from targeting their missiles.

Navigation equipment was borrowed from other national forces – and soldiers, for whom the army had not provided basic amenities, clubbed together to buy their own campbeds and showers. Then we learn that the SA80 rifle, standard issue in the army, jams in extreme temperatures or rapid firing. That was particularly bad news for my generation, taught at primary schools during the war that rapid firing and quick marching were the reasons why, in the words of the old song: "We always won."

The pattern persists. On Sunday, more than a week into the Mozambique flood disaster, the RAF helicopters – sent by the Ministry of Defence after the argument about the cost had been resolved – were being assembled on the Tarmac at Maputo. One of the British "Emergency Response Officials" explained that the liferafts, which had just arrived, might still be of use, even though the floods had subsided. He was considering having them dropped on to dry land with the suggestion that they might be turned upside down and used for shelter. He made no suggestion about the outboard motors.

Embarrassment at Britain's serial incompetence should not encourage the mistaken belief that we are terminally less efficient than our neighbours in Europe or North America. The problem, for the British psyche, is that we were all brought up to believe that Britain is superior to every other country in virtually every respect. To a nation which remembers that the First Lord of the Admiralty once told the Prime Minister, "I do not say the French will not come. I only say they will not come by sea", the announcement that half the fleet must remain in port because of the high cost of fuel comes as a nasty shock.

We had an empire on which the sun never set. After initiating the industrial revolution, we became the workshop of the world. And after the empire was lost and our manufacturing industry began to slide into historic decline, we found new reasons for patronising other middle-sized countries. During the war we stood alone against Nazi tyranny and when it was ended, we created a health service which became the envy of the world. The clichés of national superiority went endlessly on. Some of them, as is the way with clichés, were true. But they did not prepare us for the sudden discovery that, not only is gross domestic product per head lower in the United Kingdom than in the Republic of Ireland, but that (in all sorts of ways) we are a hugely inefficient lot.

The errors are not confined to the government. Our building industry finds it almost impossible to complete any major development – public or private – within the contract price. The Jubilee Line was supposed to cost £2.1bn. The final bill was £3.5bn. The estimate for the new parliament building in Scotland has escalated from £50m to £109m. The new Covent Garden Opera House really did rather well. It cost only £4m above the original figure. Unfortunately, when it was completed, much of the complicated backstage machinery did not work. If Christopher Wren had got his sums so badly wrong, half of the great churches of London would have been left unfinished.

Wren competes with Watt and Stephenson for a place in the pantheon of British genius. We invented the steam engine and the railway train and British-built locomotives belched fire through the night on tracks as far apart as India and Argentina. We now can boast what is almost certainly the least efficient railway system in the developed world, with a level of incompetence which was literally lethal at Southall and Ladbroke Grove. Tragedy is matched with absurdity. We have developed a vocabulary of incompetence. Signals, badly positioned and unverified by ancient safety equipment, are so often ignored that we now speak of "spads" (signals passed at danger). Punctuality has become a joke, not least because of the explanations that the railway companies provide. Leaves on the line really do reduce the speed of express trains. But a nation brought up to believe that Britain produces the world's best engineers finds it hard to understand why the heirs to Watt and Stephenson did not anticipate the problem.

A great deal of nonsense is talked about the nation's deteriorating educational standards. In fact we are more literate and more numerate than we have ever been. These days we are inclined to forget the generation of university graduates who spent their national service teaching new recruits to read and write. But, again, the performance of the leaders is not always as good as that of the much criticised led. Ofsted, under the command of Chris Woodhead, has sent out notices urging teachers and pupils to do better – which contained grammatical and spelling errors. Whilst David Blunkett is complaining about bad examination results, many GCSE examiners are finding marking the papers beyond their capabilities. Scripts have been lost, taken on holiday in the boots of cars and forgotten, and so many simple errors made in marking and classification that many schools are automatically appealing against their students' bad results.

An appeal was not possible for 70-year-old Graham Reeves, who died after the wrong kidney was removed during an operation in the Prince Philip Hospital at Llanelli. Accidents will happen. And naturally both the BMA and the hospital authorities mounted inquiries into how the mistake had been made. Unfortunately, the BMA's investigation ground at least to a temporary halt when it was discovered that the doctor in charge of the inquiry had himself been involved in a similar tragedy, and the adjudication on cause and blame for that incident was still being awaited. It later transpired that the same hospital had "lost a patient" for 10 days. Geoff Francis was told that he had leukaemia and then, to his relief, discovered that a blood sample had been wrongly labelled. It took almost a fortnight for the Prince Philip to discover to whom it really belonged.

Unfortunately, Britain's reputation for things going wrong has been intensified by what amounted to a public display of national incompetence – itself the product of the hubris which has led too many of us to believe that we avoided the mistakes which were common in France and Germany, America and Japan. No other country in the world took the millennium so seriously. Britain designated itself special because the meridian line, which runs through Greenwich, confirms our historic role in the calculation of both time and space. So the government built the Dome and British Airways erected the giant Ferris wheel which came to be called the London Eye.

Credit where it is due, the Dome was completed on time and within budget. But the opening ceremony became a glorious fiasco – and a public relations disaster. Dozens of VIPs, whose tickets had not arrived, were forced to queue at the box office and miss parts of the celebration. Humbler citizens who crowded the banks of the Thames to see "a wall of fire" race along the river, read in the next day's papers that the pyrotechnic spectacular had been magnificent, if viewed from a helicopter. Unfortunately, it was invisible to people at ground level.

Meanwhile, BA's millennium wheel resolutely refused to rotate. First, its erection was delayed by concerns about the structure's safety. Then there were some doubts about the construction of the capsules in which the paying public were to be carried round the great circle. In its way, the millennium celebrations were a perfect example of what so often goes wrong. There may have been millennium disasters in Stockholm and Singapore, Berlin and Brussels. But in those capitals they did not make grandiloquent announcements about the "greatest show on earth". In London we did. So the temptation to draw attention to the biggest anti-climax of the year was irresistible.

There will be those who say that pride and patriotism require loyal British citizens to ignore the errors and concentrate instead on examples of national success. Unfortunately, history has prevented us from doing that in suitable moderation. We persist in thinking of ourselves not so much as different but as superior. That is why our ambassadors have bigger motorcars and more luxurious residences than are enjoyed by representatives of similarly-sized powers. It is why our newspapers expect sporting triumph in every competition – until the very day we are trounced. And it is why we make intemperate claims about what Douglas Hurd, when foreign secretary, called "punching above our weight".

What we now need is a little old fashioned reticence. "Those who were down," said Bunyan, "need fear no fall." Nations which are humble, however great their achievements, need not be afraid that the rest of the world will draw attention to their inefficiency. The time has come to put the United Kingdom in proper perspective. We are a medium-sized European power, doing often as well, sometimes better and occasionally worse than the countries which surround us. It helps if you think that way, but I can't guarantee it will stop you feeling frustrated and even a little embarassed that it took a week to get four British helicopters to a disaster-stricken Commonwealth country. •

12 January 2000

Jon Henley

Tide of oil pushes Brittany to the edge of despair

Exactly a month ago today, 60 miles from the windswept dunes and white-painted, slate-roofed holiday villas of this neat Brittany village, a 24-year-old rusty Maltese oil tanker broke her back and sank in a midwinter gale. Two weeks later, in thick, foul-smelling black slabs, the Erika's cargo began washing up on the long pristine ribbon of Les Moutiers beach. And every day since Boxing Day, Guy le Pavec has been cleaning it up. The deputy mayor of Les Moutiers, grey-haired and crinkle-faced, looked at the scene with tired eyes. Four bulldozers were at work, digging out a fresh mountain of sludge that had arrived with the morning tide.

"It's desperate", Mr le Pavec said. "Every day we break our backs, and every morning we come back wondering how much of yesterday's work will have been undone. But you can't let it get you down. You just have to keep going."

It is revolting stuff, heavy fuel oil. It stinks and it sticks to you and it gets everywhere, and on a bright, sunny day the ugliness of it, splattered along a wild and beautiful coastline, turns your stomach. On big expanses of flat sand, like up the coast at the chic La Baule resort, the oil spreads out like a pancake and can be shovelled up by machine. But on the narrower, pebble-strewn, less fashionable strands like this one, every rock has to be cleaned by hand.

That is what 350 figures in waterproofs, wellingtons and rubber gloves were doing yesterday – soldiers from nearby Saint Nazaire, firefighters from the far south and south-west, trainee policemen from Nantes, a class of young nurses from down near Valence, and a small group of pensioners.

"At least it's a fine day," said Jean-Paul, 66, crouched over the edge of the oil-encrusted promenade, chipping away at a congealed splash with a small trowel. "I can't come here when it's cold or raining."

Raynaldo, 24, graduated last month from police college and was waiting to be assigned his first job. He was wielding a heavy shovel, filling up his mate Gregory's wheelbarrow. This beach was harder than the last, he said.

"Apart from all the rocks here, oil has got in under the sand," he said. "You see what you think is a little pebble and it turns out to be the tip of a huge lump. You wonder whether it'll ever be gone."

Sophie, 20, volunteered for a week with the rest of her nursing class, driving 11 hours through the night to get here. She was trying hard not to get depressed. "The worst is when you find a dead bird mixed up in it," she said. "But even when you don't, it's terribly hard. We don't seem to be making an impression at all."

Up and down 250 miles of the Brittany and Loire-Atlantique coast, similar groups are having similar doubts. The soldiers, police and firefighters will keep going – on a good day, they can clear two tonnes of sludge per person. The volunteers, though, are ebbing. Still, Mr le Pavec thinks that with a bit of luck they might be done in a month. The tides are bringing in less and less new oil each day, and the 20,000 tonnes still in the Erika are not, apparently, escaping.

But if that is good news for most of the village's 923 inhabitants, who rely for their income on 10,000 tourists a week in summer, it is too late for the two dozen men and women in Les Moutiers and neighbouring La Bernerie who cultivate oysters for a living. Their oyster beds, a mile or so out in the shallow expanse of Bourgneuf bay, produce 500 tonnes of shellfish a year. It takes three or four years for each new crop to mature. And last week a thin film of oil was floating inches over the beds. Some had already been coated.

"That's three seasons' work and three seasons' profits gone," spat one Les Moutiers grower, Virginie Girard. "Who will buy Bourgneuf bay oysters now? I've got 11 years of loan repayments ahead and I'm not going to sit around paying for the idiocy of an oil company that charters wrecks."

The bay's freelance shellfish fishermen, who collect cockles, mussels and clams at low tide and make a precarious living at the best of times, have also been banned from selling their produce until the necessary laboratory hygiene tests have been completed.

"Whether we survive depends on how quickly we get compensation," said Arnaud Roger, 24. "If it comes in two or three months, maybe we'll pull through. If not, that'll be another local job gone."

The government is doing what it can, they admit. The agriculture minister, Jean Glavany, is touring Bourgneuf bay this week to discuss compensation. The secretary for tourism, Michelle Demessine, has said she will send a bill for the clean-up to TotalFina, the Franco-Belgian oil company which chartered the Erika.

But on Les Moutiers beach yesterday, the sweating line of oil-smeared workers was talking of only one thing. Three miles out, a coastguard helicopter had spotted a thick new half-mile slick. Where would that one land? •

8 November 1999
Christopher Hitchens
Beautiful behemoth

Who looks at an American book?" asked the Reverend Sydney Smith scornfully in the Edinburgh Review of the mid-Victorian epoch. He went on to enquire whether anyone would care to attend an American play, or cast a glance at an American picture, or in general take even a bar of a tune from an American melody. As one of the more muscular and quotable critics of his time, Smith was by no means alone in his contempt. Dickens, in his fictional Martin Chuzzlewit and his journalistic American Notes, did his best to ridicule and discredit the notion of the United States as the land of opportunity. Lesser writers, such as the Boy's Own Captain Marryat and Frances May Trollope (aunt of John Major's allegedly favourite author), returned from the former colonies with similar tales of condescension and disdain.

Well, the Reverend Smith has now got his answer. Not only do we all look at American books, but we have scant choice about whether to view American films or American television series. Thanks in part to the universality of cable TV, and to the contingent fact that the language of the web and the internet is American English, the lifestyle of the United States middle class is the norm to which millions of immigrants and strivers now aspire. The word is out.

So far from being able to be patronising about America, some of her former rivals now fear her. Joseph Conrad saw it coming in 1904, with his impressive character Holroyd, the Yankee businessman in Nostromo who has "the temperament of a Puritan and an insatiable imagination of conquest". Holroyd looks at the world through globalising eyes and says, as he surveys the paltry efforts of lesser powers: " We can sit and watch. Of course, some day we shall step in. We are bound to. We shall run the world's business whether the world likes it or not. The world can't help it – and neither can we, I guess."

This used to be called "manifest destiny" and became known, a little later, as "the American century". Coined by the media tycoon Henry Luce, the latter slogan was often satirised for its complacency. After all, Mr Luce thought that the defining event of the century would be the American-sponsored Christianisation of China. But even Gore Vidal, who was rightly withering at the expense of that notion, wrote an essay not many years ago entitled "The Day the American Empire Ran Out of Gas". This postulated the rise of Japan as the new superstate. It's brave and decent of him to reprint it still in his collections, because it is only one of the many premature obituaries for an American century that may, in fact, be opening rather than closing.

Just take stock for a moment. The United States has the Atlantic and the Pacific as its sea walls, and Mexico and Canada for its neighbours; an almost unbelievable geopolitical felicity. It has an abundance of every agricultural, mineral and human resource.

It possesses an unchallengeable military superiority. It is the host country of the United Nations, the World Bank and the International Monetary Fund. It regularly scoops the Nobel prize pool when it comes to medicine and physics (and doesn't do too badly at the literature award either) and has labs that are aeons ahead of any probable rival. Its university libraries bulge with the letters and manuscripts of authors from a dozen other countries. Its consultants and techniques are regnant wherever elections take place; indeed, the grammar of American Tammany politics is now the baseline of democratic or at least electoral discourse everywhere. Its model of skyline and down-town is the glass of fashion and the mould of form, everywhere from Hong Kong to Sydney to Buenos Aires. Its courtroom dramas and celebrity traumas are the staple of light conversation everywhere.

I have purposely mixed the sublime and the ghastly in the foregoing, and haven't by any means exhausted the scale and scope of the thing. Educated and sophisticated Americans, returning from travels overseas, are wont to complain that they simply cannot escape the products and practices of their native heath, however far they stray. Nobody despises the McDonald's landscape more than an upscale New Yorker or Angeleno. Nobody winces more – at some atrocity like the recent ban on Darwin in the Kansas school system – than the American who has a time-share in an apartment in Paris or London.

Currently, a version of the old argument between "isolationists" and "internation-alists" is under way again, providing much facile fodder for editorialists and columnists. Actually, the United States has never been, and never will be, isolationist. Even as it was trying to put tariff and other barriers between itself and Europe in the 1920s and 1930s, it was making strenuous efforts to expand in the Pacific and in Latin America. The term that people need to employ instead is "unilateralist": the combination of a provincial mentality with an imperial one. Those who voted down the test ban treaty in the Senate did so not in order to create a "Fortress America", but in order to preserve a global nuclear superiority, and to insist that America may conduct inspection of other countries while refusing it for itself. Alas, these tough-minded conservatives were confronted only by a pseudo-internationalist; a president with the soul of a governor or a mayor; perhaps the most parochial and timorous president of modern times.

One can see the same irony at work in the attitude to new populations. American English is fast becoming the language in which the world does its business. It is the tongue of the internet and of the stock market, and of air-traffic control. Objectively, if not officially, it has deposed French as the language of diplomacy. Yet the parochialist-imperialists (like Pat Buchanan, who combines xenophobia with an unbroken record of support for war in Vietnam and Nicaragua and Grenada) worry ceaselessly about dilution and multiculturalism, and propose laws to make "English only" the official language, with penalties for those who can only stutter it. Meanwhile, sunrise corporations in Silicon Valley petition Congress to relax immigration restrictions, so that they can hire more science and computer-chip graduates from India, most of whom speak English rather better than the natives do.

This quarrel, between those who regard the American experiment as essentially complete and those who do not, is one that the rest of the world has to watch with breathless interest. Professor Benjamin Barber at Rutgers University has postulated a sort of reverse dialectic between "Jihad and McWorld", whereby the only resistance to the commodification and standardisation of everything is offered by traditionalists and fundamentalists. More familiar as a conflict outside American borders – the Saudis want an American alliance but they don't want their society saturated with cable-borne temptations – the fight actually replicates itself within them.

The only sizeable American constituency to have proposed a boycott of Disney, for its values of greed and hedonism, is the southern Baptist leadership. (I know a few urban sophisticates who moaned, if only in private, that it had come to something when only the rednecks were prepared to take a stand against corporate America.) For the moment, Disney is impervious to such sanctions. Though it doesn't do to forget that there is a traditional, pious America, several layers below the glitz, and that it feels itself alienated from the turbo- charge of modernism, it is likewise a mistake to overestimate it. The free-enterprise ethos crushes cultural conservatism as well as many other kinds of culture.

For part of the summer I was in Alaska, the last great "frontier" state of the union. Here, atop unimaginable riches of oil and minerals, sits a small population that could feature in no sitcom. Russian Orthodox churches minister to Inuit Indian congregations; the state capital of Juneau is inaccessible by road; prehistoric landscapes manifest the scars of the last earthquake and suggest the contours of the next one.

A pipeline snakes its way through wolves and moose. You can, if you really want to, swim to Russia from here. (During the cold war, I used to be able to win bets in Washington by asking which country was the nearest to the United States after Mexico and Canada. Nobody ever said the USSR, any more than anybody could answer the question: which country has the largest military base in Cuba?) Originally purchased from Russia for pennies by Seward, once Lincoln's Secretary of State, Alaska has recently and seriously discussed purchasing Siberia, or at least a part of it, from Russia. This almost certainly won't happen now – America's stewardship of the Russian economy has been the single most calamitous failure of the post-cold war period – but the mere fact of its being thinkable is testament to the astonishing reserve capacity, and astonishing confidence, of the system.

Over the border in Canada, the perennial question of dissolution also suggests that America's bounds might yet be set wider and wider. The Quebecois, if they attain independence, will seek recognition first from the United States. The Atlantic provinces, in response, may seek assimilation with it. (Pat Buchanan, among others, recommends accepting this proposal, at least for the white and English-speaking applicants. He's in favour of annexing Greenland while they're at it – another indication that the so-called "isolationists" are by no means the stay-at-home type.)

Meanwhile, at the opposite end of the continent, the life of the Fidel Castro regime continues to move peacefully towards its close. And there are those, among the Cuban exile opposition, who would like to have Cuba become a state of the union also. It's a stretch for the imagination ("The Chair recognises the honourable senator from Havana") but it does revive an old dream from the days of the Monroe doctrine. It is, in any case, a near-actuarial certainty that the United States will soon, once again, be playing the decisive role in Cuban affairs. (The other day, the US "interest section" in Havana announced a lottery for a few thousand visas. Practically everybody on the island applied for one.)

Back in the Victorian era, when the Reverend Sydney Smith and Dickens and Marryat and the rest were sneering at America as an experiment in gross vulgarity, the great exception was Karl Marx. In his essays on the civil war – when the London Times was a cheerleader for the Confederacy – he held up the United States as an example of liberty and opportunity, and staunchly supported the Union in its attempt to become a Continental power. (That he and Engels took this view of the US, and viewed Russia as a swamp of despotism and aggression, must count as one of the ironies of history.)

The radical paper Reynolds' News, one of the most eloquent voices for the London labour movement, wrote that "anything that adds to the power and authority of the United States among the nations of the earth is to the advantage of all mankind". It called for Canada to be annexed by America, on the grounds that "all good Radicals" should "look to the Great Republic for their precedents, and not to the corrupt and snobbish Dominion".

The long cold war, and the rise of plutocracy and imperialism in America, separates us from the folk memory of the new world as the last, best hope of mankind. But it's as well to remember that, at the close of the last century, the United States was in fact viewed by millions in the naive but inspiring words of Emma Lazarus on the base of the Statue of Liberty: "Give me your tired, your poor, your huddled masses... " Just as the metaphysical poets would refer longingly to "my America – my new found land" when they wished to convey yearning and longing. And now, even after Vietnam and Hiroshima and Senator McCarthy and all that, the towers and turrets of Miami and Los Angeles and Chicago still act as a beacon and magnet, perhaps now more than ever, to anyone with an eye to the future. As John Steinbeck once wrote about New York, its climate and its politics may be so bad that they are used to scare disobedient children, but once you have have been gripped there is no other place. •

Christopher Hitchens is a columnist for Vanity Fair and the Nation.

....

8 November 1999

John Hooper
@ **Berlin**

Davaa was once huge in Siberia. A light comes on in her eyes as she fixes on a point over your shoulder and recalls the applause and bouquets, the impassioned fan letters that followed her through what she calls her "beautiful years". An irrepressible, strikingly beautiful Mongolian, Davaa used to front a rock band that crazed timber cutters and hydroelectric workers as it plied the Trans-siberian railway in a specially chartered train. Later came a spot of bother with the Moscow mafia. One day, Davaa thought: "Hey, how about Berlin ?"

The same thought occurred to Nicole when she woke up to find that her provincial German home town had all of a sudden become unbearably small. Nowadays, she works at finding flats for the thousands of politicians, government officials, diplomats, business executives and journalists who have been pouring into Berlin since it became the capital again.

It occurred too to half-Romany Lou from the Black Forest, who came to learn to dance and makes a living waiting in one of the trendy cafes in the Mitte district of east Berlin. At times, indeed, it can seem to have occurred to every drifter, dreamer and go-getter from Wuppertal to Vladivostok.

Berlin is a city that was once an island and is now a bridge. The transformation is changing not only the character of the place but the composition of its population.

In the days when it was locked in the sea of old East Germany, Berlin exerted an irresistible fascination for all sorts of people in search of a refuge: drop-outs, draft dodgers, dopeheads and drones. Now in their 50s, they can still be found in areas like Kreuzberg, hanging out in evil-looking bars adorned with faded posters of Frank Zappa and Jim Morrison. Some are in pretty bad shape: if you want a glimpse of the long-term effects of narcotics abuse you could do worse than catch any late-night U-bahn on the line that leads to Alt Mariendorf.

The fall of the wall 10 years ago did more than just put an end to Berlin's isolation. For one thing, it made it a natural point of entry for anyone trying to sneak into Europe from the east. There are nowadays large numbers of suspiciously prosperous Russians living in the fashionable Charlottenburg district of the city.

The subsequent reunification of Germany also made it thinkable that Berlin could once more be the capital, and that has drawn in two new groups of outsiders. One is made up of people from Bonn, though they remain oddly invisible. Most seem to want to live in suburbs like Gruenewald, an area described by Christopher Isherwood as having villas "in all known styles of expensive ugliness".

The other group is made up of people alive to the possibilities offered by this city's new-old (and sorry about the last time) status. The erstwhile dropouts, who detest the newcomers, call them "yuppies", though that is misleading because a lot are seeking fame, particularly in the arts or the media, more than fortune.

There is a political and economic significance to all of this. Much of the concern over German reunification, particularly on the right, is rooted in a fear that Europe is about to come under the leadership of a country that has failed to embrace fully free market values; a country where welfare provision counts for more than entrepreneurial gusto.

That fear may yet prove to be justified, but by making Berlin the capital again, the Germans have exposed their leaders to a very different climate of thought. This is a town in which you go to change money and find yourself being given a concise history of the bank teller's career before she asks you point blank if you could offer her a better job; a city in which you go to transact official business with a member of the German civil service and are shown the plans of a most desirable flat you just might be interested in renting.

A "proper little New York", our landlady calls it. •

---

11 December 1999

Bernard Kops

A letter from America

It's taken me 72 years and nine months to travel to America. But finally I've made it. I'm here, in the middle of nowhere. Middle class, Midwest America. Nebraska, of all places. "Nebraska? You must be out of your mind. Nobody goes to Nebraska. Everyone leaves," was everyone's reaction.

I'm in Wayne. It is not even a dot on the map. There are no records of any white man hereabouts prior to 1869. Here stretched the boundless plains of the Sioux nation. Bison stampeded across the now deserted Main Street.

I stand on the porch of this clapboard wooden house looking out over the dry-cleaned empty streets. Wayne! Hampstead Garden suburb of the corn belt, seen through the wrong end of a telescope. The air is so pure you dare not breathe in, the sky so astonishingly sparkling you cannot look up. Wayne has a college, the hub of its universe. The student population is 4,000. The human population 5,200.

We're staying at Grandma Butch's bed and breakfast, $50 a night in a squeaky-clean, blushing room so sweetly pure it smiles down upon you, trusting you won't get up to anything other than sleep.

The American Dream started with my father. It was 1904. Struggling to survive grinding poverty in Amsterdam, he scraped and saved to buy a ticket to escape to God's Own Country. Later, examining the ticket, he read that it was one way from Rotterdam to London. Why didn't it mention New York? He was told he would receive the other half of the ticket in London from Mr Smith. But Mr Smith wasn't there. He searched frantically all night, then collapsed in tears.

He was one of the yearning masses who never made it. He yearned for the rest of his life, in Stepney. He died yearning, shadowed by the nightmare that he had been cheated out of the dream. My childhood was dominated by the dream that never was.

But I had another dream. There was the little matter of joining the Communist Party in 1947. I resigned from the party six months later, but the consequences of having belonged follows me like an albatross for the rest of my life.

My first play opened off Broadway during the heat of the McCarthy plague, and with that current mood I didn't even try to get there. Several plays and novels later, I was asked to do a lecture tour. But there was always that horrendous form to fill in. Besides, when I left the Communist Party, I went even further left, to anarchism. How could I possibly explain that away?

And soon, the matter of a visa became academic, because I developed an overwhelming fear of flying. My affliction lasted for 25 years. I simply could not swallow Bernoulli's theorem on why planes stayed up in the sky.

Then, one morning, I woke up, and the malady was gone. I looked up at every plane high over Swiss Cottage and thought "What the hell!" The very worst thing a plane could do was crash. Anyway, you never get out of life alive.

After a few short trips to boring old Tuscany and those terrible Canary Islands, I decided that abroad was nothing much to write home about after all. I suppressed all my travel dreams and settled for the Jubilee line.

But a few months ago, an airmail letter arrived from a place called Wayne. A small state college in Nebraska wanted to prodouce my newest play, Café Zeitgeist. Would I go there to do workshops with students and dazzle them with brilliant chat and lectures? It was an offer that I simply could refuse.

But the offer lingered, niggling in my mind. I simply had to prove that I could survive a long flight. And I simply had to prove that America existed before I died.

But would they let me in? Surely their computers still had me cornered. Young Bernie Kops selling Daily Workers outside Aldgate East station. 1947.

The letter from the college said they would pay for everything. All my doubts evaporated. That was it! I flew straight out of the window, second star on the left, straight on to morning. And Nebraska!

We didn't fall out of that sky, so there I am in a queue at the airport, having to remember to tell immigration that I wasn't there to work but to visit old friends. No visa. Not necessary. Just sign a form to say that I was not a Nazi and that I did not intend to overthrow the government of the United States all by myself. And that I was not suffering from a mental illness. Oh God! Where am I now that I need me?

The young, efficient female machine does not smile as she processes the passports ahead of us. We shuffle over. I immediately stoop and manufacture a benign old man and hold my breath for 20 seconds. The burnished female scans her infernal machine. She's got me! This is it! They'll frog-march me to the next plane back to civilisation.

But her face actually cracks into a smile. "Thank you. Have a nice stay." I bite my tongue and do not reply: "I shall have any sort of stay I desire." I'm through! The last of the tired masses has finally made it.

It's breakfast time at Grandma Butch's. Ardyce, our landlady, knows her statistics: 3% of the English go to church, 30% of Americans go to church, but here in Nebraska it's 80%. And that includes many of the professors of Wayne State College.

She must know I'm Jewish, but that never floats to the surface which is covered with dishes of bacon and eggs, Nebraskan potato cakes, packets and packets of cereals, crushed fruit ice and a pyramid of still-steaming muffins.

She comes up with such wonderful non-sequiturs. "I love church. We do such wonderful square dancing there. We have such happy times in Wayne." The clock ticks timelessness; the house has escaped from a Louisa May Allcott novel.

Ardyce speaks so soft, with no hurry in her voice. Come to think of it, everyone here talks as if being controlled from outer space. But then, we are in outer space.

Beaming Ken breezes in; he has a half share in the B&B. "Would you folks care to ride round town in my Model A Ford?" History may be bunk, but soon we are in this creaking time capsule taking in Main Street and every leafy lane in the town. It's all of seven minutes to make our way through everywhere. Ken honks at everyone in every street. All 10 of them. We wave out. They all wave back. They all know Ken.

A few Stepford wives lean out of windows grinning, as we honk past. Rosy-cheeked kids giggle as they swing on the porches of their clapboard houses. The sheets and the streets of Wayne are spotless, and a golden aura of autumnal trees shield it from the universe. The Holocaust hasn't happened. Paedophiles have not yet been invented. These few days are an oasis of absolute peace, like rehearsing for death.

The students here in Wayne are now well into rehearsals. Café Zeitgeist? Here of all places? The play is set in Budapest during the war. It is about prejudice, about gypsies and Jews and other people wanting to escape their inevitable fate. The style is expressionistic and hardly appropriate, I would have thought, to anything happening around here. So far I have found not one single soul who wants to escape from this place. Indeed, most of the kids have never been outside Wayne.

The next day, we have been honoured with a special place at an atavistic gathering. The football match. The game is totemic; indecipherable. Girls are thrown into the air. They've all got the same face. The home side wins. The town goes crazy. Next evening, those same faces are crammed into the theatre. It's the first night. Can Café Zeitgeist come anywhere close to the thrill of a hometown win?

To my astonishment, I am moved. And the play is a success. Due largely to Andre Sedriks, the brilliant Latvian-American director. What's he doing buried in this place?

"Do you love us?" Everyone here wants to please; desperately needs to be loved. "Do you love America? Isn't it just the greatest country on earth?" They remind me of my grandchildren whom I just cannot disappoint. "Yes, you are the greatest, happiest, most tolerant, beautiful and kindest people on this earth, and I love you with all my heart. Forever and always. Amen. Have a nice day."

"Goodnight Mr Kops. Thank you for coming. It was our privilege meeting you." They have such a sweet innocence and absolutely no concept of anywhere else. To them America is the only country that God created. Their teeth glint in the moonlight. The young and happy kids go rushing into the dark. It's all so unnerving.

As I leave the campus for the last time, I just wonder what the reaction would be if a group of gypsies parked their mobile homes on the campus lawn overnight.

Driving out of Wayne on our way to Omaha, and home, I saw the town slowly slipping away. A dream of the past. The dazzling sun on startling green-painted lawns and a few happy children, up early, giggling on the swing in the front garden. Andrew Wyeth was here, and Norman Rockwell. But David Lynch and the Coen brothers are yet to surface.

Nebraska was time out from life. They were not at all the redneck fascists I expected, so, at my time of life I have to start re-evaluating my ideas. It is all rather late in the day for an old dog to be thrown yet again into confusion, but at least I have become an inveterate, long-distance traveller. And thus am even able to drop in on New York on the way home.

I want to see Quentin Crisp, an old friend from Soho. We hadn't met for 15 years. On the telephone, he commands me to meet him at Coopers Diner. I ask him how he is.

"Falling apart," he replies.

We have corn beef hash for lunch and he devours a huge glass of ice cream. "What will you do for the millennium?" I ask.

He smiles, raises his eyes to the heavens and folds his arms across his chest.

Who could know that he will be dead within days? His dialogue is as sprightly, scintillating and original as ever. We fly back into the past, gossip about friends and monsters. It's so good to be back in the real world again. •

....

4 March 2000

Jon Henley

A century of eating has left Michelin overstuffed

Back in 1900, petrol cost 50 centimes a litre, a Georges Richard two-seater Poney automobile cost 3,500 francs, a night in a two-star hostelry including three-course meal with wine cost 10-13 francs, and the Michelin tyre company published its first Red Guide to the hotels and restaurants of France.

"This present work," that first booklet declared, "aims to provide information useful to the motorist travelling in France... We promise to be pitiless in striking from our lists any establishment whose cuisine, accommodation, water closets or service are notified to us as being defective."

Pitiless they may have been, but there is one restaurant in France which Michelin's feared inspectors, despite a century of trying, have been unable to fault. This week, le Grand Monarque in Chartres celebrated the unique achievement of appearing in all 100 annual Red Guides.

"We only realised when all the papers started calling," said Bertrand Jallerat, 29, who with his wife Nathalie took over the running of the 19th-century coaching inn two years ago from his father Georges. "I'm grateful for the accolades, but really it's a tribute to the two families who've run the place for the past 10 decades."

Much may have changed in the world since the dawn of the last century; the Michelin guide itself, for example, has grown from a give-away pocketbook about how to repair your punctures into an awesome 1,800-page foodie's bible whose coveted stars are so sought after that chefs have been known to commit suicide on losing one.

But the recently refurbished dining room of le Grand Monarque remains a modest monument to the only three things that have ever really mattered in this realm: good food and fine wine served in pleasant surroundings. Most of its customers – local businessmen, elderly ladies, even tourists in town for the famous cathedral – have been before.

"The menu's a bit more adventurous than it was in 1900," said the chef, Michel Menier. "Then, of necessity, it was strictly regional; now with modern-day transport we can get fresh ingredients every day from anywhere in France. But we still serve a few of the same dishes."

Today's £23 three-course menu features paté de Chartres – a long standing speciality – and the pièce de résistance, côte de veau Curnonsky. This was the pseudonym of one Maurice Edouard Saillard, an all-time star in the galaxy of French foodies who was known as the Prince of Gastronomes. His early 20th-century recipe for veal cutlet? Simply, "In the manner of le Grand Monarque at Chartres".

Nor have the three cellars, containing 35,000 bottles, changed very much.

The Jallerats and the Drouets before them have always bought selected Loire valley and Bordeaux wines the year they come on to the market, allowing the restaurant today to offer 20-year-old vintages of Chateau Petrus and Chateau Haut-Brion at £200-£300 a bottle – a lot of money, but maybe half what a Paris wine merchant would demand'.

There is just one small fly in le Grand Monarque's soup (as it happens, a lobster consommé served with wild mushrooms): although it has been listed in all the Michelin guides it did, some 15 years ago, lose the single Michelin star it had held for many years. No one knows quite why; perhaps the chef had an off-day.

Whatever the reason, Mr Jallerat is not so sure he wants it back – and sadly for Michelin these days, he is not alone in feeling that a star can be more trouble than it is worth. Critics, even in France, are increasingly arguing that the centenarian guide has failed to move with the times and rewards tradition rather than innovation.

More important, several top chefs have recently broken rank and complained vociferously that the guide's practice of rating comfort as highly as cuisine means they are bankrupting themselves on fripperies rather than food. Mr Jallerat shares their view.

"This isn't a chi-chi restaurant that charges the earth, it's a hotel restaurant that fills its dining room by providing decent eats in a nice atmosphere seven days a week," he said.

"A mention in the guide is very, very important – but if I get a star, I'll have to buy crystal glasses for 10 times the price and the customers will start expecting three different kinds of appetiser. It's not my priority." •

24 December 1999

Martin Woollacott

Our past is diminished but the future remains unclear

W hen the young journalist Philip Gibbs was nosing round Clerkenwell, the London area in which the Guardian now has its offices, at the beginning of the century, he found "a little Naples in its colour, its smells, its dirt. The women, as beautiful as Raphael's madonnas, sing at their washtubs, surrounded by swarms of bambini". Gibbs, later a famous correspondent during the first world war, almost got himself killed investigating insanitary conditions in the icecream factories around Leather Lane.

A century later, most of that Italian community has moved elsewhere, but many still return each week for Mass at the two fine Italian churches, and more still come at times like Christmas. They come to worship and also to pay homage to history, to their English as well as to their Italian roots. History interested Gibbs, and it interested the people he reported, even the criminal classes.

He gives an account of the scenes just before the old Old Bailey was due to be pulled down. Crowds of criminals, says Gibbs, arrived for a last look at the place where they had been sentenced and in some cases imprisoned, for the old premises had also been a prison, "and staged a mock trial in the main courtroom".

Gibbs noted an "epidemic" of historical pageants in towns and villages in the years before the first world war. "At Bury St Edmunds there was a scene depicting the homage of 22 gentlemen to Mary Tudor. Each actor there bore the same name and held the same soil as those who had actually bowed before the Tudor lady."

What a characteristically British note Gibbs strikes. History real, history confected, and history that lies somewhere in between the two, has always been part of national self-description. Leonard Woolf applied the thought to newspapers, arguing that "few things, indeed, are more interesting than an old newspaper, and it is a curious fact that the Times of a year ago, if you happen to find no more than half a sheet of it, makes better reading than that of today".

The special twist which the British in recent times gave to this reverence for old things was their insistence that it be combined with a command of the modern and the new. A half century later, that was the precise theme of the Festival of Britain, which paid extensive tribute to the past, while insisting that the country also lived on the technological frontier.

The Standard Motor Company, advertising in the official guide to the festival, asserted: "All that's best in Britain – the State Opening of Parliament – truly a Royal occasion with its colour and pageantry – yet symbolising the very essence of our British Democracy – all that's best of the Past joining with, and giving authority to, the needs of the Present." Only a British car firm, surely, could have advertised its products under a picture of a coach and horses.

Something has shifted since then, even though Tony Blair and his ministers still give us their sing-song version of this old and new discourse, as John Major did before them. The country's grasp on the old has loosened. Partly that is because it probably would no longer be possible to find 22 families in Bury St Edmunds to re-enact a ceremony their ancestors took part in more than 400 years ago. Partly it is because the value of the past is not as obvious as it was in 1901 or 1951. Then, it was precious baggage, even if some of it contained the intellectual equivalent of bricks; now, it is more problematic.

Modern historians puncture Britishness rather than affirm it, like Norman Davies in his recent account. Of course puncturing Britain is not new: Lytton Strachey did it dramatically in Eminent Victorians. Yet the British have become increasingly cavalier about their ancient ways: the Blair government's eagerness to change things is more forthright than that of its predecessors but is, in fact, a continuation of a process of often ill-planned "adaptation" that is now in itself quite old. It gathered pace under Mrs Thatcher, it idled under Major, it threatens to race along under Blair.

One of the saddest losses, in this age of supposed devolution, is that of the idea that institutions have their proper autonomy, and are not mere instruments or fields of action for the central government. It is remarkable that American institutions, for instance, are now far more sacralised and far more protected from substantial change than are those of Britain.

What is notable, too, is that, as the past is deemed of less account, the value of the future for Britain is also less clear. In the years around the turn of the last century, there was a great chorus of predictions. In particular, people in 1900 and 1901 applied themselves to the question of what life would be like a hundred years ahead. There is not much of that this time, in Britain or anywhere else. The Millennium Dome's zones may probe ahead 20 or 30 years, yet neither there or anywhere else is there a sustained effort to imagine the country, or the world, at a much later time. It seems that 2010, when the pension money may run out, is a more interesting date than 2100.

Everybody agrees that yesterday's predictions are fascinating stuff. Some imagined the conquest of Mars, but thought that, like Africa, it would be divided into British, French and other national zones. Some thought, like HG Wells in one of his many future scenarios, that after a terrible war there would be a revolution in the way the world lived, but had it led, improbably, by a young British monarch named Egbert who "read books and went about asking questions". The point is not the "mistakes" but that the intensity of 1900's curiosity about 2000 was much greater than our curiosity now. The Dome, for example, has a feeling of finis about it, rather than any great sense of beginning or becoming.

As a national exhibition, it has to bear comparison with the 1951 festival, when Britain was a more important power, politically, technically, and culturally, than it is today. The "best of the old and best of the new" ideology, slipshod and often fraudulent though it could be, was then a living thing.

Some would argue that the problem is that the concept of harmony between past and future no longer sits all that well within a purely national framework. Others might say that what Britain has lost is its sense of danger. Five Days in London, John Lukacs's wonderful book about the critical period in 1940, recently published, recaptures the moment when the British national project, and with it much else of worth in the world, could have come to an abject end. It is not beyond bounds to imagine that Britain could recover the sense that, as a nation, it is both vulnerable and valuable, in which case past and future might well assume a different meaning. •

Five Days in London, by John Lukacs, is published by Yale University Press.

19 June 2000

Gary Younge
Strangers at the gate

A black face can still turn heads in Nether Stowey. Walk into a pub in this small Somerset village, even when Euro 2000 is on the big screen, and there will be that same momentary silence you will hear in just about any rural bar in Britain as you single-handedly integrate a social space.

A tiny stretch of time when the dart seems to hover at the dart board and beer remains suspended between tap and glass – just long enough so that everyone notices, but short enough that anyone could claim you were imagining it. Not hostile stares, for good-natured conversation soon follows, but the overlong glances from people not used to strangers and for whom a non-white face denotes not just ethnicity but geography. It means "You are not from here."

This is the Mild West – Coleridge country – where hills roll, roads wind and only the bleating of sheep and rustling of leaves disturb the silence on a balmy summer's day. But recently this apparent tranquillity has been disturbed by an attempt to house up to 74 asylum seekers from Kosovo, Sierra Leone and Sudan in a former boarding school in nearby Over Stowey – a tiny hamlet of 314 people.

Planning permission for the centre was refused by Somerset council. The inquiry into that decision, which was held last week, is being viewed as a legal test case for attempts to disperse asylum seekers around the country. It also risks being turned into a moral test case on the rights of asylum seekers to exist at all.

The proposal, which has been made by the Baptist charity Kaleidoscope, has aroused the kind of blatant xenophobia that most thought had been laid to rest with Love Thy Neighbour and the Robertsons golliwog. If some locals are to be believed, the arrival of people fleeing terror in their home countries will cause house prices to tumble, crime to escalate and even compromise the virtue of local young women.

The right has tried to portray these fears as emblematic of the Tory-led assault on asylum seekers – a bastion of essential, monocultural Englishness, according to the Telegraph and the Mail, is about to be "swamped" by unwelcome foreigners thanks to a group of do-gooding liberals. They have created not only a mythic sense of what Over Stowey is, but a demonic sense of who the asylum seekers are too.

These attitudes do not come from nowhere. William Hague has sown the seeds from which this particular strain of bigotry grows and the Labour leadership has so far proved itself too spineless to get its hands dirty and pull his work out at the roots. As a consequence, we have turned into a nation that can stand up for "humanitarianism" when it comes to sending soldiers to the Balkans and Africa but is incapable of dealing with the actual humans who flee the self-same conflicts. We have learned how to export righteousness at the barrel of a gun, we just cannot bring ourselves to distribute it through the Home Office on our own doorstep.

In the church in Over Stowey there is a picture of Msusi Nyanzi – a young boy they have sponsored from Uganda. One wonders what reception he would get if, like Clare Boylan's Black Baby, he turned up one day and asked for his benefactors to provide him with the kind of Christian charity that actually made a difference to their daily lives. Probably the same reaction as the displaced families of Bujumbura, whose pictures stand nearby on the board devoted to the Mothers' Union.

Not that everyone in Over Stowey is a bigot: far from it. Some express concern that the area is not equipped to cope with such large numbers – the nearest pub, shop or post office is more than a mile away from the hostel and the bus to the nearest big town, Bridgwater, comes only twice a week.

They have a point. The location of Quantock Lodge, where the asylum seekers would be housed, is more suitable for a hospice than a hostel. It is set in woodland off the road and a good 15 minutes walk from Over Stowey itself. True, there is a swimming pool, sports pitches and arts centre in the former school – which paradoxically some local people also resent – and Kaleidoscope plans to run a minibus to Bristol,

Bridgwater and Nether Stowey. But it remains extremely isolated – possibly ideal for people suffering from traumatic experiences but hopeless for those who want to exercise some independence.

Somehow, however, one gets the feeling that if the asylum seekers were white Zimbabwean farmers on the run from Mugabe, we would not be talking about bus services and walking distances. It is also a very small community in which to place a relatively large group of people. But then Over Stowey has already shown that it can cope with this. The idea that it has been a haven of pure, lily-white Englishness is bogus, not the asylum seekers. The Lodge used to be a private school that took in a large number of Hong Kong Chinese. But they were wealthy and not, at the time, national hate figures.

There is little doubt that the arrival of asylum seekers will change Over Stowey and the surrounding area. The trouble is the automatic presumption that it will change for the worse, the notion that all that 74 people from different parts of the globe can bring to a small, ageing, rural area is crime and destitution, that an area where black people are still to be stared at has nothing to learn about the modern world.

Not everyone in the area believes that. Several local people are strongly in favour of the plans. The debate has pitted the vicar (pro) against the head of the parish council (anti) and split families. There have been petitions and heated meetings.

"It'll be great to have people here," said Suki Ince as she weeded her garden. She says those who oppose the hostel are a vocal minority; they say most of those who back it are outsiders. "Some of the things people have been saying have made me ashamed to be from this village. One person said they'd moved here from London to get away from all that. That kind of thing really surprised me."

When a visitor expressed envy at the fact that transport in the area is bad and yet the asylum seekers will get their own bus, Ince retorted: "Well, great. Then maybe we can use their bus."

Her visitor had not thought of that. And in just one sharp response, the focus had shifted from asylum seekers being people who will definitely take something away to people who had something to add. From a problem to an opportunity.

And then she went back to her weeding – seeking out the problem plants and yanking each one out by the roots. •

8 January 2000

Sam Wollaston
Harley street

*"You see things vacationing on a motorcycle in a way that is completely different
from any other. In a car, you're always in a compartment, and because you're
used to it you don't realise that through that car window everything you see is just
more TV. You're a passive observer and it is all moving by you boringly in a frame.
On a cycle the frame is gone. You're completely in contact with it all. You're in the
scene, not just watching it anymore, and the sense of presence is overwhelming."*
Robert M Pirsig, Zen And The Art Of Motorcycle Maintenance

It had to be a Harley-Davidson. I don't care for them much normally – big, cumber-
some, noisy things with all the disadvantages of motorcycles (you get cold, you
might die) and none of the advantages (they're neither fast nor good for weaving in
and out of traffic). But to cross America, coast to coast, by any other means would
have been ridiculous. Peter Fonda and Dennis Hopper did it on Harleys, so I was going
to do it on a Harley, too.

And they have good names: Night Train, Dyna Low Rider, Fatboy, Electra Glide.
Mine was a Heritage Softail Classic. Heritage, I imagine, means that this bike has a lot
of pedigree. The Softail bit refers to the rear suspension. Classic speaks for itself. I
rented it in New Jersey for three weeks, to be returned in Los Angeles.

It was red, and there was a lot of chrome about the place, and black studded leather
– nothing like my Vespa at all. For a start, it had a 1,340cc – or bigger than a lot of cars.
And I had absolutely no idea how to operate it, but I wasn't going to let them know
that. Right, here's a button with "Start" written on it... Brrrmmm. There's that pneu-
matic drill noise. Now, which way to New York?

That was probably the scariest bit of all, that first ride into Manhattan. Before I had
a chance to think about it and do something more sensible, we were out on a highway
with an absurd number of lanes. (Note that the bike and I have already become "we".)
I was pretty sure we would make a wrong turn somewhere and do a Bonfire of the
Vanities. But then we got on to one of those wonderful skyways, and there was
Manhattan stretched out in front, glorious in the autumn sunshine. I let out a whoop
(the first of many), a mixture of sheer joy and extreme terror.

Twenty days later, we rolled into Los Angeles. Twenty days, 4,283 miles, 13 states,
one-and-a-half breakdowns, one wedding (not mine) and one dead chipmunk. I tried
to avoid the chipmunk, promise, but like I said, Harleys aren't really bikes for swerv-
ing. Oh, and half a suntan – because when you go west for a long time, only the left side
of your face gets done.

I'm not sure how it worked out as 4,283 miles (that's London to Delhi, or Chicago even, if you're a crow and you have a lot of stamina). In my Rand McNally Road Atlas, it says New York to Los Angeles is 2,824 miles. We did avoid the interstates, the big multi-laned roads, where possible, and took a few detours. And detours in the US tend to be about 400 miles, generally.

We stayed a day and a night in New York, then set off up the Hudson River – or next to it rather – past Bear Mountain, where Sal Paradise turned back for the first time in On The Road because it was raining. But it wasn't raining, so we kept going, up through New York State with all the trees doing their big fall show-off display. Woodstock for bad art and very good blueberry pancakes, Ithaca for the finger lakes, Niagara Falls for the big waterfall (good, but not as good as the fountain display in front of the Bellagio hotel in Las Vegas). After that, it was pretty much west: Buffalo, Cleveland, Chicago for the wedding. Then the big skies and cornscapes of the Mid-West – like Lincolnshire, except forever. (And there's Lincoln right in the middle, just to prove it.)

Route 66 only exists in parts now, and anyway we were a long way north of it. But we found lots of other good, romantic roads. Like Route 28 through the Catskill Mountains, 92 across the plains of Iowa, or 2 through Nebraska. The road is every-thing in America; it has a romantic quality you just don't find on the M6. This is because they are much, much longer; you spend a lot more time on them, so they do assume characters. Most states even have an "Adopt a Highway" scheme. In this country, we adopt elephants at the zoo. Americans adopt American roads.

It's a big, old place, the States. I think that really struck me round about Nebraska, probably on Highway 2 – lonely Highway 2 – which meanders through Nebraska's sand hills. This is how lonely Highway 2 is: at the start of the trip I reserved my waves strictly for other Harleys (not so much a wave, actually, more of a subtle gesture with the left hand). But as you get further into the heart of the country, there aren't so many around, so you have to wave at any old bike. And then you start getting roads where even a car or a truck is so rare it deserves a wave. On highway 2, I was waving at trees.

Trees and trains, because Highway 2 runs beside the railroad. Some trains they were, too: 120 wagons of coal coming east from Wyoming. That's a mile long. And they blasted their horns back at me when I waved – that sad noise only American trains do properly. I can't explain how special it is to have a mile-long train say hello to you.

As you get further away from the coast you start to notice stuff – like how the people get friendlier and less attractive. And their jeans fit less well. I discovered the place with the worst fitting jeans in the world: Iowa 80 (named after the state it's in and the road it's on). It's a huge truck stop; a glorious city of arcade games, Wendy's, shops selling soft toys, model cars, games.

We cut a little corner of Wyoming, then Colorado and over the Rockies, and down through the canyons and deserts of the southwest to California.

The southwest was best to ride through – Colorado, Utah, Arizona – where deserted roads twist along the bottom of red canyons, or run straight across big coun-try, scenery you recognise from a thousand films. This was, I realised, what I'd come for. And it was here that I began to understand what Harley-Davidsons are all about.

They're the Bentley Continentals of the two-wheeled world. They're not for nipping about town; they're for effortless, comfortable cruising across big countries, preferably America.

In Colorado, I discovered the throttle lock. You pick your favoured engine speed, lock on to it, and then there's nothing to do at all. You can study the map, take photos, or just sit back and watch as America slides under that big, fat, chrome headlamp up front. And in Colorado, you don't need to wear a helmet, so you've got the wind in your hair as well. Truly wonderful. Now, if I'd had an Electra Glide I would have had a cassette player, too, a journey with a soundtrack...

There were lots of good times. Like going over big bridges – it's a wonderful thing to go over a big bridge on a motorcycle. And crossing big rivers, rivers you know all about from school: the Hudson, Mississippi, Missouri, Colorado. We went through bridges, too – little covered ones, in Madison County, Iowa. Yes, those bridges.

Carhenge was a good time – a copy of Stonehenge made from old cars, in a remote cornfield in the panhandle of Nebraska. And Mesa Verde National Park, high up in Colorado, was wonderful, once home to the Anastasia people who lived in towered dwellings in the sides of cliffs. And the Grand Canyon, Bryce Canyon, it goes on.

There was, of course, the odd bad time. Like the girl at the Super 8 motel in Kingston – she was definitely a bad time:

"We're all full."

"Yes, I know. You said. But are there any other motels in Kingston?"

"They're all full."

"Where do you think I might find a motel that isn't full?"

"I don't know."

And so it went on. She was very determined not to pass on any information that might be of any help to me. They weren't all full either. I hope you rot in that reception in Kingston the rest of your life, honey.

The wind in Wyoming was a bad time, too, so strong we had to ride at an angle just to stay upright, if that makes sense. And it was cold at 12,000ft in the Rockies, but we missed the snow by a day and the hot springs at Idaho Springs, on the other side, soon warm you up.

Breaking down on Interstate 80 going into Cleveland started off being bad. There was a popping noise, and we just stopped. Now I'm no expert in the art of motorcycle maintenance, so I just sat there, wondering what the hell to do... for about four minutes: then state patrolman Art Demico showed up in his patrol car and got on the radio. "Got one from London here, and I don't mean London, Ohio." Art also said I should have been on a Honda; where's your patriotism, man?

Within an hour, I was on the back of a tow truck, on the way to South East Harley-Davidson, where I had to say everything twice because the way I spoke cracked them up so much. I was happy to keep them amused so long as they fixed it – an electrical problem they said.

The other half time I broke down was when the starter motor packed up in the Rockies, which just meant I could only stop on slopes until I got it fixed in Vegas. But that wasn't so bad because it's mostly downhill to Vegas.

It got a little lonely at times. I'd done a long motorcycle trip before – Madras to Colchester – but I'd forgotten how little there is to do except think. And sing, but I don't know more than the beginnings of many songs. So I just read the signs by the side of the road: "Re-elect Fox sheriff", "Single-shot training rifles at $59.95" (tempting), "We fought four wars for this land", "The 10 commandments aren't suggestions".

And I like American place names, too. Generally it's obvious how they came about: Muddy Creek, Red Lake, Pleasant View (though Disappointment Valley I thought was wonderful). But you do get the odd one: What Cheer, Normal, Hygiene, Paradox.

I also found the fastest way to dry socks in the world: tie them to the handlebars and drive them at 75mph through the Nevada desert.

I knew my way round Los Angeles before I got there because I'd driven a Harley round it on an arcade game in the Harley-Davidson Café in Las Vegas a couple of days earlier. Interesting that on a day off, while the bike was being fixed, I'd gone to the Harley-Davidson Café and sat at the bar on a Harley-Davidson seat. But it got like that; after a while, you just want to go on and on.

Arriving in LA was exciting and a little sad. Exciting because we'd made it across, and sad because it was all over. We went to see the sea at Santa Monica, just to prove we'd made it all the way across. And then it was like when Dean Moriarty said in On the Road: "We can't go no further 'cause there ain't no more land!" •

Telly ho!

3 January 2000

Nancy Banks-Smith
Let there be light entertainment

A couple of lines, forgotten for 60 years, have been on my mind lately. 'I said to a man who stood at the gate of the year 'Give me a light that I may tread safely into the unknown'.' I doubt if anyone but a couple of queens remembers it now. George VI said it during a Christmas broadcast in 1939. We had no idea if we would reach 1940 or, more immediately, if he would reach the end of his sentence, given as he was to prolonged silences struggling with a stammer. The quotation propelled an unpretentious poetess called Minnie Haskins blinking into the light.

The gate of the year was a revolving door during the BBC's live coverage of the millennium around the world, described as the biggest and most ambitious programme ever made.

Everyone on earth wanted light. Nelson Mandela, walking stiff-legged and set-faced, lit a candle in his old cell. Those with money to burn frightened the night with fireworks according to their temperament. Sydney showily. Paris elegantly. Moscow economically, having a more sinister use for gunpowder. Stonehaven swung great balls of fire. Those with no money at all summoned the sun with song and dance.

John Simpson, seasick and out of sync, had clearly had a bumpy five days on a tramp steamer reaching Millennium Island, the rising sun's first port of call. Only coconut crabs live there so both celebrants and TV crew had to be bussed in. One singer died on the boat and had to be briskly buried on an offshore island. The survivors refreshed themselves with a magic potion. It had a visibly cheering effect. Substantially built dancers in stout, cotton bras greeted the sun as, he translated, a young woman greets her lover. Their faces shone gold like buttered crumpets. This is Millennium Island's swan song: it is drowning from global warming.

I live opposite the Millennium Dome. One day it appeared like a jellyfish washed up on the shore but recently, to my surprise, it has taken to palpitating at night, freckled with shifting spots, flushing like an octopus, which communicates with colour. The sense of a deep sea creature, defined only by light, is very strong. Professor Quatermass would have been interested.

The Queen sailed down the river in the kind of boat that often passes at night, throbbing with music. As she approached, something happened which neither the BBC nor Sky seemed to notice. The Dome was clearly all of a flutter. Agitatedly, it changed its spots from orange to blue to green and, finally, flushed perfectly purple. The higher row of lights on its crown are always red but the lower row seem to flash emotion. As the Queen arrived, they threw beams of light upwards then, visibly in a tizzy, spun round repeatedly. One of the entertaining aspects of monarchy is that this is exactly how even the most self-assured react on meeting the Queen.

When PG Wodehouse heard the first American jazz, he said he heard the 20th century. As you watched the samba spectacular in the Dome, you seemed to hear the 21st. After the show, a reporter stopped one dancer in skin-tight lycra saying "Where are you from?" "Harlesden" it replied and whirled away.

In the heart of Greenwich is the church of St Alphege, Archbishop of Canterbury around the last millennium and the world's worst public speaker. Alphege was captured by Vikings, who celebrated with a feast in Greenwich. Candid to a fault, he rose to reproach them for drunkeness, using the wrong fork and various other failings of character. They beat him to death on the meridian line with bones. Some say stones. I like bones. The audience at the Dome, while not exactly bloodstained, were plied with Tesco champagne. The present archbishop kept it very brief and conciliatory. The mike caught his sotto voce advice to the children with him 'Wave to them!'

In Sydney food stores farsightedly opened to help mop up the Fosters. In Britain, as no shops were open, legal commercials fervently appealed for clients who had, as they put it, tripped or fallen. I draw this to the attention of the three blokes who fell off London Bridge.

The revolving door of the year reached an illuminated Hollywood sign (I am very worried about 20th Century Fox. What can we call it now?) and, last of all, Samoa, down to its last grass skirt, invoking the dawn in dance. The Samoan national anthem, according to Peter Ustinov, goes 'Well done, Samoa! Well done, Samoa!! Well done!!!' •

....

14 October1999

Peter Preston
History hopping

I t is the ultimate wonder of the century; perhaps, emotionally, even of the millennium. Yet its mechanics are mundane, unremarked. You turn on the desultory wasteland called daytime TV, channel hopping from party conference to Jerry Springer. ("Can I love Gordon Brown and cheat with John Prescott?") And then, suddenly, without warning, you are in tears.

The afternoon film on Five was The Mississippi Gambler. I last saw it in 1953, sitting alone one Wednesday matinee in the cavernous stalls of the Victory Cinema, Loughborough. I saw Piper Laurie decide that she loved Tyrone Power after all and run – in a great sweep of a tracking shot – through the crowds on the New Orleans dock as his paddle steamer pulled away, hurling herself aboard and into his arms. I wept then; and now, in another life, another world, I weep again.

It isn't a great movie, just a gentle burp after Gone With The Wind. The Victory Cinema (because it was the biggest, grandest building in town) became a hole in the ground 40 years ago. Tyrone Power is long, long dead. Laurie still lives and works like a demon. Who can tell what became of the weakling heavy, Ron Randell? Wasn't he chairman of What's My Line? But this is the flotsam of memory.

The point is that here, for 99 minutes, Power is forever lean and saturnine: and that Piper Laurie is forever 21, pink-cheeked, clear-eyed, with the supple bound of youth – the girl called Rosetta Jacobs from Detroit (and Son of Ali Baba) who went on to be Lady Macbeth. The point is that time can stand still. For half a century, we have been able to make films which – in the technicalities of sound and colour – don't age. To see them now is to see them then. There is no sense of distance. The tears, like the laughter, can be constant.

What else, though, was happening in 1953? President Eisenhower was practising his golf swing. The Korean War was over, peace signed in Panmunjom. The Conservatives (elected on a manifesto called "Britain Strong and Free") were working minor economic wonders around the exhausted volcano of Churchill. Industrial production rose 5%. Harold Macmillan built a lot of houses. The Shah of Iran was out of a job – and then back in power. The Queen got crowned. John Foster Dulles was incandescent because France (and Britain) wouldn't form a Common European Army. And a baby called Anthony Charles Lynton Blair was born.

Such men, and such events, are history. They come from another, not greatly relevant, era. The homes Supermac threw up are falling down. Ike belongs to the middle American ages BK (Before Kennedy). No Shah; no job. The Queen's first born has lost his hair. France wants a European army but has utterly forgotten Dulles. Though the words Attlee and Bevan might, by accident, have been mentioned somewhere on the fringes at Bournemouth last week, there will be no Edens, Selwyn Lloyds or Maxwell Fyfes in Blackpool this week. They are dodos.

One day, maybe, some Channel 4 documentary will resurrect the distant holders of routine office and, in the flicker of old newsreels or the cringing deference of some TV interview, give them the kiss of fustian life. But it will be cold-lipped and fleeting. Politicians are no part of folk memory. They are piled, generation by generation, in the dustbin of forgetfulness. Only their clichés and banalities aspire to eternal repetition. William Hague's vision: a Britain Strong and Free.

And so begins a fascinating dislocation. Once upon an earlier time, the past was gone with the decades. Gladstone, Disraeli, Asquith, Marie Lloyd, Little Titch. The plaque on the wall of the house I pass in South London says "Dan Leno lived here". Dan who? The boys playing ball in the street below barely remember Bob Marley. Time consigned the great performers of the age to equality of oblivion. No longer. Those who – by and large – lived and worked from 1940 on have not in any true sense died. Is Jimmy Stewart dead? Or John Wayne? Is Alfred Hitchcock only a memory? Has age withered the Marilyn Monroe who slept with JFK and RFK and still commands tabloid obeisance? How old Cary Grant?

The obit columns of the broadsheets tell the story in a sense. A few weeks ago, one of them gave two-thirds of a page (something over 2,300 words) to the demise of

Marguerite Chapman. Not a brain surgeon or a sculptor or the Prescott Professor of Horse-Drawn Transport at the the University of Hull.

This was the Hollywood star of Charlie Chan at the Wax Museum (1940); Parachute Nurse (1942); and Mr District Attorney (1948). You may or may not recall her as Alita, the Martian love interest, in Flight to Mars (1951). When Chili Bouchier died, some days later, she got double the coverage of Janet Adam Smith.

Here, at first sight, is a potty inversion of values. Adam Smith was editing the poems of Robert Louis Stevenson in 1948 – when Chapman was making Coroner Creek and Bouchier was filming Old Mother Riley's New Venture. Yet there is a perverse logic in there somewhere, working. For Marguerite Chapman is not dead, either. She was alive only yesterday morning on Sky, embracing Paul Muni in Counter Attack (1945).

And 1953 lives in abundance. Susan Hayward this morning, Rhonda Fleming tonight at six; with Richard Widmark, William Holden and Eleanor Parker queueing to fill up the rest of the week. I make it 10 hours and 34 minutes of TV available 1953 movies versus 11 hours and 15 minutes of Conservative party conference coverage.

Nor, of course, does the dislocation diminish: it grows as the channels proliferate. Television itself (from the late 60s on) was technically proficient enough to make recycling possible, and thus The Persuaders, Professionals and Avengers stalk each other constantly through the channels called Gold. The soaps turn on an everlasting belt. Randall and Hopkirk are never deceased.

We do not, as the century ends, have to wonder what the popular culture of the departed decades was like. It circles us every day. The songs of Ella and Sinatra, the Stones ever rolling; the screens filled again, just as they were. The Beast from 20,000 Fathoms (and 1953) rises again this week. Piper Laurie jumps in love from the dock side, Tyrone Power opens his arms.

This is the gift of complete recall never before granted in human history. Accreting without end, it fills our lives – and gradually banishes the transients of governance to the peripheries, shadows wafting across a flimsy stage. 1999? Ah yes, the year of The Sopranos. And William Hague. Now who the heck was he? •

25 March 2000

Nancy Banks-Smith

Police, fire brigade
or veterinary?

Six years ago a jumbo jet crashed on the ITV soap Emmerdale. This week a runaway lorry collided with a supermarket bus, crammed to the rafters with colourful locals. As a London fireman said, when told there was a blaze in Pudding Lane, "Not again!"

Imprisoned in the tangled tomb were Seth Armstrong and his memorable moustache; Sarah Sugden, who is having an affair with her lodger; Butch Dingle, who was on his way to ask for his girlfriend's hand in marriage; and Kathy Glover, who was recently driven over a cliff by a murderer. (When I asked Yorkshire TV to describe Kathy, they said, "Unlucky.")

Sudden, obliterating and deafening disaster seems peculiarly characteristic of rural soaps. It is the country way. All this week, day by day, body after body was extracted from the rumpled bus. There was no sign of a doctor, though an ample sufficiency of vets. Vets are, of course, mainly familiar with anal exploration but this was no time to be picky.

You could tell the survivors were in a bad way because you had never seem them before without their caps. I didn't know they were removable. Without them, they looked pitifully incomplete, like boiled eggs with the tops lopped off. Bookies were taking bets on the bodies. I fancied a fiver on little Victoria Sugden, an overly chatty moppet, but the one fated to get it in the neck was Butch Dingle.

The Dingles are the Grundys of Emmerdale. They lower the tone of the place at the top of their voices and are far more entertaining than the gentry. Butch is the one with the perfectly circular head, like Charlie Brown.

Everyone likes Butch (Paul Loughran) and his girlfriend, Emily (Kate McGregor). They remind you of the Start Rite kids, skipping innocently hand in hand into the sunrise, but frankly it's a bit of a blessing they won't now have that large family they talked about. If Butch were a light bulb he'd be 40 watts and Emily, even by Emmerdale standards, is widely considered a daft dimmock. I think Emmerdale makes up dialect as it goes along, but you get the general idea.

Even if you are away from Emmerdale for years, you soon feel at home again. The same people are still locking horns with their lifelong enemies. So, once the temporary truce of the crash was over, they rounded on each other refreshed. Was it the fault of the driver? Or the woman who delayed the bus? Or – as we confidently expect – Chris Tate, still in a wheelchair from the jumbo jet, whose hobby and pleasure is grinding the glowering faces of the peasantry ("There is nothing I enjoy more than winding up a few bleeding heart do-gooders. Heh-heh!").

There only seemed to be one doctor in 'Otten General 'Ospital and she was candid to a fault, advising Butch to cancel his summer holiday. Taking this broad hint, he married Emily on his deathbed. Kathy tactlessly offered Emily the wedding dress in which she was jilted by Biff, Mandy wildly suggested they attempt something bridal with a sheet, but Emily, who knows what suits her, chose a cardigan.

It was virtually unique in soap weddings. The groom didn't walk out, the bride didn't change her mind, no one raised a just impediment and they lived happily ever after. Though not for long.

Butch said, "Emily, I don't feel so good. Come and lie down beside me." "Budge up then," said Emily. "Make room for a little one." But, as she told the Dingles, she couldn't keep him warm.

A hot water bottle to whoever guesses Butch's real name. •

....

12 January 2000

Gary Younge
Is it 'cos I is black?

When it comes to Ali G there is one, and probably only one, thing on which just about everybody agrees: he is very funny. His racial identity may be unclear. Views over whom his jokes are directed at may differ. And the jury may be out on whether he is reinforcing or subverting stereotypes. But he makes you laugh. He makes you recite his lines and then laugh as though adulthood never happened and with an intensity you cannot quite explain. Ask people why they find him so funny and they will hide behind truisms. "Ali G is what he is," they say. "He speaks for himself." "He is no more complicated than that."

The idea that a white, Jewish man, Sacha Baron Cohen, could impersonate an ignorant, black misogynist who interrogates the rich, famous and influential, and not run into complications is an intriguing notion in itself. The most amazing thing about the litany of black comedians who branded Ali G "racist" and "offensive" earlier this week is that they took so long to come forward. Their detractors, however, have been quicker off the mark. Within 24 hours Jonathan Margolis was using Ali G as a Trojan horse to resurrect old-school racists like Bernard Manning. "What people like Lenny Henry, Meera Syal, Sacha Baron Cohen and even Manning on a good day demonstrate, is that if comedy's racial stereotyping has a basis in accuracy, it rocks," he wrote in the Evening Standard yesterday.

The debate will, hopefully, continue, and in so doing it will illustrate precisely why Ali G has been so successful. Like the racial equivalent of a gender-bender, he stands on a precipice. On one side is the relatively steady ground of alternative comedy;

on the other is the sheer drop in to racist buffoonery. It is an awkward place to be, not least because he finds himself at the epicentre of an awkward debate. But, so long as he can keep his balance, he will remain above the fray, if not beyond reproach. Move too far inland and he will be predictable and worthy; stray too close to the edge and he might topple over and land in the lap of Jim Davidson or the black and white minstrels.

Baron Cohen does not give interviews himself and so we are left guessing – the first guess of many – which way if any he might fall. So he perches on the edge, leaving the key questions of "What are we laughing at" "Whom are we laughing at" and "Whom are we laughing with" either unanswered or with contradictory responses.

For those who are already reaching for their set texts on "political correctness", please turn the page now. Those two words – which are used to lambast everyone from non-smokers to apartheid apologists – have stifled precisely the kind of fruitful discussion on issues such as race and humour for the best part of a decade. No one is suggesting the black experience in this country is out of bounds for comedians – be they black or white.

But the idea that we should never draw an ethical line between what is acceptable and what is offensive when it comes to comedy is as disingenuous as it is bankrupt. We can argue about where we should draw the line on certain jokes, but there is little argument as to whether we should draw one at all. We do not broadcast jokes about paedophiles, Holocaust survivors or the mentally disabled because there is a general, popular view that those people are not fair game. Black people were once considered absolutely fair game simply because they existed. In the mid-70s, the sitcom Love Thy Neighbour fed off a regular diet of jokes about "honkies" and "nig-nogs". Such jokes would not be acceptable now. And in 20 years' time, we might watch Ali G or Goodness Gracious Me and wince. The line is blurred and it keeps on moving. That is what is so impressive about Ali G. The debate he has sparked is forcing us to consider redrawing the line.

At its most basic level, it's not difficult to grasp what we are laughing at when we watch Ali G. Like Dennis Pennis, Mrs Merton and Dame Edna Everage before him, Ali G is the voice of spoof. He picks out members of the establishment, asks them stupid questions for which there is no sensible answer, and then watches them dissolve into a pit of their own pomposity. "Why was Diana knobbing that Pakistani?" he asks royal-watcher James Whittaker; "What about marrying a Catholic girl?" he says to George Patton, the grandmaster of the Orange Order in the north of Ireland. "Possibly because of my faith I would not," replies Patton. "But what if she was fit?" asks Ali G. "What if she had her own car and sound system and wasn't gonna be stealing money off you all the time?" He is breaking taboos and ridiculing vanity. The less his interviewee gets the joke, the funnier the joke is.

But that is not all we were laughing at. This would not be funny if Ali G was played by a black character. Part of the joke with the likes of Dennis Pennis and Mrs Merton is that they had to adopt a special persona which had nothing to do with the real-life actors. Pennis was an orange-haired geek; Mrs Merton was a nosy old lady; Dame

Edna was a saucy, antipodean gossip queen. Because we knew who they were, we knew where they were coming from. The first problem with Ali G is that nobody really knows who, or rather what, he is supposed to be. The most common assumptions I have heard is that Baron Cohen is playing a black man, a white man trying to be black, or an Asian man trying to be black. Among the rank outsiders are that he is Turkish, Greek and Middle Eastern. After I wrote a piece assuming he was supposed to be white, one reader wrote an impassioned letter insisting: "Ali G is ASIAN. That's half the joke; Asian guys trying to be cool like black guys."

Those who have not read profiles of Baron Cohen are equally uncertain of the actor's own racial identity. He covers his hair with a Tommy Hilfiger head band and often hides his face behind ringed fingers. Guesses range from mixed-race and Asian to caucasian and any number of variations in between. "He's not white, he's Jewish," said one acquaintance at a dinner party.

Herein lies an understandable source of tension. We do not exactly know everything that we are laughing at. Ali G works on so many different levels that you can have two different people watching the same video and laughing at completely different things. One might be finding it funny the way this white comedian is poking fun at white people who overdo their impression of black youth culture. This is the most commonly held view, which casts Ali G as an exaggerated version of Tim Westwood, the popular, white Radio1 DJ who has feigned a black street accent for his hip hop slot.

With black styles at the core of British youth culture, it is argued that Ali G is not poking fun at black people at all but "wiggers" – whites who want to be, or even think they are, black. As such, the argument goes, it reflects a sense of racial ease among younger generations of Britons, who all speak the same language, wear similar clothes and listen to similar music. It is a joke which could not exist without our lives being racially entwined. When Ali G asks Sir Rhodes Boyson whether he thinks children should be "caned" in school the joke is generational, not racial. Most over-40s think he is talking about corporal punishment; most under-40s know he is talking about drugs.

But it is equally possible that somebody else might be laughing at his rendition of what stupid, sexist, drug-taking layabouts black men are. It is not as though these stereotypes are not out there and waiting to be exploited. Imagine the tables were turned and a black comedian created a white, Jewish character who made jokes about being a tightfisted, highly ambitious mummy's boy. Would it ever get screened? And if it did, would it be offensive?

The difference between just these two interpretations – and there are many more – of what Ali G is about is crucial. Is he a white man impersonating a black man or a white man impersonating a white man impersonating a black man? One could reasonably be interpreted as a joke on the black community which conveys black male culture as misogynistic and ignorant; the other is a joke on that section of the white community who over-identify with black culture and make themselves look ridiculous in the process. One feeds a long-established prejudice against a minority; the other highlights a relatively recent phenomenon among a majority.

The truth is that nobody knows. Baron Cohen is wise not to talk about his work, since to pontificate would be to take all the mystery from his character. His silence leaves us with many an unanswered question. But whatever his intention, he could not control how it is interpreted anyway. In some parts of the country his catchline, "Is it because I is black?", might be just one more surreal jingle for the playground; elsewhere it might be a line that bigots use to taunt someone who has complained about racial discrimination.

The issue is not whether we should be laughing at Ali G or not; we are. Even the black comedians who said he was offensive admit that he makes them laugh. Nor is the question whether some people should be uneasy at Ali G; they are. In such a nebulous, subjective and sensitive area the true mark of our racial sophistication will be whether we can have an intelligent discussion about what makes us laugh and what makes us uneasy. ∎

Letters

14 January 2000

'Nuff respect

You 'as grabbed 'old of da wrong end of da stick an' beginnin' to beat around the bush with it, innit? Ali G am extractin' da mick from da fashion victim (black, white or whatever) who 'tends to be clever cos 'e wears rank, overpriced gear. An' meanwhile 'e make an ass out of yo famous pillars of da 'stablishment. Is it because 'e is white?

Richard B George
Stockport

I thought Ali G was showing brilliantly how much more real and intelligent street culture is than the arrogant intellectual middle-class establishment. Gary Younge now tells me he is "impersonating an ignorant black misogynist" asking "stupid questions". But then I'm over 50, so probably don't get it.

Anne Geraghty
London
anne_geraghty@hotmail.com

Do your correspondents (January 13) want a society where no one could possibly be offended by anything? That would be offensive.

ST Parkin
London

6 December 1999
Nancy Banks-Smith
Tacky, but the girl
just can't help it

Miss World always arrives with her skirt tucked in her knickers. The girl can't help it. Tackiness follows her, fascinated. Miss World 1999 started with a feminist demonstration ("Stop this sexist cattle market".) Furious men with egg on their dinner jackets doubled their fists. It snowed flour. Channel 5 News reporter Simon Vigar said it had turned ugly, which is bad news for a beauty contest. "But to put it in context, more than two people ... er, two billion people will watch worldwide."

Yesterday the gamier tabloids reported another bump in the corrugated love life of Miss World's presenter, Ulrika Jonsson. They did not report Miss World.

Miss World has been wandering the world for 10 years and come home to die on Channel 5. She has worn that crown longer than the queen and, like the queen, tries to be trendier, but her heart is not in it. Thus, while gambolling in a bikini, Miss Lebanon confided her ambition to become a judge.

Unfortunately, Miss World's idea of a judge is Luciana Morad, described as "the stunning Brazilian supermodel" or, as you may know her better, Mick Jagger's bit on the side.

This year the presenters and commentator were women. Well, ladettes, really. Tragic Ulrika, Mel S from the Boddington beer commercials, and Mel G from the rude panel show Casting Couch, who added a happy dash of Tabasco ("Here's Miss Ireland with a pheasant strapped to her front.")

To emphasise their intellect, finalists were asked taxing questions like: "Where would you most like to go in the whole world?" And, of course: "Where would you most like to go in the whole world?"

Miss USA – you would know she was Miss USA – said the biggest challenge in her life had been figuring out who she was.

There was a short, sharp struggle when Miss Spain, sprouting purple feathers, took the microphone from Mel S ("Let me hold that! It's my job!") while explaining she would like to be Neil Armstrong.

She liked very much the moon. "I like a good moon as well," said Mel G, who could lower the tone in a space rocket.

This modern emphasis on intellect can be counterproductive. Miss Bosnia, booted out for posing for Playboy, did it, her mother said, to further her studies.

The winner, Miss India, Yukta Mookhey, was embraced by her grey-haired old granny or a very worried mother. •

Wonderful world

16 March 2000

David McKie
On the road to nowhere

When in April, says Geoffrey Chaucer – I use the Coghill translation here to make things easier – the sweet showers fall and pierce the drought of March to the root, and all the veins are bathed in liquor of such power as brings about the engendering of the flower, and other necessary conditions have been met, then people long to go on pilgrimages; as his knight, wife of Bath and others did from Southwark to Canterbury, down what we nowadays think of as the A2.

Now Pieter Boogaart, who is Dutch, has written a biography, as he calls it, of what he claims is another pilgrim route: the A272, which nowadays starts in the outskirts of Winchester and expires in East Sussex when it comes face to face with the A265. Since this endearing, eccentric work is written not just with love and diligence but also with honesty, Boogaart is forced to admit that his evidence for asserting that this was a pilgrim route is "scant". Some would go further than that. Indeed, I rather doubt if the A272 is a real road at all.

Roads in Britain are categorised in various ways. There are motorways, and As Bs and Cs, in descending order of magnitude. Among As there are primary and secondary roads. The most notable are stewarded by the Highways Agency; the remaining 96% come under the DETR. The most famous of all is the Great North Road from London to Scotland, which is why it is called the A1. Most of the following dozen fan out from London to the south, west and north. The A7, though partly in Cumbria, is essentially a Caledonian A6. The A8 and A9 are exclusively Scottish. The English collection resumes with the A10 (King's Lynn), A11 (Norwich), A12 (Ipswich and Lowestoft) and A13 (Southend). After that one descends to the second rate. The A17 (Newark-King's Lynn) seems especially feeble.

There is a distinction here more significant than anything under the aegis of Mr Prescott. Some roads are deliberate, created because people in A were eager to get to B, or vice versa. Some of the great roads which span the north, like the A68, belong in this category. Others – like the A272, I'm afraid – are accidental, cobbled together by transport planners from a network of roads which may not in essence belong together. The A1 carried armies north, the A2 took pilgrims to Canterbury, the A3 from London to Portsmouth served the navy. Roads like these litter our history and crop up time and again in great works of fiction. Even the A13 has its celebrants. "If you ever have to go to Shoeburyness," a Billy Bragg lyric advises "take the A road,/the okay road that's the best/Go motorin' on the A13... It starts down in Wapping/There ain't no stopping/ Bypass Barking and straight through Dagenham/Down to Grays Thurrock/And rather near Basildon/Pitsea, Thundersley, Hadleigh, Leigh-On-Sea/Chalkwell, Prittlewell/ Southend's the end."

Deliberate roads start at somewhere substantial, like London, and head for somewhere definitively terminal, such as Southend. We expect them to end with a bang, like a Beethoven symphony. The A272 used to begin at Stockbridge in Hampshire, a strange, wild west town with an inexplicably broad main street, out of which you half expect to see cowboys backing into the street with guns blazing – though that section has now been deemed by some bureaucrat to be the mere B3409. It ends in the middle of nowhere at a spot I would call Blackboys, though Mr Boogaart says we must call it Poundford. There is always something demeaning about a great highway expiring at a spot of no particular consequence. This tendency sometimes magnifies places of minimal interest. Hertfordshire, for instance, is full of road signs pointing the traveller to Puckeridge. I have never been, nor have I ever aspired to go, to Puckeridge. But Puckeridge is where the A120, now a road of some importance because it serves Stansted airport, expires. So its name is undeservingly blazoned across the county.

The ring roads of inner London demonstrate what I mean. Like it or not, the North Circular (A406) is a deliberate road, built for a purpose. The South Circular (A205) is accidental: a ragbag affair, some of it purpose-built, but much of it tacked together from existing roads of varying credibility. There is no finer example of the way that the north of London lords it over the south. The word transpontine usually means "on the other side of the water". Not in London. In London, it has the special meaning "south of the river" – in other words, on the wrong side of the tracks. Mr Boogaart has done a fine job for the A272. But even his ingenuity could never save that horrible accident, the A205, from perdition. •

A272: An Ode to a Road by Pieter Boogaart, Pallas Athene, £14.95

....

8 April 3000

AC Grayling
The last word on Age

Growing old is a bad habit which a busy man has no time to form – André Maurois

One is so used to seeing irrationality prevail that it comes as a surprise, and a welcome one, to see the opposite. Reports this week show that a number of leading companies, including supermarkets and B&Q, have begun to employ older people. One of the banks is rehiring retired managers because of a skill shortage, and some companies, like BT, are planning to raise their compulsory retirement age to 70.

Anti-ageism campaigners, in welcoming these developments, say that the point is choice: there are many who do not wish to retire, at least at the now young age of 60 or 65; and there is much evidence that retirement is as bad for individual health as it is for the future pensions burden of the country.

Some, of course, yearn to give up the daily tie of work, either to pursue their own avocations, or – a scarcely comprehensible desire – to put their feet up once and for all. No doubt the victories over challenges and the feeling that one is productive and valued that go so far to make life worth living can be supplied by hobbies; but hobbies have to be good to compare to a role in the real thing.

The Romans of classical antiquity saw retirement and value as linked, on the principle of "seniores priores"; the respect due to experience gave it a front seat at the counsels of state. Even if it is true, as La Rochefoucauld observed, that "old men like to give good advice to console themselves for no longer being able to set bad examples", it is nevertheless useful to a society to have the fruits of experience available if required.

The Chinese take this to an extreme; in their gerontocracy no one under 75 is regarded as yet fit for power. They think time induces perspective, as exemplified by Zhou En Lai's celebrated comment on the French Revolution; when asked whether he thought it had been a good thing; he said (after a deliberative pause): "It's too soon to say".

The fashion in recent times has been for the young to hold centre stage, as if they were the only important form of human being. The main reason is that advertisers know the young have beliefs they are prepared to back with money, chief among them that everyone else is having fun, and that if they are to have fun too they must go somewhere smoky and noisy and wear the same clothes as all the others there. They therefore flock to clubs or Ibiza in search of stupefaction by a combination of decibels, drink and drugs, and mock their elders for flinching from the scene.

They do not see that "nobody loves life as much as the old do", as Sophocles remarked, and that accumulated years confer wisdom of the kind possessed by the old bull in the fable (which goes: a young bull sees that the gate into the next field, full of cows, is open. In delight he says to the old bull, "Look! The gate's open! Let's rush down there and mount a few!" To which the old bull replies, "No; let's go down there slowly, and mount them all.")

There is, incidentally, no such thing as "middle age". This is the period of life allegedly defined by the exchange of geometries between your broad mind and narrow waist, or when, as Franklin Adams observed, you are too young to take up bowls but too old to rush up to the net. Some people are born old, and some die young in their nineties: it is entirely a matter of attitude, which, as the Stoics long ago pointed out, is something wholly at your own command. What happens as the years pass is that folly somewhat abates, and the bank balance improves; on both counts, getting older is a desirable activity.

There is much false propaganda about age. "Age has a good mind and sorry shanks," said Aretino, confusing the ability to run for a bus with good health and the right kinds of vigour. Most of the saws and sayings that apply to age, making it a concoction of trembling limbs and forgetfulness, are drawn from a time when people were old at 40. A person must now be at least double that to have the honour of being properly old. And honour it is: "Life is a country that the old have seen, and lived in", said Joseph Joubert; "those who have yet to travel through it can only learn the way from them." •

5 April 2000

Madeleine Bunting
Let's wear our frills with pride

For the discerning trend spotter, there were harbingers of the revolution. Last summer, virtually every female between two and 35 sported sparkly butterfly hairclips. Last autumn, the fashion shock was that after a decade of shoulder pads, the jacket tottered on its pillar as the essential prop of every self-respecting career woman's wardrobe. No, no, not a jacket, very passé; try a cardigan, sweetie.

These early signs have now flowered in the most gorgeous reassertion of femininity seen in fashion for years. There's not a self respecting pair of jeans in the shops without more than its fair share of beads, embroidery and feathers. Polka dots, tropical flowery prints, brilliant deep pink are filling the shops. Jewellery is obligatory – bangles, several earrings, bead chokers, brilliant waistbands – the more the merrier. Suddenly, hairties which wouldn't look out of place in South Pacific are appearing in the office.

The sense of relief is enormous. For months, the hangers and shelves have been like the school uniform outfitters of one's childhood nightmares – a relentlessly uniform mixture of grey, black and white with the odd bit of khaki or beige. A palette which wouldn't look out of place under Oliver Cromwell's interregnum. Whether you were a net freak in cargo pants and trainers or a high-flying executive, women have been aping men's clothes. Our wardrobes have been barely distinguishable from our partners: the same dull mix of understated tailoring and discreet good taste. It was all screaming: "Please boys, take me seriously, I'm just like you." As a strategy, it was a dead end. It never washed with the boys, and we got to miss out on all the fun women have had with colour, pattern and texture for hundreds of years.

What's most appealing is that women are reclaiming the whimsical and the frivolous. Nowhere is this more blatant than in accessories such as shoes and handbags. Forget sensible flatties and those huge black holdalls; think dainty, probably covered in flowers, frills, diamanté and bows. True, you can hardly walk on your kitten heels and your bag won't hold much more than your lipstick, but what the hell.

There are two ways to read all this. The first is that it is a great step forward for womenkind; we can be feminine and still be taken seriously. We don't have to look intimidating and drum our immaculately painted nails on the desk to be taken seriously. If

Martha Lane Fox can get away with messy hair, lots of earrings, chokers, an impishly coy smile and no suit, and still become a multi-millionaire, then the world is our oyster.

The second is that women have lost their senses and have adopted a Barbie aesthetic; we're in the process of being duped into reassuming an ornamentalism which we have been trying to shake off ever since Betty Friedan. Now, my five-year-old daughter and I can happily admire each other's outfits, squabble over accessories and end up not looking too dissimilar.

The fact that pussy-bows form part of this reassertion of femininity blooming on the catwalk has got to be proof of a conspiracy. If there was any part of 20th fashion which has absolutely no redeeming feature, this has to be it. Even the name exposes its horribly patronising, poodle-type connotations.

The second is plausible, but optimistically I'll plump for the former. Seventies' kinky was never around long enough the first time for me to enjoy it. I enviously watched older sisters in peasant blouses, Indian skirts, beads and bangles. Now we can look east again, border our jeans in Chinese satin, and turn saris, with their gorgeous gold woven borders, into skirts. Or, we can stick with home, English chintz (the kind your grandmother put in the bathroom) is recycled into hats and shoes. I'm fed up with puritanism, and dream that there might now be room for femininity in the boardroom. Bring back some of the radicalism of early 70s gender politics. All is forgiven.

What young feminists (and those disdainful of the label) lost sight of in the 80s and 90s was that those early pioneers wanted to claim recognition and respect for the difference of women. Wrapped up in individual ambition, we got sidetracked into wanting to prove we could be the same as men. Work as long hours (even with children), be as ruthlessly competitive, as tough bosses ...

But there's still a nagging anxiety that we're being duped. All this peasant stuff, orientalism and flowers could be the equivalent of comfort food. Reassuringly familiar and uplifting to reconcile us to all the hard grind that the speed of technological change demands of us. Is this Aldous Huxley's soma? The subliminal message is: "Go on, be naughty, treat yourself to a deliciously dinky Moschino bag for a few hundred quid ... you deserve it." •

30 March 2000

Leanda de Lisle
My brief encounter

Could I have plotted to kill Colonel Gadafy? If the former MI5 officer and newspaper trainee, David Shayler is to be believed, that's the kind of thing MI6 agents get up to. However, I don't recall bumping off foreign heads of state being in the job description when MI6 interviewed me for a post with the "coordination staff" of the Foreign and Commonwealth Office.

Our foreign intelligence department goes under a number of different names: SIS, MI6 and this "coordination staff". However it was not a term I recognised when I saw it at the top of a note that had arrived in my pigeonhole at Somerville College, Oxford.

The letter explained that I'd been recommended for a post as a junior diplomat with additional "special duties". I guessed that meant spying. For I had never applied to join the FO and we all knew that university dons with intelligence connections were used as talent spotters by secret service chiefs.

Most of these talent spotters were misogynists. But at Somerville our principal was Daphne (now Baroness) Park – a woman who looked as innocent as Margaret Rutherford, but had been MI6's woman in Hanoi during the Vietnam war.

Furthermore I had, unwittingly, met someone who was still a senior member of MI6. I've heard this soft-voiced chameleon being compared to John Le Carré's Perfect Spy. But his days as an operative were now behind him and he worked behind a desk in London. A liberal, Guardian reader, he was keen to see more women in the service.

Unfortunately, I did not arrive for my interview at Carlton Gardens, SW1, in an entirely serious frame of mind. It all seemed quite unreal and there were many moments during that afternoon when I had to try not to laugh out loud. The handsome stucco house that confronted me looked like a gentleman's club.

The image wasn't dispelled by the dark hall, where I waited before being taken upstairs to meet Mr Pink Rabbit, or whatever you would wish to call him. He proved to be a dark, handsome man in his thirties, who welcomed me into an office empty save for a Formica table and two plastic chairs.

Mr Pink told me that MI6 did not exist – officially. That being the case there was no written job description and he was to tell me what was expected. First I would join the Foreign Office in the usual way, by passing the Civil Service exams and FO interviews. A special induction course would follow (spouses are also given courses on how to cope with being married to a spy). Then you are sent abroad, posing as a diplomat, but in fact seeking to recruit agents and gather information. Our human targets were the weak, the greedy, those with financial problems, or a grudge against the government of their country.

I asked about the potential dangers, but was told the bad guys "keep themselves busy killing each other". I asked about our own dirty tricks and – if I recall correctly

– was informed that MI6 officers may not do anything that breaks British law, since as agents of the state they were answerable to parliament. I asked whether we spied on our allies and he smiled and said: "We would not do anything to harm our friends."

What I didn't ask was what kind of talent it was that they had spotted in me. But a witness to my first encounter with my recruiter assures me that it happened when I mentioned to him that I did not have to shave my legs and so forth because I was naturally unhairy. I fear it is the kind of thing the 20-year-old me might have said to confuse and provoke an elder.

But while some men might have given up their secrets to hear more from me about that, there are plenty of hairy spies out there and the fact I now seem to be growing it all over my face shouldn't make any difference.

Spies, like journalists, are not brilliantly paid (they get the standard Foreign Office wage plus expenses). And it seems likely that they share similar characteristics. Both the profession I joined – journalism – and the one I didn't – spying – attract idealists who are also cynical and manipulative.

I suspect that I'm less self-contained and also less of a team player, than would be good for a spy. However, unlike many journalistic colleagues, I don't regard spies as bogeymen. MI6 is as much a pillar of democracy as the Guardian, and if an assault on free speech can be an assault on democracy, so too can an assault on secrecy. We should be united in contempt for David Shayler – a man who has failed at both professions. But then, behind closed doors, many of us are. ∎

....

15 September 1999

Francis Wheen
The paranoia pantomime

To judge by her undimmed admiration for Uncle Joe Stalin, Melita Norwood is a political cretin. Why, then, are spy-hunting newspapers so eager to flatter her? I am told by someone who knows the old girl that she was delighted with the Times's huge front-page splash last Saturday: "The most important British female agent ever recruited by the KGB is disclosed today..." The effect of this portentous announcement is sabotaged, however, by that qualifying word "female": the KGB was never an equal opportunities employer. One might as well describe Rupert Murdoch as the most handsome billionaire media baron of Australian extraction and American citizenship to marry a Chinese woman half his age.

The depiction of Norwood as the woman who gave Russia the Bomb is also too generous by half. No one who knows anything about the history of atomic weapons believes that a secretary at the Non-Ferrous Metals Research Association could have provided Moscow with anything more than a few titbits. The fact that the Soviet Union beat Britain to the Bomb by three years speaks for itself: the really important information was coming from elsewhere – from Los Alamos, to be precise.

On Monday, I asked a friend who was instrumental in exposing Kim Philby what he made of the latest spookfest. "I reckon Philby probably was a fairly effective spy, and so was Maclean," he replied. "But if I had realised what a bunch of drunken (if murderous) pantaloons they were working for, I'd have taken them much less seriously. I am very sceptical that Grandma Whatshername did anything substantial to postpone the fall of the USSR."

He added that he now shares the view of Senator Daniel Patrick Moynihan: the cold war was always going to be won by the west, and the only achievement of the CIA, FBI, MI5 and MI6 was to delay the victory and increase its human cost. This they did by infecting the west with the ailment which dominated and destroyed the Soviet Union – the disease of secrecy and paranoia.

Melita Norwood herself is a figure of no great significance. But the hysterical tumult created by her exposure may have serious consequences. Grizzled cold warriors are already seizing the chance to resume their quest for "the enemy within". Even the 85-year-old Chapman Pincher has emerged from retirement. "Confirmation that Tom Driberg, the MP and former chairman of the Labour party, was recruited by the KGB must embarrass the government," he wrote in the Observer, "because, when I revealed this treachery on the authority of MI5 sources, it was denied with contempt... The huge scale of the conspiracy revealed by this astonishing haul of documents shows that, if anything, we underestimated the threat."

I know a thing or two about Tom Driberg, having written his biography 10 years ago. I am also regrettably familiar with the work of Chapman Pincher, who was once described by EP Thompson as a kind of pissoir in which, side by side, high officials of MI5 and MI6 stand patiently leaking in the public interest. It may be worth studying the history of the Driberg myth before we all get drenched.

The first version of the tale appeared in Pincher's book Inside Story, published in 1978. "The Labour Party leadership has been fully aware for many years of the infiltration by dedicated communists posing as socialists," he claimed, "and has done little that is effective to counter it." The only suspect who was safely dead and could therefore be defamed with impunity was Driberg: "He remained a Kremlin agent of sympathy, sponsoring various communist front organisations, urging the withdrawal of troops from Northern Ireland, and there were deep suspicions inside MI5 that he was an active agent of the KGB."

Note the urine-scented syllogism: Driberg disapproved of the British presence in Northern Ireland, therefore he was working for the Kremlin. This is a classic smear technique during epidemics of spy fever. Last weekend, the Sunday Telegraph observed that at Melita Norwood's house in Bexleyheath "CND and anti-Kosovo war posters in the window hint at a lifelong faith in the virtues of Stalin and the Communist Party of Great Britain".

In 1981, after a thorough briefing from the demented ex-MI5 officer Peter Wright, Pincher wrote another book, Their Trade Is Treachery. Driberg had been a double agent, he now alleged, who was employed simultaneously by MI5 and the KGB: "He did this from the moment he first entered the House in 1942 to when he finally retired in 1974, and thereafter when he became a member of the House of Lords. Both MI5 and the KGB had no illusions about the fact that he was working for the other side..."

Common sense would suggest that this must have made him all but useless to either side – especially since Driberg, a notoriously unreliable and indiscreet character, was not privy to state secrets anyway. But Pincher was convinced. Even Driberg's book about Guy Burgess, published in 1956, had been written as a favour to both intelligence agencies. According to Pincher, British officials lacked enough evidence to prosecute Burgess should he try to return to London; and so, to keep him away, Driberg was sent by MI5 to Moscow, where he tricked Burgess into revealing a few details about his work for the wartime Special Operations Executive (SOE). MI5 then announced that Burgess had broken the Official Secrets Act and would be arrested if he ever came home. Having served its purpose, the reference to SOE in Driberg's manuscript was deleted before publication.

As Pincher explained in Their Trade Is Treachery, everyone was happy. "Driberg's book contained enough lies and slanders against MI5 and the political system of the west for the KGB to be pleased with it, while MI5 regarded these as a worthwhile trade-off to prevent the return of Burgess."

The truth is rather different. Admiral Thomson, the secretary of the D-Notice Committee, insisted on one deletion from Driberg's manuscript – not of the SOE reference (which survived) but of a paragraph about a botched post-war attempt by British intelligence to overthrow the government of Albania. Driberg pointed out that since his source for this was Guy Burgess himself, the Russians must already be aware of it. "Good heavens old boy," the admiral laughed, "it isn't the Russians we worry about. It's the British public we don't want to know about it!"

Nothing has changed since then – except that the "British public", as defined by the spooks, now includes the prime minister and home secretary. For more than two years, Jack Straw has refused to listen to David Shayler's complaints about MI5, insisting that no inquiry is necessary because he personally invigilates all the security service's activities. "I know what they're doing," he told a television interviewer in January. "I go round the building, I talk to people, say, 'What are you doing? Show me the file...' I've got down in the engine room to see how it ticks." Despite all this hands-on supervision, however, Straw learned only a few months ago that, since 1992, MI5 had been sitting on the largest collection of KGB documents ever smuggled out of Moscow.

Straw's gullibility is matched only by that of professor Christopher Andrew, who appears to believe that KGB archives can all be treated as gospel truth. Having read the Mitrokhin files, he confidently informs us that Driberg was recruited by Soviet intelligence in 1956 after being "entrapped" while propositioning a KGB agent in a public lavatory during a visit to Moscow. Driberg "gave way to blackmail" and served the Soviet Union faithfully for the rest of his life.

Case closed? Not at all. The KGB couldn't have blackmailed Driberg by threatening to tell the British press or prime minister about his homosexuality, since this was already common knowledge throughout Fleet Street and Westminster. The fact that Moscow regarded him as an asset is neither here nor there: KGB officers routinely exaggerated their achievements in "recruiting" public figures, to impress their superiors and justify their expenses.

During the 60s, for instance, such respectable characters as Denis Healey, the Tory MP Nicholas Scott and the conservative journalist Peregrine Worsthorne were wined and dined by Mikhail Lyubimov, a KGB colonel from the Soviet embassy in London. Somewhere in the Moscow archives there may be a document identifying these men as agents of the Lubyanka. But that wouldn't make it true.

Tom Driberg regarded the spying business as a game. He liked games, from croquet to canasta, and he sometimes enjoyed gossipy lunches with a friend from MI5 or drinks with a Russian journalist. But he was no more a "KGB agent" – or "MI5 agent" – than I am. Unlike Chapman Pincher, Christopher Andrew and the other awestruck chroniclers of the intelligence pantomime, he knew that there was life beyond games. On the last page of his Burgess book, Driberg quoted Shelley: "The world is weary of the past,/Oh, might it die or rest at last!" He proposed the verse as "an apt epitaph on the cold war and all the other wars of our time". Even in 1999, it seems, the epitaph is premature. •

....

15 April 2000

Dea Birkett
No shelter from the swarm

I heard them before I saw them – an incessant hum, loud enough to make it seem as if our tiny aluminium boat was vibrating. But within a second, they were on us. And not just on us – but in us. In our hair, up our nostrils, trying to crawl inside my ear. We were being attacked by a swarm of killer bees.

Only moments before, we had been peacefully gliding up a tributary of the Rio Nosara in Costa Rica, the near-silent throb of the battery-powered boat drowned out by the calls of birds rising from the mangrove swamp. Eckhard, our guide, had been pointing out a crab-eating buzzard resting on a branch only feet above us. We felt like real explorers – my boyfriend, my six-year-old daughter, and I – yet utterly safe. Only the spot where the alligators sunned, leaving long outlines of their bodies like giants' footprints on the sand, suggested a pleasant soupçon of danger.

We were quite close to the shore, and hardly moving, looking for toads at the water's edge, when I heard the hum. Then the bees descended on us, hundreds of them, smothering our skin until it was all bumpy and black. My boyfriend was the first to be stung. He lashed out instinctively, brushing the bees from his forearm. It was a mistake. "Don't move! Don't move!" screamed Eckhard. A killer bee regards any movement as an act of aggression. The bees retaliated, and my boyfriend was stung again.

Eckhard attempted to steer us away from the swarm. This was truly heroic; he knew that even the gentle sway of his hand on the tiller meant he would be stung. The killers went for his uncovered face as he steered a path through the twisted roots of the mangrove trees. Their stings first broke like little splinters, quickly becoming craters of red. We watched. We were not heroes. If we tried to help him, we would be stung again, too.

Eckhard's hand began to wobble on the tiller. He could barely steer. The stings were beginning to make him feel woozy. We couldn't shake off our attackers; killer bees can pursue intruders up to half a mile. Eckhard's panama hat was a black furry umbrella of bees.

"They're still on me, aren't they," he groaned. "Yes," was all I said, my mouth as tight as a ventriloquist.

Eventually, our feeble boat began to outrun the bees. A few stragglers hung on, determined to punish us for invading their territory. As soon as we were free from the swarm, my boyfriend, bitten but less so than Eckhard, tried to remove the stings around Eckhard's face and neck. My daughter, who had been totally silent even when she was stung, suddenly cried. Her wail echoed along the creek, as animal as any sound from the wild beasts.

Despite their ferocious reputation, killer bees do not often attack. In eight years as a guide in Costa Rica, Eckhard had been attacked only once before. Most victims survive. Estimates of the number of fatalities in South and Central America vary from 20 to more than 1,000. But when the swarms started migrating northwards, they began to make headlines in the world's press.

The bees claimed their first Californian victim on May 20, 1998, a pit bull terrier called Killer. The news led to near panic across the country. Last month a 77-year-old woman in Las Vegas suffered a massive attack.

These bees are monsters of our own making. In 1956, African honeybees – Apis mellifera scutellata – were imported from Tanzania to Brazil, in an attempt to improve the honey production of the imported European bees. African bees were used to hot weather, and produced five times as much honey as the Europeans. A year later, 26 colonies of African bees escaped from a research apiary in Brazil and mated with the Europeans to produce Apis mellifera adansonii . Their progeny began to spread throughout South and Central America.

This new strain was different from its parentage, but not as hoped. The hybrid, soon known as the killer bee, is smaller, more vigorous, swarms more often, and is up to 10 times more likely to sting than the European bee. In technical language, killer bees have an "excessive level of colony defence". It was probably the vibration of our tiny engine that attracted them; they are often provoked by power equipment. In California, there have been two attacks on tree trimmers.

Back on the balcony at Nosara Lodge, my stoic daughter scribbled a sign and stuck it to our bedroom door – "Be Ware of Bees". My boyfriend's arms had ballooned up. Eckhard's eyes were so swollen they were nearly shut, and his ears twice their normal size. He was muttering to himself as if on a powerful drug. I strained to make out he was saying. "It's always the small animals, not the big ones, that get you," he burbled. "Better five sharks than 20 killer bees." •

27 April 2000

Tim Radford

Not for the squeamish

Ever since his riding accident five years ago, the actor Christopher Reeve has vowed that he would one day walk again. Until the moment in November 1998 when two American teams announced that they had "immortalised" human embryonic stem cells and were growing them in laboratory dishes, it seemed a dream.

Stem cell therapy sounds like the ultimate in transplant surgery. You don't commandeer someone else's tissue so that you can live, with a little help from immunosuppressant drugs. You grow your own in a dish, treat yourself and walk away, at ease with the new bit of you inside.

There are no polymer implants, no alien grafts, no synthesised drugs on prescription. Just a fresh bit of you, fashioned by the same natural machinery that took you from a single fertilised cell to a whole human being in nine months. Five years ago, it was unimaginable. Two years ago, it was just impossible. Now there are a dozen biotech companies doing research on human stem cells, taken from foetuses, embryos and adult human tissue.

With these cells, they believe they could one day offer hope for people with Alzheimer's disease and atherosclerosis, heart disease and Huntington's, macular degeneration and multiple sclerosis, strokes and spinal cord injuries.

Stem cells are life's magic cauldron: they go on providing more. Humans begin as one single cell, a fertilised egg. They end as several trillion cells, of more than 200 different kinds. The process in between is a display of evolution's wizardry. First the embryonic egg clones, and clones again and again, and with each division, the cells contain the potential for twins, or quadruplets, or octuplets and so on. Then, at some finely balanced point, the nature of the cells begins to change. Some of them become stem cells. They can no longer become a whole human, but they can become anything a human might need, launching a cascade of changes that end with teeth and toenail tissue, or nerve cells, or the inner lining of the arteries, or the tough outer skin of a foot, or the tissue of a heart valve.

If there were some way of keeping such cells alive, scientists reasoned, they might be a new weapon in the war against degenerative diseases. If there were some way of understanding how and why cells differentiate, there might be a way of turning the clock back, of making new stem cells that would replace failed tissue. And then things began to happen. In some cancers, cells can somehow turn their own clocks back, go haywire, start making the wrong tissue in the wrong place. If cells can do that in the wrong place, at the wrong time, maybe they could do it to order.

In 1996, scientists at the Roslin Institute in Scotland took an adult cell from a fully grown sheep and persuaded it go back to square one, and produced from it Dolly the clone.

And at Johns Hopkins University in Baltimore in 1998 – paid for by the Geron Corporation of California – and at the University of Wisconsin, teams of scientists separately isolated and kept alive human embryo stem cells. Words like "holy grail" were used. To illustrate the possibilities, commentators seized on celebrity sufferers who might – just might – benefit. One was Muhammad Ali, with Parkinson's disease. And one was Christopher Reeve himself, who had gone from being Superman to wheelchair-bound.

Right now, a little private company called Layton BioScience in Atherton, California, is working with a neuroscientist from the Harvard Medical School to test the effect of neural stem cells in laboratory rats before possible tests in humans. Right now, Geron BioMed at the Roslin Institute is waiting for the word from the British government before it marries the technology that led to Dolly with stem cell research and opens a new pathway in medicine, towards "therapeutic cloning".

Therein lies the catch. In the US, there is no federal money for human embryo research or anything that might seem like human cloning. On the other hand, there are no restrictions on what private companies might do. In Britain, there is a government appointed body that authorises experiments with human embryos, but only to help with infertility or certain tragic inherited diseases. The US hastily banned human cloning research in the world outcry after the announcement of Dolly the sheep. And the British government – reeling at the public reaction to the idea of genetically-altered soybean – found an excuse not to authorise new research but instead to refer the whole problem to a committee led by the chief medical officer of health, Liam Donaldson. Hope, as some see it, is blocked by red tape and squeamishness.

But there is more to it than squeamishness. The first step towards such research involves experiments with human eggs, human embryos. They will be at a very early stage – just bundles of cells – but to many they will be potential humans. Their use right now is justified because the research has led not just to new life, but to desperately longed-for life. It might seem a huge step to use what some people will see as potential life to do engineering on behalf of people who have had a life, and want to enjoy an even longer one. But each day brings new ethical puzzles: today, European fertility experts report a new way of fusing human eggs to make babies possible for women whose pregnancies have failed, and this, too raises problems of embryo research.

The chances are that stem cell therapy will go ahead. The betting is also that the use of five or six-day-old embryos will only be a stage in the adventure. Just as there are not enough donor hearts to meet demand for transplant surgery, so there will not be enough donated embryos to meet the demand for therapeutic cloning. So the dream answer is to isolate the stem cells from the patient, and use them to make the new tissue that could be injected into, or stitched into, the patient. There are huge obstacles. But if the stem cell machinery can conjure up a whole human in 40 weeks from a cell the size of a full stop, then, scientists reason, it ought to be able to conjure up a new heart valve, or endothelial cells for arteries, or eliminate damage done by diabetes, or cirrhosis, or hepatitis.

And, they think, in five or 10 years, there could be human trials for stem cell therapy – for Parkinson's, and, yes, spinal cord injury. Christopher Reeve can see the future, and from where he sits, it must look good. ∎

3 February 2000

David McKie
Far, far from Bohemia

Kathleen Hale, creator of Orlando the marmalade cat, died last week at the age of 101. Her early life was exotic: she was briefly (at 22) the mistress of the famously lecherous painter Augustus John, before settling for the possibly less exhausting role of his secretary. All that changed when, in 1926, she married a bacteriologist called Douglas McClean (she had wanted to marry his father, but made do with the son instead).

"Gradually," wrote the obituarist of the Times of this marriage, "she distanced herself from bohemia, moving to Hertfordshire in 1931."

This sentence has haunted me all this week. What is it that gives it its tragic grandeur? The sense, I think, of a life thrown irrevocably into reverse, almost as if she had moved from Tooting to Timbuktu. From bohemia, with its wine and its taste for ravishing metaphor and its overflowing ashtrays and unpaid bills and its debates through the early hours about Nietzsche and Baudelaire and Madame Blavatsky, to decent, orderly Hertfordshire, with its mile upon mile of law abiding semi-detacheds, and its modest suburban trains and obedient buses plying their trade between Watford and Ware.

Let us define bohemia, which is not the same as Bohemia, now part of the Czech Republic. Bohemia is an invention brought to our language by Thackeray, though borrowed like so much bohemian practice from the French. "She was of a wild, roving nature, inherited from her mother and father, who were both Bohemians, by taste and circumstances," he wrote in 1848. The term had come to mean a kind of literary Gypsy in retreat from conventionality, the Westminster Review reported 14 years later, thus anticipating the cyclists' touring club handbook of April 1886, which referred, in the context of somebody now long forgotten, to the "Bohemian-like contempt he harbours for all conventionalities".

How different is the image of Hertfordshire, a place which may strike the innocent visitor as harbouring more conventionalities than most. In a book called Victoria Glendinning's Hertfordshire, the biographer of Trollope and Swift recounts how a deaf old man assumed she was doing a book on Herefordshire. "Hertfordshire?"he grumbled when at last he heard her correction, "why do you want to write about Hertfordshire? It's near London." This, I fear, is a prevalent view of the county, made worse by the fact that one so often goes through to it on the way to somewhere more compelling.

If you go by train to the cities of northern England or to anywhere in Scotland, Hertfordshire is a place that you rattle through, perhaps just managing to register somewhere like Hitchin or Tring as it flashes past. Much the same is true of its many miles of motorway: Hertfordshire is a mere prelude, or if you're returning, a coda. Other counties have this transitional aspect too, but are saved because they are bigger. Essex and Kent stretch down to the sea and Surrey at least to the downs.

The planners have made things worse in our present century (that's the 20th) by establishing so many overspill towns in the county. The novelist EM Forster, when someone remarked that Stevenage had become a satellite town, said "meteorite town" would describe it better as it seemed to have fallen out of the sky. Towns like these, by definition, cannot have the history or the flavour of the counties they occupy. They are new, different, and alien. That does not make them bohemian.

This is not to deny a bohemian presence in selected sectors of Hertfordshire. One imagines strong bohemian trends in a place like St Albans, to which most of this newspaper's staff seem to have moved or be moving. The wild and fecund novelist Bulwer-Lytton lived at Knebworth, adapting the house he inherited to look like something out of one of his novels. GB Shaw, no friend of convention, settled in unexciting Ayot St Lawrence. And Graham Greene grew up at the far end of Herts, in Berkhamsted. But here we have to confront another problem. Too much of the county seems to belong to somewhere else. Even as fervent a Hertsian as Victoria Glendinning admits this is so. Tring ought to be in Bucks, she accepts, and Bishop's Stortford in Essex, while Royston "has an air of not being quite sure whether it should not be in Cambridgeshire" (hardly surprising, that, since until 1897 it was split between Cambs and Herts).

My favourite spot in the county is Ashwell, classed as a village but clearly a town, with its sweetly eccentric main street and a whopping great church with a boastful tower – a building which loudly announces: this is a place of some consequence.

But Ashwell is lodged in one of those curious protuberances which Hertfordshire thrusts out into other people's territory. It ought to be in Cambridgeshire, or even in Bedfordshire. I call in evidence the river Rhee, which rises in Ashwell, but swiftly looking about it makes off with all convenient speed into Cambridgeshire, where it changes its name to the Cam.

Kathleen Hale would have known why that is. I think it has caught a scent of Cambridge. It is looking for somewhere bohemian. •

11 December 1999

Smallweed

An extraordinary card from Oxford reveals that much-maligned Slough was formerly Upton-cum-Chalvey. Why did they change? They must be kicking themselves. John Betjeman, whose assault on Slough has entered the language, could not have done the same kind of damage to Upton-cum-Chalvey. "Come friendly bombs and fall on Upton-cum-Chalvey; it warrants the fate of Roberto Calvi" does not have the same ring (and in any case Calvi met his fate very much later). Even worse, it appears that Chalvey was pronounced Charvey. "Come friendly bombs and fall on Upton-cum-Chalvey; It's a slough of despond and crawling with larvae" is the best I can do before Christmas.

Not since I appealed for the words of the once-famous popular song, What Will Della Wear, Boys, has an issue stirred up readers as much as the matter of pear-shapedness. A whole gallimaufry of explanations for this usage have sent my poor postman Soames staggering time and again up the long crooked path which leads to the creaking door and jangling bell of Smallweed Towers. The verdict is clear: this expression long predates the Falklands war. The most favoured explanation is that it's RAF slang. One ex-RAF man says that, when checking temperatures, they used to signal that things were OK by making a circle with thumb and finger; if they weren't, they signalled the shape of a pear. Another source says it comes from the engineering trade and refers to misshapen bearings, the victims of overheating. For reasons I don't understand, "pear-shaped" bearings could be restored to shape by dropping worms into them. (Please don't try this experiment.)

A Manchester reader is more specific than most. He says he experienced it first some 40 years ago in a British comedy film featuring Richard Wattis, though since almost every British comedy film of that era featured Richard Wattis, that gives us rather too many to choose from. This one was about a collection of RN ratings planning to steal some money. When their plans were going awry, Wattis soothed them by saying they were going to "play it pear-shaped" (ie it would all go smoothly). If this explanation is right, pear-shaped is one of those usages which has changed its meaning from one extreme to the other, like silly, which once meant wise. Others claim it has something to do with Louis-Philippe (1773-1850), an aristocrat who renounced his titles, styled himself Egalité, and moved to Twickenham, Middlesex. Recalled to Paris as the "citizen king", he alienated all and sundry by his authoritarian practices and fell victim to the revolutionary spirit of 1848, escaping to England under the wildly inventive soubriquet Smith and dying at Claremont, near Esher. Cartoonists invariably portrayed him as pear-shaped, in the original dictionary sense of shaped like a pear.

Last week, you may remember, this column adopted Winsford of the Unibond League as its team to cherish, in succession to Cowdenbeath.I had qualms about that on Saturday evening, when I saw that the Metropolitan Police, a rugby union team I had at one point considered espousing, had lost 104-7 to Esher, the team on whose touch-line, enthusiasts tell me, Louis-Philippe used to wave a supportive rattle, whereas Winsford had come pretty close to holding their own in their home match with table-topping Leigh RMI, losing only 5-0. The crowd, if that is the word, numbered only 101, which suggests that few had responded to Smallweed's appeal to support them. I would have been there myself had I not felt bound to stay in and read some novel by some-one called Proust which keeps cropping up in newspaper features in which people are asked to pick their Book of the Millennium. I half expected a fierce editorial blast from Hysteria House, home of the Telegraph, blaming the Met's recent run of poor form on Lord MacPherson, who wrote the report on the Stephen Lawrence case which they rail against almost daily. But not so. Standards there must be slipping.

Mo Mowlam, I see, has been elevated to tsardom. Tony Blair has named her as poverty tsar. Suddenly the world seems to be full of these tsars, from the drug tsar upwards and downwards. It is good to be spared the term supremo, but this is getting ridiculous. Before very long, I predict, some half-crazed spinner, desperate to draw media atten-tion away from Ken Livingstone, will whisper into our prime minister's complaisant ear a tsuggestion for a tsummit of tsars. What a preposterous tsight they will make, all crammed together in tsome tsmall hotel in Tsomerset. Our irreverent popular press, I forecast, will swiftly rename them tsardines.

The probation service is understandably miffed at Jack Straw's plans to rename it the community punishment and rehabilitation service (CPRS). No use telling him that he's giving in to the Daily Mail: he knows that already. They'd do better to concentrate on the scope for confusion. Ted Heath's think tank, the central policy review staff, has gone out of business and there is happily no council for the preservation of rural Scotland alongside England's CPRE, but already we've heard of a possible clash with the crown prosecution service (CPS). If that is a threat, what are the implications for the perform-ing rights society (PRS), the cereals research station (CRS) the Canadian Pacific rail-way (CPR) or even the canons regular of Premonté (CRP) and, in football, Chalfont St Peter reserves? If he wants to invoke Victorian values, Smallweed thinks Straw should settle for the Service for the Training, Reform and Admonition of Wastrels. •

8 January 2000

Peter Tatchell
Homo heaven

I am standing on the steps of the Sydney Opera House on a glorious sunny afternoon in early February, surrounded by 22,000 revellers. Descending from the sky on a crane is a Sister of Perpetual Indulgence, the order of gay male nuns. Dressed in a fresh-starched habit and clutching a pink rosary, his blessings ceremonially launch the Sydney Gay & Lesbian Mardi Gras – three weeks of non-stop parties, plus parallel sporting and cultural festivals, culminating in the grand parade and post-parade party.

During Mardi Gras, Sydney becomes the queerest place on Earth – the closest thing to Homo Heaven. Mardi Gras totally dominates the city. Yet heterosexuals don't feel threatened. They join in. More than 600,000 line the streets to watch the night-time parade of glittering floats and costumed marchers. So many straight people want to go to the end-of-parade party that the organisers have had to restrict sales to gay outlets. Mardi Gras is, my dear, The Event in the Sydney calendar. Everybody who's anybody wants to party with the faggerati.

So many parties, so little time. Will it be the Blue Hawaii Pool Party? The theme is South Pacific, as Victoria Park swimming pool is transformed into a tropical island paradise and everyone splashes around in their bikinis – even the boys.

Or should I wait for the Chinese New Year Party? To the sounds of Chinese techno, the city's Asian gay community is celebrating The Year of the Rabbit in Sydney's stunning oriental gardens, reputedly the finest outside Beijing.

Or how about the Harbour Party? Staged in the Royal Botanic Gardens, on a spit of land jutting out into Sydney Harbour and overlooking the Opera House, this has to be the most spectacular dance party location in the world. On a balmy summer's evening, as tugboats spray water jets 100 metres in the air, 3,500 gorgeous fags and dykes party the night away. Showing off their bronzed, gym-honed bodies, most are stripped to the waist.

Call me greedy, but I did all three. Afterwards, I squeezed in Fair Day as well. This open-air Oz Pop festival and picnic-in-the-park pulls in 60,000 people. But the side events grabbed my attention most, especially the dog drag show – it was toss up between the spike and leatherette SM bulldog and the poodle in pink tights and tutu. Ms Fair Day competition was also a hoot. More drag. This time human, though some may disagree. Boys dressed as girls dressed as boys. So confusing, but that's part of the fun.

As for the costumes: how on earth did he/she manage with those four-foot high sequinned platforms and that three-tiered wedding cake hat with a groom and groom on top? As we all know, queens love to shop, and Mardi Gras has a tailor-made event to fulfil every big spender fantasy. Shop Yourself Stupid is nirvana for shopaholics, and all for a good cause. More than 300 of Sydney's most stylish stores join forces to donate a share of the day's takings to the Aids charity, the Bobby Goldsmith Foundation. Sixty drag queens on stilts mince up and down the main shopping thoroughfares all day, urging everyone to "Spend! Spend! Spend!" The result: $80,000 raised for the care of people with HIV.

In Sydney, the pink dollar has real clout. Mardi Gras is sponsored by the national airline, Qantas, and by the national telecom corporation, Telstra. Bus shelters and billboards all over the city advertise the festivities with the slogan "Gay Icon", a reference to the official online Mardi Gras guide, which is sponsored by the leading daily newspaper, Sydney Morning Herald. Big bucks are at stake. Mardi Gras earns nearly $100 million for the local economy, generating more income than any other cultural or sporting event in Australia.

Much more than a three-week party, Mardi Gras also offers unexpected treats for Mr and Ms Butch. The sports festival is a mini-gay Olympics, ranging from big girl's blouse events like softball and golf, to the hardman sports of ju-jitsu and triathlon.

For those who love the wilderness, the Southern Cross Outdoors Group organises special Mardi Gras "queer treks" in the nearby Blue Mountains – Australia's version of the Grand Canyon. I joined 50 designer-label-wearing gay bushwalkers for an 8km hike at Wentworth Falls, retracing the steps of Charles Darwin in 1836.

For the cerebrally-minded, Mardi Gras has some absolute gems. The cultural festival brings in audiences of 250,000, and showcases some brilliant avant-garde performances. Move over Xena! Razor Baby, performed by the dykon aerialists of Club Swing, fuses martial arts, dance, gymnastics and trapeze dare-devilry, backed by an all-women big percussion band.

If it's laughs you want, look no further than the Mile-High Club: cabaret hosted by Pam Ann, "the world's greatest celebrity air hostess". And for the highbrow, there is the Opera House. I made sure I didn't miss the stunning homoerotic production of Billy Budd, with its semi-naked, all-male cast tenderly vocalising Britten's tragedy of sexual repression and class privilege.

But all these events are just foreplay, leading up to the orgasmic grand finale: the spectacular street parade of floats and marching ensembles, followed by the mother of all dance parties. Tonight is that night. It is 8pm and getting dark. Rev Fred Nile (Australia's Mary Whitehouse) is still praying for rain. But God refuses to punish us sodomites. Who cares? We're here to party. And so is half of straight Sydney. Mums and dads, and loads of kids. Japanese tourists. Mardi Gras transcends all barriers.

And they're off! More than 200 entries, led by Dykes on Bikes, the 30-strong, leather-clad lesbian motorcycle club. On come the massed ranks of the marching ensembles: the Bassey Bitches (30 Shirley look-alikes belting out Hey, Big Spender), the George Michaels (40 women dressed as LAPD officers escorting a George Michael clone) and the Monicas (50 Lewinsky impersonators wearing stained blue dresses and waving moist cigars).

Then there's some political satire with a float featuring a two-faced caricature of Labour State premier, Bob Carr, condemning his failure to deliver same-sex partnership rights. Can satire change the world? A couple of months later, Carr granted legal recognition to gay couples. Poking fun at oppressive religion, the Temple of More Men float is a take-off of the Mormon Church, featuring the "More Men Tab-of-acid" male choir singing "hims", shouting "A mens!", and "promoting faith in disco devotion".

Two dazzling hours later, the parade is over and the party begins. Twenty thousand people pour into four aircraft-hanger-sized pavilions at the Showgrounds for the biggest queer rave in the world, lasting from 10pm to 10am the next morning.

The Big Top has an "Aloha Dot" South Sea islands theme and hosts the costume pageant, presided over by Jean-Paul Gaultier. With giant wind machines, The Dome is the "Temple of Thunder". Topping both is the Horden Pavilion – "Satellite of Love" – where a towering silver laser gun sends shafts of shimmering light ricocheting off the walls, ceilings and floors.

But the big daddy of them all is the Royal Hall of Industries, which hosts a staggering 9,000 party-goers. Here the theme is red: "Vegas is Burning". Probably the greatest light show in the world, its 5,000 spots and lasers arc the colours of the rainbow flag across the dance floor. Just when you think nothing can top this, disco diva Dannii Minogue descends from the rafters on a sparkling silver crescent moon, belting out her chart-topping hits to the accompaniment of 20 drag queens, 70 dancers and incandescent pyrotechnics. Unforgettable! •

13 July 2000

Polly Toynbee

Time to turn cameras on the media mob

As a spin stopper it was the only way – the prime minister in person talking over the head of the lobby straight to camera, on the record, 30 questions in a full hour. How else to get the story out there? One million more people are now in jobs than when Labour took office. Things have got a lot better for the unemployed than anyone dared promise in 1997.

That was the story. How did the Press Association put it out on the wires at first? "Blair Denies having Annus Horribilis." Did the prime minister mention anything about an annus horribilis? No. When asked if he was having one he said just that one word, "No". Who asked the question that created this 'top story'? Why, the guy from the PA of course. Second item in his report? "The prime minister today ruled out a snap election." Did Tony Blair talk about that either? No. When asked if he might make a dash for it this autumn, he just said "No." Who asked that one? Reuters. (When did he stop beating Cherie?)

For journalists not in the lobby and for people watching this unusually televised event at home, it was a glimpse – albeit sanitised – of the famous lobby at work.

Usually it meets in a dingy cubby hole under the No 10 stairs where Alastair Campbell, or more often these days, civil servant Godric Smith feeds the cabal that convenes twice a day to create some kind of story out of the frenetic buzz.

It's a wild game of fact and fiction bouncing around in a whirlwind of spin. A rare female lobby denizen whispered, "Oh, they're behaving quite differently today. Best behaviour, because it's the prime minister, but mainly because the cameras are here. They wouldn't want to be filmed behaving as they usually do."

For instance, Trevor Kavanagh, political editor of the Sun, didn't dominate the scene with his customary rant about the euro. My source said George Jones of the Telegraph usually pumps himself up into a bright red froth, ready to explode when Alastair's teasing habit of winking at him sends him off like an apoplectic rocket.

As for the rival television stars, if none of them say anything it's OK. But they play this game: if Robin Oakley of the BBC speaks, then John Sergeant of ITN, Eleanor Goodman of C4 and Adam Bolton of Sky all have to have their say too.

Paul Routledge of the Mirror thugs it out with the rudest questions: "How much longer are you going to lead this country?" he asked yesterday. "That's in part up to the country to decide," replies Blair. "Only in part!" harrumphs Routers. Daily lobby briefings are now posted on the Downing Street website, no longer off the record. The spokesman is quoted verbatim, for all the world to read – though, sadly, with no identification of the members of the press asking questions.

The magic cartel of accredited lobby correspondents is already busted, no longer the exclusive recipients of secret Downing Street wisdom. So why can't we see it happen each day on television? The only people left to be discomfited are the press themselves – their questions, their faces, their demeanour for the first time on daily display to the public. Not before time.

Unsurprisingly they hated the intrusion on their world by the BBC cameras of Michael Cockerell for his film to be shown on Saturday evening charting the backstage life of Alastair Campbell and his daily adversaries.

Did the cameras change behaviour? Yes, say insiders. Everyone was politer, not just the press. "We had Campbell on Prozac, not a hint of nasty Alastair, only nice Alastair."

Until recently Campbell has refused the cameras for fear they would yet further focus attention on himself and not the message. But now he is largely disappeared to the back rooms there's scant danger sober Godric will be magicked into the story instead.

It's time to bring in the cameras and turn them for once on the media itself. Downing Street insiders hint that the Cockerell film is a stalking horse for doing just that.

Unaccountable, immensely powerful, driven by trivia, the press and especially the lobby holds every government to ransom, but worst of all a Labour government besieged by an ideologically hostile Tory army.

Turning the cameras on the way they behave, the way they think, the way they yawn at most matters of substance might show the public how their news is mediated through such grossly distorting mirrors. Let them see the mob in full cry, observe the making of factoid and fantasy.

Voters should be sceptical about any "news" the government puts out which may or may not be honest – but let them also see how often it has become unrecognisable by the time the headlines land on breakfast tables next morning.

Of course the real stuff of politics, the briefings down the phone and the whispers in corridors would continue unabated, as they do in the White House and every other democracy – the stuff of politics.

But this mad spin hysteria needs the camera lights shining full in the face of both lobby and prime ministerial spokesmen to calm it down. •

19 April 2000

Francis Wheen

Champagne socialists unite

"**W**here are the New Statesman's priorities?" demands an indignant letter in the magazine's current issue from one Lorraine Hewitt of Whitstable, Kent. She describes the NS's excellent food correspondent, Bee Wilson, and its wine critic, Victoria Moore, as "intelligent, elegant writers on worthless themes", whose "trivial, indulgent musings have no place in a journal that is supposed to explore social justice". Hewitt cannot understand how a left-wing journal allows space for articles on such "selfish and silly concerns".

The idea that socialists shouldn't enjoy the pleasures of the table is remarkably hard to dislodge. In the 1930s, Lord Beaverbrook wrote a sneering article for the London Evening Standard about "Cafe Communists", whom he defined as "the gentlemen, often middle-aged, who gather in fashionable restaurants, and, while they are eating the very fine food that is served in those restaurants and drinking the fine wines of France and Spain, are declaring themselves to be of Left Wing faith". (One of the Cafe Communists named in the piece replied, with admirable presence of mind, that he didn't see why he should be "a victim of the malnutrition which is an endemic disease of capitalism".) When Aneurin Bevan was dining with him, Beaverbrook used to bawl at the butler: "Bring the Bollinger Bolshevik a bottle of young, fizzy, cold champagne!"

But, as Lorraine Hewitt demonstrates, it isn't only rich right-wingers who believe that champagne socialism is an oxymoron. The left in this country has its own regiment of puritan zealots who regard any form of fun as a decadent distraction from more urgent tasks.

The late Cyril Ray, a lifelong socialist who edited the Compleat Imbiber annuals, had a simple reply to these killjoys: "There is no more virtue in not minding what you eat and drink than in not minding whom you go to bed with." Though he refused on principle to allow the Daily Telegraph into his house, and once resigned from the Sunday Times because of an editorial supporting capital punishment, Ray saw no incongruity in his authorship of a book on Bollinger. As he pointed out: "They don't say 'How dare you call yourself a socialist and love good books, good painting and good music?' Socialism is about a fuller and richer life for everybody, and God knows there's plenty of good cheap wine about today." His Guardian obituary – written by Christopher Driver, another radical foodie – was headed: "The people's wine is deepest red."

Raymond Postgate, founder of The Good Food Guide, was jailed as a conscientious objector in the first world war, took to the picket lines in the general strike and received a fan-letter from Lenin for his book on The International During The War. None of this was enough to save him from being regularly attacked by pious fellow-lefties for his gastronomic enthusiasms. "Confounded nonsense," he retorted. "I should like to remind puritanical objectors that Major Cartwright, the first of the Reformers, was an expert on raisins and on gin; and that Marx himself on occasion even got drunk."

Just so: when Karl Marx had had a few he sometimes behaved in a manner more usually associated with Bertie Wooster on boat-race night. Engels, too, was a serious tippler who admitted that in 1848, the year of revolutions, he "spent more time lying in the grass with the vintners and their girls, eating grapes, drinking wine, chatting and laughing, than marching".

What Marx and Engels understood, even if some of their grim-faced followers didn't, was that there's nothing selfish and silly about shared pleasures, whether in the long grass or at the kitchen table. There are few things more conducive to comradeship than decent food and drink. It is, I think, no coincidence that the creator of the first top-class champagne was not some bloated plutocrat but Dom Perignon, a Benedictine monk of the 17th century who devoted his life to caring for the sick and needy. "He loved the poor," according to his epitaph, "and he made excellent wine." Note the conjunction: "and", not "but".

Those who yearn for a better future need all the sustenance they can get. Pessimism of the intellect, Antonio Gramsci advised, must be accompanied by optimism of the will; and how can one not feel optimistic at the sound of a popping cork, or the taste and texture of a perfect peach?

THE GURU HAS SPOKEN

After Friday's plunge on Wall Street, share-dealers had an uncomfortable weekend wondering if meltdown had begun or if this was merely a "correction". They would not know until Monday morning, when the world's greatest market guru was due to pronounce.

William Rees-Mogg (for it was he) duly obliged. "Last week's falls on Wall Street are likely to be followed by further falls in New York," the Somerset sage announced in The Times. "This is... the end of the bull market of the 1990s." Frabjous day, calloo callay! The Dow-Jones and the Nasdaq bounced back immediately.

Mogg has become something of a legend on Wall Street for his prognosticatory skill. Nine years ago he published a book called The Great Reckoning: How The World Will

Change In The Depression Of The 1990s. As he noted recently, few heeded his warning: "Indeed, people got rich during the boom by rejecting it."

An infallibly fallible tipster is just as useful as one who always picks the winner. "Although Mrs Thatcher's majority was not quite large enough to avoid a second ballot, the victory was clearly a decisive one," Mogg wrote after the first Tory leadership election in 1990. "Of course many people will doubt that she really has won... I take the contrary view that a mandate is a mandate and that she will derive real strength from having overcome so tough a challenge." I quickly placed a large bet that Thatcher would resign at once, and so she did.

In May 1993 he tried again: "It is now as probable that Mr Major will have to go as it was nine months ago that Mr Lamont would have to." This time I bet my entire life savings that Major would lead the Tories into the next election; once again, thanks to Mystic Mogg, I cleaned up.

Mogg-fanciers made another fortune on the last US presidential election, after reading his confident forecast that Colin Powell would win the Republican nomination and "be elected by a large majority in November 1996".

In his latest oracular bulletin, Mogg admits that "many of us have been wrong in the past decade about the durability of unsustainable growth in the Western stock markets". Too modest, my dear chap: you have been wrong about absolutely everything – which is why we punters love you so.

IRVING'S SHORT HISTORICAL MEMORY

Did David Irving really lose his libel case? The "revelation" of his Nazi sympathies, which have been well known for decades, is about as newsworthy as dog-bites-postman; yet, after years as a media outcast, he now finds himself a welcome guest on Today and Newsnight, and the subject of innumerable full-page profiles. No wonder his website has such a jaunty, almost jubilant tone.

Irving's hunger for publicity is insatiable. One need only recall his antics during the affair of the Hitler diaries: when Lord Dacre was declaring the documents to be authentic, Irving condemned them loudly as forgeries; when Dacre came round to his point of view, Irving then announced that they were genuine.

Why? I tackled him on this point a few years ago, and he cheerfully confessed that his eccentric volte face was "purely commercial" and "very much tongue-in-cheek". Having pocketed large fees from television companies for rubbishing the diaries, he decided he could double his money by becoming the only historian who would publicly defend them. And so it proved. During the month after the story broke, he told me, he earned £30,000.

Now that he is again in need of cash, can it be long before the wily old villain does another U-turn – and informs an astonished world that, er, Hitler was a bit of an anti-semite after all? •

....

8 March 2000

Michael White
The name game

Lucky Ken. Love him or hate him, the papers and the public remain on first name terms where Candidate Livingstone is concerned. "Ken gets the sack as he bids for mayor," said yesterday's Sun. "Red Ken kicks off with 55% lead over Dobson," declared the Mail's later editions after reading the Guardian's opinion poll findings.

Note that "Dobson". Sometimes it is "Dobbo", a nickname with amiable overtones. But it is almost never "Frank", though the official Labour candidate's first name has fewer letters than his surname, a factor which ought to help in the space-constrained art of headline-writing.

In their domestic setting, as parents or a couple, the Blairs sometimes get the friendly treatment as Tony and Cherie. But yesterday's Daily Mirror – which is anti-Livingstone – sported a splash headline which declared: "Nightmare: Blair faces civil war as Ken splits Labour."

There it goes again. Ken and Blair, not Ken and Tony. Thus the Independent's splash headline yesterday struck a slightly false note for well-intentioned reasons. A triple-banner proclaimed: "Ken says: 'I'll let London decide.' Frank says: 'The ego has landed.' Tony says: 'He would be a disaster.' "

But Tony, when used in both headlines and conversation, is often used ironically, for instance to mock the vicar's touchy-feely style in Private Eye's St Albion's Parish News. It is the same with "Mandy" Mandelson, the diminutive is ambiguous in the extreme, implicitly homophobic in the wrong hands.

"Paddy" (as in Ashdown) might also have been pejorative if anyone regarded the MP for Yeovil as a real Irishman. But Ken is Ken even to Blair and those Westminster colleagues who loathe him – quite a lot of them, actually – and do not see him as a latterday Charlie Chaplin, the lovable cockney underdog, Labour's irrepressible cheeky chappie.

They see him as an unprincipled opportunist, a loner and a liar, an egotist, not really a party man. There is truth in many of the accusations. But there is little evidence so far that they will do him much harm. Ken is a brilliantly-marketed brand, which means different things to different people, from newt-fancier to Blair-baiter.

Advertising agencies would pay – do pay – a fortune to gain such name recognition for their clients. How often do we observe this phenomenon in politics and why? Not often. In recent times there was "Maggie" Thatcher, a cheeky diminutive which did not sit easily with the Iron Lady's daunting public personality.

Her friends called her Margaret. Indeed old-school Tories tend to frown on vulgar diminutives among their leaders. Chris Patten's use of "Chris" was a black mark against him. Anthony Blair (as he styled himself during the 1982 Beaconsfield byelection) became something of a class traitor when he became plain Tony.

The Rt Hon Anthony Wedgwood Benn's demotic crime was even greater after he not only refused to become Lord Stansgate, but rebranded himself in Who's Who as plain Tony Benn. Yet, even in the heyday of his fame and influence, he was rarely spoken about as "Tony" without self-conscious intent, friendly or foul.

In the same era, Sir Edward Heath's friends call him "Ted", but not voters or editorial writers. William Hague's colleagues self-consciously refer to him during TV interviews as "William" – not Mr Hague – but the trick does not work. As the Australian expression goes: "If his name was William you wouldn't call him Bill."

Maggie was an attempt to humanise the prime minister of the day. With Ken Livingstone it is different, he is human already and people like him for it. He has "pintability" – the sort of bloke you'd happily have a pint with.

Coincidentally Ken Clarke – who calls him Kenneth? – has many of the same qualities, though the Labour MP for Brent East is clearly the senior Ken in the public mind. We see Ken in a headline and know which one we mean. There may be a deeper reason for that. Clarke is a serious political heavyweight who cultivates a bloke-ish, populist style.

Voters enjoy it, but they are not deceived. The ex-chancellor may boast that he has not read the Maastricht Treaty, and he really does like pints and cigars. But he is not really like most of us. Ken really is a populist who expresses better than most people the gut instincts and prejudices of a significant section of voters.

There have always been politicians who can do this sort of business, but not very many. They do not even have to be populists, though they do have to be able to communicate their thoughts, lofty or low, in terms which the rest of us can understand and, preferably, be moved by. Gladstone was "the People's William", Churchill sometimes Winston or even Winnie.

Thus when he returned to be first lord of the admiralty when war broke out in September 1939 a simple message was signalled throughout the Royal Navy: "Winston is back." He had held the same job in 1914. It helps, of course, to have a distinctive name. Winston, Enoch, Harold . . .

Harold Wilson was probably the last Labour politician to evoke such feelings of affection among ordinary voters. They felt that, despite being prime minister and being so clever, he remained one of them. Wilson played on it, no brandy and cigars in public, he drank pints on camera.

Changing standards of public decorum have a bearing on all this. Nye Bevan passed muster as a much-loved (and loathed) orator, democratic socialism's great romantic hero, and a funny name too. People spoke of "Nye and Jenny" – Jenny Lee MP, his formidable wife – but not in a Kennish way. He was Bevan or Mr Bevan. Harold Macmillan was Supermac.

It is a sign of the times that the Tory candidate for London mayor can be referred to in print and on the air as Shagger. No one ever said that about Lloyd George, who won an Archer-ish libel case merely because his wife turned up in court. She didn't even have to give fragrant evidence.

That was before women had the vote, let alone exercised political power. Is it a coincidence that two prominent women in Anglo-Saxon political culture pass the Ken test? Dr Marjorie Mowlam is famously voter-friendly and has been rewarded with the fetching soubriquet Mo.

No wonder that Downing Street has intermittently eyed her up as a Dobson-substitute. Across the pond the former Hillary Rodham Clinton first dropped the Rodham, now she has dropped the Clinton as she courts New York voters. Is it a populist move or top-down marketing? We shall find out in November. But Hillary still has a long way to go to catch up the cheeky chappie. His brand name is all over London, South Ken, Kennington, Kenwood, Kentish Town . . . •

Sporting strife

5 September 2000

Matthew Engel
Early risers marvel at new dawn

The most dangerous word in cricket is "unprecedented". The moment you suggest something has never happened before, someone will announce not only that it has but that it were all a damn sight better in them days too.

Well, the scenes at the Oval yesterday were as near to unprecedented as makes no difference. Here at last was the Amazing Millennium Experience that London was promised. England not merely beat West Indies, they crushed them.

Only a handful of people in the ground had witnessed England win a series against West Indies before: Henry Blofeld, Tony Cozier and Bill Frindall for sure; a few grey-beards in the crowd, no doubt. Six of the England team were not even born 31 summers ago. Nor, gratifyingly, were many of the spectators. As Nasser Hussain lifted the Wisden Trophy, kids – repeat, English schoolboys – were playing makeshift games on the Oval outfield with bags and Thermos flasks as wickets. This is what boys are meant to do. And no one chased them off.

They had to go a long way back to find room. The whole of the field south of the square was covered in humanity, and some supporters had to try to squint at the presentation from the Vauxhall End. No one could recall a crowd anything like this. Traditionally the fifth day of a Test match – no matter how excitingly poised – is played out in a near-empty stadium. Tickets are never sold in advance. This time, to unanimous astonishment, the crowds began forming outside shortly after 7am. Before the start they were massing five abreast on the Harleyford Road. By midday the gates were shut, making the match an official sell-out for the fifth successive day.

Something similar was witnessed at Headingley two years ago when England beat South Africa. Never mind that the victory was tainted by appalling umpiring. Ten thousand turned up on the last day to watch half an hour's cricket – which was amazing even if admission was free.

And yesterday cannot entirely be put down to the cheap rates either: a tenner admission, free for children and seniors (a reaction to the criticism about high cup-final prices). People were hungry, no, starving, even ravenous for success. The English had not fallen out of love with cricket: they had just grown contemptuous of the national team. Headingley 1998 aside, one of the few men on the ground who could remember winning anything was John Major – and that was 1992, and received with less unanimous acclaim than this result.

But it's amazing what the anticipation of victory can do. The famously officious Surrey stewards barred the entrances – with some glee, I thought. Touts offered £10 tickets for £60 but even they were struggling to get a supply. Hundreds of plaintive victims stood outside the gates as though they had missed the last helicopter out of Saigon. "But my mother knew Jack Hobbs," wailed one victim.

Congestion was eased when the empty hospitality boxes were opened and made available to the Great Unwashed, who rushed in and committed the ultimate corporate-day-out solecism: *They watched the cricket.* The Revolution will be like this.

There are famous pictures from 1953, when Denis Compton and Bill Edrich were cheered off by a vast throng (all wearing jackets and ties). England had just clinched the Ashes for the first time in a mere 20 years. That win came very early on the last day and there is no record of a full house.

In 1926, England's previous home Ashes win, and 1938, when Len Hutton scored his record-breaking 364, the Oval Test did not even go to the fifth day. OK, let's say it. Unprecedented. ∎

13 April 2000

Ian Aitken
Cricket for comrades

Brooding on the state of world cricket in the dismal light of the Cronje affair, and contemplating where the greatest of all games can go now, a memory of my long-dead father came unexpectedly to mind. Once a professional revolutionary as well as a Marxist scholar, he was also a very Scottish Scot, so he hardly fitted the traditional image of a flannelled fool.

Yet he loved the game with no less passion than any of the straw-hatted chumps who parade their MCC ties in the pavilion at Lord's. Thanks to a war wound which removed two fingers from his right hand, he had to abandon a promising career as a fast-medium bowler. But his enthusiasm was such that he managed to develop a weird spinning action with the stumps of his missing fingers. The jagged bits of bone which stuck out seemed to give him extra purchase on the ball, so that he could turn it like an early version of Shane Warne. Or so my memory fondly tells me.

Such was his belief in cricket as a civilising influence that he – with me in faithful tow – set out towards the end of the second world war to teach the complexities of the game to Italian PoWs lodging in an open camp on Royston Heath, Hertfordshire. These bemused but utterly delightful young Latins would try desperately to follow his instructions as he carefully placed his field before bowling his crafty fizzers at me.

In fact, he had surprising success with several of the "prisoners". Most of them learned to catch the ball quite competently, and a few managed to throw it fairly straight. One or two even mastered the elements of batsmanship, although none really

got the hang of the odd business of bowling the ball rather than chucking it – a difficulty they share with some world-renowned players today.

With steady progress being made, my father had begun to think about forming a
team of what the locals called, with genuine affection, "our Eye-ties". He had visions
of arranging fixtures with the local RAF station and (wildest of his ambitions) the
nearby USAF base. But it was not to be. One night, shortly after D-day, the Italians
were bussed out of Royston, to be replaced by a long column of dejected Germans.
The camp gates clanged shut again, and the fun was over.

My father often wondered what might have happened if he had had a bit longer to
complete his course of instruction with the Italians. He liked to think that they might
have gone home and spread the gospel of leather and willow among their sun-kissed
villages. And who knows, but for those Germans they might by now be playing World
Cup cricket, just as they do in the Six Nations Rugby Championship.

Disappointments of this sort were not new to my ever-optimistic father. As I have
said, he was a professional revolutionary, and he learned his rather specialised trade at
the Marx-Engels Institute in Moscow, dubbed by the tabloids as the "school for spies".
Early in his stay, he noticed that some of the American students were trying to teach
baseball to their Russian hosts. This acted like... well, like a red rag to a bull. For my
father thought baseball was little better than a girls' game played with a hard ball. The
revolution, he decided, deserved better – ie cricket.

Being a man of action, he sent home to Communist party headquarters in Covent
Garden to request an urgent shipment of cricket balls, bats, pads and gloves, plus six
stumps and four bails. Goodness knows what the stern apparatchiks of King Street
thought of this bizarre request, but – amazingly – they did as they were asked. So a
large parcel was dispatched to Moscow, to be delivered eventually to my father by a
clearly puzzled policeman.

On opening the parcel, my father found everything he had asked for. But there was
just one snag. The balls had been slit open, the pads and gloves had been emptied of
their stuffing, the stumps and bats had been sawn in half. Clearly, the ever suspicious
NKVD imagined that these strange artifacts might be the tools of counter-revolution.

So ended my father's first attempt at being one of the world's few Marxist ambassadors of cricket – in failure, just like his Italian enterprise was to be 20 years later. But
the mind boggles at what might have happened if he had succeeded in Moscow. He
liked to imagine that it might have had a civilising influence on the Stalinists. In the
light of events, it seems much more likely that the Russian mafia would be running
world cricket by now – hardly an improvement on Mr Cronje's Indian bookies. •

17 April 2000

David Davies

Seve puts the lid on his own trophy

The lasting image, as so often in the past, will be of Severiano Ballesteros: of Seve in the trees, Seve in the sand, and Seve, somehow, triumphant. Yesterday in a new competition that bears his name he won one of the most unlikely victories of an extraordinary career.

Now the world No590, he exhumed his game from some far-flung golfing grave, played again as he always used to, and beat – glory be! – the world No3 Colin Montgomerie.

In doing so he produced the vital point that gave his Continental Europe team victory over Great Britain and Ireland in this inaugural match by 13 to 12.

Montgomerie said later: "This was a point that we felt was secure, I have to be honest. I mean, we felt 85% sure that I would win my game, and I haven't." If he had, of course, the result would have been reversed, such was the magnitude of this latest manifestation of Ballesterian magic.

It is difficult to convey the growing sense of incredulity not only as Ballesteros continued to prevail but as Montgomerie continued to fail. The 43-year-old Spaniard began with three birdies in the first four holes and was two up. The prevailing thought was, well, at least that will keep the match going for a bit.

Then Montgomerie missed a short putt on the 10th to go one down again, stalked off angrily and the thought was that, roused, the Scot would raise his game. Instead Ballesteros holed from nine feet at the 11th to go two up and the wondering began: could he really keep this up? He did, through some typical Seve golf.

Take the 15th, for instance, a short hole at which Ballesteros was still not on the green in two. He got down in two more, Montgomerie made a hash of an easy chip, missed from six feet and halved a hole he should have won.

Take the 17th. Ballesteros, still two up, deep in trees left off the tee; Montgomerie down the middle. Ballesteros spots a gap, finds the green, has a putt from 40 feet; Montgomerie on the green to nine feet. Ballesteros putts dead; his rival, for the umpteenth time, misses to lose the match.

Given that Ballesteros has not earned a single world ranking point for two years, nor won a tournament for five, this is a defeat which Montgomerie will have to rank alongside those in the Dunhill Cup by the likes of Paraguay's Raul Fretes, India's Gaurav Ghei and China's Zhang Lian-Wei.

There was more to it than just Ballesteros, of course. In the second match Sergio Garcia birdied the last two holes to take an important half-point from Darren Clarke.

The young Spaniard won 3 points from five matches, the same as in the Ryder Cup, and Lee Westwood was the leading scorer for the home team with four from five.

There were some wonderful matches along the way. Bernhard Langer, playing as well as he can, went to the turn in 29, six under, then birdied the 11th – and was only two up on Ian Woosnam. Similarly Phil Price had five birdies and no bogeys going to the turn and was only one up on Alex Cejka. Langer and Price won eventually but it was no walk in the park.

It fell to Jose Maria Olazabal to hit the winning putt, when, with two to win the trophy from 10 feet, he dribbled one safely short and was conceded the win by Gary Orr.

The morning greensomes had seen off the last of the players with 100% records, Garcia and Westwood. Westwood, with Clarke, was on the wrong end of a seven-birdie burst by Langer and Thomas Bjorn, and Garcia and Jean Van de Velde could not match the four-under run over the last five holes by Montgomerie and David Howell.

But for all that, the teams were locked at 8-8 at lunch and when all the singles matches had played at least one hole, the teams were still level with Great Britain and Ireland leading in two, Europe in two and six matches all square. ▪

6 November 1999

Jacqueline de Gier
The beautiful, deadly game

Before Hada Dahmouni runs on to the football pitch, she spits on her knuckles and blows into her clenched fists; then she kick-boxes her way around the field. "It is nothing personal or political, I just get very angry," says the number four of Jeunesse Sportive Kabylie, or JSK, Algeria's national champions and three- times holders of the Coupe Afrique. Hada scrunches up her face; a deep scar joins her eyebrows.

"Is football your hobby?" I ask. The 24-year-old medical student bursts out laughing. She taps her chin, jutting it forward, as if to say, "Come on, punch me, then."

JSK is the Berber team, the Berber battle-axe; supporters expect a show of muscle-flexing from the players. And Hada looks like what the Algerians call "a typical Berber woman": she is tall and sturdy and loves bull-fighting, a reminder that Spain is but a short hop from troubled Algeria. If mischief has a face, it is women's football in Algeria. Around the world, women footballers attract jokes, sneers and prejudice, but not in Algeria.

Here, they attract fame and – at least until recently – killers. There are six top teams, and their players are both stars and villains: they are hugely popular because they are very good at the game and because they are so tough. They also stand as a symbol of women unencumbered by religion. And, beyond that – by thumbing their nose at authority, by standing against the conservative family tradition that unites all politicians, from the left to orthodox Muslims and modernising Islamicists – they are an inspiration to secular, rebellious young Algerians. Their matches fill stadiums with tens of thousands of mostly male spectators: fathers with children in football kits; oglers; "amateur photographers", and hordes of teenage boys and girls who wave flags, blow whistles and sing "Olé, olé" after a goal.

But there is a thin line between death and glory. The women players with their shorts and bare heads are anathema to extremist Islam. There were times when a breakfast news item featuring a triumphant team with a piece of silverware would be followed by pictures of a player in a ditch with her throat slit. Male fans gave Algeria's most famous female player, Naima Laouaddi, the highest accolade: they called her "Maradona". Naima was so popular, such a fine player – such a public affront – that she had to leave the country. She now lives in France, and plays for a German amateur team. Hada and her team-mates talk about "Maradona" with pride and admiration. They speak as if she had been transported into the world of transfers and mega deals. But she was not. "Maradona" got caught up in the world of extreme violence.

Since 1992, the war in Algeria has cost around 75,000 lives. Initially, it was described as an "Islamic insurrection", after the Algerian army staged a coup to prevent the fundamentalists of the FIS, the Front Islamique du Salut, taking power after the elections. Since then, whole villages have been massacred. Everybody was a target: football players, pop stars, shopkeepers, journalists, civil servants, men with and without beards, women with and without veils, children, babies, dogs, goats, songbirds. The graves in the cemeteries around Algiers do not have names on them, they are simply numbered. Those slaughtered were burned alive in their homes, sometimes mutilated or tortured, or killed by the now signature method of slitting the throat. The cutting of throats carries great symbolism in Islam. It is like the Sword of God at work, so this method can be used if the killers want to make their crime look "Islamic".

Officially, the conflict was between the armed forces and "the terrorists" of the Groupe Islamique Armée, or GIA, and other fundamentalist groups. Many of the massacres happened within shouting distance of army barracks, yet cries for help went unanswered. In this war fought in the shadows, no one knew who was the enemy. It also created a natural playing field for gangsters, drug dealers, pimps, family feuds, petty criminals and psychopaths.

Eighty per cent of the victims have been women and children, so to play football as a woman against that backdrop was always beyond sport. Football for women is popular all over Africa, but especially in Algiers. The sight of girls kicking and heading balls in the streets is fairly common, even in fundamentalist neighbourhoods. Every community has its stars, some of whom will never make it on to the nation's television screens, not even when they die. Everybody in Bab el Oued, an Algiers coastal neighbourhood, knew 17-year-old Samira. She was the tomboy who played football in the streets. "She always dressed in football clothes," her father says. "There were people here who were angry. But how could we stop her? She was not doing anything wrong. She was good at school. She wanted to become a pharmacist." In 1997, she was one of 400 people murdered during Ramadan, the month of fasting and alms-giving.

Since the presidential election in the spring of this year, there has been relative calm. Abdelaziz Bouteflika, Algeria's civilian president, was the favoured candidate of the military, and many Algerians expected the pattern of purge and counter-purge to continue. In fact, the new president called a ceasefire with one of the main Islamic groups in June and has managed to distance himself from the army to establish a peace platform. Following a referendum a month ago, an amnesty has been granted to most of the rebel fundamentalists, some of whom now support the government. But entrenched attitudes die hard; the women football players remain a provocation.

Algiers used to be described as a "delicious city". It still has its delicacy. By day, it makes you wonder what Monaco would be like if it fell on hard times. A Grand Prix circuit and a casino overlooking the Bay of Algiers would be natural additions to the elegant French architecture and the flair of the people, to the cafes, the patisseries, the smell of lemons, fresh coffee and croissants.

Palm trees wave while people stroll in the sea breeze. French styles and what is cool in Barcelona still inspire the street fashion. Teenage boys and girls, dressed for the safer side of the Mediterranean, hang around Peace Burger, with Boyzone blaring from loudspeakers. But by night the streets are mostly empty and eerie – there is no curfew any longer, but it is still there in the mind. Isolated groups of men hang around, talking and smoking Algerian Rym cigarettes – which mark out the "loser". Unemployment is around 30%. Two-thirds of the population is under 30 years of age and cannot find proper jobs. They scratch a living from street peddling and a little smuggling, while the well-educated and the professionals become *trabandistas* – traders who import a suitcase of cheap Chinese jeans or "genuine" Dunlop socks. They are the new merchant class. The talk in the street is not of Islam, but about the shameless corruption of a "small clique" – the military and their cronies, whom Algerians refer to as le pouvoir – hanging on to power at all costs.

"What we have here is a mafia behind the curtains, as if the place belongs to them," says Benamirouche Zahir, a 22-year-old psychology student and fanatical supporter of JSK. The overwhelming sense in the streets is that *le pouvoir* do not want to share the cake. At night the rich go to their well-protected venues. Booking a table is a must at Le Bardo, Algiers' best restaurant. To get through its door, complete with spy-hole, in the Rue Franklin Roosevelt, you need money and connections. There is no such door policy at the dark, smoky dives simply known as Les Bars, where men come to drink and listen to Rai, a mix of local music and rock that has recently been invaded by reggae beats. Most of Les Bars are in the shopping mall beneath the Monument des Martyrs, which commemorates those who fell fighting against the French. The mall is also the main hunting ground for street prostitutes. Prostitution (like satellite dishes and mobile phones) is a growth industry, providing extra cash for many female students.

In the casbah, the old part of town, once a haven for fundamentalist extremism, there is little talk of Islam either. Graffiti here shows some support for the GIA and the FIS, but admiration for JSK football club is also writ large. You see men with crescent beards, skullcaps and jellabas in the casbah – a statement indeed – and veiled women; but they move through a street scene that clearly doesn't care. Table football is played in the street, the songs of Cheb Hasni, a popular Rai singer, waft in the air. The casbah chebab – the Arabic word for a group of young men – hang around, cruise on mobilettes, talk on mobile phones, whistle at girls and smoke Rym. The girls, meanwhile, flirt. And play football...

JSK's main footballing rivals are NHD d'Alger and Kouba. Both teams are based in Algiers and neither is predominantly Berber. The Kouba stadium is near the airport, and the team trains in the stench of paraffin, and overlooked by mouse-grey apartment buildings covered with satellite dishes in one direction and a huge mosque in another. Mohamed Chalal, the Kouba coach, is not concerned about the symbolism of this clash between modernity and religion. What he's worried about is the championship football matches. JSK are winners, he says, because of their diet. "It is the olive oil. The Berbers eat a lot of olive oil. We call it the 'Berber Medicine'. My girls prefer pizza and burgers and other rubbish." Coaching is a hobby for Mohamed (he is an accountant by trade), but he takes it very seriously.

The players jog around the field. They are from middle-class families. Charazed Touati is 17, and has played for two years. She is sulking on a bench. The coach has sent her off. She is plump and a little sluggish. Mohammed shouts, "Stop eating that rubbish." Charazed's sister, Amal, is Algeria's karate champion. "She does not eat pizza," Mohamed says. But he is proud of his star player, Aisha Berrechid, who is 18 and taking her high-school exams. She travels two hours every day to train after school. "She is devoted," says Mohammed. "And she doesn't eat pizza?" I ask. He shakes his head: "I talk to her parents."

Aisha's football is a family affair. At her home in the grey concrete high-rise suburbs that frame Algiers, her medals are on display. She is shy but football has made her a neighbourhood star, and a stream of locals come to see who is visiting the famous girl. Her father shows pictures of her with a ball. Then Madame Oum el Kheir, her teacher, makes her entrance in a veil. She sits herself down, as if for a TV interview, and says: "Aisha was always a good student. I knew she would be going far. I want her to go to university. I am telling her parents that. I am also telling monsieur Chalal that football should not keep her from her studies." What does she think about football? "Women have many opportunities now, that is very good. The women of Algeria have a very big job to do."

JSK, Kouba and NHD d'Alger are the teams that make it on to the sports pages of the French-language dailies, or the national Berber newspaper. They are not professional, unlike some Algerian men's teams, but they take the game as seriously as if they were. As I make my way to meet Hada and her JSK team-mates, I skim the morning papers for news on the competition, or maybe a titbit on the lesser team, MC Oran. The coastal city of Oran is where *les papas* of the 1954 War of Independence congregated. During the worst of the civil war, it was a killing ground. One article is asking,

"Are our stadiums becoming a political battleground?" But it is a short piece, hidden on page three, that catches my attention.

Thirty *gorges* – people slaughtered by having their throats cut – have been discovered in a wine-growing region close to Oran. The story is told in one chilling sentence: "The killing was swift and sure, three people were injured but survived, and are said by doctors to no longer be able to speak." I have come to Algeria for football, but violence permeates everything. There may be less killing, but it has not stopped.

The authorities claim that 6,000 "terrorists" have surrendered so far, but desperadoes still go to the desert to sharpen their knives and regroup, and the infamous "ninjas" – the anti-terrorist heavies dressed in black with balaclavas – are still observing and "cleaning up" the suburbs. Men with guns and lists of names are no longer working the traffic jams of Algiers and executing the doomed, but their memory is still vivid. "Their shadow isn't gone," says one shopkeeper who sells aluminium couscous steamers. "I go to bed and think, 'Will I wake up tomorrow?'"

Foreign journalists are rare in Algeria these days; dozens of local journalists have fled to France or Tunisia, or even England; some were killed. As a foreigner, I was provided with bodyguards who looked like hitmen from a Tarantino movie. Leaving town presented logistical problems. I am going to see the JSK girls in their stadium in Tizi Ouzou, east of Algiers, in the company of 12 armed gendarmes in combat gear. I'm travelling in a rusty old taxi, and they are escorting me in Land Cruisers, their headlights flashing to bully the other traffic out of the way. It's hard to feel anonymous.

The drive from Algiers to Tizi Ouzou takes about two hours, through a fertile, lush-green strip of land skimming the Mediterranean, full of vine stock on rolling hills, apricot and almond trees. The desert, so close, feels far away. It is easy to forget that Algeria is mostly desert. The land is freshly ploughed. The scent of jasmine washes in. Boys and girls with ginger hair sell bunches of spring onions, fresh baguettes and fruit by the roadside.

Tizi Ouzou is a small, pleasant town in the foothills of the Grand Kabyl mountains. Kabyl is the heartland of Algeria's Berbers, with a relaxed atmosphere and a largely young population. The older Berber women and the little girls still wear the colourful Berber dresses of folklore and henna patterns on their hands, but the young stroll around in bootlegged Dolce & Gabbana clothes bought from the trabandistas. Street peddlers from Senegal offer "magic potions".

The Kabyl like to see themselves as an open-minded people who are very much not Arabs and, in the face of increased Arabisation imposed by previous governments, they campaign for Amazigh, the Berber language, to become the national language. The Kabyl people form 16% of Algeria's total population of roughly 31 million, but they are not like the Kurds in Turkey – they are not a marginalised minority; they are at the heart of political and cultural life and debate. They formed a formidable block when they boycotted the last presidential elections, and see themselves as the champions of democracy and modernity in Algeria.

Their politician, their Berber-in-the- middle, is Saad Saadi. I met him in Algiers, where he told me: "This country is never going to be an Islamic republic. Jamais. But the young want change. They don't want the old class in charge any longer, who are disconnected from the young." This is one reason why JSK women's football team gathers support well beyond the Berber world.

In the main stadium the women are training; they share the same pitch, the same facilities and the same coach with the JSK men's team, and they attract equally big crowds to matches. JSK women are Algeria's champions year after year, and frequently play international matches against teams from other African countries where the women's game is popular, notably Nigeria. Today, it is high noon and hot. Packs of little boys in JSK football kits have gathered to watch the training session.

Coach Mohamed Dubabas makes his girls bend forward with arms spreadeagled. This coach is held in great esteem (the Kouba coach, Mohammed Chalal, confesses to being envious of him). His players listen intently, but remain on the wild side when they implement his orders. One player breaks her hand, howls, and is then back on the field. Dubabas says that there is no difference in terms of strategy between men and women. But "the girls play a purer football. I cannot push them physically as much as the men, but they are technically better players."

During the match, played a few days later, they play football, but more like rugby players. They psych themselves up in the bare changing rooms, waving their bras in the air. For goalkeeper Amal Hassoun football is a "passion". She studies videos of the Brazilian star Ronaldo, whom she admires for his "pure style". Her male admirers call her Sophie Marceau, after the French actress who appears in L'Etudiante, a popular comedy on Algerian TV. Amal says:

"I am not interested in politics, I don't have some political message." But that is not how the rest of the town sees it. In folk history, Berber women are known for their prowess, and are portrayed in Orientalist watercolours in colourful dress and veils, armed with rifles and sabres. The footballers are their modern counterparts: they are remarkably free – and this is what has made them targets. Amal played for Algeria in France during an international tournament. She recalls jogging on to the field with her team-mates, alongside the French national team.

"I was almost in tears. The lights were so bright; it was like a dream. The crowd was singing, they were waving French and Algerian flags. Then the French girls started to applaud us. We were all very emotional, that's why we lost. Well, that's what happened with Ronaldo as well, during the World Cup. He was too emotional. It does not mean he is not a great player. You should see how big and subtle he is." She stretches her hands and plays an imaginary piano. "We did not mind losing to the French. They were the better side. We exchanged shirts. I cried my eyes out... the beautiful stadium, the lights..."

Malika Aigoun does not have time for technique and emotion. The politics of football consume her. She is very thin, with taut skin over her cheekbones. She launches straight into a diatribe against the controversial Family Code, which is based in large part on the shariah. Introduced in 1984, when Algeria was still a socialist one-party state ruled by the military and the FLN *papas*, it strips women of most rights. Malika's point is that the code was introduced by secular Algeria, not the imams. "Do you think we need an Islamic state for that? The Muslims did not do that, did they – did they?" she asks. "Football is important. They are trying to stop us. It is the only way we can show that we want equality. We are just as good." She even thinks that male behaviour has improved thanks to the women's success. "Men are more like gentlemen now." My local bodyguards snigger. They are Berbers themselves and quite happily leave me alone.

It is easy to fool yourself into thinking that violence has passed Tizi Ouzou by, but the town is equally renowned for slaughter as for football. The talk in the street is of the notorious Hassan Hatab, leader of the GIA, who had been replaced. His "commander" for the Tizi Ouzou region is calling for fighters to join a truce. Nobody trusts it. There is hot debate in streets and parks and shops. "Then we still have the other terrorists to get rid of." They mean *le pouvoir*.

The next JSK match is to celebrate the Berber spring. The streets are packed with tens of thousands of people; they carry banners which read Qui a tué mon fils? (Who killed my son?) Huge portraits are shown of Matoub Lunes, the Berber singer, murdered last year by "unknown assassins". But there are smaller pictures too, of small children who have been snatched and killed. As we arrive at the ground, there is furious kicking and banging on the iron gates and the shouting of abuse. Amal simply says, "This is Algeria", but Hada "cuts" her throat with her hand and roars, "Come on then." •

· ·

24 February 2000

Matthew Engel
Why I'm quitting Wisden

Wisden 2000 made its way to the printers on Monday night. It will be published on April 6. And then my ability to comment on events from the most wonderful pulpit in sport will come to at least a temporary end. I'm taking a year off. Someone else (Graeme Wright, from whom I took over the job eight years ago) will edit Wisden 2001.

I don't believe in digging in forever, and eight years is a pretty decent term. Of the 13 men known to have edited Wisden since 1864, only three have lasted longer. (Six of the 13 have died in office, most of them with disconcerting suddenness.)

The United States constitution prohibits holders of the presidency from staying on beyond eight years. It's fair to say that modern US presidents are more likely than Wisden editors to get literally shagged out. The Wisden job, though, is tiring enough, especially for someone who also has responsibilities to the Guardian and to a family.

But any cricket-lover knows that bowlers can keep going far longer if they're taking wickets. I have been obliged to edit Wisden against a background of failure. This is not failure on the part of the almanack itself – we have, miraculously, maintained our annual sale of nearly 40,000 – but of English cricket.

Sydney Pardon, the greatest and longest-serving of all Wisden editors (1891-1925), did not have to report and explain defeats against New Zealand. He did have to deal with some pretty hefty Ashes defeats. ("Humiliating," he wrote in 1922, "… never before was an England side so slow and slovenly.") But it has been the relentlessness of the failures in the 1990s which has been unique.

In the 1980s, when I was the Guardian's cricket correspondent, England lost an awful lot of matches. But they won the Ashes three times and, when they failed, they did so on a more heroic scale.

That was a time when English football was in eclipse: defeat on the field worsened by hooliganism, bordering on terrorism, off it.

The best footballer in the country was Bryan Robson. As a headline figure he wasn't a patch on Ian Botham, or David Gower, or Graham Gooch. Cricket was fashionable, and the talk of the public bar and the bus queues. Now the nation is more interested in what David Beckham wears under his shorts or sarong than in anything Nasser Hussain or Alec Stewart might do.

The World Cup last summer was England's great opportunity: a once-in-a-generation chance to play in the game's top tournament in front of their own people with conditions skewed to their advantage. They blew it, and followed up by losing, appallingly, to New Zealand.

Given that there are 1,600 pages in Wisden 2000, England's affairs are only a small part of its content. Indeed, the book has been planned not as an inquest on English cricket but as a celebration: of the game throughout the 20th century. We shall be announcing, for instance, the Wisden Five Cricketers of the Century.

But you can't hide in the past. The England team creates the mood and sets the standards: young people need role models, stars to emulate. They need a Warne or Tendulkar or Lara to inspire them. England have had no such player in years.

It's tiresome for the England players to keep being slagged off. After all (give or take the odd aberration from the selectors), they're the best we've got. It's even more tiresome for Mike Selvey and the rest of the cricket correspondents who are expected to watch every day of every Test, which the Wisden editor is not. But I've done my best to home in on what I thought was wrong. It seems like time to let someone else have a crack.

These things change. With my luck it will probably change this summer, when England take on another fading team, West Indies (for the Wisden Trophy, as it happens); maybe Graeme Wright will get the chance to celebrate the moment. But, frankly, it doesn't matter who the singer is; the song has got to change. •

Matthew Engel is a Guardian columnist and a former Guardian cricket correspondent.

14 April 2000

David Hopps

Leicestershire left armer bowls Wisden a googly

"**H**e's out!" exclaim the first words of this year's Wisden Almanack, and indeed it does appear that he is. But Wisden was soberly reflecting upon the unrivalled batting merits of Sir Donald Bradman, one of its five cricketers of the century, and it failed to spot that that was equally true of a certain Matthew Brimson.

Wisden, as far as can be ascertained, has never had a flasher. There is just a chance that the same remains true today. But many who turn to Leicestershire's team photograph on p657 of this year's edition will be convinced that Brimson is taking guard on middle.

Brimson is a left-arm spinner, which cricket history suggests makes him automatically a touch unconventional. To his mortification, picture editors were having to blow up the photograph yesterday to discover the truth. In his defence, pre-season photographs are traditionally taken in the Arctic nip of early April, which is a challenge to any man.

Brimson, it has to be said, is a county cricketer who has never before drawn such attention to himself: as left-arm spinners go, he has occasionally struggled to maintain a good length.

Wisden will make an official complaint about Brimson's exhibitionism. Matthew Engel, who has temporarily retired as editor with the hope that the millennium edition will prove to be among Wisden's finest, described it as "an insult to county members", which seemed a touch personal.

"I can see the funny side like everybody else," he said, "but I think you have to be a damn sight better at your profession to behave like this. It is all part of the syndrome that is affecting county cricket."

The same photograph, sources suggest, was innocently hung in the Lord's dining room throughout last summer. Leicestershire met inquiries yesterday with a dead bat.

"We have had a meeting with Matthew Brimson and we have accepted his explanation that it is not in his character to do anything that would cause offence," they stated. "He wishes to apologise to anyone who may have misinterpreted the published photograph." •

1 November 1999

Ian Malin

Technicolor game

NEW ZEALAND 31 FRANCE 43

This was the greatest game in the history of the World Cup. In 30 second-half minutes France fired a 33-point salvo without reply that destroyed the favourites New Zealand and rescued the reputation of the game in the northern hemisphere.

For sheer drama it left for dead France's 30-24 defeat of Australia in the 1987 semi-final when Serge Blanco scored the winning try in the last minute. Now France meet the Wallabies again, in Saturday's final at the Millennium Stadium, while the All Blacks and the Springboks, the finalists four years ago, must somehow recover from a desolate weekend to fight out third place in Cardiff two days earlier.

In terms of style, there could not have been a greater difference between this tour de force in the sunshine and what Twickenham had seen in a gale 24 hours earlier. Australia and South Africa had given us an awesome war of attrition. Here seven tries were shared in a Technicolor game that took the breath away. Vive la différence.

And one man stamped his indelible mark on the game. Christophe Lamaison, the Brive fly-half, would not have played at No10 if Thomas Castaignède had been fit. He only returned from injury himself this summer after missing a Five Nations in which a wretched French team had ended with the wooden spoon.

Yesterday Lamaison had a personal haul of 28 points and completely outplayed Andrew Mehrtens, the world's best attacking fly-half, scoring the day's first try and taunting the mighty Jonah Lomu with a series of booming touchfinders that sent the giant wing scurrying backwards. He converted all four tries and landed two imperious second-half drop goals. In fact, Lamaison did not miss a single kick at goal in his virtuoso display.

Other Frenchmen who missed the Five Nations covered themselves in glory. Abdelatif Benazzi's body may be swathed in more bandages than Boris Karloff but his mighty charges forward swept the All Blacks pack off their feet. Olivier Magne, the seriously quick openside flanker, was everywhere, setting up the final try for Philippe Bernat-Salles and having what looked a legitimate score of his own disallowed in the first half.

The day, it must be said, also belonged to Lomu. This extraordinary man has scored in all five of the All Blacks games in the World Cup. He scored two here for a personal haul of eight, and when after the break he crossed the French line for the second time, France looked set to be submerged beneath a black tidal wave.

Lamaison had made a rare error when his clearing kick fell into the arms of Jeff Wilson. The full-back exchanged passes with Lomu before giving the wing a second touch 30 metres from the French line. Lomu powered through the tackles of Xavier

Garbajosa, Bernat-Salles and Fabien Galthié. All three were left lying like dead wood in an autumn gale. Mehrtens landed the conversion to make it 24-10 to the All Blacks, and the crowd awaited the inevitable.

It was then that rugby's world order was turned upside down. France threw caution to the wind, went on the attack and Lamaison dropped two goals effortlessly. In the feeding frenzy the All Blacks panicked, with Lamaison landing two penalties when they strayed offside. Suddenly France saw a gap.

Counter-attacking, the scrum-half Galthié kicked a teasing up-and-under down the left touchline to the corner. The left wing Christophe Dominici thundered after it, ran around Mehrtens and scored. Lamaison converted, France were ahead, and pandemonium broke out.

On the hour the French pack rumbled forwards with a massive drive. They won quick ball from a ruck and Lamaison's perfect chip forward bounced fortunately into the arms of the centre Richard Dourthe, who beat Wilson to the line.

The All Blacks looked devastated but attacked the French with verve; Wilson was only just bundled into touch before the line by Garbajosa and Galthié. Then, with five minutes left, and the tackling now ferocious, the Kiwis made one last desperate charge.

Mehrtens flung a pass to Tana Umaga but the wing could not hold it, and Lamaison kicked on from the French 22. Magne hacked ahead into the New Zealand half and Bernat-Salles won the race with Wilson to plunge over.

The game was up, Wilson's last-minute try notwithstanding. The All Blacks had conceded more points than any New Zealand Test team in history.

From the start it seemed France had sensed that with the ball in hand they could rumble this young All Blacks side. Sure enough, after Lamaison and Mehrtens had swapped early penalties, France showed what was to come with a fine apéritif try.

Dominici had the defence turning every which way before being tackled 10 metres short of the line. Dourthe dug the ball out of a ruck and cleverly adjusted the line of attack with a pass that wrongfooted New Zealand and gave Lamaison room to dart over.

Lomu's first try in reply was devastating as he swatted Lamaison aside and battered a path through five Frenchmen. Perhaps Lomu's majestic power is the true measure of France's achievement here. •

13 March 2000

Jamie Reid
Jumping to the summit

There may be other racetracks in Europe as spectacular as Cheltenham but the list would not be a long one. Goodwood and Chantilly are places of rare beauty on a high summer's day but neither can match Cheltenham's stunning natural amphitheatre with its undulations and raking turns and its majestic backdrop of Cotswold hills and sky.

This is not charisma-free Kempton Park or visually challenged Newmarket. This is the home of the National Hunt Festival and the setting for the most stirring battles of the racing year. When the runners reach the top of the hill for the last time and it is suddenly apparent that one market leader is cruising or that another has "gone" or that there are three or four challengers still in there fighting, the tension and the drawing-in of breath in the grandstand are palpable. And there is still that punishing uphill finish to come, the scene of so many dramatic reversals of fortune such as Dawn Run's emotional Gold Cup win in 1986 and Pendil's last-gasp defeat 13 years before.

Flat racing's extended and increasingly international season has numerous peaks from 2,000 Guineas day in May to the Breeders Cup and the Japan and Melbourne Cups in November. But jump racing's lines converge all winter on the glittering terminus of the festival. To be a great name in National Hunt racing you have to prove you can win at Cheltenham, and the fact that so many of the truly great horses – from Arkle and Flyingbolt to Persian War and Istabraq – have won there not once but three or four years running helps give the meeting its allure.

It would be difficult to exaggerate the contrast with the Flat, where for every durable character such as Daylami or Swain there are so many explosively brilliant horses who may be seen no more than three or four times as a three-year-old before being whisked off to a career at stud.

It was just after the second world war that the Cheltenham Festival, previously of secondary importance to the Grand National, began to gather momentum. And it was Vincent O'Brien, the greatest trainer of the 20th century and the godfather of the Irish breeding industry, who did the most to raise its profile.

The shy genius from Churchtown in Co Cork was a brilliant tutor of racehorses but lacked the capital to expand. He needed to bet to get going. He was shrewd enough to look beyond Ireland and began targeting Cheltenham. Between 1948 and 1959 his raids netted four Gold Cup wins, three Champion Hurdles in a row with Hatton's Grace and no fewer than 10 divisions of the Gloucestershire Hurdle.

This was when the trainer's compatriots started making the annual pilgrimage to the Cotswolds, safe in the knowledge that one of Vincent's carefully prepared gambles would pay their expenses. The meeting's fierce betting exchanges, its sociability and the infectious Irish dimension stem from that era.

When O'Brien turned his attention to high-stakes Flat racing the baton was passed to other great Irish trainers, Dan Moore, Paddy Sleator and in particular TW "Tom" Dreaper, whose unsurpassed record of 26 festival victories included the three successive Gold Cup triumphs of Arkle of 1964-66. The first two of those races, both epic duels with the great English champion Mill House, remain etched in the memory as perhaps steeplechasing's finest hour.

Irish racegoers, with their love of horses, willingness to gamble and disinclination to bow and scrape to pompous officialdom, have shown how to enjoy Cheltenham. Nowadays the meeting attracts a teeming cross-section of cheerfully intermingling enthusiasts from all corners of the land and all social classes.

The great unsaddling enclosure invasions of five and 10 years ago have been cracked down on, sensibly from the point of view of safety if a little sadly from the perspective of entertainment. Who can forget the scenes after Dawn Run's 1986 Gold Cup when a euphoric but largely well behaved crowd surged all over the paddock? A small posse of stewards led by Lt-Col Sir Piers Bengough, all wearing sensible tweeds and bowler hats, mounted an inadvisably small podium and attempted to keep the riffraff at bay. As one steward saw his bowler go west in the melee, the scene resembled a cross between Rorke's Drift and Carry On Up The Jockey Club.

Rules about admission badges and bar closing times may be strictly enforced but the festival's mid-March date provides the ideal chance to defy puritanism and celebrate the onset of spring. Evening carousal spreads out into every town and village within 50 miles. The small local pubs, many happy to shut their doors and keep the beer coming long after closing time, are often the most convivial places to relax in.

The social focal point used to be the Queen's Hotel at the top of the elegant Regency Promenade. It would be fair to say that the atmosphere there has gone greyer in recent times, especially since the management clamped down on the big poker and backgammon games that used to take place each night in the back room.

In the 70s card sharps straight out of The Cincinnati Kid would descend on Cheltenham, sleep during the day, eat a steak and drink a bottle of mineral water around 5pm and then be ready, ice-cool and sober, when the punters returned flush from the track.

Now the sport's high rollers have mostly moved away from Cheltenham and into luxurious outlying hotels such as the Lygon Arms in Broadway and the Wyck Hill House near Stow-on-the-Wold, which is the favoured watering hole of Ireland's former Taoiseach Charlie Haughey and his entourage. Needless to say, the craic is always more memorable if the gambled-on favourites have delivered on the track.

Charlie Swan, who has ridden 13 festival winners, has known many high-pressure rides on such horses as Istabraq, Danoli and Mucklemeg, all blessed or cursed with the tag of the Irish banker. There are few more spine-tingling moments than when the massed ranks on the terraces and in the betting ring start roaring "Go on Charlie" as their hero hits the front.

But the jockey admits: "The knowledge that thousands and thousands of ordinary people have had not just their festival money but their entire winter savings on these horses makes it more a feeling of relief than jubilation when you win. The party starts later."

There can, of course, be moments at Cheltenham when you can feel you are the only person not invited to the ball. Especially if you are a first-time festival-goer or if you are a woman lost in the scrum and facing a 20-minute queue every time you want to go to the bar or the toilet. This is the point to abandon any attempt to do everything and to walk out into the centre of the course, stand by a fence and let yourself be swept away by the noise, drama and sheer passion of horses and riders jumping at speed.

On Friday morning the real devotees will wake up with the biggest and most anticlimactic hangover of the year. Some boy scout of a commentator will trot out the old cliche that "little fish are sweet" and that there are just as many betting opportunities at Hexham as at Prestbury Park. We may even be encouraged to look forward to next week's opening of the turf flat season at Doncaster. Festival addicts will ignore these encouragements to be cheerful, crawl back beneath the duvet and start dreaming of Cheltenham 2001. •

20 June 2000

David Lacey

Even the last resort is better than a return to Heysel

Supposing several thousand people from another European country descended on, say, Mansfield and ruined its day. First they drank heavily and then they began swearing at the locals, singling out ethnic minorities for particularly vile abuse. When the police intervened there were running street battles, with chairs thrown, windows broken and bottles smashed.

It is reasonable to assume that, on hearing the visitors were in Mansfield to watch their football team, the government of the day would be unimpressed. Promises that something would be done in future would probably not wash. Not only would the rowdy offenders be kicked out, their footballers would be told politely but firmly to go home.

Swap Mansfield for Charleroi and you have a point fast being approached by England and the ullage among their travelling fans. Normally Lennart Johansson, the Swedish president of Uefa, has the lawyer's mastery of the non-committal statement but on Sunday night he was unequivocal: any more violence when England play Romania in Charleroi tonight and the team will be thrown out of Euro 2000, lock, stock and two smelly socks.

For Kevin Keegan and his players this would be a fearful price to pay for one minute's confrontation between English and German supporters and the five minutes it took mounted Belgian police and an armoured water cannon to disperse them. After all, the scenes captured on television so far hardly bear comparison with the violence that accompanied English visits to Rotterdam, Paris, Brussels and elsewhere during the 70s and early 80s, culminating in the Heysel tragedy of 1985 when Liverpool met Juventus and 39 fans died.

This, of course, is Johansson's point. Having suffered nearly 30 years, on and off, of bad English behaviour abroad Uefa is not about to condone another generation of violence.

Some may feel that slinging England out would be giving in to the hooligans; it is an old response. But surely turning quiet towns into armed camps and causing considerable disruption to their routine activities merely because an international football is being played amounts to the same thing.

True, this does not apply only to English supporters; the Germans, Dutch and Belgians have their own hooligan problems. Yet it is an established fact that when England do not qualify for a European Championship or a World Cup the atmosphere is infinitely more relaxed.

The argument between those who would like to see potential troublemakers kept at home by the confiscation of their passports and others who see in this a denial of the basic liberty to travel unimpeded until an offence has been committed is as old as football hooliganism itself.

For several days before England and Germany met in Charleroi on Saturday German security turned back hundreds of undesirables at the Belgian and Dutch frontiers. Small wonder, then, that Alain Courtois, the director of Euro 2000, asked how it was that so many rowdies were allowed to leave an island called Britain.

Of the 800-odd English fans arrested by Belgian police some were innocent and many were guilty of being no more loud and obnoxious than the average pub on a Saturday. But what is regarded at home as an integral part of England's yob culture is not acceptable in a sedate Belgian town that believes that being able to walk along a street uninsulted and unmolested is the most civil of liberties.

It will be a pity if England have to go home to prove the point and the disgrace would do nothing for the 2006 World Cup bid but Uefa is entitled to make the stand it has. And, if Johansson is lucky, Romania will do the job for him before the prospect of English hooliganism returning to what used to be called the Heysel Stadium for a quarter-final against, of all teams, Italy darkens Euro 2000 further still. •

1 December 1999

Donald McRae

A hard day's night
for Billy Schwer

t rained steadily on Monday in London and for Billy Schwer, two days on, that same dark and soaking rain is still falling inside his stitched head and broken heart. His memories of a hard and bloody night are raw enough to make the tug of the stitches knitting together the skin on his face seem meaningless.

The swollen bruises will fade and even the slashing cuts across the bridge of his nose and under both eyes will heal. But as an authentic fighter, with a world championship dream as deep as his immeasurable courage, it will take far longer for him to get over the pain of losing.

Monday was meant to be the night that Schwer, at the age of 30, finally won the WBC world lightweight title in his 42nd fight. We met in hope at seven o'clock, exactly two hours before he stepped into the ring to face the brilliant American southpaw Stevie Johnston.

"Hello, mate," Billy said softly in his dressing room. He held out his hand. "I slept until half 10 this morning. Only problem was that I'd been awake till four. But I was chilling. I lay there in the dark, listening to music, thinking about tonight. I've visualised this fight in my head a million times, right through to the post-fight interviews and the party back home in Luton. Guess what? I win every time."

At 7.30pm, he lay on the floor. He began his elaborate stretching routine. The noise of the crowd outside rose as another fighter headed for the ropes at Wembley Arena.

Billy's 67-year-old trainer Jack Lindsay drifted over to the adjoining mirrored room. Jack spoke thoughtfully. "Dangerous situations bring out the best in Billy. Johnston might have met classier fighters but he won't have met anyone with Schwer's resolve. Johnston has lovely movement, a natural sense of positioning and quick hands, but I hoped he might underestimate Billy. But he looks ready for a tough fight."

Billy shadow-boxed to the music track that would accompany his lonely walk to the ring. It was called Love & Happiness. He lifted his arms in the air. "Destiny!" he exclaimed as he saw his triumphant pose in the mirror and shuffled his feet to the garage music.

Jack could hear heavier rhythms in his head. "Johnston's a very good finisher," he murmured. "When he hurts someone he climbs in. But they've both got implacable wills. We could be in for a dour struggle."

At 7.55, the man from Sky wandered in to say that the fight might begin in less than an hour: "8.45 at the earliest," he said smoothly, "9 o'clock at the latest."

"C'mon," Billy muttered, "let's get me bandaged." It was time for that strange ritual where an official and an observer from the opponent's dressing room watch a fighter having his hands taped.

At eight o'clock exactly a squat, black American man opened our door. At the end of his left arm, in place of a hand, a metal hook swung gently as he moved across the room. He wore a blue satin robe, emblazoned with the words Stevie "Lil' But Bad" Johnston.

Billy sat astride a chair, his arms leaning over the back with one hand cocked. Two lines of tape were stuck to the mirror, in which Billy watched his own reflection.

Jack took hold of his fighter's hands and began to cover them. Jack and Billy seemed engagingly English then, as they tried to put the American at ease.

"Do you like London?" Jack asked. "Ain't had time," Johnston's man grunted.

"Do you find it cold?" Billy asked.

"Nope. We're from Colorado. It'll be snowing there tonight."

We all laughed uncertainly, except for the man with one hand, his hook suddenly seeming like a terrible warning of Johnston's own slashing fists.

Billy Schwer Sr and I walked back into the main room. The fighter's father patted me on the back. "My stomach starts turning over now," he said. "It's even worse when they're fighting. It feels like I take every punch."

After Billy's hands had been wrapped and the gloves checked, we were down to the last 30 minutes. Billy sat down with me one last time.

"The hangman's coming now," he said, half joking. "He's not far away. I can almost see him, waiting for me . . ."

I tried to smile but asked about Johnston instead. "He's a great champion," Billy insisted. "The best lightweight in the world. I won't have to go looking for him. He's also slippery and awkward. But I want to beat the best. If I win this, I'm there. I'm really there."

There were many moments over the next hour when, sitting at ringside, I stared into his unseeing eyes as he slid on to his stool at the end of each round.

It was not long before his face began to be sliced. The cut across his nose was a hideous gash, making the open weals around his eyes seem tiny incisions. The blood turned his blond shock of hair a pale pink. A darker red stained his white satin shorts as, for 12 brutal rounds, Billy Schwer showed unbreakable bravery.

Afterwards, as we waited in the corridor while they stitched Billy's face, Jack hesitated. "Billy wasn't at his best. Maybe I should rephrase that: perhaps Johnston didn't allow his best. He was too fast and elusive. I always liked Johnston as a fighter and as a man. But he was even better than expected. He's exactly what a champion should be. But, oh Billy! What heart!"

Billy's dad shuddered. "You could hear the thud of each Johnston punch," he confirmed. "That terrible sound of leather on flesh. After eight rounds I could see that Billy wasn't going to pull it out. In my heart I hoped they'd stop it but we knew Billy wanted to keep on till the end."

If there were still crimson streaks on the trainer and the father, Billy's mother, Wendy, looked in shock. Her face was almost bloodless as she waited for her son to return. Eventually he did. We started to clap and as he walked through his dressing room a wry smile opened up his battered face.

He turned to his dad first and then to Jack – and finally to his mother. Then he headed for the room where his hands had been bandaged almost three hours before. Billy's dad, Jack and I followed him. The two old men knelt and began to unlace his boots. With his lowered head watching them, Billy looked like a little boy who was too tired to undress after a long afternoon of football.

They each tugged at a boot. The socks came next. Billy's feet looked very white.

"You really came out firing in that 12th round," Jack marvelled. "It was everything or bust."

"Yeah," Billy said, "but he always went one gear higher than me. He was good, wasn't he?"

"He was impressive," Jack said.

"You have to take a drug test, Billy," his dad reminded.

"What? Even if you lose?" Billy chuckled, his sense of humour happily intact. "Those drugs didn't do me no good tonight, did they? He wasn't a devastating puncher but he was hitting me with sharp and accurate punches. They felt solid."

He offered his hand again to me. "Next time," I tried, "you'll have to fight someone who's . . ."

"Shot!" Billy said. "I better take on an old and worn-out champion. But I wanted to fight the best – and I did tonight. But it's not over yet. I'll fight again, once we get over this . . ."

As the first small step in helping him recover from his bloody hurt, they all danced with Schwer until four o'clock yesterday morning in Luton. •

2 December 1999

Michael Walker

One-time safecracker captures the Cup

It must constitute one of the most spectacular gestures of faith in the history of ex-offenders. At four o'clock yesterday, in the ambassador suite of third division Darlington football club, the club chairman George Reynolds – a one time safe-blower with four years in prison on his CV – was handed the most treasured prize in football, the FA Cup. That it was given to him by the Cup sponsor AXA, an insurance company, surely made Mr Reynolds's rehabilitation complete.

It is more than 30 years since Mr Reynolds's days smuggling gelignite under the fridge of his Mr Softee ice cream van, and he has acquired the respectability and authority of a self-made millionaire since then. So when Darlington became the first so-called "lucky loser" in the FA Cup yesterday morning, AXA representatives had no qualms about speeding up the M1 to Co Durham to hand over their most precious silverware.

But it should be said that the trophy's lid was stuck down. "I'm taking it all home," said an AXA spokesman.

Darlington's good fortune was the result of Manchester United's government-inspired betrayal of the Cup. United's withdrawal to compete in the World Club Championships in Brazil in January meant that only 63 teams would go into the famous third round draw instead of 64.

The Football Association came up with the idea of holding another draw featuring the second round losing teams to find the 64th competitor, which would play against Aston Villa. Darlington came out of the hat. Their odds of winning the competition are 1,500 to 1.

It was the second striking piece of luck this year for the underachieving club. In May, as liquidation threatened, Mr Reynolds, 62, walked into the club's ground, Feethams, and wiped out the £5.5m debt with a single cheque. He also paid off seven employees' mortgages and gave each of them a new Mercedes. Mr Reynolds then took the club into his vast kitchen worktop and chipboard business, a slice of which he had sold earlier in the year for £40m.

To say his has been an unlikely rise is like saying Jeffrey Archer is occasionally economical with the truth. Indeed, it would take the combined imaginations of Archer and Catherine Cookson to create a maverick character like Mr Reynolds.

Born into 1930s poverty in Sunderland's Dock Street East, George Reynolds was sent to a workhouse aged eight. By the time he reached his first prison cell, sentenced for blowing safes, he was an illiterate. But in prison the inmate learned to read and write, while also making money selling contraband. His hero is Norman Stanley Fletcher. On his release Mr Reynolds's entrepreneurship blossomed. He estimates his wealth today at £300m.

In May, while Mr Reynolds was out buying a car for his son, the dealer asked why the businessman had not come to the aid of his struggling local club. A few days later Mr Reynolds handed Darlington a large cheque.

The club is progressing well in division three but in the FA Cup lost out to Gillingham. Yesterday's redraw offered the new club chairman another second chance and, as he held on to the trophy, he said: "I had a feeling it would be us. I've got a direct line with him upstairs. It's ex-directory and I'm the only one who knows it."

He was holding on tight. ∎

31 December 1999

Frank Keating
The sportsman of the century

Utter and unparalleled achievement is taken for granted. But charm and chivalry, a clear and glistening inborn spirit and nature for fair play, is the crucial ingredient and yardstick here. Sheer fame and a peerless mastery at a pursuit is one thing, but this judge and one-man jury dwells on aspects more ethical and pure than solely super-eminence at sustained performance.

Only irreproachable sportsmanship makes this shortlist. Nobility is our gauge. We seek the century's very best performer, but the most gallant and courtly too: Le preux chevalier. This at once rules out a supposed favourite, the self-styled "greatest". For all his ticket-selling bombast, the prizefighter Muhammad Ali well understood, and usually displayed, a fearless foe-honouring heroism but he forfeits any claim to this shortlist – he can be "personality of the century", a different thing altogether – for the remembrance of his two shaming performances against Floyd Patterson in 1965 and Ernie Terrell two years later. With a vicious spite and no end of illegalities, Ali toyed with both men for allegedly addressing him as "Clay", asking "What's my name?" between each humiliating assault.

Even two of Ali's ringside fans were sickened: after the first contest against the decent, outclassed Patterson, Robert Lipsyte of the New York Times compared Ali's conduct to a playground bully "sadistically pulling the wings off a butterfly"; against Terrell, the Daily News's Gene Ward called Ali's "a disgusting display of calculating cruelty, an open defiance of decency, sportsmanship, and all the tenets of right versus wrong." Those two condemnations toss Ali from this list.

Mind you, greybeards of the fancy roundly dismiss Ali's claim to be the century's greatest anyway – pound for pound, the two Sugar Rays, Robinson and Leonard, would have had his measure, they say; and of those his own size, the all-round technique and fluid menace of Joe Louis, the intellect of Gene Tunney, and the relentless bombardments of Rocky Marciano would also have ambushed Muhammad.

At his very different sport – cricket batsmanship – there can be no shred of doubt, however, that Don Bradman was the century's utter and unarguable champ of champs. His indelible figures in Wisden still defy all imagination.

He averaged 99.94 for every time he went to the crease in a Test match. In 52 Tests he scored 29 hundreds. In all, in 338 innings, he hit 117 hundreds. His cricket brain and his captaincy was second to none, so was his ruthless allegiance to the game's ethics.

Bradman's batting made pygmies of the art's previous totems, Jack Hobbs and Victor Trumper. He all too often turned his contemporaries, the glorious likes of Hammond and Headley and Hutton, into bit-part characters, cricketing versions of "attendant lords that will do to swell a progress, start a scene or two".

Yet I fancy there was something bloodless about Bradman's merciless concentration. As a boy, Neville Cardus saw WG Grace play once; and in the year before he died he saw Ian Botham play once – but it was enough for him to tell that they both "played cricket with the whole man of him in full action, body, soul, heart, wits, and pomp." He would never have said that about the remarkable ascetic calculator that was Bradman.

As the veteran Australian writer Les Carlyon put it last year: "You might wish your son might bat like Bradman, but you don't necessarily want him to take on Bradman's persona. Such a kid would be rather fussy and finicky and not a lot of fun to be around." But the Don unquestionably makes our shortlist of five.

In the middle segment of the century, between the 30s and 70s, the world's most popular pastime was blessed by two very different paragons, Stanley Matthews and Pele – and such was the nobility of standards they set that around them gathered almost as talented courtiers of civility, grace and charm: Finney, Puskas, Di Stefano, Garrincha, Best, Charlton, Beckenbauer, Cruyff and Platini. There was also the supremely gifted Argentine, the chancer Maradona.

But if all the virtues of both simplicity and grandeur which made soccer so compelling in most every cranny of the universe were to be embodied in one supreme practitioner, that footballer has to be Pele, who wanted only that his unparalleled resplendence on the field serve as an earnest of the rapture he stored in his heart for his "beautiful game."

The same sort of thing went for another consummate beau ideal – golf's emperor Jack Nicklaus. He won 20 majors – a street ahead of anyone else – and was runner-up in an astonishing 19, but such was his smiling sportsmanship as the last putt fell that you had to check with the scoreboard to see if he'd won or lost.

One used to be able to feel the same about the century's host of grand Olympians, the runners and throwers and jumpers of sporting competition's most antique manifestation. Not any more. The pill-popping moderns have wrecked it. Is he or she "on it" is the question now, not who won or lost?

They have not only smithereened the records of yore, but besmirched with doubt as well their famed and honest predecessors, like Nurmi and Zatopek and Bannister, Thompson and Lewis and Coe... even those who ran so heart-wrenchingly not so much for themselves but for their whole race, Jim Thorpe, Jesse Owens, Wilma Rudolph, Tommy Smith, Lee Evans and John Carlos.

If the cricketer Denis Compton illuminated for Britain the drab, grey, bomb-scarred and still scared post-war late 40s, so in the following decade a tennis player lit up with warmth the whole world. Lew Hoad was the very best player at tennis as well, simultaneously, as the very best sportsman at sportsmanship. From 1953 to 1956, Hoad won an astonishing 13 grand slam titles, 10 out of 12 Davis Cup singles for Australia and seven out of nine doubles – inevitably with a grin on his face and always contemptuous of caution, nervousness or any mannerism remotely connected with gamesmanship, meanness or sly endeavour.

I used to watch him win at Wimbledon on fuzzy-pictured monochrome television, but his power and purpose, speed and smile, imaginative fearlessness and chivalry, came over in Technicolor. I worshipped him as only the young can worship – and much later got to know him, and realised that his generosity was as genial as his immense talent and that losing never bothered him overmuch if it happened dead on opening time.

Hoad's compatriot, that enchanting fawn Evonne Goolagong, is this page's Sportswoman of the Century even though she lost more Wimbledon finals than she won – three and two. But she won with grace and happy naturalness and lost with grace and happy naturalness and, well, simply the earth would have stopped turning on its axis if Evonne Goolagong had been heard to grunt in a tennis match.

We have four on our shortlist of five – Bradman, Pele, Nicklaus, and Hoad.

Our fifth, born peasant and pauper, was to become the glistening monarch of a game which supposedly rooted its whole existence in fair play and chivalry. For at batting and bowling and fielding, for sheer and utter presence and sense of theatre, history's nonpareil has to be Garfield Sobers, of little Barbados and all the big wide universe. He began laying down his markers in the game when West Indies still had to have a white man as captain – and then for 15 years from the late 50s he was, simultaneously, the world's best batsman, best fieldsman, best left-arm swing bowler, best left-arm spin bowler – as well as the best foe-honouring and smiling ambassador any institution, let alone a game, could possibly wish for.

Sir Garfield Sobers, gallant knight, played his ravishing cricket with a radiance which transcended the simple boundaries of games-playing. He was beloved and esteemed as much by those he played against as with. Expressing this theme many years ago in these pages the Guardian writer Alistair Cooke wrote an obituary of his hero, the shining American amateur golfer Bobby Jones:

"What we talk of here is not the hero as sportsman, but that someone the world hungered for and found – the best performer in the world who was also the hero as human being, the gentle, chivalrous, wholly self-sufficient male. Jefferson's lost paragon: the wise innocent."

Sir Donald Bradman... Jack Nicklaus... Lew Hoad... Pele... all hail... Step forward – with a smile and that unforgettable feline gait – the Sportsman of the Century: Sir Garfield Sobers. •

Passing through

23 May 2000

John Mortimer
Dear John

I always thought you were immortal. Ten years ago, when you were well over 80, we were in Tuscany and you were playing the disreputable, lecherous old journalist who insists on going on a summer holiday in order to embarrass his family, in a filmed version of Summer's Lease. You went home, had a small operation and came back a week later still chain-smoking, gossiping, talking endlessly, acting with a faultless touch, as though there had been no interruption.

I remember a long night shoot with you talking in a dark garden. We got on to your great comic creation, John Worthing and your memory of Bosie. "Lord Alfred Douglas was a beautiful young man who ended up sour and ugly. Can you believe this? He was at the first 'The Importance' and he couldn't remember whether it was played as farce or comedy. He was Wilde's closest friend and he couldn't remember a single thing about the production."

I suppose I was not much more than 10 when I saw your first Hamlet, an intelligent, witty, sensitive and poetic prince, for me the Hamlet of all time. "I played other characters," you said, "but I always thought of Hamlet as me." I can still see you as Richard of Bordeaux, a spoiled king, bathed in a golden light. I wrote for a signed photograph of you wearing a trilby hat and the star of the Good Companions. I never dreamed that I'd grow up to sit with you in the canteen of Thames Television and have you tell me that you learned more from your failures than your successes. When you were at the Old Vic, playing all the great roles in your youth, James Agate came round to congratulate you in the interval on Macbeth because, he said, "I might have changed my mind by the end of the play". As you talked your hands moved to the rhythm of your speech. "Ken Tynan said I only had two gestures, the left hand up, the right hand up – what does he want me to do? Bring out my prick?"

The pre-war theatre was dominated by two great stars. You and Olivier. You were the master of the poetry, easily moving the audience because you were so effortlessly in tears yourself. You told me that your mother cried "almost constantly like a wet April". Olivier, with the clipped delivery, was the physical actor, dropping from a great height to kill Claudius and rolling down a long staircase as Coriolanus. The rivalry became a collaboration when you and Olivier alternated as Romeo and Mercutio in an unforgettable production.

Shakespeare hadn't been played in the West End since the days of Irving and Tree, but you made him a box office hit on Shaftesbury Avenue and then, in the 50s, the theatre changed, Look Back In Anger came to the Court and poetry seemed to be no longer wanted. Luckily, it was Tony Richardson, also from the Court, who cast you as Lord Raglan in the Charge of the Light Brigade and a great player of film comedy was revealed.

You said that you had three besetting sins, on and off the stage, impetuosity, self-consciousness and "a lack of interest in anything not immediately connected with myself or the theatre". This lack of interest extended to horses. You played the King of France on horseback during the filming of Becket. The director told you to say the line and the horse would move one pace forward. At the first take you said the line, of course impeccably, but the horse remained immobile. By the seventh take the horse had still not moved on cue, or at all. Then, extremely puzzled, you asked the director: "Do you think the animal knows?"

It was true that you took a somewhat vague view of matters not connected with yourself or the theatre. One night in wartime you were seen to look sadly up at the barrage balloons which protected London and say: "I do feel so sorry for our poor boys up there. They must be terribly lonely." I remember a dinner long ago at Tony Richardson's house. My actress daughter Emily was a baby then, and we had brought her with us in a carrycot and left her in a spare bedroom. We were lugging this pink plastic box out of the front door when you saw us and said: "Why on earth didn't you leave your child at home? Are you afraid of burglars?"

You were also, of course, the most famous brick dropper of all time. Having directed Richard Burton in Hamlet, you went into his dressing room meaning to say, "We'll go to dinner when you are ready" but your critical subconscious made you come out with, "We'll go to dinner when you're better". Your classic dropped brick came when you were having lunch in the old Ivy with a pre-war playwright whose name, curiously enough, was Edward Knoblock.

A man came in at the door and waved to you and Knoblock asked you who he was. "That," you said with great confidence, "is the second most boring man in London." "So who's the first most boring man in London?" the playwright asked, to which you unhesitatingly replied, "Edward Knoblock, of course". And then, realising you had said exactly the right thing, you tried to mend matters by adding, "Not you, of course, I mean the other Edward Knoblock".

Apart from Summer's Lease you did a radio play of mine and you were unforgettable as Charles Ryder's father in a television adaptation I did of Brideshead Revisited. The scene in which, with barely concealed malice, you mock your son's unwelcome need of money must rank among the great comic performances of all time. You had that essential quality of all comedy performers. The scene must always be played absolutely seriously, and the actor must never think he is being funny.

So I have been extraordinarily lucky. You introduced me to Shakespeare on the stage, and you said lines I have written. More than that you were, as everyone who knew you or worked with you can testify, an inspiration to all of us and a constant, unexpected, unpredictable joy to be with. I suppose we must accept the idea that you are not immortal, but irreplaceable you most certainly are. •

4 March 2000

John Ezard
A hero passes into folklore

Sir Stanley Matthews, the Pied Piper of English football, worked his magic one last time yesterday when his light, deft winger's body returned in state to his beloved and adoring cluster of towns in the Potteries. His memory conjured 100,000 people – last night's official Staffordshire police count – of all ages on to the streets despite a wet, cramping wind for a funeral parade fit for a Victorian monarch. And all this for a prodigy whose prime 50 years ago, as his soccer colleague Jimmy Hill said in wonder, is known to young people only from scratchy old newsreels.

An estimated 10,000 were at Stoke City's Britannia stadium, another 20,000 in or outside St Peter's church, where his quick spirit was laid to rest, with his great fellow players Nat Lofthouse, Sir Tom Finney, Sir Bobby Charlton and Gordon Banks among his pallbearers.

Others lined pavements often 10ft to 12ft deep and mounted the roofs of department stores along the 14-mile route as the cortege passed places dear to him in the six Potteries towns: Longton, Fenton, Hanley, Burslem, Tunstall and Stoke itself.

In one of the drabber parts of Stoke, miles from the official route, someone had tied a bouquet to a wire fence with a card saying "Stan the Man, Rest in Peace – from an Evertonian".

Hundreds more bouquets were more conspicuously left outside the front door of Britannia stadium, although his family had asked for no flowers. Along the two-mile road to the ground, Sir Stanley Matthews Way, red and white shirts and scarves in the Stoke colours were wrapped round lamp posts and pavement bollards like heraldic banners in a mediaeval court.

The note of wonder and informality continued in church, where the first hymn listed was And Did Those Feet?, usually called Blake's Jerusalem, and the second, chosen by Matthews' family, was Lord of the Dance. Many of the 300 fans who were given a third of the church seats draped Stoke City scarves over their gallery balcony.

But the watchword of the day was respect. Cheers began in a few throats and a few fists punched the air. But these gestures were choked off by the collective mood of the crowds.

Instead, there was applause. It started in the cortege's journey of honour through the three-year-old, £14.7m stadium, on an exposed hill above the towns. Hands were at first too cold to clap loudly or without pain.

But they persisted and warmed into the first of a series of great, solemn, minutes-long ovations of respect which were repeated wherever the motorcade travelled on its 75-minute tour.

Noticeably, they were as warm for the cars carrying members of Matthews' family as for the leading hearse, decked with red roses and white carnations in the shape of a football jumper carrying the number seven, his playing position.

As the rector of Stoke, Canon Edgar Ruddock, said in St Peter's, the day marked "the passing of a hero into the folklore and mythology of Stoke City, Port Vale, Blackpool – and through them into the worldwide community of sport".

It also marked the passing of a different kind of England, one which was thought to have been almost forgotten long before he died, a country in which modesty was respected or worshipped almost as much as popular virtuosity.

Matthews was a hero of 1940s and 1950s children's cigarette cards and comic books as well as newsreels. He was the real-life counterpart of Wilson the Wonder Man who – long before Roger Bannister – once ran a mile in a still unbeaten 3min 43sec, wearing a black, long-sleeved Victorian bathing costume. Matthews' wizard dribbles were viewed as almost as remarkable.

But his was a more accessible magic. Anyone could grow up to be like him if they trained very hard, went to bed at 9pm and never got big-headed. His fitness was again drummed in by yesterday's speeches.

"I never once saw him out of breath in the football field", said the former England player Jimmy Armfield. Peter Coates, ex-Stoke City chairman, said: "He never criticised the modern game. He never said players weren't as good as in his day."

His world has been dismissed to the remote past. But yesterday among the street crowds and at Britannia stadium there was a sense even among younger fans that its virtues ought to be brought back.

Duncan Bagnall, a 35-year-old local government worker, said: "It seems like something's gone now. He embodied something that was perfect. Later people like Gary Lineker have tried to do it but never quite managed it".

Yesterday's turnout was not only for the wizard of dribble, or Der Zauberer (the sorcerer) as German players called him, but for a local hero who was given his nickname by Keele students in a song they wrote after his 1965 knighthood: "You've heard of Greaves and Puskas and Pele from Brazil/But Stanley Matthews of the Potts is the greatest of them all."

And so his funeral procession, looping and dog-legging through the small brick streets and ring roads of the modern Potteries, took in not only his statue, where spectators stood with bowed heads as the hearse passed, but his primary school and his birthplace in Seymour Street, Hanley.

The house stands only just over half a mile from the birthplace of Arnold Bennett, novelist of five of the towns. Bennett, influenced by sombre French realists, said: "Pessimism – when you get used to it – is just as agreeable as optimism."

Matthews' feet spoke for the more gladsome side of Stoke, which gave him back full-hearted gratitude at his funeral. "The ball ran for me," he used to say after a good match. As it did, for him and for his kind, on one final farewell day yesterday. •

....

18 April 2000

Francis Beckett

One woman's journey from revolutionary idealism to Stalin's slave labour camps

Rosa Thornton (née Rust), born 26 April 1925; died 2 April 2000

When Rosa Thornton, who has died aged 74, was born in London, her young, East Ender father, Bill Rust, was leader of the Young Communist League. He named his daughter after the murdered German revolutionary, Rosa Luxembourg, but was himself soon facing a 12-month prison sentence for sedition and incitement.

Three years later, in 1928, Rust, the epitome of the dedicated British communist, set off for Moscow with his wife and child to work for the Comintern. Once there, Rosa, aged three, promptly went down with scarlet fever; she recovered, but came out of hospital having forgotten how to speak English.

By 1930 the Rusts' marriage was over, and, back in London, Bill Rust was appointed as the first editor of the Daily Worker. In 1937, as Stalin's great terror reached its climax in the Soviet Union, Rosa's mother also came back to England. She promised to return for Rosa, but Bill suggested that the child would be better off in the Soviet Union. So their daughter was left at a boarding school for the children of top foreign communists, a few miles from Moscow – other pupils included the offspring of the future Yugoslav leader Marshal Tito, the future Hungarian leader Matyas Rakosi, and China's Mao Tse Tung.

By 1940, Rosa was living in a Moscow hostel for political immigrants, and loving it, with morning classes and evenings taken up with theatre, music and cinema. Then, in June 1941, came the Nazi invasion of the Soviet Union, and, within a month, the Luftwaffe was bombing Moscow. Her parents assumed she was safe but, amidst the chaos of war, the Soviet bureaucracy sucked her in, put her with a group of German exiles and sent her to the Soviet Union's Volga German republic, near the frontline.

On the Volga, Rosa made friends with Hannah, an older German Jewish woman. Hannah, weighing little more than seven stone, was physically weak; Rosa looked after her, and Hannah taught Rosa about survival. They shared a deserted house, and the 16-year-old worked 12-hour shifts in a canning factory.

Then, three months later, the militia came calling. Hannah, as a German, was to be deported to Kazakhstan. Rosa stood by her friend, and stumbled into one of Stalin's greatest crimes – the forced migration of hundreds of thousands of Volga Germans to the far corners of the vast country. For the rest of her life, one of Rosa's most insistent questions was, where are they now, the Volga Germans?

The two women travelled on horse and cart for 36 hours to Astrakhan, a transit centre for thousands of deportees. Then came three days on an open boat along the Caspian Sea to Guryev, followed by six weeks in railway cattle trucks. En route, a young woman nursing her four-month-old daughter left the train to search for hot water. The train started without her – and Rosa was left, literally holding the baby. It took the mother a week to catch up, whereupon Rosa returned the infant alive and well.

Lice-ridden and close to starvation, they arrived in Kazakhstan, where Hannah and Rosa were separated. For two years, Rosa was worked close to death in the copper mines, pushing and emptying metal-laden rail trucks from 6am until after dusk. She never saw the sun. Back in London, oblivious to this suffering, her father was at the Daily Worker, still extolling the Soviet Union.

Malnutrition made Rosa half-blind, and turned her skin yellow. She avoided death only thanks to a letter that she wrote to a Moscow friend, asking that it be forwarded to someone in authority. It found its way to Georgi Dimitrov, general-secretary of the Comintern, and later ruler of communist Bulgaria. In spring 1943, a pass arrived, signed personally by Dimitrov. Weeks later, Rosa arrived in Moscow.

She told Dimitrov that she wanted to go to England, but would not leave until Hannah, and a dozen or so other Volga Germans, were rescued. Hannah was released, and Rosa boarded a convoy for Leith, from where she was sent to London. Neither the British government – then the wartime ally of the Soviet Union – nor the British Communist party had any interest in revealing what had happened to Rust's daughter, or news of cattle-trucks and deportations.

Rosa Rust was 19 before she had mastered English – after studying at the Regent Street Polytechnic – and, in later years, recalled how, in those early days, she had tried to post letters in bins marked "litter" and thought railway stations were called "Bovril" because that was what the posters said. After leaving the polytechnic, she worked as a translator for the Soviet news agency, Tass, until the Foreign Office closed it down in 1951. She married George Thornton, a brilliant young historian, whose career was later damaged by his association with Rosa and leftwing views.

Rosa soon discovered that she loved English poetry as much as she loved Pushkin, and became one of the most fluent and articulate people you could meet. All her life she could recite, among great swaths of other poetry, her first ever English poem: GK Chesterton's The Donkey. The passion and intensity of her voice, and the rhythm of the words, were given an extra dimension by her Russian accent.

Anyone who met Rosa sensed the inner strength that brought her out of Russia alive. And they too sensed the instinct of loyalty and rebellion that got her into the camps in the first place. She talked of it in a deep, clear voice full of great, gay Russian-sounding gusts of poetry and laughter.

She starred in the drama group she set up near Redcar, Yorkshire, where she and her husband lived. The actress Anna Calder-Marshall, who planned to present a one-woman show about Rosa's life, observed that there was only one person who could really play Rosa – and that was Rosa. She was, Calder-Marshall added, one of the most brilliant actresses she had ever met.

Rosa and George Thornton were devoted to each other for more than half a century, sharing a passion for drama and poetry, cricket and music, and walking by the sea. She died a Yorkshire grandmother with a Russian accent, leaving her husband, four grown-up children, and five grandchildren – who always called her "Babu", short for babushka, the Russian for grandmother. •

27 March 2000

Robin Denselow
Essex philosopher

Ian Dury, singer, songwriter and actor, born 12 May 1942; died 27 March 2000

Ian Dury, who has died of cancer aged 57, was one of few true originals of the English music scene, the only man to successfully combine the energy and excitement of rock 'n' roll and funk with the bawdy humour, wit and home spun philosophy of music hall and of his native Essex. The fact that he had been crippled since childhood, and was severely ill during his final years as a performer, merely added to his stature. He was truly brave – both physically and in the way he approached his music.

That bravery was evident at his first major London concert, at the Hammersmith Odeon in May 1978, at the height of the punk era. The audience were told to prepare for "one of the jewels in England's crown", and on came not Dury but his hero, the veteran music-hall star Max Wall, who was barracked by the boisterous crowd until Dury stormed on to quieten them down. When he reappeared with his band, he hobbled across the stage, supported by a stick, looking like some spivvy Cockney update of a Dickensian villain. The punks were suitably impressed.

Here was a man already in his mid-thirties who looked crippled but dangerous, and had an armoury of quite extraordinary songs, ranging from the realistically romantic to the outrageous. He could belt out a thoughtful rock song like Sweet Gene Vincent, and then introduce a distinctive Essex spin. Even hardcore punks were taken aback by the stories of Plaistow Patricia or Billericay Dickie, dealing as they did with the life and loves of losers, chancers and wide-boys from the East End and beyond. No one then, or since, could match lyrics like "a love affair with Nina in the back of my Cortina, a seasoned-up hyena couldn't have been more obscener".

The man responsible was born in Harrow. His father was a bus driver and later a chauffeur, who split up with his university-educated mother soon after the war. The young Ian went to live in Upminster with his mum, but was struck down by polio at the age of seven. He spent several years in hospital and at a school in Sussex for the disabled, and then moved to the Royal High Wycombe Grammar School. He left with three O-levels and moved back to Essex, to Walthamstow Art School.

Then came the Royal College of Art, a stint teaching art in Canterbury, and in 1970 the formation of his first band, Kilburn and the High Roads. They developed a minor following on the emerging London pub-rock scene and their first album, Handsome, in 1974. It included some distinctive Dury lyric but was not successful. Dury had yet to fully develop his exaggerated Cockney stage persona.

The transformation came after Dury started writing with pianist Chas Jankel and signed to the independent Stiff label, co-founded by David Robinson, one of the great showmen and the godfather of British funk.

Dury toured with his fellow Stiff artists including Elvis Costello, and in October, 1977, released his classic New Boots And Panties. The album, which went on to sell over a million copies, included the erotic Wake Up And Make Love With Me.

In April 1978 Dury notched up his first Top Ten single, What A Waste, followed later the same year with the number one hit, Hit Me With Your Rhythm Stick, and a year later Reasons To Be Cheerful (Part 3). In 1980, the compilation album Juke Box Dury packaged these hit singles along with Dury's best-known stage anthem, Sex & Drugs & Rock 'n' Roll.

At the time, Dury insisted to me that, as an unlikely pop star, he was merely continuing his career as an artist: "I was a painter for seven years, a successful illustrator for two years, and now I'm a rock 'n' roll singer. I still feel I'm doing the same thing, but I'm not painting with paints." As for his physical disability, he had confidently used it as a part of his stage act.

"I'm charismatic and I'm not ashamed about my physical appearance," he said.

"Even good-looking people have got a weakness. My weakness is so obvious that there's no point in worrying about it. Luckily I'm quite interesting to look at. I know 'cos I painted myself as an art student about 500 times."

He succeeded partly because of the care and attention he put into his work, explaining: "I ain't a poet, I'm a lyricist," and spending weeks carefully perfecting his songs. He described his influences as "the Stax and Motown labels and Max Miller, with a lot of television thrown in".

During the 1980s, with the waning of the punk era and rise of the New Romantics, Dury gradually fell out of fashion, despite some glorious tours with his band the Blockheads. But he still continued his policy of musical bravery, collaborating with trumpeter Don Cherry on the 1980 set Laughter, and travelling to Nassau the following year to record with the reggae rhythm section Sly and Robbie for Lord Upminster.

This was the Year Of The Disabled, and Dury contributed the thoughtfully realistic Spasticus Autisticus. The song, which contained lines like "I dribble when I nibble," was considered to be in such bad taste that, despite Dury's own disability, it was banned from radio play.

The departure of Chaz Jankel from the Blockheads proved a more serious blow and, in 1984, after the release of the unsuccessful album 4000 Weeks Holiday, Dury took a rest from live performance, and concentrated on acting. He appeared in a series of unremarkable films, including Polanski's Pirates (1986) and Hearts Of Fire, a vehicle for Bob Dylan.

He had more success on stage the following year, in the Royal Court production of Jim Carter's Road. Two years later, he was back at the Court with a musical, Apples, which he had co-written with the former Blockhead Mickey Gallagher. It was not a success, but Dury had continued with his policy of doing exactly what he wanted.

Never too concerned about personal wealth, he had turned down an offer from Andrew Lloyd Webber to provide the lyrics for Cats – a commission that reportedly earned millions for Richard Stilgoe. Dury had a simple explanation for turning Lloyd Webber down: "I can't stand his music."

In 1990, the Blockheads came together again, initially to play a benefit for their former drummer Charlie Charles, who was suffering from cancer. The reunion was so successful that further shows followed over the next two years, and several members of the band collaborated on Dury's 1993 album, The Bus Driver's Prayer And Other Stories. Then, just as his career was heading for another upswing, Dury was diagnosed as suffering from cancer. In 1996 a tumour was removed from his colon, but two years later, further tumours were detected on his liver.

He reacted, in typical fashion, by plunging himself back into work, and 1998 will be remembered as his finest period since the glory days of the late 1970s. Once again reunited with Chas Jankel and the Blockheads, he embarked on a series of concerts that showed he had lost none of his old verve, wit or musical skill. Their songs ranged from the funk and black humour of Mash It Up Harry and Jack Shit Georgie (an attack on the education system) through to an unashamedly emotional, semi-spoken love song, You're My Baby. ∎

23 November 1999

Simon Hattenstone
Flirting with happiness

Three weeks ago I thought Quentin had died on the phone. We spoke frequently, and he was often in a bad way. But this time it was different. Even the wonderful elongated "Oh yeeeassssssssss" as he answered was shrivelled in misery. He tried to talk about his upcoming trip to England, but suddenly stopped. " Oh no, oh God, oh no. Oh, oh oooohhhhhhh ." The cries were pitiful and terrifying. The phone went dead. I felt as if I'd murdered him.

Ten minutes later, I rang back. " Oh yeeasssssssss ," he said. Followed by the lovely abrupt: "Oh. Hello." Quentin had made another miraculous recovery. I asked him how he was. "Oh well. I have cancer now, cancer of the prostate," he said. And then there was the hernia, and the eczema that left him scratch-crazy, and the paralysed hand that brought his film criticism for the Guardian to a premature end earlier this year.

Why are you coming to England?, I asked. Because I've been told to, he answered. Quentin always said that he did as he was bid, his was not to question, that he could never turn down a request. And although he told it like a joke, it was true.

Around three years ago his long-term agent Connie died, and he was taken up by a man he simply referred to as the policeman. The policeman turned out to be a police-man-turned-agent who had put Quentin on his books and sent him out on the road. He had never worked, or rather been worked, quite so hard as over these past three years. Quentin was sent all over America to perform his one-man show to packed houses. In a way, his reinvigorated career made the end of his life fuller and more appre-ciated. He died playing to packed houses. But Quentin said he was being worked into the ground, and packing him off to England was different from sending him to San Diego. Not only was England such a distance, it also held appalling memories for him.

Shortly after the terrifying phone call, I met up with him in New York. He felt a thousand years, and looked gorgeous. The lipstick and mascara were applied more tenderly than in the louche days. We were meeting at a restaurant close to his apart-ment on East Third Street, but he was in too much pain to walk. It was Halloween, and a stunning waitress was dressed in a flimsy towel. We were too busy staring to talk. I thought she may have been a he, but Quentin scanned her ankles and promised me she was a she. He said, as he had done so often before, how much easier it would have been if he had been a woman. He ordered chicken soup and fish cakes, and mash and a Scotch. Right to the end, Quentin had a proud appetite.

I told him he wasn't well enough to travel to England, and that he should cancel. He said he couldn't let people down, and I wondered whether he meant the audience or his agent. Ah well, it will be great playing to an adoring audience, I said, pathetically trying to jolly him along.

"No, no, no," he said ferociously. "They hate me in England, hate me. You see that is the difference between England and America." He loved contrasting the cruelty of England with the generosity of America. "In America people would only come to see you if they liked you, if they wished you well. In England they will come because they despise you, to laugh at you. In England, they stopped me on the streets, they beat me, they spat at me." The fear was fresh on his lips.

"Not only are they sending me to England, I am being sent to dreadful places like Manchester and Leeds." His lips thinned with magnificent contempt. I reminded him I was from Manchester and he apologised. Quentin would have hated dying in Chorlton-cum-Hardy.

I first spoke to Quentin about seven years ago when I asked him to go and see some movies for the Guardian. "Oh. Lovely," he'd say. Ratatattat. His reviews were acerbic, elegant and very funny. You never read them for the argument (there wasn't one) or for his taste (the basic rule was that a movie was only good if someone died within the first 15 minutes, and the bloodier the death the better). They were just packed with amazing one-liners, instant aphorisms.

After seeing Pulp Fiction, he said: "Now I know what Mr Travolta has been doing all these years away – eating."

At first, I found the relationship frustrating and one-sided. Things changed when I became nosier and more demanding. Why don't you ever call me by my name?, I asked. "I daren't." He said that when he was young if he ever called a man by his first name, it was a confession of intimacy.

Why don't you ever ask me about my life?, I complained. "Oh dear," he replied again. "I don't know how to." He felt that would be a presumption, that he was there to perform for people, to tell them the stories they wanted to hear. They took him out for lunch, and he repaid them with the most intimate of one-man shows.

Quentin was terrified of real intimacy. He was desperate for company, a benign smile or wave, the kindness of strangers. So long as he could walk away from it. That's why he loved New York, where he was celebrated in peace.

He started to talk quietly. The performance was over. He lay on his bed, and smiled over old memories – even nasty ones. I told him I thought he was scared of intimacy, and he agreed. Then we began to talk about love. Quentin was a desperate romantic. He would have done anything for the love of a good man, but he thought it impossible that it could ever be granted to a "sinner" like him. He said he had gone into prostitution looking for love, not money, and only after six months of brutal sex with self-loathing married men did he give up looking.

A couple of years ago I visited him in his apartment, which was tinier, darker and less hygienic than even he had led us to believe. The previous day we'd had a night on the town and he'd been done up to the nines. But the Quentin that answered the door was a shocking apparition. His short dressing gown showed off impossibly skinny legs and a trail of weeping sores, his toe-nails were like whelk shells, his thin hair wrapped round his head in sad circles. When I wrote a piece about my visit, describing his appearance, a couple of readers wrote to say it was a cruel unmasking.

But I think he wanted me to see the unpainted Quentin, the raw material. Only then was it possible to appreciate the genius that went into the daily creation of himself. After a few minutes, when the shock had subsided, he looked more beautiful, more delicate than ever. People asked whether he was sad or lonely. Yes, both. But at the same time he knew more friendship and happiness than many of us experience.

Last time I saw him, at the Halloween table, he told me I looked different, more American. I think it was a compliment. He said how nice it was to chat quietly, rather than perform. At the end of the evening he apologised for his body, and struggled out of the cab with a few whimpers. "It's been such a lovely night," he said.

Next day he had another agonising attack on the phone. I told him he had to see a doctor, and was amazed I could be so bossy. When he said he couldn't afford one, I told him not to be so daft, and to promise he'd book himself in straightaway.

I rang him a few days ago just before he was leaving for England. " Oh yeeeesssss," he answered with all the old bounce. He told me he'd been to the doctors, his "patron" was going to pay for treatment, and he was going to have his hernia operated on as soon as he got home. He sounded delighted that he'd done it, and, I think, that some-one cared enough to give him a good bollocking. Again, I told him he shouldn't come here, but he said it was already decided. How could he start letting people down at the age of 90? •

14 October 1999

Leading article
Alastair Hetherington

In at least a hundred different ways, the Guardian you are reading today is different from the paper which Alastair Hetherington handed over to Peter Preston in 1975. Some of it – pre-eminently the presence of tabloid sections alongside the broad-sheet main paper – would have been inconceivable then. But technologies and the tastes of readers change, and so do editor's preferences. If they don't, papers die. At a deeper level, though, things do not change. A new editor of the Guardian is charged with main-taining the paper's spirit "as heretofore". And to those who know it best, the paper you hold in your hand this morning could not have been what it is without Alastair. Indeed, without Alastair, it very probably would not be here at all.

Alastair moved the editor's chair to London, and was in charge when the Guardian first ran on London presses. Inheriting it as the pride of Manchester, he made it a national paper. Taking over just as the Suez crisis broke, he laid down a line of firm and principled opposition which alienated some readers – and advertisers – but for most of this newspaper's constituency did exactly the job their paper existed to do. He needed courage, for sometimes the paper's problems looked terminal. In the middle 60s, some on the business side despaired, and saw its best hope as merger with the Times. Alastair, above all others, saved us from that – though, as he would have wished us to emphasise now, in determined and decisive alliance with Richard Scott, grand-son of one editor, son of another and chairman of the trust which owns the paper.

Today we publish a wealth of tributes from people in and outside the Guardian. There could have been many more. But above all it is here, at the very heart of the news-paper, in the columns where he wrote so often and so powerfully, that we honour Alastair's memory and commemorate with gratitude the indelible imprint left on it by his 19 years as editor. •

Letters

The deservedly generous tributes to Alastair Hetherington all rightly underline his remarkable personal tolerance, even of those with sharply different opinions to his own. Apart from his unfortunate change of view to support the United States' bombing of Vietnam, he rarely used his editor's prerogative to override strongly dissenting opposition from colleagues.

During the 1960s, when I worked with Alastair as a leader writer and as his administrative deputy, I certainly had reason to appreciate that quality of tolerance. Not only did we disagree very strongly about issues such as Ireland and Vietnam, without rancour on his part, but he reacted with mere bemusement when some of his young leader writers even took time off to organise and speak at anti-Vietnam war demonstrations in London. When, as a former parliamentary Labour candidate with far leftwing views, I fell foul politically of the powers-that-be in the Labour party, he was unconcerned that this might affect his own relationship with Harold Wilson and the party leadership. Indeed he told me: "I am regarded in those circles with suspicion myself as being something of Scots nationalist." At the time I thought this improbable. But I was less sure in later years when Alastair was sacked from his post in BBC Scotland for being, in effect, a "premature devolutionist".

John Palmer
Brussels

Alastair Hetherington was the editor I most wanted to work for. He was an outstanding journalist, a great editor and one of the finest human spirits I have encountered in journalism.

I almost did work for him. In 1969 when my old newspaper (the Odhams Sun) closed and Murdoch bought the title, Alastair offered me a return to his paper (I had worked for the old ManchesterGuardian) in a job of considerable status. Mistakenly I chose elsewhere. He forgave me – though I always had difficulty in forgiving myself.

He was also a splendid companion on walks: I vividly recall a walking expedition I had in his company during a press visit to Georgia in the old USSR. It was a memorable conversation with a seriously memorable companion.

We will miss him and I salute his memory.

Geoffrey Goodman
Editor, *British Journalism Review*

Your report of the death of Alastair Hetherington says that when the Guardian stood out against the 1956 Suez campaign Hetherington was isolated with the Observer. Not so.

The Daily Mirror, *then the paper of Hugh Cudlipp and Sydney Jacobson, also opposed the war. It wrote: "There is no treaty, no international authority, no moral sanction for Eden's war". As a result, it lost 70,000 in circulation.*

Terence Lancaster
London .

7 March 2000

WL Webb

Leader writer who split the Guardian

Newspaper leader-writers have never had academia's comfortable pauses for reflection, but need something of the scholar's instincts and equipment if their judgments against the clock are to have weight and effect.

Frank Edmead, who has died aged 80, exemplified these special gifts: a good linguist, an omnivorous reader, a careful student and meticulous analyst of affairs, with a particular passion for Chinese history and culture. One of the most perceptive and well-informed Guardian leader-writers throughout a difficult post-war decade, and largely responsible for steering the paper's policy through the minefields of the Middle East and south-east Asia, his resignation as a matter of principle in 1967 was felt by many colleagues to be a tragedy for the paper, and perhaps for its editor, as well as for Frank.

How it came about is set out in Changing Faces, Geoffrey Taylor's history of the Guardian from 1956-88: "Before the start of the six-day war in June 1967 Frank Edmead had established an editorial line on Palestine against which all future comment would have to be measured. Most people on the paper would say he had done the same for Vietnam. The editor altered course on both subjects" – and within a space of less than three weeks.

On Vietnam, Edmead had argued a line of careful but consistent criticism of the American engagement, less emotional than, but consonant with, most reporting by the paper's staff and special correspondents, among them Clare Hollingworth and Martha Gellhorn. The editor, Alastair Hetherington, after a visit to Vietnam – during which he had been given free and welcoming access to the American generals – wrote endorsing the American presence as the force most likely to produce peace.

In the case of Palestine, Edmead, in a signed column on May 29, had produced what Taylor called "the dialectical half-nelson from which no subsequent Guardian leader-writer was able to escape". Why, if the Jews claimed the right to return after 2,000 years, had the Palestinian refugees no such right after only 20 years? Given that Muslims had not generally persecuted Christians, why should the Palestinians suffer for the wickedness of European Christians? "At the receiving end, Zionism looked like yet another European colonial movement; settlers flowed in, to acquire much of the land and all of the political power."

But again, in a long leader on June 12, Hetherington wrote that it would be "neither surprising nor wholly wrong" if Israeli policy were to include the keeping of the Old City of Jerusalem and most of the west bank.

When Edmead left shortly afterwards, the feeling of many colleagues was expressed in a letter that the then features editor, Christopher Driver, wrote to Hetherington. "We are shaking off irreplaceable individualists at an alarming rate and the latest and most lamentable departure looks to the rest of us directly attributable to the fact that generals and politicians have your ear more than historians or students of Asian behaviour. I doubt whether your arguments on Vietnam will outlast a year, let alone a decade."

Edmead and Hetherington had both joined the Manchester Guardian in 1950. Hetherington, who served through the war as an officer in the Royal Armoured Corps, made his name as defence correspondent, and defence remained an abiding interest. Edmead, a Quaker, had driven an ambulance across Europe following the Normandy landing (once crossing a minefield to rescue a wounded German soldier), and had been promoted from a talented reporters' room when Hetherington became editor in 1956.

Very different in many ways, each was a believing Christian, and each respected the other. Indeed, Edmead said later that he thought Hetherington, in his memoirs, had treated their differences with admirable fairness. History gives Edmead the better of the argument, but probably both of them could really be seen as victims of the cold war.

Frank was a Kentish man, educated at Borden school, Sittingbourne, and University College, London, where he read English. After his war service, he worked with German children evacuated to Austria (some of them from the Adolf Hitler school for the children of Nazi elite), shepherding hundreds back to ruined Germany in journeys that required resourcefulness and ingenuity.

After his break with the Guardian he returned to University College to do postgraduate work in conflict studies, eventually teaching systems science at the City University, where, unsurprisingly, he developed a special interest in catastrophe theory.

In retirement, this principled but gentle and sweet- natured man returned to his old love, China, spending every other year teaching at the universities of Shanghai and Xi-an and travelling widely in remote territories, intriguing people with his Shanghai accent.

No use asking him what he was going to write. Nothing, he said; he had undertaken not to. Anyway, he'd written enough, and there was so much to see and do. On a final trip to Yunan in 1996, he caught pneumonia, and several times nearly died following complications on his return. At the end, he seemed to be not much more than spirit. But frail as he was, he usually got to meetings at the old Friends' house in Hemel Hempstead; and was not to be discouraged from turning out on a cold day in January to attend Alastair Hetherington's memorial service.

His wife, Joan, died in 1974. He is survived by his daughters, Mary and Madeleine. •

26 June 2000

Harold Jackson

A masterful eye
for gentle ridicule

William 'Bill' Papas, artist, born 1927; died 19 June 2000

William Papas, for many years the Guardian's principal political cartoonist, has drowned following a flying accident in British Columbia at the age of 73. Harold Wilson's political secretary once described one of his cartoons as "the worst blow the Guardian struck against the Labour party".

Papas was born in Ermolo, South Africa, to a Greek couple who had emigrated there in the early years of the last century. In 1947, at the age of 20, he came to England to complete his art training at St Martin's and Beckenham colleges. He returned home in 1949 to be faced with the most profound political change since the Boer war.

The 1948 elections had brought the avowedly racist Nationalist party government to power. More or less coinciding with Bill's return came the first of its apartheid laws, the Citizenship Act, which forbade marriage between blacks and whites. As the government unrolled its repressive legislative programme, Bill, not instinctively the most political being, was obliged to sort out his attitudes. He opted to work for two of the principal opposition publications, the Cape Times and Drum magazine.

After six years, with the political climate getting ever more difficult for anyone of liberal views (he was eventually banned by the Pretoria government), Bill decided to try his luck in Britain. Within a year, he was taken on by the Guardian, though it was not the easiest time to join the paper as a political cartoonist. David Low's hugely influential work was still appearing regularly on the leader page and Vicky, who had just joined the Evening Standard, was casting almost as long a shadow.

As Papas slowly found his feet, he developed the habit of button-holing me on the newsdesk at around 4pm each day to mull over topics for his nightly cartoon. As we talked, he would sketch out potential offerings at lightning speed. They rarely, if ever, bore the slightest relation to anything we had discussed, but he clearly needed this contact; sometimes, he would even ring me at home on my day off.

Once the session ended, he would take his preliminary drawings to the duty editor for a final decision. Then, in a windowless hovel off the newsroom, he turned the chosen topic into finished artwork with quite astonishing speed and elan – though we had to be equally fast to spot the spelling mistakes before he shot out of the office.

He was best, of course, on South Africa and Rhodesia but, as he hit his stride, he lashed through the British political and social scene with happy assurance. He was also contributing to the Sunday Times, with which the Guardian shared a building, and to the old Punch magazine. But he was never completely happy with abstract debates on public policy.

He loved to get out to such events as party conferences, where he could pen his wonderfully wounding portraits (many of which are now on the walls of their victims, and some in the National Portrait gallery collection).

This need to get out and about evolved into a series of large and detailed impressions of major cities – Amsterdam, Avignon, Jerusalem. He was the author and illustrator of Instant Hebrew (1979) and People Of Old Jerusalem (1980). In the 1980s and 90s, he produced Papas's America and Papas's Portland. Always a classy entrepreneur, he somehow persuaded the paper to fund poster-sized colour reproductions of these works, which he then marketed through Papas Prints.

In 1967, during the six-day war, I had just got back to Tel Aviv from the Golan Heights, when I saw a familiar figure across the hotel lobby. It was Bill, covered in the dust of Sinai, just back from producing an artist's impressions of the conflict. He was uncharacteristically subdued, having been with an Israeli officer when they encountered some Egyptian stragglers near the Suez Canal. One had been slow to discard his weapon and the Israeli had simply shot him dead. The incident cured Bill of any further ambitions as a war artist.

The following year, we dreamed up a splendid scam, charging off to Finland for a couple of weeks for a words-and-pictures feature about the Laplanders' reindeer round-ups. We did not stop to consider that these events take place in December, and failed to realise that culling reindeer is a highly secretive market operation, which Lapps do not reveal to strangers. We therefore covered most of deep-frozen Lapland on various wild goose chases, and could only console ourselves by thawing out in hotel saunas.

In one, we discussed the claim that Finns roll in the snow to cool off, and Bill promptly rushed into the night to try it for himself. He soon reappeared as a sort of transparent, blue wraith, quite unable to speak. It took 20 minutes to get him back to human form. "No", he stuttered out, "I think it's just one of those stories". But he had to establish that for himself.

It was on the Lapland trip that he also showed his effortless grasp of human nature. He had filled the car boot with booze – totally illegal under Finland's spartan alcohol regulations – and, within days of our arrival, the word was out. Suddenly, the Lapps became extraordinarily friendly and informative as they posed for Bill, sipping great mugs of illicit firewater. Within a couple of days we were wallowing in the gore of one of their supposedly secret reindeer culls.

Back in London, I could sense that Bill was getting restless, and was not surprised when he sold up in 1971 and set sail with his wife, Tessa, for the Greek village his father had left 60 years earlier. Their next 12 years were spent cruising the Aegean, assembling a mammoth collection of watercolour portraits and landscapes. I once stumbled on one of Bill's exhibitions in Chicago to find the gallery full of pictures showing all the old sureness of line and lightness of spirit – at prices a long way beyond my pocket.

In 1985, Bill and Tessa moved to Portland, Oregon, where they established their own gallery. Bill concentrated on book illustration and watercolour paintings. He also mounted exhibitions in such varied locations as the military museum in Khabarovsk, the US Senate, and the Old City museum in Jerusalem. By the time of his death, he had established a secure reputation across the United States.

His wife survives him. •

----

29 March 2000

Melvyn Bragg

A lifelong devotee of the Lake District, he mapped its geography, history and culture

William Rollinson, historical geographer, born 2 August 1937; died 22 March 2000

William Rollinson, who has died aged 62, was the leading historical geographer of the Lake District – probably the best there has ever been. He published a number of books, one of which, Life And Tradition In The Lake District, is a classic which will endure as long as anyone is interested in Wordsworth's patch of ground. He was an outstanding lecturer with a substantial personal following in the north-west. In an area carefully combed and commented on over 250 years, he made an original and substantial contribution. He spread the word on local radio and Border Television, never lowering his standards.

Bill Rollinson was born in Barrow-in-Furness in 1937. His father was a bricklayer at the Barrow iron and steel works. After Barrow Grammar School for Boys, he took a first in geography at Manchester University. In 1962, he became a lecturer at Liverpool University, eventually moving to the department of continuing education, from where he retired in his late 50s. He continued to lecture to local societies in the far north-west, increased his published output and found a niche in local broadcasting.

Rollinson's first public work was an article on the Lost Villages And Hamlets Of Low Furness. His last, a trio of booklets on Making Charcoal, Making Drystone Walls, and Making Swill Baskets. Between those typically local and particular concerns came several outstanding works on the landscape, traditions and language of Cumbria. These were what fascinated him, particularly the Scandinavian connection.

Although he was, in a very competitive field, supreme in his work on the Lake District, there was perhaps an even deeper pull to Norway, especially to the Fjord Mundal. Probably Rollinson's best television documentary, and most charming book, compares Mundal and Wastwater – uncannily similar in look and history. Bill was entranced by the connections and, year after year, hauled boatloads and busloads of hardy audiences to Iceland and Norway to examine the origin of the folk who, more than a millennium ago, became the core settlers in the lakes, giving it its unique language and character.

I first met Rollinson more than 30 years ago, when he came to see me at the small, half-derelict cottage in north Cumbria in which I was hoping to live. I was hopelessly digging out some obstinate raspberry canes. Bill rolled up his sleeves – literally – gave me a hand, stayed for tea, then for supper, and from then on he became a closer and closer friend of the family.

He was an old-fashioned, unreconstructed bachelor. Doctor Watson would have recognised a fellow spirit. My family, especially our children, welcomed his kindly, adult, wise presence, and were as shaken as I was when they learned that an early death was inevitable.

I worked with Bill on several television and radio programmes, most ambitiously a series of six one-hour documentaries on the history of the Border Television area – the lakes, the borders themselves, and the Isle of Man. He was determined that images – of which he had a robust distrust – should not eclipse content, and his incisive interference was often a pain in the neck, but one which the whole crew genuinely appreciated because we knew he was aiming for something that mattered. The result, I think, was a series that is both authoritative and lively on a subject that lends itself too easily to scenery, lush music and undemanding thought.

When you walked with Bill along, say, Buttermere to Haystacks, you walked through millions of years of geology, centuries of history and, above all, a landscape of language. He had a deep pleasure uncoupling words and showing where they came from – usually from Norse; if this sounds boring, believe me, it was gripping. Sometimes, when he chatted on as we concentrated on getting up something steep, it encroached a little too much, but even that was memorable.

Bill was a man who gave. He never came to see us without bringing gifts of some sort, but when you gave back to him, he was abashed. Although he was as welcome as spring, he had to be importuned to stay overnight, even after 30 years. This was shyness, perhaps a deeper loneliness at the heart of a man abundantly endowed with friends and always true to his Barrovian working-class roots. His politics were Labour, his characteristics were north British, yet he enjoyed meeting the great and influential in the county, as he did in the course of his comprehensive scaling of the lakes.

It is difficult to see Bill Rollinson being replaced – that devotion, that scholarship, that happy "narrow cell". Whenever I thought of the lakes, I thought of Bill, and that will not change. His ashes will be scattered on Westmoreland Cairn Great Gable. •

6 April 2000

Duncan Campbell
So long Charlie Kray

His autobiography was entitled *Me and My Brothers*, but in reality Charlie Kray always knew that it was really My Brothers and, very far behind, Me. If ever there was a man haunted by a famous family name it was the Kray twins' elder brother. It followed him around from the 50s to his death, like a tightly fitted electronic tag.

When he last appeared in court, down in the bleak and characterless wastelands of the top security Belmarsh complex in Woolwich in 1997, Charlie was already 70 and cut a sad figure. It was no surprise that his defence counsel, Jonathan Goldberg QC, sought to portray him to the jury as such. He was, said Goldberg, "an old fool, a pathetic old has-been, an utterly washed-up figure made to appear something he is not at all". Charlie had been caught offering cocaine to undercover officers but Goldberg suggested that he was, in fact, "anti-drugs, anti-crime and a man with a heart of gold".

Gold was certainly always heavily in evidence if you met Charlie Kray, the rings and the bracelets a sign of at least some success in the various small livings he carved out for himself while his brothers served their life sentences.

He was the oldest of the Krays and had it not been for the explosive folie a deux that followed him, he would probably have ended his days running a bar selling Carling Black Label and crabsticks on the Costa del Sol, involved in nothing much more criminal than passing off a few dodgy watches and a bit of Moroccan blow. But in the early 60s the Kray name had more of an upside than a downside and Charlie was happy to take advantage of it.

As a young man Charlie had been a promising boxer, but he was soon overshadowed by his twin brothers whom he had coached. His mother Violet had said that "Charlie was always a different kettle of fish" to the twins. While at the end of the 50s Ronnie and Reggie were trying to establish their little empire run from Vallance Street in the East End, Charlie was trying to establish a modest little furniture business and settle down with his wife, Dolly. But when Ronnie was jailed for an assault, Charlie found himself drawn into what was becoming the real family business: extortion.

He was soon helping to run the Double R club, which the twins had set up in the East End. He told me he had invented the club's name himself as "a cowboy, lone plains drifter tribute" and although he was never feared in the way the twins were, it was known that he was part of The Firm and, as such, had to be treated with respect.

While Charlie took some of the modest benefits of the rackets – and the Krays were remarkably unsuccessful when it came to amassing money from their exploits – he was also in line for the penalties that went with it. When the police finally cracked the Kray empire in 1968, following the murders of George Cornell and Jack "the Hat" McVitie, Charlie was one of the sprats caught in the net along with the great white sharks.

In 1969 Charlie received a 10-year jail sentence for his part as an accessory after the death of McVitie – who had been stabbed to death by Reggie – and he was released from prison in 1975. Since then he has never quite escaped from the Kray aura, despite separating himself geographically by moving to Spain for a while, hanging out in Ibiza and Benidorm and dabbling in the worlds of pop music and clubland.

When I first met him in a West End hotel in the 80s, he was marketing his book, the first of a series of attempts to parlay the family name into loot. He made £100,000 for being a "consultant" on the 1990 feature film, The Krays, but the money soon ran out.

"It was like the wild west," Charlie said of the early days with the twins, whose notoriety made them targets. "It was 'let's kill Billy the Kid and then we'll be Billy the Kid'." Some of his descriptions of their criminal exploits had a farcical element, and he seemed to enjoy the joke in a way that his brothers would never have done. He once recounted how he had had to burn a number of stolen bonds in his mother's dustbin because they had become too hot to handle.

Charlie made a number of public appeals for the twins to be released but ran into frequent problems, particularly with Ronnie. Charlie never seemed to be sure whether he was in favour with the twins or not and Ronnie used to issue proclamations from Broadmoor before his death in 1995 disowning his big brother over some perceived liberty taken, only to "forgive" him within a few months. This bewildered Charlie, who was the most sociable of the three brothers and was always keen to get on with people.

When I met him, Charlie was tanned and in good trim for a man of his age. He was the classic East End get-a-round-in-this-one's-on-me-show-respect-to-the-ladies kind of guy. He followed the party line of suggesting that, bless 'em, the twins had only ever harmed their own, they had been soldiers in a war and it was kill or be killed. But in reality, Charlie seemed perfectly happy working in a civilian rather than military capacity – his first job after leaving prison was on an Ideal Home exhibition stand, demonstrating cutlery. (Jack the Hat, who had once blotted his copybook by arriving drunk at one of the Krays' clubs wearing a pair of Bermuda shorts, his trademark hat and carrying a bayonet, would doubtless have appreciated the joke.)

Although his first wife left him for George Ince, who had had his own problems with the police, Charlie never seemed to be without an attractive woman on his arm. The small crowd of supporters who gathered outside the courtroom three years ago always seemed to include at least a couple of handsome women of a certain age. From Barbara Windsor to headmaster's daughter Judy Stanley, who attended his final trial, women saw a charming side of Charlie that clearly eluded the flying squad.

Charlie was one of the four pallbearers who lowered Ronnie's coffin into the ground in 1995 and at the time he spoke of various music production projects and schemes connected with the Kray name. But while he kept his body in trim as a good old boxer should, it would seem his mind was wandering when he was approached by undercover cops in the mid-90s and asked to find them some cocaine. He found himself playing the part of a big drugs broker and walked straight into the pit that had been dug for him. At the time he was on his uppers and driving a Vauxhall Astra – hardly the flash gangland figure he was painted as.

His funeral will not be as massive as Ronnie's – a strange event that hovered half way between Pulp Fiction and the Lavender Hill Mob – and in a way his epitaph has already been written for him by his lawyer. His mourners – and there will be plenty – will wonder whether, without the existence of the terrible twins, people would have seen a different person, or whether the one sent down for a final stretch was the proper Charlie. •

30 March 2000

Norman Shrapnel
A comic writer in the English tradition

Anthony Dymoke Powell, writer, born 21 December 1905; died 28 March 2000

Anthony Powell, who has died aged 94, is inevitably regarded as the English Proust, on the strength of the massive novel sequence A Dance to the Music of Time – 12 volumes and a million words – that became his central life's work. The Proust impact was more dominant and more obvious than that of other great European novelists and assorted influences from Petronius to modern Americans. Yet he will stand as essentially a comic writer in the English tradition – comic in the least uproarious way imaginable, reflective and often melancholic, the strong social spine to his work being the one distinctively uncommon feature in a branch of writing remarkable more for eccentricity than togetherness.

In fact, Powell has a measure of both. He goes in for no deep psychological dredging, yet his novels rest on a firmer base of instinct and belief than is usual among the English comedians. He is fascinated by the play of time and chance on character, and it is by no means time and chance that always win. His narrating hero and anchorman, Nicholas Jenkins, is constantly being mildly surprised by the way things and people turn out.

The unpredictability of life, as Powell himself described, is built into his structure as an essential part of it. Coincidences, so irritating to some readers, often happen in life, so why should they be forbidden to fiction? They are not excluded from Powell's novels, nor are all manner of trivia other writers might scorn or mishandle. It was his belief that with the right cook in charge anything could go into the cauldron. A novelist never lacks material – only the capacity and energy to handle it.

Silver spoons, in the Powell kitchen, were never in short supply. The world he deals with, upper middle-class life from the 1920s onward, is his own world. The son and grandson of distinguished soldiers, he spent part of his childhood with his mother in rented accommodation in the home counties following his father, a lieutenant-colonel in the Welch regiment. He was at Eton, where he was a contemporary of Orwell and a founding member of the Eton Society of Arts, and then at Balliol College. After Oxford, he got a job with Duckworth, a small London publishing house, but left after nine years to write scripts for Warner Brothers, even paying a six-month visit to Hollywood.

His first novel, Afternoon Men, appeared in 1931 and there were several others by way of prelude, followed by a long silence through the war – he joined his father's regiment before being transferred to the Intelligence Corps – and for some years after it. Then, in 1951, came the start of The Music of Time sequence, the title deriving from Nicolas Poussin's allegorical painting. The books emerged at roughly two-yearly intervals.

The sequence, stretching across a quarter of a century from A Question of Upbringing (1951) to Hearing Secret Harmonies (1975), is more than a successful fictional marathon. It achieves a coherence, a central vitality which runs sluggishly at times but is never extinguished. His vast army of characters, clubmen all, pursue their power games through peace and war, marriage or divorce, in sickness and in health. War – as memorably described in the ninth volume, The Military Philosophers – is for Powell-people an extension of ordinary life; the flow is diverted but not stemmed, and rank is merely a crude token of what always existed in this elegantly competitive world. Some characters may only be glimpsed before disappearing from view, perhaps springing up like blades of grass in another volume years later. But nothing is lost or without its effect on the total pattern, while the allegorical master of the dance – as in the Poussin picture – smiles a shade malignly.

Other characters are as perennial as the unreliable Dicky Umfraville, often in hot – or at least very warm – water, first noted leaving school under a cloud (not actually expelled, it was insisted) and last seen masquerading as an octogenarian drug-addict. Or the ever-indulgent Lady Molly, whose house in South Kensington, more than the Ritz, is really open to all.

With Powell's known writing method and this roving cast of hundreds there was naturally much speculation about who were the originals, in whole or more usually in part, of the characters appearing in the Dance. Sometimes the guess-who game was easy, as with the well-known Fitzrovian writer and reviewer Julian Maclaren-Ross who became the character X Trapnel. He appears as a novelist who holds forth at length about the art of the novel to the narrator Jenkins, also a novelist. He insists, and Jenkins doesn't contradict, that naturalism is only natural in the right hands and that reading novels takes almost as much talent as writing them. It can hardly be carrying presumption too far to assume that some of these ideas, as from novelist to novelist, are shared by the club's founding member, Powell himself.

Others are more mysterious. Above all – literally so, if he had his way – there is the preposterous, the ever-haunting Widmerpool. Writhing with self-contradiction – a shade pathetic, a little absurd, more than a little sinister – he pervades the book, occupying a full half-century even of Powell's ocean of time. Where can this strange creature have sprung from?

"I am perpetually badgered about Widmerpool," Powell said when he was being interviewed for his 80th birthday. All sorts of originals have been suggested, from a recent lord chancellor down. Actually, so far as the character was drawn from life, "he was drawn from somebody I served under during the war". Powell tells us, in Journals for 1982-1986 (1995), that he first came across Widmerpool as a Cromwellian Captain of Horse in Hutchinson's Memoirs of the Civil War. Further volumes of the Journals were to appear, covering the years 1987-89 and 1990-92.

If any character was going to beat time you felt it would have to be the apparently indestructible Widmerpool, but he goes in the end – suitably weirdly, collapsing (it seems) on a ritual jog at dawn.

The inextricable mingling, in such a world as Powell's, of life and literature is made doubly apparent in the memoirs, To Keep the Ball Rolling, which Powell brought out in four volumes between 1976 and 1982. So happily do fact and fiction marry that it is easy to forget at times that you are reading about a real character in an actual place, and imagine you have slipped back into one of the novels.

This reaction is particularly strong in the account – laconic and uninhibited like the fiction – of the early days in London when Jenkins is finding his feet in the literary world. The real-life memories develop, as the novels do, a sense of the significance of trivial and seemingly casual events, while large ones may pass invisibly by. Real people surge on to the scene like figures from a fantasy world: Augustus John, JC Squire, Rosa Lewis of the Cavendish, Maclean and Burgess ("a notorious scallywag"), the seedy diabolist Aleister Crowley at Simpsons, Tallulah Bankhead in a nightclub.

We watch him becoming a Territorial recruit in the Royal Artillery ("I felt that if the gunners were good enough for Tolstoy they were good enough for me") and, rather more dangerously, pursuing a friendship with Evelyn Waugh. There are drinks with the Sitwells. The air of clubbishness, a cool, bookish intimacy, persists. Most of the way, that is. Just once in a while togetherness fails: "In the flat below mine lived EM Forster (a writer whose books have never greatly appealed to me), but we never met."

The trivia of the memoirs can be as funny as anything in the novels, and that means very funny indeed. Powell was of the opinion that most important writers, unlike most critics, have been well equipped with resources of humour; he even seems to have regarded it as a touchstone in evaluating them.

Powell began as a writer for addicts – clubmen too, members of the Powell Club – but they increased rapidly. Or was it more like an open prison, in which Powell was governor and his readers were condemned to life sentences? They never wanted to be anywhere else for long, and they always came back at call.

For a single writer to have put such a stamp on his day, and against the prevailing mood and style of the time, is a huge achievement. Powell didn't stand quite alone. Kingsley Amis was with him, dealing bold strokes in defence of the comic spirit; but the Amis comedy, though by no means all belly-laughs, was of a rougher order and failed to carry the approval of the bookish establishment. While Amis sold books, Powell won praise. It was ungrudging and well-earned.

Largely it was a triumph of tone. A fastidious satirist, he never shouts and seldom mocks – or (except in the physical sense) moves very far. Powell's ideal hunting-ground seems a mile square and an inch deep, and there are bound to be some – particularly when so little, for such long spells, manages to happen – who get to find the inflexibly well-bred narrative voice a shade wearing. This is surely part of the fun. Powell's descriptive powers are clinically accurate and searching, and he is constantly putting himself in the way of good material.

He is a conscientious mixer in the interests of his profession. It goes beyond club-land and the haunts of off-duty politicians, bureaucrats and important artists, though even lower life has its standards and good manners survive in unlikely places. Powell's world is well supplied with pubs without being beery, and there are times when the streets are thronged with well-born paupers conscientiously dodging their creditors. In taxis, of course.

Violence, public and domestic, in peace and war, is muted by the modulated tones of civilised life. This relentless gentility would risk serious tedium without that sharpness of eye and wit. The head, you could say, remains as cool as the heart. He lacks what Amis and most of the later English humorists have possessed – sentimentality. That would have destroyed the work.

He has a strong indulgence towards fantasy and eccentric behaviour, always with the assumption that it is observed and not invented. He can be ruthless, not always in expected settings. There are funerals, not necessarily particularly mournful occasions; death seems no more serious than life, which is indeed serious enough in so inflexible an English comedy world. There is an inclination for ritual, with serious sacrificial moments such as the drowning of a key manuscript in the Regent's Park canal (Books Do Furnish A Room), or the death – could it be possible after all? – of Widmerpool in the final volume of the sequence.

The fiction adds up to a marvel of skill, originality, patience and sheer longwindedness. Technically the challenge, brilliantly met, must have been the handling of that enormous flock of free-range characters and the disposing of the maddening, mysterious, apparently indestructible Widmerpool. No wonder the face in Poussin's ritual dance came to look more malign than ever, for the Powell version must have called for a kind of anti-choreography remote from dancing. These hundreds of performers had to be trained to collide with each other as much as possible for fear that they might otherwise stray off and never be seen again.

There must have been many who wished that for Widmerpool. Did Powell ever wish he had never created the man, if man it was? Keeping track of Widmerpool through 12 volumes and a million words, not really knowing whether he was ink or flesh, whether his true existence was inside the book or out, could have been a lifetime's job in itself

He popped up everywhere: something in the City, something in the army, employed in many an advisory capacity. He was a Labour MP under Attlee, an admirer of Mrs Ernest Simpson. Hugh Gaitskell – though nobody seems quite sure about this – was thought to have been instrumental in getting him a peerage. He influenced people's lives though not in the traditional way; more a kind of one-man quango. He would always be in touch. There was no danger of his getting lost.

After the Music of Time sequence Powell continued to write – he had also been literary editor of Punch after the war and a long-time book reviewer for the Daily Telegraph – until immobilised by a series of strokes in the late 1980s. There was a short novel in 1983 dementedly entitled O, How the Wheel Becomes It! (Ophelia's mad scene, it fittingly turns out, provides the clue). And in 1986 he published The Fisher King, an elegant modern version of an ancient myth. He was made a Companion of Honour in in 1988.

Powell had married Violet Packenham, sister of Lord Longford, in 1934 after a brief acquaintanceship. For many years they lived in a handsome regency house near Frome in Somerset. He is survived by Lady Violet and two sons. •

Envoi

....

24 June 2000

Michael Frayn
Late night final

No one, for some reason, has ever been able to remember the title of my novel Towards The End Of the Morning. By the common consent of almost everyone who has mentioned it to me since it was first published in 1967, it seems to have been rechristened Your Fleet Street Novel. What surprises me a little is that anyone can still remember what the phrase Fleet Street once signified.

Fleet Street now is just the dull, busy thoroughfare that connects the City to the West End. When I first arrived to work in it, in the last few months of the 50s, it was synonymous with the newspaper industry. It referred not just to the street itself, but to the whole close-packed district around it – to a way of life with its own style and philosophy; a world that has now vanished as completely as the Fleet Ditch that gave the street its name. (The notoriously foul stream was incorporated by Bazalgette into the sewerage system, and concealed in a culvert that runs beneath Ludgate Circus, at the eastern end of the street; certain parallels with the newspaper industry, however, continued to be visible to its critics.)

It even had its own characteristic smell. Just as Southwark, where my father worked, on the other side of the river, was immediately identifiable by the delicately sour smell of the Kentish hops that were warehoused and factored there, so the alleys and courts of Fleet Street were haunted by the grey, serious smell of newsprint. I catch the delicious ghost of it in my nostrils now, and at once I'm back at the beginning of my career, struggling to conceal my awe and excitement at having at last arrived in this longed-for land.

By that time, actually, Fleet Street was coming towards the end not just of the morning, but of the afternoon as well, and the shades of night were gathering fast. On the street itself there were only two real newspaper offices left: the modernistic black glass box from which the Daily and Sunday Express improbably dispensed their archaic patriotics, and the white imperial slab of the Telegraph, looking more appropriately like the Tomb of the Unknown Leader-Writer. The London offices of various provincial and foreign papers maintained Fleet Street addresses in cramped rooms up staircases above tobacconists' shops – the Manchester Guardian, where I worked, had a few rooms over the post office at the Temple Bar end of the street.

The real life, though, was in the narrow lanes just off the street, in Fetter Lane and Shoe Lane to the north, and Whitefriars Street and Bouverie Street to the south – in the grimy, exhausted-looking offices of the Mail and the Mirror, the News of the World, the Evening News and the Evening Standard. The Observer, to which I moved in 1962, occupied a muddled warren down in Tudor Street.

Other papers had ventured a little further, though they all remained in pubbable range – the Times at Blackfriars, the Financial Times up the hill by St Paul's, the Sunday

Times and Sunday Pictorial a bleak half-mile away in Gray's Inn Road. The Sun and the Independent were still undreamed of, and the appearance of anything new in this run-down world seemed as unlikely as the birth of a baby in an old folk's home. Even when the Daily Telegraph did manage to give birth to the Sunday Telegraph in 1961, the new infant had a suitably grey and elderly air.

A few terminal cases were still coughing their last in odd corners. The Daily Herald up in Endell Street, being slowly suffocated by its affiliation to the TUC; down in Bouverie Street the poor old News Chronicle, the decent Liberal paper that everyone liked but no one read, and on which I had been brought up, kept going by its rather more successful little brother, the Evening Star. On the masthead of the Chronicle lingered the titles of a whole succession of defunct and forgotten papers that had been interred in it over the years, like the overgrown names of the departed accumulating on a family mausoleum: the Daily News, the Daily Chronicle, the Daily Dispatch, the Westminster Gazette, the Morning Leader. I'd scarcely been there a year when the whole vault finally collapsed, taking the Star and all the old names with it.

All the same, the forests of the sub-arctic north were still being steadily digested each day through this tangled alimentary canal. Great cylinders of newsprint went swinging above your head from the articulated lorries blocking every side-street. Through grimy pavement-level skylights here and there you could glimpse the web racing on the huge machines thundering in the basements. In every loading-bay there loitered underemployed gangs left over from some earlier industrial age, waiting to pass the product out, bale by bale, hand to hand, like sacks of grain from a medieval mill, to the the vans that raced the more and more clamorously titled Late Extras and Late Finals of the evenings to the street-corner vendors, then the Irish and country editions of the dailies to the main-line stations. And, wafting from every bay and ventilator and seedy lobby, that intoxicating scent.

Mingling with it was another characteristic smell – the warm beery breath from doorways with titles above them as familiar as the mastheads on the papers themselves. The Mucky Duck, aka White Swan, where the Chronicle and I think the Mail drank; the Printer's Devil, favoured by the Mirror; the King and Keys, in Fleet Street itself, that refreshed the Telegraph opposite. I was passing the King and Keys one day when I was almost killed by a projectile emerging from it like a shell from a howitzer. It was a man being ejected by unseen hands, in a high trajectory that took him clear above the pavement and into the gutter beyond; whoever it was, somebody evidently felt quite strongly that it was time for him to be on his way back to the office.

From the windows of the Guardian on another occasion I watched a very large and distinguished journalist slowly emerge from Piele's, the pub opposite, totter a few dignified steps, then abruptly sit down on the pavement, where he remained, with a surprised but resigned look on his face, plainly not the shape of person to be able to get to his feet again unaided, until the news got back to Piele's, and a team of rescue workers came straggling out to hoist him up and carry him back inside again for medication.

The Observer drank in Auntie's, though I've forgotten whether it had any other name, and even who Auntie was. The Guardian had a foot in two camps. One was the Clachan, a rather undistinguished Younger's house grimly decorated with samples of the different tartans, where we drank our best bitter watched by a mysterious official of one of the print unions, who sat on his own at a corner of the bar every day from opening to closing time, wearing dark glasses and referred to in respectful whispers, but speaking to no one, apparently paid by either union or management just to sit there and drink all day.

The other was El Vino's (always so-called, with an apostrophe s, like Piele's or Auntie's, as if it had a landlord called Elmer Vino). This was quite different – not a pub at all, but a wine-bar before wine-bars had been invented, where we drank not bitter but Chablis-and-soda, alongside not trade-unionists but florid Rumpoles from the Temple and the sort of fellow-journalists who had pretensions to be members of a learned profession themselves – ruined scholars who could review you at short notice a book about Lord Northcliffe or Hugh Kingsmill, or knock you out a belligerently authoritative think-piece on the proper constitutional relationship between Crown and Woolsack. Women were strongly discouraged from entering. Any woman who insisted was not allowed to disturb the collegiate atmosphere of the bar itself but was directed to a room at the back furnished with chairs and tables, where Elmer's grand head-waiter would ritually shame her by forcing one of the more elderly and infirm old soaks taking refuge there to give up his seat to her.

There was something symbolic about our alternation between these two different establishments. On the one hand we were simple craftsmen and trade-unionists; on the other we had certain social aspirations. I was a member of the National Union of Journalists, certainly, but my only contact with it by the time I had moved to the Observer, apart from paying my dues, was an occasional plaintive note from the branch secretary asking why we had no union chapel at the office. I would pass the queries on to colleagues who knew more than I did about the paper's rather idiosyncratic workings, and back the same answer would always come: we didn't need a chapel because we were all, staff and management alike, gentlemen together.

We mostly worked at a rather gentlemanly pace by the standards of today's journalists. We didn't have quite such a limitless acreage of newsprint to fill, and we hadn't yet got bogged down in the endless union negotiations that darkened the last days of Fleet Street, before Rupert Murdoch side-stepped them, and in 1986 broke out of that increasingly hobbled and embittered little world to the brutal simplicities of Wapping.

Now the rest of the newspaper industry has followed Murdoch's lead, and scattered across London – to the Isle of Dogs and Clerkenwell (where my two former employers have taken refuge under the same roof at last), to Old Street and Kensington High Street; even, at one point, to South London and Heathrow. I don't know who's getting thrown out of the King and Keys these days, but no one, I imagine, with that astonishing ability to drink until the floor tips and still write a thousand words on the shocking decline in standards of behaviour.

Long before newspapers were out of Fleet Street, though, I was out of newspapers. Leaving behind that small memento, My Fleet Street Novel. The unnamed paper where the story is set is located in one of the street's more obscure backwaters. From the sound of it, I imagine that Hand and Ball Court was on the site of a yard where an early fore-runner of fives was played. Perhaps it had been part of Henry VIII's Bridewell palace that Edward VI made better known when he turned it into a penitentiary for vagabonds and whores. I can't find it on the current A to Z, so I suppose it has vanished in its turn to make way for a splendid new palace of commerce, perhaps also housing a few modern rogues of one sort or another, just as the paper itself has presumably been relocated to a more remote and less congenial environment, if not to the footnotes of media history.

I have been authoritatively informed by some people that it's really the Guardian; by others that it's the Observer. It doesn't seem to me much like either. So far as I can tell, it is itself, as things in fiction so often are, though no one believes it. In which case its editor bears no resemblance to any real editor of my acquaintance? Well, yes, he does, as it happens – to a most distinguished editor, though not one who ever, so far as I know, set foot in Fleet Street, or any of its surrounding byways. So are any of the other characters based on real people? I borrowed a few features, I have to confess: a nose here and an eye there. Some of the characteristics of John Dyson, the head of the department that deals with the crossword, the nature notes, and other miscellaneous features, I took from the wonderful leader-page editor of the Observer, John Silverlight, who used to handle my copy, and of whom I was very fond. Gradually everyone in the office but John guessed. He wasn't one to keep a thought to himself, any more than John Dyson is, but he never noticed even when one of our colleagues used to embar-rass me by performing lines of his dialogue in front of him – "Oh, Michael, you write like an angel!" etc. I never owned up. Not, at any rate, until I wrote his obit a few years ago, just as poor old Eddy Moulton, the ancient who is sleeping out his last years in the corner of John Dyson's office, was no doubt doing for his contemporaries.

The story begins with a premature and premonitory nightfall, and I suppose that with hindsight the book does look a bit like a valediction: though in the case of Fleet Street itself, as it turned out, the darkness that settled in was not going to lift in time for lunch. •

A new edition of Michael Frayn's *Towards The End Of The Morning* has been published by Faber.